Research Design in Aging and Social Gerontology

Research Design in Aging and Social Gerontology provides a review of methodological approaches and data-collection methods commonly used with older adults in real-life settings. It addresses the role of normative age-related sensory, cognitive, and functional changes, as well as the influence of generational cohort (age-period-cohort) upon each design. It discusses the role of older adults as true co-researchers; issues uniquely related to studies of persons residing in community-based, assisted, skilled, and memory-care settings; and ethical concerns related to cognitive status changes. The text concludes with detailed guidelines for improving existing data-collection methods for older persons and selecting the best fitting methodologies for use in planning research on aging.

Features of *Research Design in Aging and Social Gerontology* include:

- Descriptions and evaluations of a wide range of methodological approaches and of methods used to collect data about older persons (quantitative, qualitative, mixed, and emergent methods: photovoice, virtual environments, etc.)
- Ways to match research questions to selection of method without a preconceived methodological preference or dominance
- Real-world and applied examples along with cases from the gerontological literature
- "How to" sections about reading output/software reports and qualitative-analysis screenshots (from ATLAS.ti) and quantitative (SPSS) output and interpretation
- Pedagogical tools in every chapter, such as text boxes, case studies, definitions of key terms, discussion questions, and references for further reading on chapter topics
- Glossary of key terms, a complete sample research report, and an overview of past methodological research design work in gerontology
- Companion website at www.routledge.com/cw/Weil where instructors will find PowerPoint presentations, additional discussion questions, and a sample syllabus; and students will find flashcards based on glossary terms, a downloadable copy of the sample research report in the text, and links to data sets, related websites, further reading, and select gerontological journals

This text is intended for upper-level undergraduates and master's students in aging and gerontology as well as students in human development, applied anthropology, psychology, public health, sociology, and social-work settings. Health care professionals, social workers, and care managers who work with older adults will also find this text a valuable resource.

Joyce Weil, Ph.D., MPH, is Assistant Professor of Gerontology at the University of Northern Colorado.

Textbooks in Aging Series

Currently, more than 617 million people are aged 65 and older, accounting for about 8.5% of the world's population. To enhance students' understanding of the issues associated with aging, an increasing number of academic programs include a lifespan perspective or opt to incorporate consideration of aging processes among the topics they include in the curriculum. The Routledge/Taylor and Francis *Textbooks in Aging Series* is designed to address the growing need for new educational materials in the field of gerontology. Featuring both full-length and supplemental texts, the series offers cutting-edge interdisciplinary material in gerontology and adult development and aging, with authored or edited volumes by renowned gerontologists who address contemporary topics in a highly readable format. The series features texts covering classic topics in adult development and aging in fresh ways as well as volumes presenting hot topics from emerging research findings. These texts are relevant to courses in human development and family studies, psychology, gerontology, human services, sociology, social work, and health-related fields. Undergraduate or graduate instructors can use these texts by selecting a series volume as a companion to the standard text in an introductory course, by combining several of the series volumes to use as instructional materials in an advanced course, or by assigning one series volume as the primary text for an undergraduate or graduate course or seminar.

Published:

Latinos in an Aging World: Social, Psychological, and Economic Perspectives
Ronald J. Angel and Jacqueline L. Angel

Research Design in Aging and Social Gerontology: Quantitative, Qualitative, and Mixed Methods
Joyce Weil

Research Design in Aging and Social Gerontology

Quantitative, Qualitative, and Mixed Methods

Joyce Weil

NEW YORK AND LONDON

First published 2017
by Routledge
711 Third Avenue, New York, NY 10017

and by Routledge
2 Park Square, Milton Park, Abingdon, Oxon, OX14 4RN

Routledge is an imprint of the Taylor & Francis Group, an informa business

Library of Congress Cataloging-in-Publication Data
Names: Weil, Joyce, author.
Title: Research design in aging and social gerontology : quantitative, qualitative, and mixed methods / Joyce Weil.
Description: New York, NY : Routledge, 2017. | Includes index.
Identifiers: LCCN 2016046380 | ISBN 9781138690257 (hardback : alk. paper) | ISBN 9781138690264 (pbk. : alk. paper)
Subjects: LCSH: Aging—Research—Methodology. | Gerontology—Methodology.
Classification: LCC HQ1061 .W377 2017 | DDC 305.26072—dc23
LC record available at https://lccn.loc.gov/2016046380

ISBN: 978-1-138-69025-7 (hbk)
ISBN: 978-1-138-69026-4 (pbk)
ISBN: 978-1-315-45016-2 (ebk)

Typeset in Minion
by Apex CoVantage, LLC

Visit the companion website: www.routledge.com/cw/weil

Printed and bound in Great Britain by
TJ International Ltd, Padstow, Cornwall

This book is dedicated to Rosemary Cooney, Ph.D., who inspired me to pursue my love of research about aging and is a steadfast mentor and supporter.

Contents

About the Author

Joyce Weil, Ph.D., MPH, is Assistant Professor of Gerontology at the University of Northern Colorado. She holds a doctorate in sociology (demography) from Fordham University, an MPH degree from Columbia University, and a Certificate in Gerontology from the Institute on Aging at Temple University's School of Medicine. Her current research focuses on aging-in-place through the use of formal supports, such as senior centers and rural aging networks; social demography of aging; and inequalities across the lifecourse. She is the author of *The New Neighborhood Senior Center: Redefining Social and Service Roles for the Baby Boom Generation* (Rutgers University Press) and co-editor of *Race and the Lifecourse: Readings from the Intersection of Ethnicity and Age* (Palgrave Macmillan). Her articles appear in the *Journal of Aging, Humanities, and the Arts*; *Journal of Loss and Trauma*; *Social Forces*; *International Journal of Aging and Society*; *PRISM: A Journal of Regional Engagement*; *Ageing International*; *Gerontology and Geriatric Medicine*; *Sociological Inquiry*; *Educational Gerontology*; and *Research on Aging*.

Foreword

Aging is one of the most important phenomena of the 21st century. Today, more than 617 million people are aged 65 and older, accounting for about 8.5% of the world's population. By 2030, that total is projected to increase to one billion older adults, or 13% of the world's total population. In the United States alone, between 2011 and 2030, about 10,000 Baby Boomers will turn 65 each day (Cohn & Taylor, 2010). By 2030, the first members of the Baby Boomer generation, born in 1946, will be 84 years of age, and the youngest members, born in 1964, will be 65 (Federal Interagency Forum on Aging-Related Statistics, 2010). Thus, with the aging of the population in the United States and across the globe, more people than ever before will be living into their seventh, eighth, and ninth decades of life and beyond.

To enhance students' understanding of the promises and challenges associated with individual and societal aging, an increasing number of academic programs are including a lifespan or lifecourse perspective along with their disciplinary focus, or opting to incorporate consideration of aging processes and outcomes among the topics they include in the curriculum. Thus, the Taylor and Francis *Textbooks in Aging Series*, an interdisciplinary set of both full-length and supplemental volumes on aging, is timely and exciting. The series offers cutting-edge material in gerontology and adult development and aging, with the volumes authored or edited by renowned gerontologists who lend their expertise to a variety of contemporary topics in a highly readable format that will appeal to both beginning and more advanced students.

Our vision for the series includes texts covering classic topics in adult development and aging approached in fresh ways as well as volumes presenting hot topics from recently emerging research findings. These texts will be relevant to courses and programs in human development and family studies, psychology, gerontology, health-related fields and professions, human services, social work, those in other behavioral and social sciences areas, and courses in humanities and arts and other fields for which background in adult development and aging would be relevant to the instructional goals.

Both undergraduate and graduate course instructors could use these topical volumes in several ways. They might assign one or two as companions to a standard, comprehensive textbook in introductory courses. Another approach would be to select several volumes to use in an advanced course that would integrate specific, complementary topics. Still another possibility would be to select one volume to use as the text for a one-credit seminar. In addition, these more specialized volumes might be of interest to researchers interested in obtaining an overview of the literature in the areas covered by the series topics.

The second text in the series is *Research Design in Aging and Social Gerontology: Quantitative, Qualitative, and Mixed Methods* by Joyce Weil. Our experience as researchers tells us that development of investigations follows a typical sequence of identifying significant questions, planning the methods, conducting the study, and interpreting the results regardless of the topic one wishes to pursue, and the same data analytic methods can be applied to myriad studies. Yet our experience as educators points to the effectiveness of presenting research methods and data analysis material using terms and examples that are familiar to students and applicable to their interests, rather than generic ones. Therefore, a text on research design specifically focused on gerontology topics and issues is pedagogically sound and should be of great help to emerging gerontology scholars.

Dr. Weil takes readers through the processes of conceptualizing, conducting, and concluding gerontological research in a systematic approach that is clear and helpful. She covers fundamental aspects of scholarly investigations such as identifying a research question in general terms, then moves into topics related to designing research specifically on aging, providing many examples from the gerontology literature along the way. After giving gerontological theories extensive attention, Weil provides thorough guidelines for qualitative, quantitative, and mixed-research designs, including associated analyses of the data and presentation of the findings. Moving beyond these traditional approaches, Weil also addresses new and emerging designs and methods that expand opportunities for data gathering and analysis. Attention to research ethics and principles for preparing publications, presentations, and applications for funding round out the volume. Overall, this text represents a comprehensive overview of best practices in gerontology research that students will want to consult frequently as they pursue their quest for new knowledge about issues of aging.

Rosemary Blieszner and Karen A. Roberto, Series Editors

References

Cohn, D., & Taylor, P. (2010, December 10). Baby Boomers approach 65 – glumly. Pew Research Center's Social & Demographic Trends Project. Retrieved from http://www.pewsocialtrends.org/2010/12/20/babyboomers-approach-65-glumly/

Federal Interagency Forum on Aging-Related Statistics. (2010). *Older Americans 2010: Key indicators of wellbeing.* Washington, DC: Centers for Disease Control and Prevention.

Preface

Purpose of the Book

You may ask, why create a book devoted to gerontological research methods? Why not just adapt a general methods book to older people and aging? Am I suggesting that we adjust and design research based on the age of the population and not the intention of the research question?

Well, I have had these and more questions asked of me: Why don't research-methods texts incorporate real, relevant examples and designs with older people to use in our field? Or, when examples are included, why are older people only part of the sample? Why do studies use a site in the aging network (the group of organizations that work with older people or do service provision) to recruit participants, but the implications of the site itself in the study or in participants' lives are often ignored? Why are studies researcher-only led and not elder centered?

I have often heard, or been told, "Older people cannot use computers or text messaging as part of a study," "Their interviews take too long, and they just want to chat," and, "They just don't see the value in participating in a study." Some even feel that doing research with older people is a one-sided favor to the older person who is too eager to participate, with the researcher or interviewer in the more altruistic role.

This book seeks to move beyond marginalization and limited ways of thinking about aging and older people in research design. A goal is to introduce some multi-, inter-, and transdisciplinary research possibilities in gerontology. Therefore, this book works on two levels: first, it provides an overview of a method, and, second, it demonstrates how to implement and execute that method. That said, traditional "how-to" elements of research design are also included along with application strategies, or ways of implementing and really doing the process of research, with real-world issues a researcher encounters in the field.

The book stems from students' direct requests and the need in my own teaching. When teaching social research-methods courses and proposal-development courses for years, and using a wide variety of methods, I have often bemoaned the lack of a comprehensive age-based guide that explains all (quantitative, qualitative, and mixed-methods) techniques in a clear, how-to way. There was a need for a text that guides the user fully through all steps of the design-to-analysis process. The text should also cover all major methodological approaches and expose students to all the design possibilities. When students asked me for direction about aspects of research design as applied to older people, I was sure a plethora of information and literature was available about methods specifically related to older adults. However, upon looking, I saw that not as much was out there as I originally thought. My colleagues in the field of gerontology confirmed these hunches.

Drawing upon and updating seminal and comprehensive gerontological research-methods texts—such as Sinnott, Harris, Bloc, Collesano, and Jacobson's *Applied Research in Aging: A Guide to Methods and Resources* (1983) and McAuley, Blieszner, Bowling, Mancini, Romaniuk, and Shea's *Applied Research in Gerontology* (1987)—this book builds on the groundwork of expert methodologists and predecessors in the field. An expanded list of past gerontological methods texts is in an Overview of Past Methodological Research Design Work in Gerontology, Appendix A.

This book explores how to design a research project—by beginning with the question the researcher seeks to explore, then matching a method and analysis strategy to that question. It improves existing data-collection methods for older persons and ways to select the best-fitting methodologies for use in future research on aging. It moves beyond past quantitative-versus-qualitative divides and beyond works that cover only one specific design (quantitative, qualitative, mixed). All methods—including true mixed-methods designs and new emergent ones—are given equal weight and prominence in this book.

Intended Audience

This book is designed as a guide for many types of researchers: those beginning their first research project, those trying to master a new method, or those working with older people and wanting to gather data or complete an evaluation. The aim is to foster a way for a researcher to develop a critical-thinking approach in addressing a research question. Grounded in social gerontological research design, this book is of value to a wide audience. This interdisciplinary audience draws from the gerontologically inclusive fields of sociology, psychology, social work, human development and family studies, nursing, public health, applied anthropology, social research methods, and the humanities. That said, the material can expand to embrace many more disciplines linked by the study of older persons or aging. Fields specializing in lifecourse and those focusing on healthy aging can benefit from this work. Professionals in the field such as gerontologists (broadly defined), health-care workers, and care managers who work with older adults can utilize this text as a resource. This work is of interest to upper-level undergraduate and master's students in a variety of programs. It also offers some translational research approaches—from more academic research to application to direct work in the field with an older population, the population of interest for this book.

Overview of Content

Research Design in Aging and Social Gerontology addresses current gerontological phenomena. First, as initial waves of Baby Boomers reach 65 years of age, methods of studying older populations are becoming increasingly varied (e.g., mixed methods, online surveys, and video-based environments). Second, there is a call to investigate rigor and appropriateness of fit in all gerontological research designs. Recent journal editorials discuss common reasons why qualitative work is not published more frequently in journals, and they concurrently call for the inclusion of more varied, inclusive methods and offer guidelines for researchers. As gerontological methods advance, journals also seek to include arts-and-humanities-based techniques and cutting-edge methods. Journal articles have called for new gerontological research approaches and outlined qualitative guidelines, ways to ensure quantitative and qualitative rigor, and the application of survey methods to older people in varied cultural settings. *Research Design in Aging and Social Gerontology* expands the discussion of rigor in gerontological research methods and discussion about design types appropriate for use with older people.

Issues of research design and methods are reexamined and evaluated through the use of real-life examples, case studies, and application of quantitative, qualitative, and mixed-research designs. This book includes a review of existing and emergent data-collection methodologies commonly used with older adults in real-life settings. It addresses the role of normative age-related sensory, cognitive, and functional changes, as well as the influence of generational cohort (age-period-cohort) upon each method. It highlights the role of older adults as true co-researchers—issues uniquely related to studies of persons residing in assisted, skilled, and memory-care settings—and highlights ethical concerns related to cognitive status changes.

Structure of the Book and Chapter Organization

Research Design in Aging and Social Gerontology has 11 chapters and is divided into three parts: (I) "Getting Started: An Overview of the Aging Research Process"; (II) "Choosing a Research Method and Selecting a Design"; and (III) "Analyzing Results and Reporting Findings."

The first part, "Getting Started," sets the stage for the book. It introduces contemporary issues in aging research, offers ways to design research about aging and social gerontology, and provides an overview of gerontological theoretical approaches to be used in research design. The second part, "Choosing a Research Method and Selecting a Design," introduces and covers the key features of each of the methodological approaches: qualitative methods, quantitative methods, mixed methods, and emerging and future methods. There is also a chapter devoted to quantitative data analysis and evaluation. The final part, "Analyzing Results and Reporting Findings," brings all the prior chapters together. It provides ways to use quantitative and qualitative software and computer-assisted research techniques with data. A latter chapter outlines the unique ethical debates and protections in aging research. The book concludes with detailed guidelines about reporting aging research in multiple venues, such as articles, presentations, and grant proposals.

Distinctive Features/Benefits

Unique features of *Research Design in Aging and Social Gerontology* include the following:

- This book describes and evaluates a wide range of existing methodologies used to collect data about older persons (quantitative, qualitative, mixed, and emergent methods: photovoice, virtual environments, etc.).
- It takes a broad methodological stance and can be more consistent and complete in describing all elements of research design and options to a reader.
- It weights the matching of research question to selection of method without a methodological preference or dominance.
- The fundamental elements and "how-to" processes of research design are offered in cohesive voice.
- Research methods for and with older populations and gerontological topics are the full focus of the book. Aging is the topical emphasis.
- Real-world and applied examples are included along with examples from the gerontological literature.

Pedagogical Features and Companion Website

Research Design in Aging and Social Gerontology offers several pedagogical features for readers. Each chapter has a chapter introduction and summary. Chapters include boxes and/or case studies to provide applications of concepts. Key terms are defined and boldfaced when first introduced. Open-ended questions for discussion (or examination use) are at the end of the chapters along with references for further reading. Chapter 9 ("Quantitative, Qualitative Software and Computer-Assisted Research") has "how-to" sections about reading output/software reports and includes qualitative-analysis screenshots (from ATLAS.ti) and quantitative (SPSS) output and interpretation. This book also offers a companion website for both instructors and students at www.routledge.com/cw/Weil. There instructors will find PowerPoint presentations, additional discussion questions, and a sample syllabus. Students will find flashcards based on glossary terms, a downloadable copy of the sample research report in the book, and links to data sets, related websites, further reading, and select gerontological journals.

Personal Acknowledgments

I would like to thank several sets of people who were integral in the process of conceptualizing and writing this book. I wish to extend a heartfelt thanks to Debra Riegert (past Senior Editor at Routledge/Taylor & Francis), Georgette Enriquez (current Editor), Rachel Severinovsky (Editorial Assistant) and Katherine Wetzel (Project Manager at Apex) as steadfast supporters with stealth guidance throughout this process. Expertise offered by reviewers commissioned by Routledge/Taylor & Francis greatly forwarded my work. I thank Phyllis A. Greenberg and Heidi H. Ewen for their insightful, thorough reviews and shared knowledge. In my academic community, I would like to express my thanks to several friends and colleagues who acted at sounding boards and encouraged my writing a book about methods—in particular, Natalie Byfield, Nancy Karlin, and Susan Hutchinson. Elizabeth Smith, who began as a graduate assistant and continued on as she embarked upon her professional career, provided invaluable support on many aspects of this project. My colleagues and graduate students at the University of Northern Colorado deserve acknowledgement, as well. Lastly, I am indebted to the kindness of those closest to me. My spouse, David Lefkowitz, served as first reader and informal reviewer of this manuscript and helped me develop a love of clear prose. My dear friend Dorothy Davisson inspired me on a weekly basis to write about ways to authentically capture the lived experience of older people.

Part I
Getting Started
An Overview of the Aging Research Process

1
Introduction

This chapter creates the framework for the basic elements and approaches to gerontological research. It defines gerontology and aging research terminology and introduces the reader to key components of developing a research question or narrowing down a topic of interest. Journal articles, existing literature reviews, and freewriting are presented as ways to create a new research question or develop an existing question further. The chapter introduces the process of choosing a research philosophy and other key decisions needed to develop a methodological stance and research design.

What Is Aging Research?

Often, gerontologists get asked who they are and what they do. Gerontologists work in a field that is called multi-disciplinary, interdisciplinary, and even transdisciplinary. They encompass many disciplines and multiple theoretical and conceptual frameworks for doing research in the field called "gerontology." **Gerontology**, or social gerontology, is the study of the biological, psychological, and social processes and changes that occur as part of aging and in older populations. Gerontology, though often used interchangeably, must be differentiated from the term "geriatrics," which has a more biomedical focus. **Geriatrics** addresses the medical, biological, and health-related aspects of the aging process and older persons (Association for Gerontology in Higher Education, 2016; Robnett & Chop, 2015).

The contemporary definition of gerontology today stems from prior works. Tracing the roots of the concept is helpful in understanding and defining the term. The origins of gerontology, as a term, are traced back to the word's more biomedical roots. In the United States, Élie Metchnikoff (1908) suggested gerontology as a study of aging as an accumulation of disease processes leading to death. Several researchers and physicians added to the medical application and expanded this term from early 1900s to the 1980s. They include L.F. Barker (1939), E.V. Cowdry (1939), Ignatz Nascher (1916), Nathan Shock (1947), several early Institutes of Gerontology, Ruth Cavan, Ernest Burgess, Robert Havighurst and Herbert Goldhammer (1949), and Elaine Cumming and William Earl Henry (1979). British counterparts in early gerontological terminology development include Trevor Howell's *Advancing Our Years* (1953), Arthur Exton-Smith's *Medical Problems of Old Age* (1955), and Peter Townsend's *Family Life of Old People* (1957) and *Last Refuge* (1962). Gerontological coursework developed in the 1980s with the rise of the critical (advocacy-based) gerontology of Carroll Estes (1979), Meredith Minkler and Carroll Estes (1999), and Chris Phillipson and Simon Biggs (1998). Three now well-known terms contributed to the modern definition of gerontology. Robert Butler's coining of "age-ism" (1969) refers to discrimination or stereotyping based on older age. John Rowe and Robert Kahn's (1997) application of their "successful aging" model added some conditions to aging well. Their model included the absence of disease and disability with high levels of physical, mental, and social functioning. Building upon C. Wright Mills's (1967) sociological imagination (and its use of personal troubles and societal issues terminology) is the **gerontological imagination.** It is an "awareness [that] allows us to comprehend the links between biological, behavioral, and social-structure factors that influence human aging. It is by definition, a multidisciplinary sensitivity to aging that incorporates the common stock of knowledge from the core disciplines engaged in research on aging" (Wilmoth & Ferraro, 2013, p. 327).

Overview of the Research Process: Developing a Gerontological Researcher's Approach

Each researcher must embark upon his or her own work to add to the body of work in the field. The history and current definitions of gerontology are a starting point for the development of research agenda. Understanding one's own view and basic research principles is the roadmap to generating or refining an age-based research topic. Gerontologists can employ a holistic approach to creating a research question.

Basic Principles

It all starts with a question. **Research** is, basically, a way or systematic process of seeking an answer to a question that arises in a gerontologist's mind, experience, practice, or time in the field. It can be "blue skies" research or research for the sake of research, without immediate application. It can be **applied research,** research that seeks a solution to an everyday issue or to solve a practical problem. Earlier authors—such as Jan Sinnott, Charles Harris, Marilyn Block, Stephen Collesano, and Solomon Jacobson (1983)—have suggested applied research began with workers at the bedside of skilled-care or home-care agencies, senior centers, meal sites, or Area Agency on Aging's direct contact with older persons. William McAuley, Rosemary Blieszner, Cynthia Bowling, Jay Mancini, Jean Romaniuk, and Laurie Shea called the distinction between applied and pure gerontological research "blurred" (1987, p. 7). For example, a researcher may want to address multiple issues. He or she may seek to do the following:

- *Evaluate how something is done.* How did the autobiographical writing group with centenarians work out? Impact the writers?
- *Describe an experience or event.* What is it like being a male caregiver to an older parent?
- *Explore practice options.* What is the impact of trademarked exercise groups or services on older adults?
- *Generate new ways of thinking.* How would older persons use visual images and photos to depict their worlds?
- *Explore something that is bothersome in the researcher's experience, training, or practice.* Why are older people objectified? Painted with one brushstroke as "old"? Why the use of elderspeak in care settings?

Research questions are exactly that, questions about the issue that is of the researcher's interest, or the phenomena he or she seeks to investigate, relayed to others in a statement. Research questions can arise from an organization in the aging network's call to do research—e.g., for a Department on Aging's need to do an evaluation of older service users' satisfaction levels with an existing program to meet the Older American's Act funding requirement. Research questions can examine conditions that are favorable for paradigm shift—e.g., test the climate for cultural change, or alter the way long-term care is provided to older persons.

Research question are aligned with a researcher's **methodology**, or approach to research. A methodological approach is the way researchers use an underlying philosophy as a basis to conceptualize and design all elements of their study—from selection of theory to presentation of findings. It includes the researcher's use of an underlying **philosophy** (worldview or epistemological perspective) that is the basis of the study's design and his or her approach and relationship to participants. Methodology includes "a set or system of methods, rules, and principles employed by a given discipline that govern how research is conducted" that is broader than the method alone (Sullivan, 2009). This means that a researcher's philosophical standpoint (**positivist, constructionist, subjectivist, transformative, and pragmatist** as defined in Table 1.1) greatly influences his or her methodological approach—as a

Table 1.1 Moving from Philosophical Paradigm to Research Design

Ask yourself	Relates to	Issues and decisions to make	Examples of specific designs
What is your view of reality?	the use of an underlying philosophy (or epistemological perspective) also called worldviews **Objectivism** **Constructivism** **Subjectivism**	**Objectivism:** objective, external reality exists and can be measured and tested. **Positivist:** Bring a traditional "scientific approach" to study people. Studies are objectively generalizable and include causality. Mostly quantitative. **Post-positivist:** use the scientific method (applied to human beings) with variables, hypotheses, and theory to quantify and explain reality.	Quasi-experiments
		Constructionist: seeks to capture the way individuals construct or create reality. Research is centered upon participants' views/ways of constructing meaning/seeing their worlds. Origins in hermeneutics. **Interpretive:** acknowledges there are multiple views of reality (including those of the researcher and those "studied"), so the "participants" are the best at describing experience, events, etc., in their own lives. **Symbolic interactionism:** understanding how people attach meaning to their experiences in the world based on their interaction with society.	Participant observation, open-ended interviews, phenomenology, case study, focus groups, life review, narrative analysis
		Subjectivism: our views of reality are filtered/seen throughout subjective viewpoints or vantage points. **Critical/transformative:** includes power and political dynamics of oppressed/marginalized groups and societal influences upon these groups. **Feminism:** an inclusive approach to include women's voices and intersectionality statuses—reflecting society's role in creating gender-based social problems.	Participatory action research, critical discourse analysis
		Pragmatism: avoids reality/construction debates and lets the researcher apply methods in the real world. Not so much interested in getting at a universal truth or being linked to only one philosophy—the real goal is problem-solving. How the data and outcomes can help solve real-world problems.	Evidence-based, outcomes research processes

(*Continued*)

Table 1.1 (Continued)

Ask yourself	Relates to	Issues and decisions to make	Examples of specific designs
Are you beginning with theory to guide data? Or are you using data to generate theory?	the use of theory (to inform the process, or as something to be formed as a result of the research process)	**Deductive approach:** begins with theory or a framework and applies those to the data (once called "top down"). **Inductive:** begins with data to generate a theory or framework (once called "bottom up").	Secondary analysis of data, hypothesis testing Grounded theory, qualitative methods
What is the purpose of your study in terms of data?	a decision about the approach (quantitative, qualitative, or mixed methods)	**Quantitative approach:** numerical data **Qualitative approach:** textual data **Mixed methods:** a mixture of data types	See Chapter 2 for a decision-making process.
Who is your sample?	research units (ranging from documents to people)	Consider the types of people, institutions, agencies, or societies you wish to study. What are your eligibility requirements for your sample? (Don't think about the number needed in your sample here; address that once you have selected a method and specific type of design.)	See Chapters 4–8 for individual sampling by method.
What is the role of time in your study?	time in relation to data collection/ analysis processes	In research on aging, time has many roles. Here consider the time(s) you wish to collect data. For now, is data collection a one-time (cross-sectional) or several-time/ongoing (longitudinal) process?	Age-period-cohort issues are addressed in Chapter 2.
What is your role as the researcher?	a decision about how you will be involved in the study	Consider your role: To what extent are you a participant in the study, observer, overt/covert, co-researcher (hermeneutics) with participants, or an advocate? How will you record and monitor your role?	See Chapter 2 for more discussion of the researcher's role.
Ethical issues?	any ethical dilemmas?	Add in any concerns about working with people in institutional care settings or possible changing cognitive-status issues.	See Chapter 10 for more discussion of ethical issues.
What do you want to do with your outcomes or findings? What is your end product?	a method of gathering data, data analysis, and writing up the findings	Are you producing a report, technical brief, manual, manuscript for publication, findings for dissemination at conferences, or follow-up report for a grant?	See Chapter 11 for ways to disseminate your findings.
Who is your audience?	how will you write your results to address your readers' expectations?	Who are your intended readers? How familiar will they be with jargon? How much of your design, analysis, and methods will you need to include? Will multiple differing groups of people need to read your work? Researchers, practitioners, lay people, those in the study?	See Chapter 11 for ways to disseminate your findings.

Sources: Babbie, 2013, Creswell, 2014, Crotty, 2009, Merriam, 2009, Sinnott et al., 1983.

quantitative approach (using numerical data), a **qualitative** approach (using textual data), or a **mixed-methods** approach (using both data types).

Methodologies are matched to a selection of research designs. Research designs are the frameworks or processes that dictate how the data will be collected and analyzed. Major quantitative research designs include the causal comparative method, correlation, pre-/post-testing and experimental designs, structured observation, and single-case research. Major qualitative designs include narrative analysis, ethnography, grounded theory, case

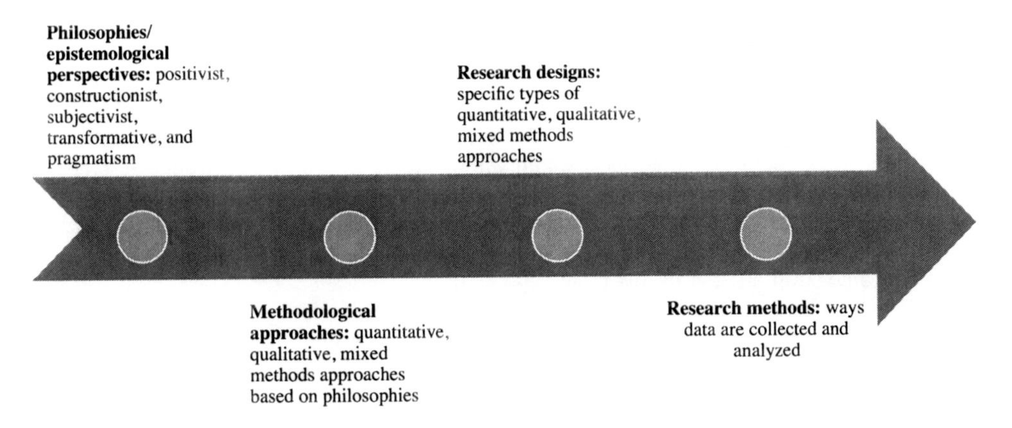

Figure 1.1 Moving from Philosophy/Worldview to Methodological Design

studies, and phenomenological accounts. Sequential explanatory, sequential exploratory, convergent parallel, embedded, transformative, and multi-level are types of mixed-methods research designs.

The **method** is the process a researcher uses to collect data as part of the study. It is the process and procedures used to collect data (e.g., quantitative, qualitative, or mixed methods). A research method is the way a researcher actually carries out and conducts his or her research. Some have described the distinction between the two terms methodology and method as becoming "hazy" (Nickoson & Sheridan, 2012, p. 2). For example, a quantitative approach, a qualitative approach, or a mixed-methods approach can be part of a researcher's overarching methodology and research design but also heavily influence the method or way he or she collects and analyzes data. Figure 1.1 depicts the path from philosophy to method.

Corresponding latter chapters (Chapters 4 through 8) are devoted to choosing a particular research design and method for each of these three major quantitative, qualitative, and mixed-methods approaches. Each element of Table 1.1 will be covered in detail throughout the book. The remainder of this chapter focuses on formulating a research question.

Have a Research Question? Or Need to Develop One?

A researcher may be reading this book because he or she is beginning a new research project; a general question or topic of interest may already be in mind. Or the researcher may want to conduct a research project but needs to generate a topic or narrow a broad topic down to a more manageable one. A few pre-planning steps may be of assistance in either case—no matter with which group the researcher identifies. **Freewriting** consists of using a fixed interval of time to brainstorm and write the first thoughts that one has about a topic. Freewriting is free from grammar and punctuation rules. The goal is to further an idea or develop a new one by writing or drawing a conceptual map. The freewriting exercise in Box 1.1 can help with thinking about potential research topics or refine the details of a topic under consideration. Box 1.2 provides an example of a conceptual map—produced via freewriting—used to generate ideas about Baby Boomers' retirement strategies.

Box 1.1 Focused Freewriting for a Research Topic/Path

Reflect briefly on a topic about which you would like to do research. If you are not sure, ask yourself: What do you like to study? What issues or topics are you most interested in? Passionate about? What projects would you like to do in the future? What are some things you are working on now?

Don't think about it too much; just write down the topic. You can freely draw a flowchart, outline, or whatever works for you and continue writing/answering the following questions:

Why are you interested in this topic?

What are the main issues you are interested in learning about?

What steps do you need to take to learn more about this topic?

Then, start to jot down ideas, notes, and steps you would take.

Use whatever approach you feel most comfortable with—an outline, conceptual map, paragraph outline, summary, etc. You have only 10 minutes, so you must work as quickly as you can.

Box 1.2 Freewriting Conceptual Map to Generate Ideas about Baby Boomers' Retirement Strategies

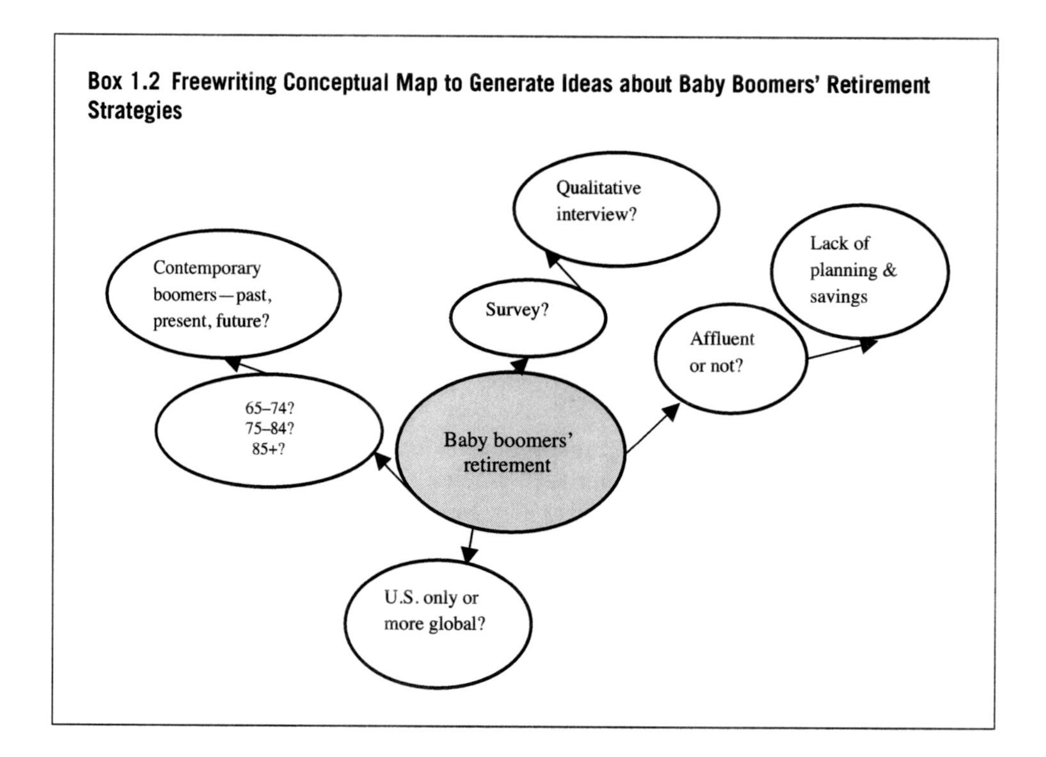

When There Is No Research Question or Proposed Topic in Mind

Sometimes, a researcher may not have a research question or specific topic in mind. If this is the case, and freewriting does not generate ideas, a researcher can try several ways to formulate a topic or research question. Philip Pullman's "read like a butterfly, write like a bee" is perfect in this case. The quote implies that researchers should read everything they can get their hands on about the topic that they may be interested in. What does the academic literature say?

Many people find meta-reviews of literature about a topic a good way to begin here. **Meta-reviews** are helpful since they summarize and provide an overview of what is published about a topic to date. Meta-reviews also outline current debates, critical issues, and key authors writing about a topic in the field. For example, a researcher is really intrigued by the many ways "successful aging" has been defined in the field. The researcher is familiar with some of the original work by Rowe and Kahn and knows about recent efforts to create more successful aging-based theories, but he or she is not too sure what exactly has been updated about these concepts. The researcher is not sure about the "hot" key issues among contemporary researchers who study successful or healthy aging. For example, Marty Martinson and Clara Berridge's meta-review article "Successful aging and its discontents: A systematic review of the social gerontology literature" (2015) provides background and analyses existing in successful aging articles. Their work can bring a researcher up to date on the four new directions in successful aging theory. The authors suggest there is an "Add and Stir group" (who seek to expand the discussion of aging theory) and a "Missing Voices group" (who seek to add older people more directly into the successful aging theory development). The "Hard Hitting Critiques" are a group who would add the impact of society and intersectionality to the body of literature, and the "New Frames" are those who favor different philosophical and non-Western viewpoints for successful aging theory moving forward.

Reading existing literature can spur ideas. **Peer-reviewed journals** are a great starting point since published articles have been reviewed for rigor and edited by other researchers active in the field. Journal articles have a general format or structure. The order may vary for a specific journal, but information is usually organized in the following way: title, author(s) with affiliation, abstract, keywords, introduction, literature review/theoretical framework, research questions/hypotheses, methodology and design (sample/participants, data collection/procedure, and concepts/indicators), data analysis (theme coding/statistical tests), findings/discussion/conclusion (limitations of current study, future directions, and policy implications), notes, references, authors' biographical information, sources of funding, statement of each author's contribution/conflict of interest, and received and accepted publication dates.

Some general guidelines for journal article review include the following:

- Describe the theoretical framework(s) used (general schools of thought, theoretical approach, etc.). Locate the article's research question(s). How does the article introduce and review existing literature about the topic?
- Which bodies of prior literature are reviewed? How is the literature review constructed? How does this article fit into the existing literature (retesting or challenging an existing theory, generating new theory, or examining theoretical gaps)? What are the research questions addressed in the article? Were hypotheses generated? Or did the article seek to generate a theory?
- What is the sampling design? How was the sample chosen? What were some difficulties in the sampling process (e.g., locating cases, non-response rates, lack of counternarratives, etc.)?
- What kind of data are used? Describe how the data were collected. What procedures were used?
- What are the major concepts studied? How are they operationalized to become indicators or variables? Describe how each indicator was measured. Or, if themes were coded, how were codes constructed? What is the codebook like? How were codes made into larger codes or code families?
- How are the data coded? What is the analysis plan?
- How was rigor ensured and addressed (in terms of reliability/validity or trustworthiness)?
- Look over the method(s) used to analyze the data. Techniques—such as multiple regression or chi-square, or co-occurrence tables—may be mentioned. Many techniques can be applied here.
- Review the Conclusion/Findings/Discussion sections. Do they seem to match the research question(s), theoretical frameworks(s), and study design?

Access to electronic journals is becoming increasingly easy. Researchers can actually sign up to have journals email their just-published or published-ahead-online table of contents to them. This is a powerful tool; if the researcher does not have access to the full articles, he or she can still see the current topics other authors are writing about and debating. Some journals offer free trial subscriptions or editor's-choice articles, in full, for free general/public access (e.g., the *Journals of Gerontology—Biological Sciences, Medical Sciences, Psychological Sciences and Social Sciences*, the *Public Policy & Aging Report*, and the *Gerontologist*). A list of many commonly used and cited gerontology and aging-related journals is found on the companion website to this book. This list is a starting place and can be tailored with journals added to it that relate to a researcher's own specific path of study or sub-discipline in the gerontology field.

Annual gerontological conferences also have research interest groups devoted to the discussion of methods, with members, listservs, blogs, and social media as resources. University or community libraries may also have a "gerontology" or "aging" research guide or a dedicated subject librarian. In addition to the published literature, organizations in the field of gerontology have newsletters addressing current issues. Age-related issues often appear in the news—these can be places that help a researcher develop initial interest.

"But No One Has Studied What I Want to Study" or "Everyone Has Studied This": Using Literature to Help Formulate Research Questions

A researcher does not need to be the first, and, more often than not, he or she is not the first person to study a topic. However, a researcher certainly needs to ground his or her work in the existing knowledge in the field. Getting into the existing literature is like taking the pulse of a topic. When understanding where a concept or theory is at in the field, a researcher should ask:

- What are the key lines of thinking?
- Who are the people writing about the issue and often cited in the literature? Generally, the same group of people writes about an issue.
- What is the history about the topic? What are the oppositional groups' stances? Then, with these in mind, the researcher can state his or her own take on the issue.
- Where does the researcher stand? With what ways of thinking does he or she agree? Disagree?
- Where are the gaps in thinking? Or in the literature?
- What can the researcher do to move the discussion forward?
- Can this new research generate or test ideas to further the thinking about this issue?

When There Is a Research Question or Proposal in Mind

Even if a researcher has a question in mind, some decisions still need to be made. After the research question is stated, the main choices are as follows:

- Where does this research question fit in the existing body and/or gaps in the literature?
- What is the scope of the question? And, then, what is the underlying philosophy, epistemological perspective, or worldview (objectivist, constructionist, subjectivist, transformative, or pragmatic [Creswell, 2013; Crotty, 1998; Merriam, 2009]).
- What is the goal of this research question (to explore, describe, explain, and/or predict)?
- How will the philosophy lead the researcher to a methodological approach (quantitative, qualitative, or mixed methods and designs), and, then, what specific types of quantitative, qualitative, or mixed methods will be used?

While these may seem like a lot of independent decisions, they are, in fact, linked and occur in a sequence as part of a process. While acknowledging that there is no one best method or one-size-fits-all path to creating an idea for a study or a research question, review Table 1.1 as an outline of all of the key components to consider and aid in a researcher's decision-making process—matching the research question to a corresponding methodology and design. While chapters in this book can help refine each research and each approach (quantitative, qualitative, mixed, and emergent), the flowchart in Figure 1.2 can aid in narrowing down a design and method from your general research goal.

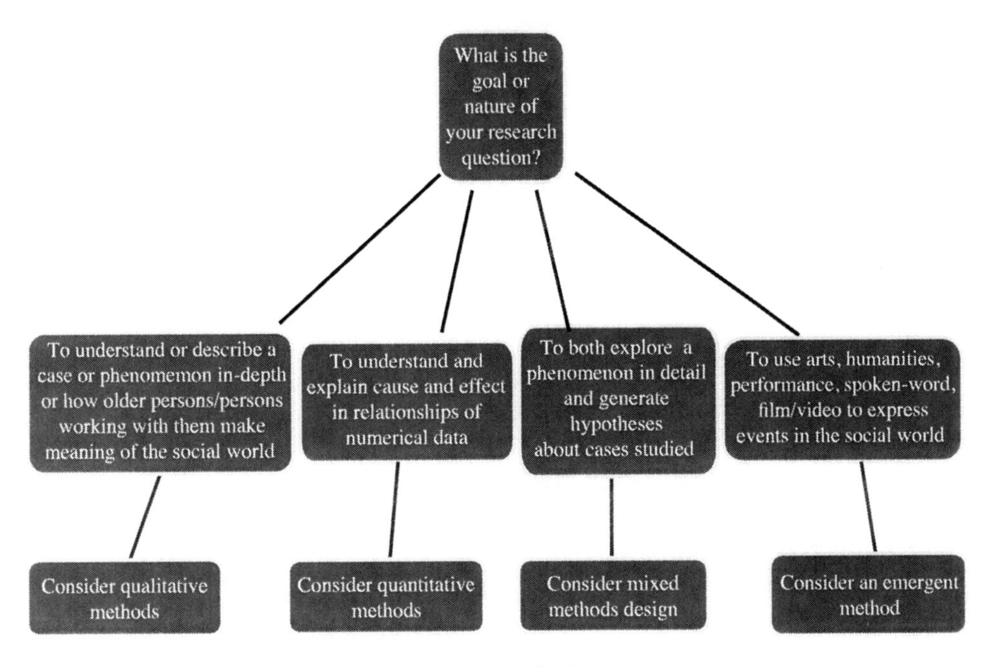

Figure 1.2 Moving from Research Question to Research Design

> Every researcher has to consider key components of his or her approach to research before conducting a study. These elements help determine a study's design. A critical element is the construction of a defined research question. Freewriting or reading journals can help create a question by highlighting gaps in existing work. But, before stating a research question, a researcher needs to consider his or her view of reality (or philosophy or worldview). The researcher's own philosophical paradigm or worldview influences all other elements of design. He or she must consider the role of theory in the study—as either a basis or an outcome—and the role of data, be they numerical, textual, or both types. Also requiring consideration is the sample and number of times data will be collected. The researcher must determine his or her role in the study and the type of interaction he or she will have with participants. Planning for potential ethical issues along with creating a research dissemination strategy for multiple audiences sets the researcher along the road to begin his or her work.

Discussion Questions

- Create your own researcher's stance. Use Table 1.1 to design a study about quality of life for those nearing 100 years of age. First, select an underlying philosophy (or epistemological perspective or worldview) that is closest to your view. Are you a positivist, post-positivist, constructionist, interpretivist, subjectivist, feminist, or pragmatist, or do you have a critical/transformative view? Describe how the choice of philosophy impacts each methodological step outlined in Table 1.1. Then, choose another, different, philosophical perspective and describe how that view would change elements of your study.
- Follow your gerontological imagination—what do you see as gaps in existing aging research? What are some ways you could use new studies to fill these gaps?
- Use the freewriting exercise in the chapter and develop three potential research questions. Rank them in terms of your interest—which would you want to move forward first?
- Use the links provided to the gerontological journals in the Overview of Past Methodological Research Design Work in the book's companion website. Choose several journal titles that relate to your topic of interest. Search through the journals' tables of contents for articles related to your topic of interest. State where your study can fill gaps in the existing literature or build upon existing work.

Bibliography

Association for Gerontology in Higher Education (AGHE). (2016). *Gerontology/geriatrics definitions*. Retrieved from http://www.aghe.org/resources/gerontology-geriatrics-descriptions#sthash.dohnJjZS.dpuf

Babbie, E. (2013). *The practice of social research* (13th ed.). Belmont, CA: Cengage Learning.

Barker, L. F. (1939). Aging from the point of view of the clinician. In Cowdry E. (Ed.), *Problems of ageing: Biological and medical aspects* (pp. 717–742). Baltimore, MD: Williams & Wilkins Company.

Cavan, R., Burgess, E., Havighurst, R., & Goldhammer, H. (1949). *Personal adjustment in old age*. Chicago: Science Research Associates.

Cowdry, E. V. (Ed.). (1939). *Problems of ageing: Biological and medical aspects*. Baltimore: Williams & Wilkins Company.

Creswell, J. W. (2014). *Research design: Qualitative, quantitative, and mixed methods approaches* (4th ed.). Thousand Oaks: Sage Publications.

Crotty, M. (1998). *The foundations of social research: Meaning and perspective in the research process*. Thousand Oaks: Sage Publications.

Cumming, E., & Henry, W. E. (1979). *Growing old*. New York: Arno Press.

Estes, C. L. (1979). *The aging enterprise*. San Francisco: Jossey-Bass

Ferraro, K., & Wilmoth, J. (2013). *Gerontology: Perspectives and issues* (4th ed.). New York: Springer Publishing Company

Howell, T. (1953). *Our advancing years: An essay on modern problems of old age*. London: Phoenix House.

Merriam, S. B. (2009). *Qualitative research: A guide to design and implementation* (2nd ed.). San Francisco: Jossey-Bass.

Metchnikoff, E. (1908). *The prolongation of life: Optimistic studies*. New York: The Knickerbocker Press.

Mills, C. W. (1967). *The sociological imagination*. New York and London: Oxford University Press.

Minkler, M., & Estes, C. L. (1999). *Critical gerontology: Perspectives from political and moral economy*. Amityville: Baywood Publishers.

Nascher, I. L. (1916). *Geriatrics: The diseases of old age and their treatment, including physiological old age, home and institutional care, and medico-legal relations* (2nd ed.). Philadelphia: Blakiston.

Nickoson, L., & Sheridan, M. P. (2012). *Writing studies research in practice: Methods and methodologies*. Carbondale: Southern Illinois University Press.

Phillipson, C., & Biggs, S. (1998). Modernity and identity: Themes and perspectives in the study of older adults. *Journal of Aging and Identity*, *3*(1), 11–23. doi:10.1023/A:1022888621674

Robnett, R., & Chop, W. (2015). *Gerontology for the health care professional* (3rd ed.). Burlington, MA: Jones & Bartlett Learning.

Rowe, J., & Kahn, R. (1997). Successful aging. *Gerontologist, 37*(4), 433–440.

SCImago. (2014). *Journal ranking for gerontology*. Retrieved from http://www.scimagojr.com

Shock, N. W. (1947). Older people and their potentialities for gainful employment. *Journal of Gerontology, 2*(2), 93–102.

Sinnott, J. D., Harris, C., Block, M., Jacobson, S., & Collesano, S. (1983). *Applied research in aging: A guide to methods and resources*. Burnaby: Simon Fraser University.

Sullivan, L. (2009). "Methodology." In Larry E. Sullivan (Ed.), *The Sage glossary of the social and behavioral sciences* (p. 324). Thousand Oaks, CA: Sage Publications.

Weigand, S. (2016). *University of Northern Colorado's gerontology research guide*. Retrieved from http://libguides.unco.edu/gero

2

Designing Research about Older People and Aging

Older persons and aging are the focus of gerontological research. This chapter presents several key issues that uniquely affect an older population. A clear understanding of normative and non-normative age-related changes in later life is essential to aging research. These changes are reviewed to paint a clear picture of older persons. Settings also vary with older peoples' participation in studies in places across the continuum of care—in the community, assisted living, skilled or memory care, and hospice. Researchers must consider their own role in the study and the involvement of older persons as co-researchers. Researchers must be aware of cultural norms and appropriate ways to study aging and older people across cultures. Time, itself, plays multiple roles in studies about aging. The age-period-cohort issue of time in aging studies will be discussed.

Now that a researcher has a research question, he or she must mix in knowledge specific to the study of older persons and aging. Gerontologists seek to capture the lived experience of older adults in their research, so the researcher must be aware of normative and non-normative age-related physical and cognitive changes in later life that can impact study design. Research with older persons also occurs in many settings, from one's home or community-based places (such as senior centers or congregate meal sites) to assisted living, skilled care, memory care, and hospice. The impact of place of research must be understood. Researchers must carefully assess their roles in the field (researcher and clinician or researcher and friendly visitor) and how to partner equally with older persons as co-researchers or conduct community-based participatory research projects with them. Time is another distinctive feature in studies of aging. Researchers have to distinguish and plan analyses to address changes to chronological age (**age effects**), changes due to a period of time experienced by all (**period effects**), or changes due to the group into which one is born (**cohort effects**). The combination of these three time elements is called **age-period-cohort effect**.

Unique Characteristics of an Older Population

Normative Age-Related Sensory Changes to Consider during Research

Physical and psychological/cognitive health changes that accompany normal chronological aging impact research with older persons.

Sensory Changes

The senses of vison, hearing, and touch change with age. **Vision changes** start in the 30s or 40s and increase when a person reaches his or her 60s. Changes can include a need for reading glasses, decrease in acuity or sharpness, and loss of near vision—especially of less than two feet (Besdine, 2015). The lens becomes more opaque, which means contrast between light and dark is more difficult (as the pupil is less reactive), and more light is needed to see (Besdine, 2015; Dagnelie, 2013). The lens yellows with age (called the **"yellow filter effect"**), and viewing color may be distorted (Saxon, Etten & Perkins, 2015, p. 104). Eyes become dry with a reduced peripheral visual field and more sensitivity to glare. **Severe vision difficulty**, being "blind or having serious difficulty seeing, even when wearing glasses," increases (He, Wan & Larsen, 2014, p. 1). About 17% of persons 65 to 74, 18% of those 75 to 84, and 25% of those 85 years of age and over have severe vision difficulty. Glaucoma, cataracts, and age-related macular degeneration may also impact older persons' vision—but these are diseases and not normal age-related changes.

Box 2.1 Sensory Links

Age-related vision changes:
http://www.nei.nih.gov/health/examples/index.asp
http://nihseniorhealth.gov/lowvision/lowvisiondefined/01.html

Age-related hearing changes:
http://nihseniorhealth.gov/hearingloss/hearinglossdefined/video/hb1_na.html?intro=yes

Hearing changes begin at age 40 or 50 with noticeable changes noted after 60, when about 30% of people report some hearing loss. Rates of hearing difficulty increase with age: 35% of those 65 to 74, 41% of those 75 to 84, and 48% of those 85 and older have a hearing disability, defined as "deafness or having serious difficulty hearing" (He, Wan & Larsen, 2014). The Federal Interagency Forum on Aging-Related Statistics (2010) found that 31% of those 65–74 had some hearing trouble, and 59% of those 85 years of age or older did, but only 11% of women and 18% of men 65 or older wore hearing aids.

Hearing loss can be caused by repeated exposure to loud noises, chronic conditions, or prescription medications, or it can be a conductive hearing loss from a physical blockage of the ear canal or due to wax. **Presbycusis** is an age-related loss of high-pitched and other frequencies. It has a gradual onset and often affects both ears. With presbycusis comes the loss of consonant differentiation, particularly of *k*, *p*, *s*, and *f* sounds (Rabbitt, 2015, p. 113). Similar-sounding words—such as "bear," "care," and "wear"—are difficult to distinguish (Gates & Mills, 2005). Background noise makes hearing all aspects of conversations problematic. **Tinnitus** (or ringing in the ears) can accompany presbycusis. Speaking clearly in a lower pitch, enunciating, and clear pronouncing are preferred. Increased volume only increases the distortion of sound. Vertigo, loss of equilibrium, and Meniere's disease are diseases that can accompany aging. Chronic illness, oral health, and medications can impact sense of taste and smell.

Physical and Functional Changes

Activities of Daily Living (ADLs; e.g., bathing, dressing, toileting) and **Instrumental Activities of Daily Living** (IADLs; e.g., completing housework, taking medication, managing finances) are used to describe physical functioning. *Older Americans 2012* summarized functional ability and limitations data for Medicare recipients 65 and older in 2009, finding 12% had IADL difficulties only. In terms of ADL difficulties, 18% had difficulty with 1–2 tasks, 5% had difficulty with 3–4 tasks, and 3% had difficulty with 5–6 tasks. Rates and patterns of functional limitations differ owing to many factors, such as socioeconomic status, race, ethnicity, advanced age, and gender. Women have higher rates of limitation in older age, though they begin with a higher baseline of limitations in midlife than their male counterparts (Federal Interagency Forum on Aging-Related Statistics, 2012; Rohlfsen & Kronenfeld, 2014).

Ambulatory difficulty—"having serious difficulty walking or climbing stairs"—increases with age (64% of those 65–74, 65% of those 75–84, and 73% of persons 85+; He, Wan & Larsen, 2014, p. 1). About 68% of Medicare recipients 65 years or older reported using assistive devices or equipment (such as a cane) as aids in ambulation. Most of those persons (38.4%) used equipment only, while 6.4% used personal assistance only, and 23.4% used a combination of personal and device assistance (Federal Interagency Forum on Aging-Related Statistics, 2012).

Mobility issues can stem from co-morbid or multiple chronic conditions and changes in body composition. Estimates suggest 67% of persons 65 years of age and older have multiple chronic conditions (CDC, 2013). Loss of muscle strength and decreased flexibility may occur (Besdine, 2015). Falls and changes in balance can occur due to loss of sensation in the hands and feet, as well as vestibular changes (Rabbitt, 2015). Functional changes in later life are different for those with an earlier disability.

Cognitive Changes

Cognition includes many functions and processes. They include thinking, perception, attention, reasoning, language, intelligence, and learning. These different aspects of cognitive function change differently with chronological age.

Anatomical changes include a reduction in brain mass/size, decrease in white matter, and pre-frontal grey matter loss affecting executive functioning (controlling organization and emotional regulation). There are fewer neurons to activate, which affects verbal recall. While some anatomical changes are linked to changes in functioning, cognition in later life can also be seen as a process of brain changes and compensation. Recent work calls for an understanding of why some people experience greater/more rapid cognitive decline in working and long-term memory (Rabbitt, 2015, p. xi).

Recently, the Institute of Medicine (IOM, 2015) produced a comprehensive summary of research to date about cognitive changes in multiple domains—cognitive speed, attention, memory, executive function, reasoning, language, spatial ability, intelligence, and wisdom. **Cognitive speed**, or the ability to process information and respond verbally, does slow with age. **Selective attention** (focusing and filtering one's social environment) and **divided attention** (splitting one's attentions to accomplish several tasks at once) do decrease with age. But, sustained attention, or the ability to concentrate or focus on a particular task, does not decline with age. Research suggests we need to explore the relationship of attention control in tests to working memory (Verhaeghen & Zhang, 2013).

Working memory "is used to plan and carry out behavior. One relies on working memory to retain the partial results while solving an arithmetic problem without paper, to combine the premises in a lengthy rhetorical argument, or to bake a cake without making the unfortunate mistake of adding the same ingredient twice" (Cowan, 2008, p. 3). This slows, as does recalling information with age (Rabbitt, 2015). Long-term memory that is **semantic** (factual, fact-based) decreases little with age, while **episodic memory** (remembering personal daily details), **prospective memory** (remembering future tasks and events), and **source memory**

(keeping memories in context—"flash-bulb memory . . . [where people] must recollect when, where, and/or from whom they learned information)" also decreases so that one may forget links between people and events or how to link information to a source (Rabbitt, 2015; Rapcsak, Verfaellie, Glisky, Cook & Davidson, 2005, p. 916). **Procedural memory** (learning new skills) is not impacted by age, but the functional changes may be at play here. **Executive function**—those higher-cognitive skills needed to perform complex tasks, organize information, think abstractly, and adapt to new situations and act appropriately—declines with age as does reasoning, logical thinking, and problem solving.

Language abilities for vocabulary and comprehension of words remain stable with age, and some say that an older person's is better than a younger person's aptitude. Aspects of language negatively affected by age include language production, having lesser idea density in speech, less ability to understand distorted speech, and word loss ("words on the tip of one's tongue"). In tests of spatial ability (rotating drawn shapes in one's mind or copying 3-D images), older persons perform less well when compared to younger persons. **Crystallized intelligence** (accumulated knowledge) is reported to increase with age or at least be stable or show little decline with aging, while **fluid intelligence** (problem solving in new settings) decreases. The study of wisdom, as a form of expertise, has begun to enter studies about positive cognitive changes with age.

While, in the past, anatomy and brain size were solely associated with functioning and absence of diseases, **cognitive reserve** is now seen as more key in preserving normal functioning than mass alone (Stern, 2012).

> Individuals who have higher levels of cognitive functioning in their young adulthood . . . will experience similar rates of cognitive decline as those who have less education and cognitive abilities. The time it takes for these individuals to reach functional levels of impairment may be longer than the average individual.
>
> (Horning & Davis, 2012, p. 50)

Concepts of **neural plasticity** (the ability of the brain to change and compensate for loss) need to be addressed, as does the norming of test scores for normal/within-range cognitive functioning (IOM, 2015). See Table 2.1 for age-related changes impact upon research.

Cognitive changes must be differentiated from cognitive impairment and not viewed as a given step-wise progression or continuum. Gradual decline in memory is common as one ages, since "a minority of people, perhaps 1 in 100, go through life with virtually no cognitive decline" (Petersen, 2011, p. 2227). Minor forgetfulness (loss of a name or word) is typical. But normal age-related memory loss and mild cognitive impairment are different. Mild cognitive impairment can be experienced as periods of forgetfulness without changes in executive function (called **amnestic**) or with changes in attention, language, and spatial tasks (called **non-amnestic**). This mild cognitive loss, beyond normal aging, is linked to increased difficulty with daily life and embarrassment, frustration, and loss of confidence (Parikh, Troyer, Maione & Murphy, 2015; Vaughan, Erickson, Espeland, Smith, Tindle & Rapp, 2014). The IOM stresses that mild cognitive impairment should not be used as a "catch-all" for any/all memory loss and that we need to explore how well tests capture impairment, realize the impact of stress and illness upon impairment readings, and begin to investigate the use of biomarkers to define "boundaries in cognitive functioning change" (p. 46).

Media may see exercise as improving cognitive ability and as a quick fix (Vandenberg, Price, Friedman, Marchman & Anderson, 2012). Research suggests training exercise may maintain cognitive function but only in those who begin with greater cognitive ability (Bielak, Cherbuin, Bunce & Anstey, 2014). Or physical training may improve cognitive function in persons who are frail (Langlois, Vu, Chassé, Dupuis, Kergoat & Bherer, 2013).

Table 2.1 Normative Age-Related Changes and Issues of Administration

Mode of Delivery/ Administration	Major Issues	Recommendations
Face-to-face	Hearing; vision; changes in cognition	Face older interviewees, at the same level, with limited background noise. Employ visual aids and "use direct, concrete, actionable language when talking to older adults; verify listener comprehension during a conversation; ask open-ended questions and genuinely listen; if computers are used during face-to-face visits with older adults, consider switching to models that facilitate collaborative use; and ask questions about an older adult's living situation and social contacts" (Gerontological Society of America, 2012). Having readable fonts on consent forms and study-documents is advised (Goodbrand & McMurdo, 2013). Types of behavior: nonverbal, spatial, linguistic, and extra-linguistic—pitch, rate of speed, interruption (Frankfort-Nachmias, Nachmias & DeWaard, 2015). Facial cues/ recognition differ by older age group and gender. Older age groups may have more difficulty using facial cues to assess emotion. Older women focus on eyes for cues, while men focus on mouths for reading emotional expression (Sullivan, Campbell, Hutton & Ruffman, 2015). Older men (69+) with higher cognitive scores preferred and followed what they perceived as trustworthy faces and expressions more so than younger persons in the study. Older persons have difficulty following eye-gaze directions/cues of others and expressiveness of eyes, which can be related to difficulty in reading expression in faces (Slessor, Riby & Finnerty, 2012; Slessor, Venturini, Bonny, Insch, Rokaszewicz & Finnerty, 2014). In terms of averted gaze and interpretation of deception (lying) and direct gaze as being honest, older persons found someone averting indicated deception (but less often than younger persons); researchers felt this indicated a lesser connection of gaze as a way to assess another's level or honesty or deception (Slessor, Phillips, Bull, Venturini, Bonny & Rokaszewicz, 2012). Stereotypes can negatively influence cognitive testing, creating poor performance, which has lasting impact (Barber, Mather & Gatz, 2015; Levy, Zonderman, Slade & Ferrucci, 2012). The difference between motor and cognitive abilities in testing must be separated and better understood (Vasquez, Binns & Anderson, 2014; Yang, Chen, Ng & Fu, 2013) as does the time of day the test is performed (Anderson, Campbell, Amer, Grady & Hasher, 2014) Speed of processing information can differ in "lab and real world" test settings (Lin, Chen, Vance & Mapstone, 2013).
Telephone	Hearing; vision; changes in cognition	For those with moderate to severe hearing loss, a telephone is not a good option when background noise is present. Listening using two ears, not only one, is a preferable strategy (See Picou & Ricketts, 2013).

Mode of Delivery/ Administration	Major Issues	Recommendations
Internet (email, video conferencing, social media)	Changes in dexterity; vision; technological concerns	Older persons see the benefits of Internet use to include connectivity to friends and family, satisfaction of accessing information, and positive learning experiences. Expressed barriers include frustration with development of new programs, physical changes in response time, hearing and vision issues, and concerns with fraud and issues of time (Tak & Gatto, 2008). Slowed typing and cognitive acuity can play a role in satisfaction of online work (Remillard et al., 2014). Researchers looking at online senior communities found older persons are a fast-growing online presence (Nimrod, 2013), while some older persons may opt out of usage for personal choice and not health issues. And there is a diversity of Internet experience and usage (Chang et al., 2014). Recommendations for web design and use for older people include less-decorated, simple pages with large targets, no pull-down menus, less green and blue colors usage, no sharp color changes, spell-checked searches, concrete error messages, time to read items, and less reliance upon recall (Zaphiris, Kurniawan & Ghiawadwala, 2007). Younger age groups (66–74) are more often Internet, mouse, and text users. Men in this age group were found to use the Internet more often than women. Those with vision and memory issues were less likely to use technology—but support (such as easy-to-use keyboards) and training are options. Researchers question whether it is the technology, itself, or the ways to access it that is the problem (Gell, Rosenberg, Demiris, LaCroix & Patel, 2013). Interactive voice response system use (interacting with a voice-prompted menu via the telephone) has been found to be somewhat difficult for older adults because the language used and required by the respondent is often non-natural speech and requires a specific pace of speech—without much room for repeated attempts or errors (Miller, Gagnon, Talbot & Messier, 2013). Recent research findings suggest tablets with their ease of use are a good tool for computer-based studies with older persons (Tsai, Shillair, Cotten, Winstead & Yost, 2015). In terms of computerized versus pen-and-paper testing, pre-testing computer skill evaluation is helpful—using screening tools like the Computer Proficiency Questionnaire (Boot et al., 2015). There may need to be new norms and cut-off values for computerized tests. And these online assessments can offer greater accessibility as they can be done with the older persons in the convenience their own homes, if they so choose (Fazeli, Ross, Vance & Ball, 2013). We need to see technology beyond supportive medical devices/ applications and look at more than barriers to use among older people and health and independence relationships (Schulz,Wahl, Matthews, De Vito Dabbs, Beach & Czaja, 2015).

Adapted from: Weil, J. (2015). Applying research methods to a gerontological population: Matching data collection to characteristics of older persons. *Educational Gerontology*, 41(10), 723–742.

The Impact of Place in Aging Research

The location of research matters. The setting can impact what a researcher learns when studying an older population. Two key considerations are the place a person is living and the way the researcher views the study site. In terms of the locale, issues of boundaries, roles, and power differentials arise.

Community vs. Continuum of Care

Community. Community-dwelling older persons are not so vastly different, per se, than any other study participant. Beyond social desirability or providing answers that meet the interviewer's perceived expectations, older respondents may use cultural scripts about health and chronic disease that they believe an interviewer may favor, feel comfortable hearing, or want to hear (Cruikshank, 2013). Since independence is a societal value, it impacts research in the community (Hillcoat-Nallétamby, 2014). The idea of independence and living on one's own may frame the topic of discussion (Freedman & Spillman, 2014). An interviewer can also foster discussion of issues of "dependency" and "frailty" or "active," "successful" aging in interviewees. Community-dwelling older persons, as they are living in the community and not in a facility, may need transportation to the study site (Goodbrand & McMurdo, 2013).

Researchers studying homebound older persons report this group may have unique issues related to the perceived therapeutic intervention of the presence of the researcher, loneliness, and increased vulnerability (Locher, Bronstein, Robinson, Williams & Ritchie, 2006). Medicare (2015) defines homebound as "having trouble leaving your home without help (like using a cane, wheelchair, walker, or crutches; special transportation; or help from another person) because of an illness or injury; or leaving one's home isn't recommended because of their condition; and [the person is] normally unable to leave their home, and leaving home is a major effort. [The individual] may leave home for medical treatment or short, infrequent absences for non-medical reasons, like attending religious services" (Medicare Glossary, 2015). The researchers suggest having a backup plan for witnessing abuse and needs in the field and a referral plan for getting the older persons help, if and as needed.

Continuum of care. Those in assisted or skilled-care residential settings (without memory impairment) may feel as if there is an incentive or tie between participation and care. Residents may feel their candidness and frankness can cause negative effects in their care or living environment. For example, would a resident feel free to tell the interviewer that the staff do not treat her well? Or meet her needs? If a resident talks about a need for additional ADL assistance or financial problems, will she fear the staff will want to move her to another facility? Social desirability pieces come back into play.

Issues of true **voluntary consent** (participating in the study by choice without coercion) also arise. Clinical researchers in English care homes found that staff can also bias who participates in a study and how the study is framed to older residents. The researchers suggest posters as recruitment tools for residents and to keep disruption on residents' and staffs' daily schedules minimal (McMurdo et al., 2011). Frail persons in care may be excluded from studies (Goodbrand & McMurdo, 2013). For those in memory care or with impaired cognitive status, a researcher must consider how the person's cognitive impairment affects his or her ability to consent to, and participate in, the research. If a **proxy** (another person other than the person with cognitive impairment) provides information in a study, the accuracy of that information must be assessed. For example, Gillian Hewitt, Alizon Draper, and Suraiya Ismail's (2013) study sought to conduct a needs assessment using a participatory-based approach with older persons and staff in an assisted-living-like setting in Guyana. They found difficulty gaining consistent support from staff for their study. Residents reported hesitation to talk about real issues in front of staff due to confidentiality concerns, saying "bush got ears and grass got tongue" (p. 9) and having fear of the staff's abuse of power. Residents often reported a better rapport with the researchers than with institutional employees.

Barbara Resnick, Ann Gruber-Baldini, Ingrid Pretzer-Aboff, Elizabeth Galik, Verita Custis Buie, Karin Russ, and Sheryl Zimmerman's (2007) Reliability and Validity of the **Evaluation to Sign Consent (ESC)** measure asks persons with potential cognitive impairment about the risks, benefits, and ways to withdraw from a study before they participate. They suggest that this test is a better option than doing mental testing and cognitive screenings alone, since the ESC questions relate to the study directly. Other researchers suggest that proxies for those with dementia have difficulty assessing present and past wishes (Dunn, Fisher, Hantke, Appelbaum, Dohan, Young & Roberts, 2013). Other times, when a proxy is present, the older person with dementia will be less involved or will let the proxy do much of the talking (Sugarman, Roter, Cain, Wallace, Schmechel & Welsh-Bohmer, 2007).

Recruitment Site vs. Study Site

Although these two terms sound alike, seeing the setting as a recruitment site is very different from seeing it as the setting for your study. As Buckwalter (2009) pointed out:

> Too few papers report recruitment outcomes or adequately identify study procedures used to recruit participants, noting instead something such as, "Subjects were recruited voluntarily from three local assisted living facilities." . . . Still fewer articles document recruitment costs or publish information on the cost effectiveness of different recruitment strategies that inform researchers about appropriately budgeting for their studies. In many cases, investigators fail to anticipate the time, personnel, and costs associated with recruitment efforts, especially those involving direct involvement of researchers with community stakeholders.
>
> (p. 256)

There are several major differences. Clinical researchers have found issues of communication, trust-building, comfort and security, and expressions of gratitude all important issues to consider when working with older persons. Other issues include mistrust of the research or researcher, stigma of a disease (e.g., Alzheimer's disease), caregiver burden, having medical conditions or frailty, or issues of cognitive status (McHenry, Insel, Einstein, Vidrine, Koerner & Morrow, 2012). In recruiting for clinical trials for older persons with hypertension, researchers found social marketing—such as "health parties," where persons learn about the study—worked, as did connecting with local non-profits and service agencies. These sites were places where the study could also be brought up during service provision. Allowing more staff time for recruitment and planning for transportation, parking, and related costs also increased participation, while medical conditions, as part of eligibility, reduced participation. The team found three principles helpful in recruiting older adults for clinical research: communication and trust-building (offering personal care and face-to-face contact), providing comfort and security (parking, navigating the medical center, member of the team as a greeter/guide), and expressions of gratitude (contact and explanation of the study, quick compensation, hand-written notes, small gifts; McHenry, Insel, Einstein, Vidrine, Koerner & Morrow, 2015, p. 846).

If the study site is primarily seen as a recruitment site only, the researcher will spend time working with a **gatekeeper** (or person that is key in getting access to the site). Contact with older participants will be more limited and formalized—e.g., mostly completing surveys and focus groups. Some refer to this as **"hit and run," "helicopter,"** or **"smash and grab" research** (Braun, Browne, Ka'opua, Kim & Mokuau, 2014). Researchers who see the setting as the site of their study will, undoubtedly, spend more time there. In the case of ethnography with extended case studies, longitudinal data collection, or some concurrent parallel designs, time spent in the field could be years. Whether a researcher sees the study location as a setting or as a site of recruitment only, some of the same principles exist. Never exhaust the field setting. If possible and practical, keep older persons in the analysis in active roles or use participatory-based designs (discussed later in this chapter).

A Researcher's Roles in the Study and Field

While the researcher's role is often thought of as something to address in qualitative studies alone, the researcher's influence or imprint can be seen in all designs. Qualitative researchers are always called to reflect on their role in the field and level of engagement with older persons they study. A quantitative researcher decides upon hypotheses and questions, variable construction, data sets and participant selection, choice of measure or statistic, level of significance, software, instrument design, and way to report his or her findings. It is not that quantitative researchers take advantage of innumeracy or "lie with statistics" as popular culture books attest (from Huff, 1954 to Best, 2005). Issues of a quantitative researcher's hand and presence in the process must be noted. Researchers using mixed methods may need to justify their own role in both portions of the study. In **emergent methods**, researchers become more enmeshed in the data and research process—using participants' words as performance or being captured in photovoice or advocating for a group as part of the group. They must be openly aware of power differentials and conflicting roles (Carter & Hurtado, 2007).

Assessing Your Own Role in the Field

The good news is the researcher is the one deciding what his or her role will be in a study. This section can help researchers assess the responsibilities associated with a role and if they are a suitable match. In the previous chapter, researchers were asked to consider their own roles in their research—to think about the extent to which they are a participant in the study, a covert or overt observer, a co-researcher with older participants, or an advocate. Now, researchers can add in ways to record and monitor their roles.

Sue Berger works as both a practitioner and an academic researcher. She is an occupational therapist who has done a qualitative study of older adults with vision loss. As part of her work, she has presented about changing role or stance from a clinician's role to that of a qualitative researcher (Berger, 2011). In her 2011 Gerontological Society of America's presentation, "Challenges in the Art of Interviewing: Transitioning from Clinician to Researcher," she discusses the similarities and differences in these two roles. Berger found that the two roles both merge and diverge. Both seek to establish trust with older participants, use self-reflexivity, and use past experiences to enrich current practice. In terms of role structure, both roles use interviewing and observational skills. But Berger found styles differ in terms of length of time, question, and prompt type. She describes conflicting purposes of listening in research: "as a clinician: listening and thinking of ways to make change" and "as a researcher: listening to understand." In "Wearing two hats" (2009), Lorraine Ritchie writes about her "role tension" as a nurse and interviewer. At times, she wore her nurse's badge and felt she needed to offer medical advice or assess symptoms as a form of reciprocity to those she studied. Other times, interviewees would directly ask her for medical advice or even for examinations—e.g., an older woman asked her to examine a leg wound during an interview.

On an emotional level, the researcher may have difficulty leaving his or her subjects and remaining "uninvolved—when privy to so much detailed, personal information" (Greenwood, 2009, p. 31). Depending upon the work, a research can experience what Linda Burton, Diane Purvin, and Raymond Garrett-Peters call **vicarious trauma**. They describe ethnographic work with domestic violence and how the transcription, analysis, and presentation processes can also traumatize the researchers working on the project.

Older Persons as Co-researchers: True Community-Based Participatory Research

Researchers describe the co-research approach with researchers and older persons along a continuum (from "user-led initiatives to users as collaborators to users consulted to users as recipients"; Gutman, Hantman, Ben-Oz, Criden, Anghel & Ramon, 2014, Figure 2.1, p. 188).

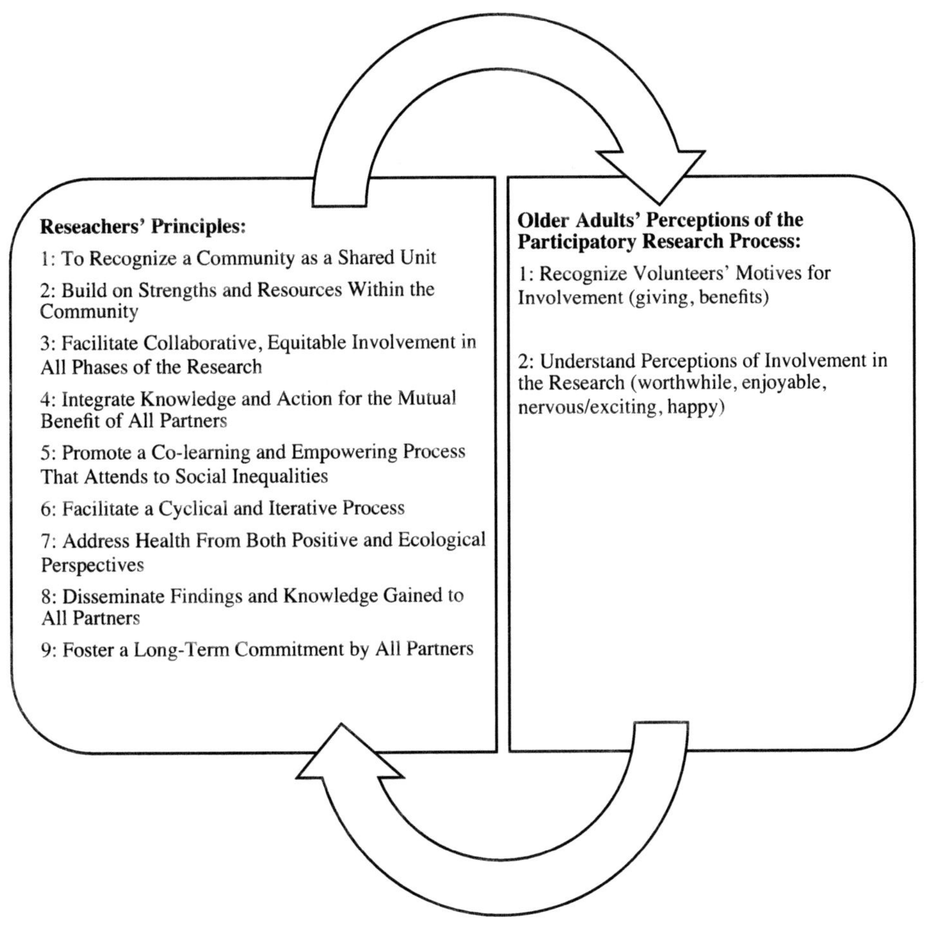

Figure 2.1 Lessons from a Community-Based Participatory Research Project: Older People's and Researchers' Reflections

Source: Doyle and Timonen (2009).

Others describe the team-building and co-led research process using collaborative journey-based metaphors: "the travel itinerary, differing landscapes, enjoying the view" (Bindels, Baur, Cox, Heijing & Abma, 2014).

True **community-based participatory research (CBPR)** keeps researchers and older community members as true equals with no power differentials (Israel, Schulz, Parker & Becker, 1998; Israel, Schulz, Parker, Becker, Allen & Guzman, 2003; Janes, 2015). Martha Doyle and Virpi Timonen explored the process of using CBPR with older persons to evaluate and improve home-care services in Dublin. Lessons learned from researchers and older persons are presented in Figure 2.1. Using CBPR, researchers and older rural persons were able define what "healthy aging" meant to them. Items generated by the CBPR (social interaction, independence, keeping active, optimistic thinking, and good cognitive health) differed from what administrators and policy makers had identified as healthy aging markers (Bacsu et al., 2014).

Other researchers used **participatory action research** (PAR), one in which the persons impacted by an issue or problem define the problem and seek to find solutions. Robin Shura, Rebecca Siders and Dale Dannefer (2011) used a PAR process to have residents address gaps in an Eden-assisted and skilled-living setting that may exist, even though the facility and principles are part of the culture-change care movement. Residents formed the Resident Research Group and created general policies of actions and behaviors to help staff and residents work together better. They include the following: "handling bumps in the in the road with grace; Using sensitivity, and being accountable; and It is never too late to say 'I'm sorry,' It goes a long way" (p. 219). The PAR project used these policies to address lessening staff involvement and low staff morale. The Population Study of Chinese Elderly in Chicago (or PINE) is an example of an academic and 20-community-organization-partnered study working to collect and assess health data about Chinese older persons (Dong, 2014).

Understanding and Acknowledging Group Differences in Aging Research

Another way a researcher can think about his or her own role in a study is the way the role can impact work with different groups and cultures. Group differences can include gender, race, ethnicity, socioeconomic class, sexuality/LGBT status, functional and cognitive ability, and many other characteristics of the researcher and older persons studied. These identifiers can even be overlapping and include cultural differences: "[T]he term **culture** refers to the way of life and attitudes of a particular group. . . . [T]he broader term ethnicity refers to a sense of group identity that can be based on race, culture, nationality, or language" (Lewis, 2005, p. 676). While there are many ways to define differences, the gerontological researcher must strive to understand and these **emic** ("behavior studied from within a system in only one culture") and **etic** ("behavior studied from a position outside the system, when it is studied in many cultures") differences when conducting research (Eckensberger, 2015, p. 112).

Working with older adults in many cultures and countries can be a topic for a separate book or volume of books. The following are some examples to generate thinking as researchers work on their own studies. In *Race and the lifecourse* (2014), Nancy Mendoza writes about her work investigating the cultural concepts or norms in studying Latino grandfamilies. She studied potentially undocumented Latino grandparents raising grandchildren and their families by using intergenerational interviewing. The setting had a history of difficulty in obtaining Latino participants and fear and distrust associated with past Immigration and Customs Enforcement raids. While exploring caregiver and *la familia* role-based norms, she found a need for additional safeguards to protect participants and used witnessed consent (not signed consent) and a NIH Certificate of Confidentiality. These safeguards are discussed in detail in Chapter 10. Participants were also consciously not asked about their legal status in the United States. Individuals were referred to by pseudonyms, and all materials were numerically coded and destroyed. Mendoza found these practices increased the comfort level of participants, gathered richer data, and fulfilled the researcher's duties and obligation to participants. Carolyn Mendez-Luck and Katherine Anthony's work (2015) examined the heterogeneity in the *marianisma* concept (or traditional roles of caregiving ascribed to Mexican women in the United States and Mexico). Toni Antonucci, Kristine Ajrouch, and Sawsan Abdulrahim (2015) found the similarities in Lebanese familial relationships—that a distinction was needed between supposed social ties and that a more "nuanced" and "less simplistic" view of social ties needed to emerge (p. 833).

Ramraj Gautam, Barbara Mawn, and Sarah Beehler's in-depth interviews with older Nepalese refugee adults in the United States found that the typical approach, where a researcher selects the person in a family to be the main participant, did not work. For Nepalese refugees, it was the entire family, led by an elder, who would decide the best participant and seek greater family input in the study and informed-consent process. Researchers in Beirut, Lebanon, found the same family-based participant selection process. The family would make the decision and select a candidate. This was in contrast to the study, where it was the researchers who sought to choose the participant (Abdulrahim, Ajrouch, Jammal & Antonucci, 2012).

Other studies have found that living through traumatic events/poverty impacts immigrants' aging experiences. Kate de Medeiros, Robert Rubinstein, and Polina Ermoshkina (2015) found that older Russian women now living in the United States but who lived in the Soviet Union during World War II were less hopeful or generative about the future. Researchers found older Somali refugees in Canada had a more positive view of aging, with men expressing more negative aspects about their new setting (Lagacé, Charmarkeh & Grandena, 2012).

Helen Fung (2013) and Michael North and Susan Fiske (2015) suggest differences in aging in Eastern and Western culture while questioning what "Eastern" and "Western" cultures signify. Min Fang Wang-Letzkus, Gail Washington, Evelyn Calvillo, and Nancy Anderson (2012) applied CBPR and a Vulnerable Populations Conceptual Model to approach research with older Chinese Americans with diabetes. The researchers stated that "vulnerable populations often bear a disproportionate burden of the deleterious effects of diseases. Age, immigrant status, financial restraints, lack of English-language proficiency, limited access to public resources, physiological decline, and frequent chronic health problems classify Chinese American elders as a vulnerable population" (2012, p. 256). Combining both CBPR and VPCM allowed researchers to collaborate with older persons with respect for cultural beliefs as a foundation of their partnerships. Other researchers have quantified the cultural-item bias in scales, such as the Center for Epidemiologic Studies Depression Scale (CES-D) for Korean-American older persons (Kim, Lee, Ko, Yoon, Kim & Jang, 2015). Group and language bias in defining terminology and creating research tools has been found for many other racial and ethnic groups (Angel, 2013; Hilton & Child, 2014).

In a study of Vietnamese and Chinese caregivers for those with dementia in Australia, researchers used a Cultural Exchange Model. "Participants were involved and contributed to all stages of the process.... The model enabled the researchers to engage the stakeholders early and to refine the implementation process based on their feedback" (Haralambous et al., 2014, p. 72). Knowledge creation was a joint process that involved researchers' and stakeholders' consultation, immersion, and collaboration, including an understanding of each group's culture, ethnicity, and values (Haralambous et al., 2014).

Researchers are actively working on ways to conduct research with indigenous older person using **decolonizing strategies** (those addressing power differentials and marginalization of indigenous people in research). Researchers suggest that quantitative questions can be culture-bound and that qualitative models can reproduce Eurocentric/ethnocentric views of participants. Both CBPR and PAR models are favored, with the best approaches to be lifecourse and resilience, or strength-based designs (Braun, Browne, Ka'opua, Kim & Mokuau, 2014). This marginalizing view can impact outcomes, as when David Hodge and Robert Wolosin found hospital staff often did not include Native-American spiritual practices in health care. Other researchers found convening listening groups of native Hawaiian elders is a data-collection method that recognizes the older person's cultural role (Browne, Mokuau, Ka'opua, Kim, Higuchi & Braun, 2014).

Time in Aging Research

Measuring Age and Time in Aging Studies

Age and time are two key issues in gerontological research. Age can be measured in several ways. The most common use of age is chronological age or the number of years lived (e.g., age-related changes). However, other ways may measure age. Subjective age, or the age a person feels he or she is, is based not on number of years lived but on the person's own assessment (Barrett & Montepare, 2015; Hummert, 2015). Functional age is based on one's level of functional abilities such as ADLs and IADLs. Life-stage categories, such as being a grandparent or widow, are additional ways of marking time (Morgan & Kunkel, 2007). There is also social aging, or how "our external experiences of our bodies" are a reflection of how society sees us aging (Holstein, Parks & Waymack, 2011 p. 48).

Age-Period-Cohort (APC) Effects

Three time effects must be considered when doing research on aging: age, period, and cohort. Authors suggest it is crucial to address age-period-cohort effects in analysis of studies including older persons so one time effect is not attributed to another (Yang & Land, 2013).

Age. Age effects can be thought of as "the individual's experience of time passing" (Jamieson & Victor, 2002, p. 102). These are the changes that happen over a person's life and include normal age-related and developmental changes that happen with the passage of chronological time.

Period. Period effects occur across calendar years or time intervals. A period effect is the result of all of society experiencing an event or phenomenon that occurs during the study period. The event or experience is not unique or restricted solely to older adults.

Cohort. Birth cohort plays a role in research about older persons and aging. One's **birth cohort** is the group into which one is born and with whom he or she ages across his or her lifespan. The cohort into which a person is born affects his or her attitudes, views and experiences, health and functional abilities, and place in society (Christensen et al., 2013). Since some cohorts can span a number of years (e.g., Baby Boomers born 1946–1964), sub-cohorts

Box 2.2 An Example of Mixed Age-Period-Cohort Effects

Quality of Life for Rural Older Persons

You read about a three-year mixed-methods study assessing quality of life for persons 80 years of age and older living in a U.S. Census–defined and person-defined rural setting. These participants are the Lucky Few generation (born 1929–1945). This generational group was smaller than prior ones. They were born during the war and Great Depression but had peace-time military service and better employment and education than earlier generations.

As part of their structured surveys, researchers interviewed older persons who were long-term residents of the area, meaning they have lived in the same general vicinity for at least 25 years. The research team also pulled some secondary data about chronic conditions and mental-health services.

The researchers mention in the article that in the second year of this study, the region was hit by a tornado that initially caused some participants to be relocated. After the Federal Emergency Management Agency (FEMA) was brought in, many of the older persons' homes were rebuilt to code (some even better than before the natural disaster). Other older persons left the area and moved into care or lived with families and friends and chose not to return. There was also an influx of newly retired, more affluent older persons into this community after the rebuilding.

The overall findings indicated that the rural older persons in this study reported high levels of happiness and had high levels of life satisfaction.

Based on the information provided here, identify the way age, period, and cohort issues may have affected the researchers' findings.

may also spring up. Cohorts are heterogeneous because they cover a wide time span and have subgroups within them.

Use of Longitudinal and Cross-Sectional Designs

Several design options are proposed to address APC that prevent a true measurement of separate age, period, and cohort effects. Traditionally, **longitudinal designs** (collecting data over several time points) are one way to separate out **confounding influences** (attributing changes to one element of time [e.g., age] when they are really caused by another [e.g., period]; Alwin, 2002). Controlling for one or two of the time-based variables is another strategy to separate APC effects involved (Yang, 2009).

Statisticians are working to develop practical ways to apply techniques to control for age-period-cohort analysis (Yang & Land, 2013). More advanced approaches—intrinsic estimator use, hierarchical or mixed-effects models for repeated cross-sectional surveys with multilevel data, hierarchical change models for accelerated longitudinal cohort data or cohort-inversion models—may not be accessible by all researchers (Yang, 2009, pp. 9–10). Other researchers echo the concern that we need to develop more effective and feasible models to test APC (Bell & Jones, 2015). Table 2.2 provides a description of three study types and which aspect of APC effects they address and APC elements they may confuse. A list of further APC-related techniques is provided in the bibliography at the end of this chapter and in Chapters 5 and 6.

Table 2.2 Review of Study Designs Addressing Age-Period-Cohort Issues

Type of Study	Compares*	Confounds*	Example
Cross-sectional	Age groups at one point in time	Age and cohort	Those 65 in 2015
Longitudinal	Same individuals at different points in time	Age and period	Those 65 in 1995, 75 in 2005, then 85 in 2015
Time-lag	Individuals at the same age in different points in time	Cohort and period	Those 65 in 1995, 2005, 2015

Source: * = Created from the narrative in Victor, C., Westerhof, G. J. and Bond, J. (2007). Researching ageing. *Ageing in Society. European Perspectives on Gerontology*, 85–112.

This chapter reviewed elements related to aging and older populations that researchers must address in their study design. Knowing normal changes in physical and cognitive functioning and recognizing how a site can impact design helps researchers create better-designed studies suited to older persons. Community-Based Participatory Research and Participatory Action Research were reviewed as ways to have older persons as co-researchers in a study. Issues related to the role of time in aging studies and age-period-cohort effects were introduced so researchers can begin to separate out findings based on a person's aging, events occurring to everyone during the time of the study, and changes due to the period in which the person was born.

Discussion Questions

- Provide a paragraph summarizing the major "normal" age-related changes (discussed in this chapter) that are likely to occur with age. Then, design three questions you would want to ask to gather additional information from an older person about age-related changes you described. Your questions should help you gain greater knowledge about the changes an older person may be experiencing that would help you in your field of study or professional work with older persons.
- Describe ways to address age-related changes in study design. How would you address vision changes in written materials? How could cueing work in physical testing? How would you address hearing changes? Address cognitive changes? (Consider accessing either of these resources: National Institute of Aging [2016], *Talking with your older patient: A clinician's handbook*, at https://www.nia.nih.gov/health/publication/talking-your-older-patient/talking-patients-about-cognitive-problems?utm_source=20160426_twyop&utm_medium=email&utm_campaign=ealert, or the Gerontological Society of America's [2012] *Communicating with older adults: An evidence-based review of what really works* [Washington, D.C.].)
- Discuss some strategies for handling both your roles (researcher/clinical or researcher/social visitor) in the field. What are other risks to researchers in the field?
- What are some ways to have older persons as co-researchers in a study? Consider lessons learned from Doyle and Timonen's (2009) community-based participatory research project and their comparison of older people's and researchers' reflections about the research process.

- Explain how the setting (as a place in the continuum of care: the community, assisted living, skilled or memory care, and hospice) and view of the site of research (study site vs. recruitment site) matter in studies with older persons.
- Describe some of the research approaches that the authors cited in this chapter suggest when doing research with indigenous peoples. How can you apply these to other groups? What are some key things for researchers to consider when studying older persons in cultures that vary from their own?

Bibliography

Abdulrahim, S., Ajrouch, K., Jammal, A., & Antonucci, T. (2012). Survey methods and aging research in an Arab socio-cultural context: A case study from Beirut, Lebanon. *Journals of Gerontology: Social Sciences, 67*(6), 775–782.

Alwin, D. F. (2002). "Age-period-cohort model." In D. J. Ekerdt (Ed.), *Encyclopedia of aging* (Vol. 1, pp. 43–45). New York: Macmillan Reference. Gale Virtual Reference Library.

Anderson, J. A., Campbell, K. L., Amer, T., Grady, C. L., & Hasher, L. (2014). Timing is everything: Age differences in the cognitive control network are modulated by time of day. *Psychology and Aging, 29*(3), 648.

Angel, R. J. (2013). After Babel: Language and the fundamental challenges of comparative aging research. *Journal of Cross-Cultural Gerontology, 28*(3), 223–238.

Antonucci, T. C., Ajrouch, K. J., & Abdulrahim, S. (2015). Social relations in Lebanon: Convoys across the life course. *The Gerontologist, 55*(5), 825–835. doi:10.1093/geront/gnt209

Bacsu, J., Jeffery, B., Abonyi, S., Johnson, S., Novik, N., Martz, D., & Oosman, S. (2014). Healthy aging in place: Perceptions of rural older adults. *Educational Gerontology, 40*(5), 327–337.

Barber, S. J., Mather, M., & Gatz, M. (2015). How stereotype threat affects healthy older adults' performance on clinical assessments of cognitive decline: The key role of regulatory fit. *The Journals of Gerontology Series B: Psychological Sciences and Social Sciences, 70*(6), 891–900. doi:10.1093/geronb/gbv009

Barrett, A. E., & Montepare, J. M. (2015). "It's about time": Applying life span and life course perspectives to the study of subjective age. *Annual Review of Gerontology & Geriatrics, 35*(1), 55–77.

Bartlett, H., Henwood, T., & Carroll, M. (2011). Mentoring Australian emerging researchers in aging: Evaluation of a pilot mentoring scheme. *Educational Gerontology, 37*(8), 703–714.

Bell, A., & Jones, K. (2015). Bayesian informative priors with Yang and Land's hierarchical age-period-cohort model. *Quality & Quantity, 49*(1), 255–266. doi:10.1007/s11135-013-9985-3

Berger, S. (2011, November). Challenges in the art of interviewing: Transitioning from clinician to researcher. *The Gerontologist, 51*, 210–211.

Besdine, R. (2015). *Physical changes with aging in the Merck manual, professional version.* http://www.merckmanuals.com/professional/geriatrics/approach-to-the-geriatric-patient/physical-changes-with-aging

Best, J. (2005). Lies, calculations and constructions: Beyond how to lie with statistics. *Statistical Science, 20*(3), 210–214.

Bielak, A. A., Cherbuin, N., Bunce, D., & Anstey, K. J. (2014). Preserved differentiation between physical activity and cognitive performance across young, middle, and older adulthood over 8 years. *The Journals of Gerontology Series B: Psychological Sciences and Social Sciences, 69*(4), 523–532.

Bindels, J., Baur, V., Cox, K., Heijing, S., & Abma, T. (2014). Older people as co-researchers: A collaborative journey. *Ageing & Society, 34*(6), 951–973. doi:10.1017/S0144686X12001298

Boot, W. R., Charness, N., Czaja, S. J., Sharit, J., Rogers, W. A., Fisk, A. D., Mitzner, T., Lee, C. C., & Nair, S. (2015). Computer proficiency questionnaire: Assessing low and high computer proficient seniors. *The Gerontologist, 55*(3), 404–411. doi:10.1093/geront/gnt117

Braun, K. L., Browne, C. V., Ka'opua, L. S., Kim, B. J., & Mokuau, N. (2014). Research on indigenous elders: From positivistic to decolonizing methodologies. *The Gerontologist, 54*(1), 117–126.

Browne, C. V., Mokuau, N., Ka'opua, L. S., Kim, B. J., Higuchi, P., & Braun, K. L. (2014). Listening to the voices of native Hawaiian elders and 'Ohana caregivers: Discussions on aging, health, and care preferences. *Journal of Cross-Cultural Gerontology, 29*(2), 131–151.

Buckwalter, K. C. (2009). Recruitment of older adults. *Research in Gerontological Nursing, 2*(4), 265–266.

Burton, L. M., Purvin, D., Garrett-Peters, R., Elder, G. H., & Giele, J. Z. (2009). "Longitudinal ethnography: Uncovering domestic abuse in low-income women's lives," In G. H. Elder, & J. Z. Giele (Eds.), *The craft of lifecourse research* (pp. 70–92). New York: Guilford Press.

Carter, D. F., & Hurtado, S. (2007). Bridging key research dilemmas: Quantitative research using a critical eye. *New Directions for Institutional Research, 133*, 25–35.

Centers for Disease Control and Prevention (CDC). (2013). *The state of aging and health in America 2013*. Atlanta, GA: Centers for Disease Control and Prevention, US Department of Health and Human Services.

Chang, J., McAllister, C. & McCaslin, R. (2014). Correlates of, and barriers to, Internet use among older adults. *Journal of Gerontological Social Work, 58*, 1–20.

Cowan, N. (2008). What are the differences between long-term, short-term, and working memory? *Progress in Brain Research, 169*, 323–338.

Cruikshank, M. (2013). *Learning to be old: Gender, culture, and aging* (3rd ed.) Lanham: Rowman & Littlefield.

Dagnelie, G. (2013). Age-related psychophysical changes and low vision. *Investigative Ophthalmology & Visual Science, 54*(14), ORSF88–ORSF93.

de Medeiros, K., Rubinstein, R., & Ermoshkina, P. (2015). The role of relevancy and social suffering in "generativity" among older post-soviet women immigrants. *The Gerontologist, 55*(4), 526–536. doi:10.1093/geront/gnt126

Dong, X. (2014). Addressing health and well-being of U.S. Chinese older adults through community-based participatory research: Introduction to the PINE study. *The Journals of Gerontology: Series A, Biological Sciences and Medical Sciences, 69*(Suppl 2), S1–S6.

Doyle, M., & Timonen, V. (2009). Lessons from a community-based participatory research project: Older people's and researchers' reflections. *Research on Aging, 32*(2), 244–263.

Dunn, L. B., Fisher, S. R., Hantke, M., Appelbaum, P. S., Dohan, D., Young, J. P., & Roberts, L. W. (2013). "Thinking about it for somebody else": Alzheimer's disease research and proxy decisionmakers' translation of ethical principles into practice. *The American Journal of Geriatric Psychiatry, 21*(4) doi:10.1016/j.jagp.2012.11.014

Eckensberger, L. H. (2015). Integrating the emic (indigenous) with the etic (universal)—A case of squaring the circle or for adopting a culture inclusive action theory perspective. *Journal for the Theory of Social Behaviour, 45*(1), 108–140. doi:10.1111/jtsb.12057

Elder Jr, G. H., & Giele, J. Z. (Eds.). (2009). *The craft of life course research*. New York: Guilford Press.

Fazeli, P. L., Ross, L. A., Vance, D. E., & Ball, K. (2013). The relationship between computer experience and computerized cognitive test performance among older adults. *The Journals of Gerontology Series B: Psychological Sciences and Social Sciences, 68*(3), 337–346.

Frankfort-Nachmias, C., Nachmias, D., & DeWaard, J. (2015). *Research methods in the social sciences*, 8th ed. New York: Worth Publishers.

Freedman, V. A., & Spillman, B. C. (2014). The residential continuum from home to nursing home: Size, characteristics and unmet needs of older adults. *The Journals of Gerontology Series B: Psychological Sciences and Social Sciences, 69*(Suppl 1), S42–S50.

Fung, H. (2013). Aging in culture. *Gerontologist, 53*(3), 369–377.

Gates, G. A., & Mills, J. H. (2005). Presbycusis. *The Lancet, 366*(9491), 1111–1120. doi:10.1016/S0140-6736(05)67423-5

Gautam, R., Mawn, B., & Beehler, S. (2014). *In-depth interviews with older refugee adults: Individualistic and family-centered approach of informed consent.* A symposium at a session "Vulnerable Populations and the IRB in Qualitative Work," November 5–9, 67th Annual Scientific meeting of the Gerontological Society of America (GSA) conference in Washington, DC.

Gell, N. M., Rosenberg, D. E., Demiris, G., LaCroix, A. Z., & Patel, K. V. (2013). Patterns of technology use among older adults with and without disabilities. *The Gerontologist, 55*(3), 412–421.

Goodbrand, J. A., & McMurdo, M. E. (2013). Overcoming obstacles to clinical research in older people. *Maturitas, 76*(4), 294–295.

Greenwood, N. (2009). Reflections of a researcher interviewing older people. *Nursing Older People, 21*(7), 30–31.

Gutman, C., Hantman, S., Ben-Oz, M., Criden, W., Anghel, R., & Ramon, S. (2014). Involving older adults as co-researchers in social work education. *Educational Gerontology, 40*(3), 186–197.

Haralambous, B., Dow, B., Tinney, J., Lin, X., Blackberry, I., Rayner, V., & LoGiudice, D. (2014). Help seeking in older Asian people with dementia in Melbourne: Using the cultural exchange model to explore barriers and enablers. *Journal of Cross-Cultural Gerontology, 29*(1), 69–86.

He, W., & Larsen, L. J. (2014). *Older Americans with a disability: 2008–2012*. U.S. Census Bureau, American Community Survey Reports. Washington, DC, U.S. Government Printing Office.

Hewitt, G., Draper, A. K., & Ismail, S. (2013). Using participatory approaches with older people in a residential home in Guyana: Challenges and tensions. *Journal of Cross-Cultural Gerontology, 28*(1), 1–25.

Hillcoat-Nallétamby, S. (2014). The meaning of "independence" for older people in different residential settings. *The Journals of Gerontology Series B: Psychological Sciences and Social Sciences, 69*(3), 419–430.

Hilton, J. M., & Child, S. L. (2014). Spirituality and the successful aging of older Latinos. *Counseling and Values, 59*(1), 17–34.

Hodge, D., & Wolosin, R. (2014). American Indians and spiritual needs during hospitalization: Developing a model of spiritual care. *Gerontologist, 54*(4), 683–692. doi:10.1093/geront/gnt042

Holstein, M., Parks, J. A., & Waymack, M. H. (2011). *Ethics, aging, and society: The critical turn*. New York: Springer.
Horning, S., & Davis, H. P. (2012). "Aging and cognition." In V. S. Ramachandran (Ed.), *Encyclopedia of human behavior* (2nd ed., Vol. 1, pp. 44–52). London: Academic Press.
Huff, D. (1954). *How to lie with statistics* (1st ed.). New York: Norton.
Hummert, M. L. (2015). Experimental research on age stereotypes: Insights for subjective aging. *Annual Review of Gerontology & Geriatrics, 35*(1), 79–97.
Institute of Medicine. (2015). *Cognitive aging: Progress in understanding and opportunities for action*. Washington, DC: The National Academies Press.
Israel, B., Schulz, A. J., Parker, E. A., & Becker, A. B. (1998). Review of community-based research: Assessing partnership approaches to improve public health. *Annual Review of Public Health, 19*, 173–202.
Israel, B., Schulz, A. J., Parker, E. A., Becker, A. B., Allen, III, A. J., & Guzman, R. J. (2003). "Critical issues in developing and following community based participatory research principles." In M. Minkler, & N. Wallerstein (Eds.), *Community-based participatory research for health* (pp. 53–76). San Francisco, CA: Jossey-Bass.
Jamieson, A., & Victor, C. R. (2002). *Researching ageing and later life: The practice of social gerontology*. Buckingham and Philadelphia: Open University Press.
Janes, J. E. (2015). Democratic encounters? Epistemic privilege, power, and community-based participatory action research. *Action Research, 14*(1), 72–87.
Kim, M. T., Lee, J., Ko, J., Yoon, H., Kim, K. B., & Jang, Y. (2015). Sources of response bias in older ethnic minorities: A case of Korean American elderly. *Journal of Cross-Cultural Gerontology, 30*(3), 269–283.
Kuypers, J. A., & Bengtson, V. L. (1973). Competence and social breakdown: A social-psychological view of aging. *Human development, 16*(2), 37–49.
Lagacé, M., Charmarkeh, H., & Grandena, F. (2012). Cultural perceptions of aging: The perspective of Somali Canadians in Ottawa. *Journal of Cross-Cultural Gerontology, 27*(4), 409–424.
Langlois, F., Vu, T. T. M., Chassé, K., Dupuis, G., Kergoat, M. J., & Bherer, L. (2013). Benefits of physical exercise training on cognition and quality of life in frail older adults. *The Journals of Gerontology Series B: Psychological Sciences and Social Sciences, 68*(3), 400–404.
Levy, B. R., Zonderman, A. B., Slade, M. D., & Ferrucci, L. (2012). Memory shaped by age stereotypes over time. *The Journals of Gerontology Series B: Psychological Sciences and Social Sciences, 67*(4), 432–436.
Lewis, T. (2005). "Race." In G. D. Jaynes (Ed.), *Encyclopedia of African American society* (Vol. 2, p. 676). Thousand Oaks, CA: Sage Reference.
Lin, F., Chen, D. G. D., Vance, D., & Mapstone, M. (2013). Trajectories of combined laboratory-and real world-based speed of processing in community-dwelling older adults. *The Journals of Gerontology Series B: Psychological Sciences and Social Sciences, 68*(3), 364–373.
Locher, J. L., Bronstein, J., Robinson, C. O., Williams, C., & Ritchie, C. S. (2006). Ethical issues involving research conducted with homebound older adults. *The Gerontologist, 46*(2), 160–164.
McHenry, J. C., Insel, K. C., Einstein, G. O., Vidrine, A. N., Koerner, K. M., & Morrow, D. G. (2015). Recruitment of older adults: Success may be in the details. *The Gerontologist, 55*(5), 845. doi:10.1093/geront/gns079
McMurdo, M. E. T., Roberts, H., Parker, S., Wyatt, N., May, H., Goodman, C., & Age and Ageing Specialty Group, NIHR, Comprehensive Clinical Research Network. (2011). Improving recruitment of older people to research through good practice. *Age and Ageing, 40*(6), 659–665.
Medicare Glossary. (2015). Home health compare. Retrieved from https://www.medicare.gov/homehealthcompare/Resources/Glossary.html?Choice=L
Mendez-Luck, C. A., & Anthony, K. P. (2015). Marianismo and caregiving role beliefs among US-born and immigrant Mexican women. *The Journals of Gerontology Series B: Psychological Sciences and Social Sciences, 71*(5), 926–935. doi:10.1093/geronb/gbv083
Mendoza, N., & Weil. J. (2014). "'Pues a mi me da gusto, porque ando con mis nietos:' Latina grandmothers raising grandchildren as an extension of the caregiving role over the lifecourse." In D. Mitra, & J. Weil (Eds.), *Race and the lifecourse: Readings from the intersection of race, ethnicity, and age* (pp. 201–221). New York: Palgrave.
Miller, D., Gagnon, M., Talbot, V., & Messier, C. (2013). Predictors of successful communication with interactive voice response systems in older people. *Journals of Gerontology Series B: Psychological Sciences and Social Sciences, 68*(4), 495–503.
Morgan, L. A., & Kunkel, S. R. (2007). *Aging, society, and the life course*. New York: Springer Publishing Company.
Nelson, I. A., London, R. A., & Strobel, K. R. (2015). Reinventing the role of the university researcher. *Educational Researcher, 44*(1), 17–26.
Nimrod, G. (2013). Probing the audience of seniors' online communities. *Journals of Gerontology, Social Sciences, 68*(5), 773–782.
North, M. S., & Fiske, S. T. (2015). Modern attitudes toward older adults in the aging world: A cross-cultural meta-analysis. *Psychological Bulletin, 141*(5), 993–1021.
Parikh, P. K., Troyer, A. K., Maione, A. M., & Murphy, K. J. (2015). The impact of memory change on daily life in normal aging and mild cognitive impairment. *The Gerontologist, 56*(5), 877–885. doi:10.1093/geront/gnv030

Petersen, R. (2011). Cognitive impairment. *The New England Journal of Medicine, 364*(23), 2227–2234.

Petrican, R., English, T., Gross, J., Grady, C., Hai, T., & Moscovitch, M. (2013). Friend or foe? Age moderates time-course specific responsiveness to trustworthiness cues. *Journals of Gerontology Series B: Psychological Sciences and Social Sciences, 68*(2), 215–223.

Picou, E. M. & Ricketts, T. A. (2013). Efficacy of hearing-aid based telephone strategies for listeners with moderate-to-severe hearing loss. *Journal of the American Academy of Audiology, 24*(1), 59–70.

Rabbitt, P. (2015). *The aging mind: An owner's manual.* New York: Routledge.

Rapcsak, S., Verfaellie, M., Glisky, E., Cook, S., & Davidson, P. (2005). Source memory in the real world: A neuropsychological study of flashbulb memory. *Journal of Clinical and Experimental Neuropsychology, 27*(7), 915–929. doi:10.1080/13803390490919335

Remillard, M., Mazor, K., Cutrona, S., Gurwitz, J. & Tjia, J. (2014). Systematic review of the use of online questionnaires of older adults. *Journal of the American Geriatrics Society, 62*(4), 696–705.

Resnick, B., Gruber-Baldini, A. L., Pretzer-Aboff, I., Galik, E., Buie, V. C., Russ, K., & Zimmerman, S. (2007). Reliability and validity of the evaluation to sign consent measure. *The Gerontologist, 47*(1), 69–77.

Ritchie, L. (2009). Wearing two hats: Interviewing older people as a nurse researcher. *Medical Sociology Online, 4*(1), 14–24.

Rohlfsen, L. S., & Kronenfeld, J. J. (2014). Gender differences in functional health: Latent curve analysis assessing differential exposure. *The Journals of Gerontology: Series B, Psychological Sciences and Social Sciences, 69*(4), 590–609.

Saxon, S. V., Etten, M. J., & Perkins, E. A. (2015). *Physical change and aging: A guide for the helping professions* (6th ed.). New York: Springer Publishing Company.

Schoorman, D., & Bogotch, I. (2010). What is a critical multicultural researcher? A self-reflective study of the role of the researcher. *Education, Citizenship and Social Justice, 5*(3), 249–264.

Schulz, R., Wahl, H., Matthews, J. T., De Vito Dabbs, A., Beach, S. R., & Czaja, S. J. (2015). Advancing the aging and technology agenda in gerontology. *The Gerontologist, 55*(5), 724.

Shura, R., Siders, R., & Dannefer, D. (2011). Culture change in long-term care: Participatory action research and the role of the resident. *The Gerontologist, 51*(2), 212–225.

Slessor, G., Phillips, L., Bull, R., Venturini, C., Bonny, E., & Rokaszewicz, A. (2012). Investigating the "deceiver stereotype": Do older adults associate averted gaze with deception? *Journals of Gerontology Series B: Psychological Sciences and Social Sciences, 67*(2), 178–183.

Slessor, G., Riby, D. M., & Finnerty, A. N. (2012). Age-related differences in processing face configuration: The importance of the eye region. *The Journals of Gerontology. Series B, Psychological Sciences and Social Sciences, 68*(2), 228. doi:10.1093/geronb/gbs059

Slessor, G., Venturini, C., Bonny, E. J., Insch, P. M., Rokaszewicz, A., & Finnerty, A. N. (2016). Specificity of age-related differences in eye-gaze following: Evidence from social and nonsocial stimuli. *The Journals of Gerontology Series B: Psychological Sciences and Social Sciences, 71*(1), 11–22. doi:10.1093/geronb/gbu088

Stern, Y. (2012). Cognitive reserve in ageing and Alzheimer's disease. *The Lancet Neurology, 11*(11), 1006–1012.

Sugarman, J., Roter, D., Cain, C., Wallace, R., Schmechel, D., & Welsh-Bohmer, K. A. (2007). Proxies and consent discussions for dementia research. *Journal of the American Geriatrics Society, 55*(4), 556–561.

Sullivan, S., Campbell, A., Hutton, S. B., & Ruffman, T. (2015). What's good for the goose is not good for the gander: Age and gender differences in scanning emotion faces. *The Journals of Gerontology Series B: Psychological Sciences and Social Sciences, 2015*, 1–6. doi:10.1093/geronb/gbv033

Tak, S. & Gatto, S. (2008). Computer, internet, and e-mail use among older adults: Benefits and barriers. *Educational Gerontology, 34*(9), 800–811.

Tsai, H., Shillair, R., Cotten, S., Winstead, V., & Yost, E., (2015). Getting grandma online: Are tablets the answer for increasing digital inclusion for older adults in the U.S.? *Educational Gerontology, 41*(10), 695–709.

Vandenberg, A. E., Price, A. E., Friedman, D. B., Marchman, G., & Anderson, L. A. (2012). How do top cable news websites portray cognition as an aging issue? *The Gerontologist, 52*(3), 367–382.

Vasquez, B. P., Binns, M. A., & Anderson, N. D. (2016). Staying on task: Age-related changes in the relationship between executive functioning and response time consistency. *The Journals of Gerontology Series B: Psychological Sciences and Social Sciences, 71*(2), 189–200. doi:10.1093/geronb/gbu140

Vaughan, L., Erickson, K. I., Espeland, M. A., Smith, J. C., Tindle, H. A., & Rapp, S. R. (2014). Concurrent and longitudinal relationships between cognitive activity, cognitive performance, and brain volume in older adult women. *The Journals of Gerontology Series B: Psychological Sciences and Social Sciences, 69*(6), 826–836.

Verhaeghen, P., & Zhang, Y. (2013). What is still working in working memory in old age: Dual tasking and resistance to interference do not explain age-related item loss after a focus switch. *The Journals of Gerontology Series B: Psychological Sciences and Social Sciences, 68*(5), 762–770. doi:10.1093/geronb/gbs119

Victor, C., Westerhof, G. J., & Bond, J. (2007). "Researching ageing." In J. Bond, S. Peace, F. Dittmann-Kohli & G. Westerhof, *Ageing in Society, European Perspectives on Gerontology* (pp. 85–112). London, UK: Sage.

Wang-Letzkus, M. F., Washington, G., Calvillo, E. R., & Anderson, N. L. R. (2012). Using culturally competent community-based participatory research with older diabetic Chinese Americans: Lessons learned. *Journal of Transcultural Nursing, 23*(3), 255–261.

Weil, J. (2015). Applying research methods to a gerontological population: Matching data collection to characteristics of older persons. *Educational Gerontology, 41*(10), 723–742.

Yang, L., Chen, W., Ng, A. H., & Fu, X. (2013). Aging, culture, and memory for categorically processed information. *The Journals of Gerontology Series B: Psychological Sciences and Social Sciences, 68*(6), 872–881. doi:10.1093/geronb/gbt006

Yang, Y. (2008). Social inequalities in happiness in the United States, 1972 to 2004: An age-period-cohort analysis. *American Sociological Review, 73*(2), 204–226.

Yang, Y. (2009). "Age, period, cohort effects." In D. Carr (Ed.), *Encyclopedia of the life course and human development* (pp. 6–10). Detroit: Macmillan Reference.

Yang, Y., & Land, K. C. (2013). *Age-period-cohort analysis: New models, methods, and empirical applications.* Boca Raton, FL: CRC Press.

Zaphiris, P., Kurniawan, S., & Ghiawadwala, M. (2007). A systematic approach to the development of research-based web design guidelines for older people. *Universal Access in the Information Society, 6*(1), 59–75. doi:10.1007/s10209-006-0054-8

3
Gerontological Theoretical Approaches

Theory is the bridge between research questions and study design. Theoretical perspectives in this chapter add to work done in prior chapters—establishing a philosophy that guides research perspective, thinking about initial areas of research and research questions, and applying approaches specific to research with older populations. Gerontological theories are divided into several groups: early and/or general theories; biomedical and health-based theories; biopsychosocial and biological theories; psychological, developmental, and cognitive theories on aging; social gerontology and life-course perspective; critical gerontology; ecological theories; social construction and phenomenological theories; and identity-based theories on aging.

Theoretical elements are another tool to add to the researcher's toolkit.

Gerontology as Discipline: Data Heavy, Theory Light? Or with Rich Theoretical Paradigms?

While gerontology may have been accused of being "data rich and theory poor," this past adage no longer holds true (Birren, 1988, p. 155). Theory can be seen as the lifeblood of the field, necessary to move it forward. **Theory** informs the research questions and methods in an investigation (Blieszner, 2016). Theory helps explain the reasons why events happen, lets the researcher integrate knowledge, guides interventions, and influences practitioners' work and public policy (Bengtson & Settersten, 2016). The 35 chapters of Vern Bengtson and Richard Settersten's (2016) *Handbook of theories of aging* attest to the abundance of theory. Theories range from more general ones to those centered on an issue, such as health, or a specific philosophical approach, such as phenomenological, critical, or lifecourse theories. Additionally, gerontological theories are becoming more interdisciplinary in nature (Alley, Putney, Rice & Bengtson, 2010). In *The need for theory: Critical approaches to social gerontology*, Simon Biggs, Ariela Lowenstein, and Jon Hendricks (2003) expanded the view of gerontological theories with micro and macro focus, those created for the field or from the field, and those adapted from other disciplines. This tradition was continued in a series of articles exploring the origins and theoretical advances of the field of gerontology (see Bass's [2013] "The state of gerontology-opus one," or Ekerdt's [2014] "Gerontology in five images").

In a study that looked at the most commonly mentioned theories in several major gerontology journals, the top five theories cited were the life-course perspective, life-span developmental theories, role theory, exchange theories, and person-environmental fit/ecological theories of aging (Alley, Putney, Rice & Bengtson, 2010). The most commonly mentioned theories in family gerontology focused on caregivers/caregiving, family relationships, social support and social networks, family structures/living arrangements, and specific family issues (e.g., transitions, end of life, or health issues; Roberto, Blieszner & Allen, 2006).

While this book is a research guide and not a theoretical text, it is important to begin by covering some basic theoretical approaches so that they can be used to (a) guide research design and (b) allow researchers to be self-reflexive about the ways their theoretical orientations can influence their design. This does require a disclaimer. While the theories are grouped in these categories below, they can also be grouped in many other ways. And, of course, it is not possible to review all theories in this book. While not all inclusive, gerontological theoretical approaches can be divided along several lines:

- Early and/or General Theories: Disengagement, Continuity, Activity, Age and Modernization, and Gerotranscendence Theories
- Early Biomedical and Health Based, and Successful Aging with a Nod to Biopsychosocial and Biological Theories
- Psychological, Developmental, and Cognitive Theories on Aging
- Theories of Social Gerontology: Lifecourse Perspective and Social Science/Sociological Theories
- Critical Gerontology: Political Economy of Aging, Age Stratification, and Cumulative Advantage/Disadvantage Theories
- Ecological Theories: Person-Environment Fit/Aging in Place
- Social Construction and Phenomenological Gerontological Theories
- Identity-Based Theories and Aging: Feminist Gerontology, Multiple Jeopardies, and Intersectionality

Early and/or General Theories: Disengagement, Continuity, Activity, Age and Modernization, and Gerotranscendence Theories

Some of the early theories discussed in gerontology texts are often paired and contrasted, such as Disengagement and Activity Theories. **Disengagement Theory** posits that as one ages, he or she withdraws from society until the final disengagement (of death). This reverse-socialization process is unidirectional and not reversible. The removal from societal participation makes the way for younger generations to fill and take over roles once held by older persons (Cumming & Henry, 1961). **Activity Theory** was developed to challenge the idea that disengagement is a natural or expected part of the aging process (Havighurst, Neugarten & Tobin, 1963). While often thought of simply as "being active keeps older people happy," Activity Theory is more complex. The theory suggests it is a participation in, or maintenance of, a group of activities that influences an older person's well-being. It is the older person's own internal view of himself or herself that is supported by this engagement with the external environment, or society (Lemon, Bengtson & Peterson, 1972). Though heavily criticized, recent works suggest that ideas from these early theories can be found in recent ones—Activity Theory's elements are present in Successful Aging Theory, and Disengagement Theory may be found in Socioemotional Selectivity Theory (Bengtson & Settersten, 2016).

The third, closely related theory, often discussed with Disengagement and Activity Theories, is **Continuity Theory**. This theory suggests that with older age comes a way to balance and adapt to changes both on internal levels (such as values, ideas) and on external levels (such as experiences within society or in social networks) to maintain a sense of the self over time. The continuity-achieving process is dynamic, flexible, and ongoing (Atchley, 1989). Later theorists called for an expansion of societal factors impacting change throughout life (Bengtson, Silverstein, Putney & Gans, 2009).

The **Theory of Modernization**—a broad, general theory—has been applied to the treatment and role of older persons at a societal level (Cowgill & Holmes, 1972). The idea is that as a society becomes more industrialized and undergoes an economic modernization, older persons lose their former, traditional, and respected roles. At the time of its introduction, this theory introduced structural elements, such as economic changes in society, into a largely individualistic and psychologically based view of the aging process (Cowgill & Holmes, 1972). Modernization theory has been expanded in its gerontological application to become one of many ways we view how societal changes influence aging (see the work of Achenbaum & Stearns, 1978; Hendricks, 1982). For example, scholars of global aging examine the treatment of older persons in "elderly heavy" and "elderly light" countries (Powell, 2012).

Social Breakdown and Competence Models theorize the relationship between an older person's social world and the view an older person has about himself or herself (Kuypers & Bengston, 1973). The two processes are often described as circular processes or wheels. Each can be seen as the opposite of the other. The cycle of Social Breakdown creates a negative self-image, while the Social Competence cycle builds that image up. In the social-breakdown cycle, a negative change or loss in role makes older persons feel society is labeling them as "other" (i.e., weak, frail, dependent), and then that role is internalized. The older person matches his or her behavior to meet these lowered expectations, which causes skills to not be used and to be lost over time. This promotes even more negative labeling. On the other hand, in the social-competence cycle, the older person's value is restored; the person is seen as valuable for what he or she can do instead of what he or she cannot. This reinforces one's sense of agency or internal locus of control, which fosters new skill building and resistance to negative labeling.

Building upon specific stage-based theories of aging that use maturity as an outcome, the **Theory of Gerotranscendence** describes changes in an older person's developmental process and relationship to the outside world (Tornstam, 1996). Gerotranscendent persons develop a more fluid sense of time—the cosmic view that the past can be felt as present or the past and present merge. The individual feels more connected to the universe and sees deeper meaning and insights into everyday events. The self, in this theory, is not fixed but changing throughout life. Personal and social relationships take on different meaning. Less superficial relationships are sought, accompanied by a broadmindedness, acceptance of all positive and negative aspects of one's life, new openness to seeing the world, and comfort with not knowing everything.

Early Biomedical and Health-Based Successful Aging with a Nod to Biopsychosocial and Biological Theories

As gerontology is often related to geriatrics (the branch of medicine addressing aging and older people), it is no surprise that the field has many biological theories of aging, anti-aging technologies, and more health-focused theoretical models. Biological theories seek to explain how and why we age and understand and debate the difference between "normal" and non-normative aging. Theories of biogerontology (or ways to slow the aging process) and anti-aging medicine have emerged, exploring aging as a disease and ways to prolong lifespan or even to eradicate aging altogether.

Early Biological Theories

Early biological theories, such as **Wear-and-Tear Theory**, posited that with time, an organism wears out (Pearl, 1924; Weismann, 1892). This was the precursor of many "failure to repair" theories that see aging as an accumulation of injury and damage from the environment. However, advances in molecular and cell biology make wear-and-tear theory outdated.

In terms of biological aging theories, some early theories fall into the Programmed Theories of Biological Aging, while others are classified as Error Theories of Biological Aging. **Programmed Theories** suggest cells have an inherent "lifespan." The Hayflick Hypothesis, as an example of a programmed theory, suggests certain cells can divide only a limited number of times: the Hayflick Limit (Weiss, 1974). Thus, lack of cell division over time can leave cells vulnerable to damage. For a time, antioxidant and other defense systems are adequate to control damage. At some point, defense systems fail, and waste products of stochastic damage accumulate. Then, a damaged cell will "blink out" and not be replaced. Another programmed theory, Immunological Aging, describes decreased vigor of immune response. Age-related decline in T cell efficiency is due not to fewer T cells but to a shift in proportion of T cells that can respond and those that fail to respond.

The past **Error Theories of Biological Aging** see aging as a mistake or abnormal change in biological processes. For example, Somatic Mutation Theory looks at random "hits" to inactivate large chromosome regions, chromosomal abnormalities, and mutations in genomes of somatic or non-reproductive cells' DNA. These mutations occur too rapidly for cells to repair; cells lose the ability to function, including the ability to divide; and somatic mutation can interfere with gene expression.

The **Free Radical or Oxidative Stress Theory** focuses on the "oxygen paradox" that cells need oxygen to live, but, if unattached (as an unpaired electron, free energy, bonded with other molecules), oxygen can damage cells. This process has been linked to late-onset diabetes, arthritis, cataracts, hypertension, and atherosclerosis. The Cross-Linkage Theory (Post-translational Protein Modification Theory) sees the accumulation of chemical changes in cells resulting in proteins in the body binding to each other and preventing affected tissues from functioning normally. This protein binding causes inflexibility—i.e., stiffness in arteries' connective fibers, increasing systolic blood pressure. Other past biological theories see telomeres as the biological clock. These genetic segments appear as "caps" at a chromosome's end and shorten progressively with cell division. When a "cap" is impaired, a DNA-damage response is triggered, causing problems with the chromosomal structure or cell death. Telomere cap changes are thought to be related to diseases such as cancer.

Recent biological theories focus on loss of cellular protein in cells as a cause of aging, while some scientists are focusing on the relationship between inflammation and chronic diseases—e.g., heart diseases, cancer, frailty, and loss of cognitive functioning.

Anti-aging medicine and the emergence of **biogerontology** as a discipline both look to halt or reverse the effects of aging (or aging, itself) and seek prolongevity, or life extension. Such groups make up an anti-aging consumer market with appearance-based products and services (e.g., the American Academy of Anti-Aging, A4M). Theories focus on stem-cell research, nanotechnology, gene therapy, and technology-enhanced aging. Theories propose ways to extend the limits of human life by studying other species or through practices such as intense calorie restriction (see De Grey, 2015; De Grey & Rae, 2007).

Health-Based Successful Aging with a Nod to Biopsychosocial and Biological Theories

Following the medicalization of aging, health-based theories expand the way we look at health in terms of biological changes. Though now often contested, at the time, Rowe and

Kahn's **Model of Successful Aging** added social components to theories of aging and health. Successful aging is defined around three domains: (1) the ability to maintain low risk of disease and disease-related disability; (2) high mental and physical functioning; and (3) an active engagement with life. The Successful Aging Model then underwent updates by many authors and now includes theories of meaningful aging, insightful aging, and harmonious aging, to name a few. Even Rowe and Kahn have created a Successful Aging 2.0, adding in the influence societal institutions have on the value society places on older people.

Healthy Aging has become a popular theme in the discourse on aging. On the national stage, healthy aging theories were featured in the United States' 2015 White House Conference on Aging and the National Institutes of Health web-based "senior" topic directory that defined healthy aging as ways to "to stay healthy, get good health care, and manage lifestyle changes as you age." Healthy aging theories see wellness as achieved through combinations of the following: disease prevention, health promotion, improving cognitive and behavioral health, aging in community, and civic engagement (Ryff & Singer, 2002). A more recent **Spectrum Model of Aging** lets older persons and health professionals create an "individualized aging plan" for each older person, increasing the diversity of ways to age "successfully." In this model, individuals choose from a wide range of interdisciplinary factors they consider key to having a good quality of life as they age (e.g., relationships, spirituality, cultural items), in addition to physical health. The Spectrum Model lets each person create a customized plan to age well with less focus on only "activity" or "ability" as the most important elements (Martin & Gillen, 2014, p. 57).

Psychological and Developmental Theories on Aging

Developmental Theories

Drawing on the fields of psychology and human development and family studies, this set of theories addresses how older people maintain a sense of self and adapt to changes occurring throughout their lives and at later periods in their lives. While a multitude of theories cover development in early life and childhood, developmental theories discussed here include a focus on continued development in the latter years of one's life. Some of the earliest later-life-inclusive lifespan-development theories are those of Carl Jung and Erik Erickson. While some theorists saw development halting in mid-life, Jung (1933) saw development as not fixed but lifelong. He suggested that midlife, the "afternoon" of one's life, involves a transition where goals and expectations are evaluated. During this time of change, concerns about one's physical self move toward achieving balance or being in harmony with nature (Lachman & James, 1997, p. 6).

Erick and Joan Erikson's original **Stage Theory of Development** (1968) divided lifespan development into a series of eight sequential stages. Each stage has two sides of a psychosocial crisis requiring conflict resolution to move to the next stage. The last and eighth stage of late adulthood (called "Old Age") has the conflict of ego integrity versus despair—with the result of this conflict being "wisdom" through reflection upon all prior lifelong stages. However, Erickson, in her nineties, suggested that the eighth stage required re-thinking. She added a ninth stage called "Extreme Old Age" in which all prior stages are evaluated (Brown & Lowis, 2003). Daniel Levinson's theory, **A Conception of Adult Development** (1986), used life-cycle eras to create what he called the adult-transition phase (ages 60 to 85) as a "season of life" where one experiences major health events and some loss of societal status. George Vaillant's **Theory of Adult Development** (1996) added a developmental task of old age as being a "keeper of meaning."

Urie Bronfenbrenner's **Ecological Model** (1979) describes lifespan development as the process of an individual's personal characteristics interacting with many levels of his or her environment. These multi-leveled social and physical environments function like "nested Russian dolls" of developmental influence (p. 22). For example, for an older person living in her home and receiving assistance with Activities of Daily Living (ADL) from Certified Nursing Assistants (CNAs), her closest relationships are to family, caregivers, and peers who form her "microsystem." The relationships of caregivers and family to each other form the "mesosystem." The policies of the home-care agency and events that occur without direct influence of the older person, such as an adult child moving out of state, make up "exosystem" influences. And larger societal policies (such as health-insurance laws regulating home-care coverage and pay) and cultural norms (such as preferences to live at home or age in place) make up the "macrosystem." An older adult's development is also influenced by the timing of personal changes that occur throughout her life (e.g., the death of a spouse or a chronic health condition creating the need for home care) and societal changes (e.g., the increased availability of home-care providers due to new federal universal health care laws) called "chronosystems."

Paul Baltes's **Lifespan Perspective** added several elements to the study of behavioral changes from birth to death. He and colleagues added the consideration of biological, social, historical, and cultural differences to the development processes throughout a person's life. His work proposed that chronological age has less predictive power in behavior over time and that inter-individual differences increased with age (Baltes & Goulet, 1970). Building upon earlier work, Paul Baltes and Margaret Baltes's **Selective Optimization with Compensation** (SOC, 1990) model defines aging well as an outcome of how one adapts to environmental changes. When aging, an individual selects important activities or developmental goals that she sees as key in defining herself. Then, she optimizes the activities she does well as part of a task to address any loss of functioning and compensate, or alter, the way she may carry out a task due to physical changes.

A theory of **Thriving** posits an alternative to the "failure to thrive" concept (Haight, Barba, Tesh & Courts, 2002). In Thriving theory, a person and his human and built environments interact to create positive ties to society, meaning in his life, and resiliency. Richard Schulz and Jutta Heckhausen's **Motivational Theory of Life-Span** (1995) made motivation to meet goals an ongoing process throughout life (Heckhausen, Wrosch & Schulz, 2010). The theory includes primary control (where older persons change the external world to meet their needs) and secondary control (where older persons adapt themselves to meet changes in the external world).

In Laura Carstensen's (1992) **Socioemotional Selectivity Theory**, older persons seek more meaningful interactions based on greater satisfaction from close friendships and less from peripheral friendships. With chronological aging comes the development of poignancy in later years (experiencing emotional extremes, such as happiness and sadness, at once) and a valuing of emotional satisfaction. Though more interdisciplinary than developmental, relationships and their changes in closeness to the older person over the lifespan are also part of Robert Kahn and Toni Antonucci's **Convoy Model of Social Relations** (1980). Gene Cohen's (2000) **Theory of Human Potential** sees just that—developmental potential in later life—and challenges the idea of developmental phases as "fixed" in early life. He finds that human potential and creativity (in many forms) increase with age. His developmental phases in the "second half of life" are midlife reevaluation (ages 40s–50s, people on a path of quest, not crisis), liberation (ages 60s–70s, brings a renewed sense of personal freedom), summing up (aged 70+, placing life's context in larger meaning), and encore (aged 80+, assessing one's final impact and completion of life's loose ends; Agronin, 2013, p. 36, Figure 4). Current theories of lifespan development now focus on **intraindividual variability** allowing for more heterogeneity in developmental processes and paths for each individual (see Diehl, Hooker & Sliwinski, 2015).

Cognitive Theories

The fields of neuropsychology and cognition have produced theories to explain why brain mass and processing speeds are not the sole predictors of cognitive functioning. This set of theories addresses why some changes in cognitive functioning with older age do not seem to be related to (as previously thought) underlying brain changes. Researchers suggest newer theories about neural and cognitive plasticity and cognitive reserve (Chapman et al., 2015). While **neural plasticity** refers to neuronal changes (the growth, change, or loss of neurons and dendrites in the brain), **cognitive plasticity** refers to the ability to learn or acquire new skills. Theories debate whether cognitive training with high-order, executive-function-based mental strategies and tasks, along with increased blood supply, help with cognitive plasticity. Other theories suggest **cognitive reserves** (or ways the brain is resilient to loss) can potentially mitigate brain losses and explore functional plasticity of aging (Greenwood, 2009; Stern, 2012).

Theories of Social Gerontology: Lifecourse Perspective, Sociological Theories, and Critical Gerontology

Social-gerontology theories seek to add the role of larger society to the experience of aging and older people. Work by Dale Dannefer and his **sociogenic hypothesis** (1984) attributed later lifespan developmental processes to being more heavily influenced by society and social structures than other factors. Early on, Glen Elder's **Lifecourse Perspective** (or approach) looks at how transitions during the early years in one's life, the time in which one lives, and social connections shape lived experiences. In this theory, individuals have agency, or the ability, to exert their influence and make changes within the worlds they live (Elder, 1994). Many researchers have followed up on the role of larger societal institutions in the lives of older people. For example, Gretchen Alkema and Dawn Alley's (2006) **Integrated Model of Social Gerontology** builds upon the inclusion of societal forces upon aging and includes cultural, economic, political, environmental, and historical influences.

Age Stratification Theories focus attention on the process of dividing members of a society into strata, or social groups (see Riley, Johnson & Foner, 1972). The various age strata form age cohorts that encompass those born within a particular time period. While the similarities of members within a stratum are thought to provide cohesion within that stratum, age-stratification theories suggest that inter-strata conflicts also exist. Conflicts may arise between strata, often framed around competing group interests such as "young" versus "old." One example of how these conflicts play out in society would be institutional battles over the allocation of economic resources, such as spending on Social Security programs for the Baby Boomers versus federal aid to families with young children. Terms like the "generation gap" or "age war" imply competition between the strata, while "greedy geezer" and "silver tsunami" cast blame on one group. The idea that older persons place an excessive burden both upon their families and upon the healthcare system also implies a conflict that pits the interests of younger groups against those of older persons. Theorists argue **intergenerational exchange**—sharing of time and resources among groups of different generations—promotes solidarity. This positive social interaction exposure buffers negative views of old groups by young groups. Yet some argue that although models of intergenerational conflict are promoted, the degree of conflict between young and old groups is overstated.

Critical Gerontology Theories stem from ideologies, or ways of thinking, from the Frankfurt school and views of Theodor Adorno, Jürgen Habermas, and Erich Fromm. Critical gerontologists adapted Marxist philosophy to include the impact of the power of social structures (the State, societal institutions) upon the individual experience of aging (Nealon & Irr, 2002). **Political Economy of Aging Theories** (Estes, 1979, 2001) contend that there is a dominant (hegemonic), negative view of older people in society. Social institutions, such as social services and laws, are designed to support and keep this view alive in debates. Social institutions, then, have the power to regulate older peoples' lives and control aging and older people by the policies they create. For example, social services agencies' policies determine who is eligible for their help, such as receiving rental assistance, or laws set a fixed retirement age when one can receive full benefits.

Cumulative Advantage/Disadvantage (CAD) Theories follow up on Robert Merton's work about social inequalities. CAD theories see these inequalities as lifelong, not simply a result of a later period or stage in life. Theorists suggest that avoiding the impact of society on lifelong development would paint an incomplete picture of aging (Dannefer, 2003). CAD theories are also known as **Cumulative Inequality Theory**. Researchers taking this inequality approach proposed a biographic structuration concept: that early adversity or inequality has a lifelong impact upon individuals and affects whether they handle later events in life in either a positive or negative light (Ferraro, Shippee & Schafer, 2009).

Ecological Theories: Person-Environment Fit and Aging in Place

Aging in place is described as the ability to remain in one's own home or community over one's life, until old age, and is often associated with the availability of resources of all kinds to do so. Aging in place is seen as a multi-dimensional concept because it looks at how place influences identity and how people adapt to both changes in themselves and in their physical surroundings. While aging in place has been thought to be universally favored, there is a movement to closely examine all aspects of the concept. Recent work calls for reexamination of aging in place as a one-size-fits-all model and draws attention to differences based on social class, gender, age group, cognitive status, and geographic differences. New studies about aging in place discuss cost, cost effectiveness, and real-model possibilities, such as designed, age-friendly communities that people move to age in or neighborhoods where residents remain in and age in throughout their lives. The definition of aging in place has been expanded to include those aging in place in the same formal, continuum-of-care institution. For example, it includes those once in assisted living moving to skilled-nursing and/or memory-care settings in the same facility (Weil & Smith, 2016).

M. Powell Lawton and Lucille Nahemow's (1973) early **Ecological Model of Person-Environment Fit** includes a sense of place with the experience of aging. A person's ability to remain in place is examined in terms of how well she fits in within her own home environment or geographic setting. The fit of person and place is assessed by the match of an older person's personal capabilities and level of autonomy to that person's environmental demands. A person's capabilities can include health, sensory or cognitive abilities, level of ADL performance, social skills, and desire and motivation to remain in place. Environmental demands, or press, can include an older person's environmental issues at many levels, from home to society, such as house-and-yard maintenance, availability of assistive devices, availability of services and programs for meal preparation, housekeeping and individual care, transportation, finances, and personal and neighborhood security.

Social Construction and Phenomenological Gerontological Theories

Both **Social Construction and Phenomenological Theories** share a common approach in understanding how an older person would attach meaning to his or her social world. Each set of theories support the idea that reality is socially constructed. Theorists are interested in how meaning is created and interpreted by the individual based on the society in which he or she lives. Social constructionists follow the tradition of earlier post-modernist theorists, such as Jacques Derrida, Michel Foucault, Chris Gilleard, and Paul Higgs (Bengtson, Silverstein, Putney & Gans, 2009). Social constructionists can also fall into the critical-gerontological view. For example, Carroll Estes's view of how society contributes to the framing or construction of what old age is can be both a social-constructionist and a critical-gerontological view. Phenomenological gerontology theorists—from Alfred Schultz to Jaber Gubrium and James Holstein—explore how an older person attaches meaning in his or her own life (or "lifeworld"). The older person self-constructs the narrative and is, therefore, an active subject and not a passive object of research.

Identity-Based Theories and Aging: Feminist Gerontology, Multiple Jeopardies, and Intersectionality

Feminist gerontological theory focuses on the difference gender creates in the process of aging. Ruth Ray (1996) traced the roots of feminist gerontology and felt that this approach lent itself to understanding the lived experience of both aging and being a woman. For example, Margaret Cruikshank (2009) discusses how society devalues caregiving work because the majority of persons providing care for older people are women. Toni Calasanti (working with Neal King and others) continues to expand the feminist gerontological perspective. Her work adds in other forms of marginalization—such as the view of older bodies—and the intersections of multiple social statuses that can come into play and influence older women's experiences of aging (Calasanti, 2008; Ojala, Calasanti, King & Pietila, 2016). She points out the lack of the study of women and aging in many academic fields. Calasanti and Kathleen Slevin's (2013) edited volume covers topics such as aging women's sexuality, age and family roles and expectations, older women workers, spousal care, and general female embodiment with age. Julia Twigg (2004) sees "feminist and cultural critics in challenging [the "othering," or objectification of older people] having regained important territory for social gerontology, and in ways that have deepened our understanding of the experience of old age" (p. 71).

Theories of Multiple Jeopardy examine the impact of a multitude of social statuses that one may occupy simultaneously upon the experience of aging or being old (Dowd & Bengtson, 1978). Old age can add to any existing group status, such as an older person's race, ethnicity, gender, sexual orientation, social class, and health. An older person with non-hegemonic (i.e., non-preferred) societal statuses in more than one of these categories faces multiple jeopardies. An **intersectionality perspective** builds upon the concept of double and triple jeopardies. It includes the interaction of many identities but does not use the concept of a master status or dominant identity as more important than other identities. In terms of aging studies, Jan Mutchler and Jeffery Burr (2011) see intersectionality as a particularly useful way to examine the impact of older individuals' race or ethnicity within a societal lens.

Emergent theories in gerontology and aging are moving in several directions. Some are focusing more deeply at the cellular levels to expose the biological agents of the aging process. Theories are developing at the societal level and adding additional political and economic determinants, as well as the impact of societal stereotypes about age. Cross-cultural and culture-based theories along with spiritual, intra-individual theories are addressing the person-based heterogeneity of aging. Vern Bengtson and Ricard Settersten (2016) suggest that a guiding principle of new theory development will be a transdisciplinary focus, embracing multiple disciplines.

Theories are an integral part of the research process. They allow a researcher to put his or her work in context and generate new explanations of events. Theories link together the phenomena or events a researcher studies. They are not static; they evolve with increased application. The theoretical approaches discussed in this chapter can form the basis of research designs discussed in the next section of the book, "Choosing a Research Method and Selecting a Design," which includes Chapters 4 to 8 and discusses qualitative methods, quantitative methods, mixed methods, and emerging and future methods.

Discussion Questions

- How would you explain the value of theory to a colleague who thinks it is "just something extra in a research project that is definitely not necessary?"
- Review the worldview or philosophical approaches to conducting research in Chapter 1. Which groups of theories introduced in this chapter match back to the different approaches? For example, would post-positivists support modernization and gerotranscendence theories; early biomedical and health-based theories, and successful aging theories; psychological developmental theories and cognitive theories on aging; theories of social gerontology: life-course perspective and social science/sociological theories; critical gerontology; ecological theories; social construction and phenomenological gerontological theories; identity-based theories and aging; feminist gerontology; or multiple jeopardies and intersectionality? Which theories would a constructivist support?
- How would a quantitative researcher use theory in his or her work? How would a qualitative researcher use theory? How would a mixed-methods researcher use theories in his or her work?
- You are asked to provide theories that can support each element of a biopsychosocial assessment with older persons. Conducting a biopsychosocial assessment of an older person includes questions about biological factors, psychological factors, emotional wellbeing, social factors and social functioning, family factors, cultural factors, sexual functioning, spiritual factors, environmental factors, and financial resources. Choose three of the areas of assessment (listed above), and find corresponding theories that could be used to generate questions as part of the interview.

Bibliography

Achenbaum, W. A., & Stearns, P. N. (1978). Old age and modernization. *The Gerontologist, 18*(3), 307–312.

Agronin, M. E. (2013). From Cicero to Cohen: Developmental theories of aging, from antiquity to the present. *The Gerontologist, 54*(1), 30–39. doi:10.1093/geront/gnt032

Alkema, G. E., & Alley, D. E. (2006). Gerontology's future: An integrative model for disciplinary advancement. *The Gerontologist, 46*, 574–582.

Alley, D. E., Putney, N. M., Rice, M., & Bengtson, V. L. (2010). The increasing use of theory in social gerontology: 1990–2004. *Journals of Gerontology Series B: Psychological Sciences and Social Sciences, 65B*(5), 583–590.

Antonucci, T. C. (2001). Social relations: An examination of social networks, social support. *Handbook of the Psychology of Aging, 3*, 427.

Atchley, R. C. (1989). A continuity theory of normal aging. *The Gerontologist, 29*, 183–190.

Babbie, E. (2013). *The basics of social research.* New York: Cengage Learning.

Baltes, P. B., & Baltes, M. M. (1990). Psychological perspectives on successful aging: The model of selective optimization with compensation. Successful Aging: Perspectives from the Behavioral Sciences, 1, 1–34.

Baltes, P. B., & Goulet, L. R. (1970). *Life-span developmental psychology: Research and theory.* New York: Academic Press.

Bass, S. (2013). The state of gerontology-opus one. *Gerontologist, 53*(4), 534–542.

Bengtson, V. L., & Settersten, R. (2016). *Handbook of theories of aging* (3rd ed.). New York: Springer.

Bengtson, V. L., Silverstein, M. Putney, N. M., & Gans, D. (Eds.). (2009). *Handbook of theories of aging* (2nd ed.). New York: Springer.

Biggs, S., Lowenstein, A., & Hendricks, J. (Eds.). (2003). *The need for theory: Critical approaches to social gerontology.* Amityville, NY: Baywood Publishing Company.

Birren, J. E. (1988). "A contribution to the theory of the psychology of aging: As a counterpart of development." In J. E. Birren, & V. L. Bengston (Eds.), *Emergent theories of aging* (pp. 153–176). New York: Springer.

Blieszner, R. (2016). Personal communication.

Bronfenbrenner, U. (1979). *The ecology of human development: Experiments by nature and design.* Cambridge, MA: Harvard University Press.

Brown, C., & Lowis, M. J. (2003). Psychosocial development in the elderly: An investigation into Erikson's ninth stage. *Journal of Aging Studies, 17*(4), 415–426.

Calasanti, T. (2008). A feminist confronts ageism. *Journal of Aging Studies, 22*(2), 152–157.

Calasanti, T. M., & Slevin, K. F. (2013). *Age matters: Re-aligning feminist thinking.* New York: Taylor and Francis.

Carstensen, L. L. (1992). Social and emotional patterns in adulthood: Support for socioemotional selectivity theory. *Psychology and Aging, 7*(3), 331–338. doi:10.1037/0882-7974.7.3.331

Chapman, S. B., Aslan, S., Spence, J. S., Hart, J., John, J., Bartz, E. K., Didehbani, N., & Lu, H. (2015). Neural mechanisms of brain plasticity with complex cognitive training in healthy seniors. *Cerebral Cortex, 25*(2), 396–405.

Cohen, G. D. (2000). *The creative age: Awakening human potential in the second half of life.* New York: HarperCollins.

Cowgill, D. O., & Holmes, L. D. (1972). *Aging and modernization.* New York: Appelton Century-Crofts.

Cruikshank, M. (2009). *Learning to be old: Gender, culture, and aging.* Lanham, MD: Rowman & Littlefield.

Cumming, E., & Henry, W. (1961). *Growing old: The process of disengagement.* New York: Basic Books.

Dannefer, D. (1984). Adult development and social theory: A paradigmatic reappraisal. *American Sociological Review, 49*(1), 100–116.

Dannefer, D. (2003). Cumulative advantage/disadvantage and the life course: Cross-fertilizing age and social science theory. *Journals of Gerontology Series B: Psychological Sciences and Social Sciences, 58*(6), S327–S337.

De Grey, A. D. (2015). Do we have genes that exist to hasten aging? New data, new arguments, but the answer is still no. *Current Aging Science, 8*(1), 24–33.

De Grey, A., & Rae, M. (2007). *Ending aging: The rejuvenation breakthroughs that could reverse human aging in our lifetime.* New York: Macmillan.

Diehl, M., Hooker, K., & Sliwinski, M. J. (2015). *Handbook of intraindividual variability across the life-span.* New York: Routledge.

Dowd, J. J., & Bengtson, V. L. (1978). Aging in minority populations: An examination of the double jeopardy hypothesis. *Journal of Gerontology, 33*(3), 427–436.

Ekerdt, D. J. (2016). Gerontology in five images. *The Gerontologist, 56*(2), 184–192. doi:10.1093/geront/gnu077

Elder, G. H. (1994). Time, human agency, and social change: Perspectives on the life course. *Social Psychology Quarterly, 57*(1), 4–15.

Erikson, E. H. (1968). Life cycle. *International Encyclopedia of the Social Sciences, 9*, 286–292.

Estes, C. L. (1979). *The aging enterprise: A critical examination of social policies and services for the aged.* San Francisco, CA: Jossey-Bass.

Estes, C. L. (2001). "The political economy of aging: A theoretical framework." In C. L. Estes, & Associates (Eds.), *Social policy and aging: A critical perspective* (pp. 1–21). Thousand Oaks, CA: Sage Publications.

Ferraro, K. F., Shippee, T. P., & Schafer, M. H. (2009). "Cumulative inequality theory for research on aging and the life course. "In V. Bengtson, D. Gans, N. Putney & M. Silverstein (Eds.), *Handbook of Theories of Aging* (pp. 413–433). New York: Springer.

Greenwood, N. (2009). Reflections of a researcher interviewing older people. *Nursing Older People, 21*(7), 30–31.

Haight, B. K., Barba, B. E., Tesh, A. S., & Courts, N. F. (2002). Thriving: A life span theory. *Journal of Gerontological Nursing, 28*(3), 14–22.

Havighurst, R. J., Neugarten, B. L., & Tobin, S. S. (1963). "Disengagement, personality and life satisfaction in the later years." In P. F. Hansen (Ed.), *Age with a future* (pp. 419–425). Copenhagen, Denmark: Munksgaard.

Heckhausen, J., Wrosch, C., & Schulz, R. (2010). A motivational theory of life-span development. *Psychological Review, 117*(1), 32–60. doi:10.1037/a0017668

Hendricks, J. (1982). The elderly in society: Beyond modernization. *Social Science History, 6*(3), 321–345.

Jung, C. G. (1933). *The stages of life: Modern man in search of a soul.* Trans. W. S. Dell, & C. F. Baynes. New York: Harcourt Brace Jovanovich.

Kahn, R. L., & Antonucci, T. C. (1980). "Convoys over the life course: Attachment, roles, and social support." In P. B. Baltes, & O. Brim (Eds.), *Life-span development and behavior* (Vol. 3, pp. 254–283). New York: Academic Press.

Kuypers, J. A. (1973). Social breakdown and competence. *Human Development, 16*(3), 181–201.

Lachman, M. E., & James, J. B. (1997). *Multiple paths of midlife development.* Chicago, IL: University of Chicago Press.

Lamont, R., Swift, H., & Abrams, D. (2015). A review and meta-analysis of age-based stereotype threat: Negative stereotypes, not facts, do the damage. *Psychology and Aging, 30*(1), 180–193. doi:10.1037/a0038586

Lawton, M. P., & Nahemow, L. (1973). "Ecology and the aging process." In C. Eisdorfer, & M. P. Lawton (Eds.), *Psychology of adult development and aging* (pp. 619–674). Washington, DC: American Psychological Association.

Lemon, B. W., Bengtson, V. L., & Peterson, J. A. (1972). An exploration of the activity theory of aging: Activity types and life satisfaction among in-movers to a retirement community. *Journal of Gerontology, 27*, 511–523.

Levinson, D. J. (1986). A conception of adult development. *American Psychologist, 41*(1), 3–13.

Martin, D., & Gillen, L. (2014; 2013). Revisiting gerontology's scrapbook: From Metchnikoff to the spectrum model of aging. *Gerontologist, 54*(1), 51–58.

Mills, C. W. (1967). *The sociological imagination.* New York: Oxford University Press.

Mutchler, J. E., & Burr, J. A. (2011). "Race, ethnicity, and aging." In R. Settersten & J. Angel (Eds.), *Handbook of sociology of aging* (pp. 83–101). New York: Springer.

Nealon, J. T., & Irr, C. (2002). *Rethinking the Frankfurt school: Alternative legacies of cultural critique.* Albany, NY: State University of New York Press.

Ojala, H., Calasanti, T., King, N., & Pietila, I. (2016). Natural(ly) men: Masculinity and gendered anti-ageing practices in Finland and the USA. *Ageing & Society, 36*(2), 356–375. doi:10.1017/S0144686X14001196

Pearl, R. (1924). *Studies in human biology.* Baltimore, MD: Williams and Wilkins.

Powell, J. (2012). The social and economic forces of global ageing in a global society. *Journal of Comparative Social Welfare, 28*(2), 165–177.

Ray, R. E. (1996). A postmodern perspective on feminist gerontology. *The Gerontologist, 36*, 674–680.

Riley, M. W., Johnson, M., & Foner, A. (1972). *Aging and society.* New York: Russell Sage Foundation.

Roberto, K. A., Blieszner, R., & Allen, K. R. (2006). Theorizing in family gerontology: New opportunities for research and practice. *Family Relations, 55*(5), 513–525.

Rowe, J. W., & Kahn, R. L. (1997). Successful aging. *Gerontologist, 37*(4), 433–440.

Rowe, J. W., & Kahn, R. L. (2015). Successful aging 2.0: Conceptual expansions for the 21st century. *The Journals of Gerontology Series B: Psychological Sciences and Social Sciences, 70*(4), 593–596. doi:10.1093/geronb/gbv025

Ryff, C., & Singer, B. (2002). "From social structure to biology." In C. Snyder & A. López (Eds.), *Handbook of positive psychology* (pp. 63–73). London: Oxford University Press.

Tornstam, L. (1996). Gerotranscendence: A theory about maturing into old age. *Journal of Aging and Identity, 1*(1), 37–50.

Twigg, J. (2004). The body, gender, and age: Feminist insights in social gerontology. *Journal of Aging Studies, 18*(1), 59–73.

Vaillant, G. E. (1996). Three models of adult development. *[H.W. Wilson—EDUC], 39*, 153.

Weil, J., & Smith, E. (2016). Aging in place in the continuum of care: Redefining "place" to include independent living, assisted living, skilled-care, and memory-care settings. *Working with Older People 20*(4), 223–230. http://dx.doi.org/10.1108/WWOP-08-2016-0020

Weismann, A. (1892). *The germ-plasm: A theory of heredity.* New York: Scribner.

Weiss, A. K. (1974). The Hayflick hypothesis. *The Gerontologist, 14*(6), 492–493.

Part II
Choosing a Research Method and Selecting a Design

4
Qualitative Methods

The next five chapters cover qualitative, quantitative, mixed, emergent, and future methods designs. This chapter covers qualitative work in gerontology. It provides the history of qualitative work in gerontology. Each qualitative design (narrative analysis, ethnography, grounded theory, case studies, and phenomenological accounts) is described along with ways to choose the method best suited to a researcher's study. Design features are compared, and details are provided for each element of research design (sampling, data collection, transcription, analysis, trustworthiness/rigor, and ethics). The chapter concludes with a discussion of best practices for qualitative researchers, an introduction to qualitative software choices, and issues to consider drawn from applied examples from the field.

Although once thought of as an opposite research design to quantitative work, qualitative work is more accurately seen as having a different methodological stance and addressing different research questions. The **qualitative design** is best used when the researcher looks to explore a topic in aging about which little is known or where more in-depth, first-person accounts are needed. A qualitative approach can be seen as a shift from a more positivistic view of reality that sees it as objective or something external that can be independently measured to a stance that believes reality and social life are socially constructed or created by individuals. There are multiple realities and viewpoints of it. Qualitative methods employ a general philosophy of constructivism or subjectivism—how meaning is attached to experiences or events.

Qualitative Aging Research in Print and Academic Journals

Work done by Graham Rowles and Nancy Schoenberg (2002) found that qualitative methods have been gaining wide acceptance since the 1980s. Since that time, many seminal books on the mechanics and application of qualitative work exist and have been printed. Despite the history of qualitative research design in aging work, a fairly recent discourse has reemerged among gerontological journal editors about the "scientific-ness" and rigor of all types of qualitative research. Rachel Pruchno et al.'s (2014) editorial "Science or fishing?" discusses common reasons why qualitative work is not published in that particular journal. There is also the desire to increase recognition of qualitative methods' strength and the need to devote more journal space to qualitative articles. Several gerontology journals offer tables of standards for writers and reviewers of qualitative research articles, from overall project design to research questions, methods, and writing up results and discussion. These editorial articles have titles like "Food for thought" (Schoenberg, Shenk & Kart, 2007), "Promoting qualitative research" (Schoenberg & McAuley, 2007), and "The qualitative portfolio at the Gerontologist: Strong and getting stronger" (Schoenberg, Miller & Pruchno, 2011), which offers detailed guidelines about publishing qualitative work in gerontology journals. Or there is "Qualitative research in Journals of Gerontology: Social Sciences—'I'll take a side of coleslaw with that'" (Warren-Findlow, 2013), offering an editor's point of view and the 12 most common critiques given to qualitative authors by reviewers.

Articles such as "Bridges and boundaries: Humanities and arts enhance gerontology" (Kivnick & Pruchno, 2011) seek to further expand the role of qualitative work in gerontology. The North American Network in Aging Studies (NANAS) and European Network in Aging Studies (ENAS) include literature and arts to overcome resistance to combining gerontology and humanities-based research (Marshall, 2014).

As qualitative research on aging expands and develops more forms and designs, we need to continue to explore those areas of aging research. In her 2014 analysis of "Qualitative research trends in gerontology: An 18-year analysis of 7 journals (1995–2012)," Áine Humble found that 33% of articles in these journals during the 2010–2012 period were qualitative, with the order of type mentioned as grounded theory, content analysis, ethnography, case studies, and phenomenology. A recent editorial, in a leading gerontology journal, called for publication to be driven by quality and topic and not a methodological preference, thus embracing more qualitative research options (Carr, 2015).

Deciding How to Choose a Research Method and Design: Qualitative Options

If we think back to Figure 1.1 in the introduction, we see that a qualitative design most closely matches either a constructivist or subjectivist worldview/paradigm but can incorporate a mixture of others, as well. For a recap of those approaches, see Table 4.1. Along with a viewpoint that the people you are studying help create their view of reality, powerful reasons emerge for using qualitative methods. Aspects of a good qualitative research question would include the need for **rich, thick description.** This term, attributed to Clifford Geertz (1973), means the recording of all events in the field in great detail. Included are taking extended, detailed quotations from interviewees, recording field notes about the

Table 4.1 Examples of Philosophical Paradigms Related to Qualitative to Methodological Design

Constructionist: Seeks to capture the way individuals construct/create reality, and research centered upon participants' views/ways of constructing meaning. Origins in hermeneutics.	**Interpretive:** acknowledges there are multiple views of reality (including those of the researcher and those "studied"), so the "participant" is the best at describing experiences and events in his or her own life. **Symbolic Interactionism:** understanding how people attach meaning to their experiences in the world based on their interaction with society.
Subjectivism: our views of reality are filtered and seen throughout subjective viewpoints or vantage points.	**Critical/Transformative:** includes power and political dynamics of oppressed/marginalized groups and societal influences upon these groups. **Feminism:** an inclusive approach to include women's voices and intersectionality statuses—reflecting society's role in creating gender-based social problems.

setting and events from the researcher's perspective, and including items from the field (newsletters, photos, etc.) in the data-collection process. The goal is to gather enough information to aid the researcher in understanding the many factors of the issue he or she is studying from the participants' point of view. Qualitative research's strength is the ability to collect detailed information about a topic (when a closed-ended or fixed-choice question would not gather the information you seek in enough detail) or when a topic could be considered sensitive—such as research questions about the impact of recent widowhood or transition in one's living situation (moving from a house to a skilled-care setting or aging as a refugee in a new country).

If you seek an intact, holistic view of an older person's experience as the focus of your study, qualitative methods work best. Other times, qualitative work can generate or "ground" theory about topics and populations where little information is known: for example, the role of grandparenting for Latino older persons with unknown legal custody and immigration status (Mendoza, 2012). Qualitative work can lead, follow, or be conducted concurrently with a quantitative design. These sequential and mixed-methods designs are mentioned, briefly, at the end of this chapter and discussed fully in Chapter 7.

Choosing among Qualitative Designs

While qualitative methods in aging are constantly evolving, the present methodological designs can be divided into five main categories used by John Creswell, Sharan Merriam, and Earl Babbie for general qualitative work. These include narrative analysis, ethnography, grounded theory, case studies, and phenomenological accounts.

Narrative Analysis

Narrative analysis is used in many disciplines. Generally, narrative analysis can be an analysis of the content of the story and how it conveys meaning on the part of the teller. Or the analysis can be about the way a story is told, of the text and dialogue itself. Narrative accounts can be spoken or written. Beginning with the work of Butler (1963) on life review and reminiscence in older persons, gerontological narrative designs have been given many names and forms. For example, interviews may produce or contain stories. There are multiple forms of narrative where an interviewer or researcher seeks to capture stories of an older person's life. These are **life histories** (an older person's self-story, told to another), **life review** (an older person's self-story, told to another with explicit evaluative or resolution-based purpose; it can be guided), or **life stories** (an older person's self-story, told to another or written by the person—a more generic term). These stories can be part of **reminiscence** (an older person's directed storytelling to another) or of **oral histories** (stories about an older person collected by another). The narrative process is not about assessing a universal "truth" but analyzing the story, itself, from many vantage points (de Medeiros, 2014).

Narratives can be self-written or collected on the part of the older person with the older person as author and also recorder of the story. Examples include autobiography, including **poetry** (older person-based, self-written) or **guided autobiography** (older person-based, self-written, led through group processes; see Birren & Cochran, 2001). Gerontological research includes the use of **diaries and journaling** (older person-based, self-written), **memoirs** (older person-based, self-written, with memories of times and events as a focus), and **biography** (older person-based, other-written). **Ethnodramatic practices** include the researchers in the narrative process and let them act out or perform stories of those they study. Ethnodramatic elder narrative can be in the form of visual stories and poetry. For

Box 4.1 Two Poems by Dorothy Davisson

Times Change

Who is that in the mirror?
She still has blue eyes
She faintly resembles someone I used to know.
And has all her own teeth, thank goodness.
But she has been known to ask questions
Then answer herself—the poor dear.
She still has energy to dance around the house
To good dance music.
She used to sing in the church choir but
I don't know where her voice went
Does talking to your house plants make them grow better?
I've heard her have those conversations.
The thing that worries me the most.
She has been known to go outside in her robe
To get the morning paper.
What will the neighbors think?

Dorothy's Comments:

As times change, at least it happened to me, I became more introspective—looking at each person to see who she is. Since I wrote this poem, times changed. I've changed. I wrote it still believing the way my mother felt in her day. She was more straight-laced, always living as if she were in a glass house and people could observe her actions. After living more honestly, I would change the last verse to reflect who I am today:

Instead of appearance and passage of time
Keep friendships close by.
Be proud of accomplishments
And wear red shoes when you choose.

Tapestry

A Craftsman
With visions of a masterpiece
Collected colors of the spectrum
Red, yellow, black, white, bronze,
And began his work.
He toiled
During wars and joyful times
Feelings
And faces of people
Interwoven.
Golden threads
Throughout the tapestry,
Connected people and events
Into a giant montage.
All were necessary
To complete the picture.

Dorothy's Comments:

I wrote the poem Tapestry as an allegory. Imagine my surprise to read a book in 2012, entitled, *To Heaven and Back* by Mary C. Neal, M.D. It is an account of her death, heaven, angels, and life again. On page 142, she quotes: "I began to visualize a reasonable allegory for our individual lives; each of us is like a small piece of thread that contributes to the weaving of a very large and very beautiful tapestry." She goes on to say: "without our individual contribution the tapestry would be incomplete and broken."

example, Box 4.1 contains two poems written by Dorothy Davisson when she was in her 70s with comments and additions in her 90s. On a larger societal scale, older persons' stories may include **master narratives** (i.e., cultural scripts for behavior or action that exists in a particular society) that may work their ways into an individual's own story or narrative (de Medeiros, 2014; Phoenix, Smith & Sparkes, 2010).

Some recent examples of narrative analysis focused on stigma in age-based housing and care settings (Roth, Eckert & Morgan, 2016) and how social support is received by older persons not having children (Allen & Wiles, 2014). Others examined the importance of narrative in cultural anthropological and gerontological contexts (Perkinson & Solimeo, 2013) and narratives in healthcare (such as spiritual distress during physical rehabilitation; Mundle, 2015). Researchers looked at multiple generations co-creating narratives (Saunders, Saunders & Amaechi, 2013) and good stories in maintaining a resilient identity (Randall, 2013). Some explored **"shadow" or hidden stories** within a story (de Medeiros & Rubinstein, 2015) and narrative analysis of poetry written by those with dementia (Clark-McGhee & Castro, 2015). There are narratives of resistance to bodily aging as decline (Phoenix & Smith, 2011) and medical students' own accounts of geriatric work (O'Donnell, Carson, Forciea, Kinosian, Shea, Yudin & Miller, 2013).

Grounded Theory

Grounded theory, developed by Barney Glaser and Anselm Strauss in (1967), develops theory from an ongoing, open-ended questioning process with participants. The inter-relatedness of concepts leads to the development of the theory of how the events of processes studied relate to each other. Glaser and Strauss's method came from their own study about how dying persons, families, and medical staff react to, discuss, or avoid discussions of imminent death in *Awareness of dying* (1966).

The grounded-theory process involves several elements in creating theory from data. These key elements are an inductive process, rich data, theoretical sampling, constant comparative method, memo use, saturation, the researcher's self-reflexiveness, theory production, and a different approach to the literature review. An **inductive process** is key. Here the data are used to generate a theory instead of a preconceived theoretical framework directing data collection. There is debate about the nature of a literature review in grounded-theory studies (which Charmaz calls the "disputed literature review" [2006, p. 165]). Journal guidelines and dissertation and thesis formats may require a formal literature review, while traditional grounded-theory models would not do so to the same extent. Applications of grounded theory often take a different approach to the literature-review process. Here, an author may review literature up to the current study for gaps and starting points for his/her own study. The existing literature is a springboard to introduce your own approach/ideas, thus setting your place in the dialogue. Rich, thick data, though an important part of all qualitative work, allow grounded theorists to understand the phenomena they are studying. These data are the building blocks used to construct a theory, so they need to be thorough and exhaustive.

Constant comparative method, or continued comparison and contrasting of the data, as an ongoing, recurrent part of the data collection and analysis process, is essential (Glaser & Strauss, 1965; Merriam, 2009). The more **types of narrative data** (from interviews, written stories, printed materials) there are, the stronger the comparative process in producing differing ideas and avenues of study. Parts of this iterative process include the use of theoretical sampling. This lets the researcher choose cases to help explore, develop, and provide alternative views for an existing theme. For example, if all participants talk about the great benefit of being a member of a senior center's "regular members," a researcher would seek those that find membership limiting. **Theoretical sampling** allows the researcher to seek out these counternarrative voices—such as "bingo" or "menu" members—and include them in the study to develop the concept of "role of senior center members" as they progress through the study (Weil, 2014).

Memos serve as ways to record decision making during the data-analysis process, to collect the researcher's reactions and thoughts, and as an analytical tool. **Saturation,** also called "theoretical saturation" by Charmaz, is what the term implies: a saturation of knowledge and ideas about the issue you are studying. So, no new themes, idea, or concepts can be generated. It is crucial that the researcher is self-reflexive, both analyzing and writing about his or her views and role in the process of theory construction. A grounded-theory method produces theory to forward the way a discipline thinks about a concept, event, behavior, or group.

In gerontology, grounded-theory-based studies look at a wide variety of topics. Some have examined how nursing-home residents define quality of care (Bowers, Fibich & Jacobson, 2001), pathways to gambling in later life (Tira, Jackson & Tomnay, 2014), and attitudes toward information technologies and Internet use (González, Ramírez & Viadel, 2012). Researchers explored the perceived stigma of hearing loss in peer groups (Wallhagen, 2010), created typologies of caregivers for persons with dementia (Corcoran, 2011), and studied the experience of becoming a caregiver in midlife (Pope, Kolomer & Glass, 2012). Others generated theory about the social lives of individuals or couples in assisted-living settings (Kemp, Ball, Hollingsworth & Perkins, 2012; Kemp, Ball & Perkins, 2016), the meaning of home (Sixsmith et al., 2014), and experiences of residents in naturally occurring retirement communities, NORCs (Greenfield, 2013). Studies have also used grounded theory about older persons with disabilities; post-hip fracture (McMillan, Booth, Currie & Howe, 2012); social and spiritual resilience (Cheung & Kam, 2012); perceptions of successful aging in lesbian, gay, bisexual, and transgender older adults (Van Wagenen, Driskell & Bradford, 2013); and persons with functional limitations (Romo et al., 2013).

Ethnography

Ethnography is a qualitative way, or method, of studying a group of people in a society or social setting. This method has been integral to the understanding of older persons and their lived experiences and social worlds from the individual's perspective. It involves the researcher becoming embedded with the persons he or she is studying and remaining with the group (often referred to as "being in the field") for a long period of time. The overall goal of ethnographic work is to understand an experience or events from a participant's point of view without having the researcher impose his or her own point of view on the events as they happen. The scope of ethnographic work can be a single case study but also range to an entire social institution or interrelated institutions in society. The **ethnographer acts as the instrument** recording data, while his or her own observations, field notes, and printed materials, as well as audio and visual materials, can act as the data. But ethnographic work can also be collaborative—with the data being co-created by the persons being studied or by a team of researchers. Usually, **key informants** (also called stakeholders or gatekeepers) are from the group being studied. They help the researcher gain access to participants by building trust and rapport with those in the field. Ethnographies of aging can be a mixture of participant observation, in-depth interviewing, focus groups, document analysis, and use of photos. Sampling can be based on **snowball-sampling methods** (with one participant suggesting others) or **purposive** (where initial participants are selected for their knowledge of an issue). Traditionally, the practice was to use **pseudonyms** (fictitious names) of those studied, but, with photographs and participant or community-based collaborative methods, actual names and images of participants may also be used (with the consent of those studied).

While early ethnography has its roots in cultural anthropology, many types of ethnographic work exist today, from **critical ethnography** (representing a multitude of participants' voices with a focus on those of groups often voiceless or centered around exposing existing inequalities) to **autoethnography** (a first-person account of an individual to also reflect upon societal structure and larger societal/social influences upon his or her life). Types of autoethnography include emotional, evocative, or heartful, where researchers include their own emotions/reactions in the writing (Ellis, 1999).

With the history of recognition of qualitative methods in gerontology (Eckert, 1988; Gubrium, Puddephatt, Shaffir & Kleinknecht, 2009; Stafford, 2001), the strength of the ethnographic process is that it allows the researcher to use data collected through a variety of methods, including in-depth interviewing, participant observations, printed materials, personal narratives, life review, reminiscence, photographs (or "photovoice"), and video.

While **traditional images of an ethnographer** present someone jotting field notes in a physical notebook while a cassette tape runs, data-collection methods can also include **digital ethnography**, or audio and video recording. Data can be collected via phone/tablet apps, mapping or geographic information systems (GIS), and video-calling interfaces, such as FaceTime or Skype. The ethnographic process is moving in several directions. Building on the team-based approach, ethnographic work is becoming even more collaborative with participants also working as researchers. A recent example is the creation of **participatory ethnographic videos** (see Jean Schensul and Margaret Diane LeCompte's *Specialized ethnographic methods*). In this case, the researchers and the community create a video that addresses a community-based issue in a shared, ongoing process. Cyberspace, applications for mobile devices (apps), and live visual and audio online, web-based interfaces (such as Skype) are expanding the ethnographic setting or field. **Performance ethnography** continues to evolve and further blend research and artistic expression (such as spoken word or dance) to address social issues.

Ethnographic work with older adults has examined transitions in housing, meaning of home, healthcare needs/decisions, experiences of medical professionals in skilled-living care, living with health issues, experiences at senior centers, and social networks in neighborhoods settings, retirement communities, and leisure. Box 4.2 provides a discussion of specific ethnographic books in gerontology by topic. A full reference for each ethnography is available at the end of this chapter.

Case Studies

Case studies and extended case studies can have one individual as a focus or include multiple persons or levels as part of the case—individuals, social institutions, societies, or even larger geographic units, such as countries. For example, at the individual level, a case study could look at the experience of a woman—from her point of view—as she moves from her house to assisted living. This case study, at an institutional level, could examine how staff working at one particular assisted-living facility aids in new residents' transitions, or it could be how the United States, as a whole, addresses transition in its assisted-living facilities.

It seems that ways to describe the qualitative case-study approach are limitless, but the elements of case studies to consider include bounded system, an intrinsic vs. an instrumental focus, the choice of a single case or multiple cases, and a single site or multiple sites. Case studies are descriptive and are uniquely critical and revelatory about the issue at hand. **Bounded**, though defined differently by methodologists, can mean that the case has naturally occurring limits (such as the case of older persons living in a particular rural county in 2015), or cases can be made into a bounded group, grouped by the researcher for his or her own purposes (the first several persons to move into elder co-housing or men

Box 4.2 Examples of Ethnographies of Aging and Older Persons

Topic	Name	Description
Early descriptive, ethnographic works	Jerry Jacobs's *Fun city* (1974)	A case study in cultural anthropology exploring a retirement community in the U.S.
	Barbara Myerhoff's *Number our days* (1979)	An anthropological account detailing lives of Jewish senior center attendees at the "Aliyah" senior center.
	Susan Sheehan's *Kate Quinton's days* (1984)	A journalistic account describing the life of a Brooklyn woman in her 80s as she and her family transition through levels of care and her return to home with home care.
	Frida Furman's *Facing the mirror* (1997)	Studies segregation by age and identity of older women—in this case, at a beauty salon.
	Dorothy Ayers Counts and David Counts's *Over the next hill* (1996/2001)	Covers older persons' use of recreational vehicles and the meaning of traveling around the U.S.
Sociological accounts	Arlie Hochschild's *The unexpected community* (1978)	She calls the work her "sociologist's diary" of social isolation and connectedness of persons 65 and over living in an apartment building California (vii).
	J. Kevin Eckert's *The unseen elderly* (1980)	An ethnographic study of the social conditions of single-room-occupancy hotels, in a city setting in California.
The role of geographic or community-based place upon older people	Graham Rowles's *Prisoners of space* (1978)	An interdisciplinary (psychological, sociological, anthropological, and literary) analysis of the geography of place.
	Maria Vesperi's *City of green benches* (1985)	Examines the social conditions and construction of age for the oldest old in downtown St. Petersburg, Florida.
	Janice Smithers's *Determined survivors* (1985)	An ethnography of the daily lives of older persons in an urban high-rise apartment complex in a California city.
	Eric Klinenberg's *Heat wave* (2002)	Analyzes the impact of a natural disaster on the lives and health of older Chicago residents and includes the roles of civil and governmental/political leaders in the phenomenon.
	Philip Stafford's *Elderburbia* (2009)	An ethnographic work about aging in place and age-friendly communities in the wake of the Baby Boomers.
	Christine Milligan's *There's no place like home* (2009)	Uses narratives of older persons to describe the meaning of home and community also seen through a larger social and political lens.
	Meika Loe's *Aging our way* (2011)	Creates life lessons from work with mostly community dwellers aged 85 years and older in parts of upstate New York about what it means to live in the community and maintain a sense of comfort and well-being.

	Joyce Weil's *The new neighborhood senior center* (2014)	Uses a multiyear ethnography of a closing senior center in NYC to explore larger social, governmental, and political issues facing senior centers.
Impact of either assisted or skilled nursing-care institutions for older persons	Jaber Gubrium and David Buckholdt's *Describing care* (1982)	Based upon observational work describing how health professionals speak of, and define, conditions of persons undergoing physical rehabilitation.
	Jaber Gubrium and *Oldtimers and Alzheimer's* (1986)	An ethnographic account of Alzheimer's disease—the way it is lived by those with it and is socially constructed by medical and healthcare professionals.
	Jaber Gubrium and Andrea Sankar's (1990) edited volume, *The home care experience*	A collection of work exploring home care as it was being created as a mode of service delivery and the creation of corresponding policy.
	Jaber Gubrium's *The mosaic of care* (1991)	Uses in-depth interviewing and case-study methods to help service professionals understand what the lived experience of frailty is to the frail and their families and care providers in neighborhood, hospital, and skilled-nursing-care settings.
	Jaber Gubrium's *Living and dying at Murray Manor* (1975/97)	Records the daily life and organizational structure of skilled-care facilities, called nursing homes, as a site of study.
	J. Kevin Eckert, Paula Carder, Leslie Morgan, Ann Christine Frankowski, and Erin Roth's *Inside assisted living* (2009)	An ethnographic group's multi-year work about the experiences of older persons transitioning into and remaining in assisted-living care for almost 400 older persons in six different facilities.
Transitions in living arrangements and care	Lee Bowker's *Humanizing institutions for the aged* (1982)	Uses observational work in four long-term care Milwaukee facilities to examine the totalizing nature of these institutions.
	Eileen Fairhurst's (1990) article "Doing ethnography in a geriatric unit"	Describes her work with staff in a British physical-rehabilitation unit.
	Philip Stafford's *Gray areas* (2003)	Is an edited volume of chapters about *Ethnographic encounters with nursing home culture.*
Lived experience of those with a specific condition or disease	Lawrence Cohen's *No aging in India* (2000)	Depicts how dementia and cognitive changes are seen in four settings in India.
	Julia Twigg's (2006) *The body in health and social care*	Looks at issues of embodiment or how institutions of health in society regulate the body as it ages through diet and other measures.
	Samantha Solimeo's *With shaking hands* (2009)	An ethnographic account of persons living with Parkinson's disease and organizations working with the disease.
	Pia Kontos's (2010) article "Embodied selfhood: Ethnographic reflections, performing ethnography, and humanizing dementia care"	Examines the construction of self and selfhood for those with dementia in an Orthodox Jewish long-term care facility.

experiencing widowhood). An **intrinsic case** focus means the researcher has interest in that specific, distinct case vs. an instrumental case, a more general case that is used to gain insight into an issue (Stake, 2008). Cases can be single or multiple in volume (ranging in scope from people to countries or systems) and have single or multiple sites (or collective case studies—e.g., the case of older persons living in several rural counties in 2015 in several neighboring states). For a full discussion of case-study classification, see Robert Yin's (2014) *Case study research: Design and methods* and Patricia Brown's (2008) "Review of the literature on case study research."

Some recent examples that illustrate the varied use of case studies (at multiple levels) in gerontology are how an activities director's view of death informed and subsequently influenced residents (Black & Rubinstein, 2005). Case studies examined the use of survey research with older persons in Beirut (Abdulrahim, Ajrouch, Jammal & Antonucci, 2012) and offered a gerontologist's account of working with an insurance company to develop long-term-care insurance options with reflection 10 years later (George, 2013). Other case studies focused on the practices of anti-aging practitioners and their view of aging in relation to successful aging ideas (Flatt, Settersten, Ponsaran & Fishman, 2013). Researchers studied the life history of an 80-year-old gay man living his life in a rural setting (Rowan, Giunta, Grudowski & Anderson, 2013). For an example of a traditional case study (such as one documenting the age and experience of a male centenarian), see John Wilmoth, Axel Skytthe, Diana Friou, and Bernard Jeune (1996). Case studies can also be used as a teaching tool, providing realism to more abstract concepts and ideas (see Clark, 2002).

Phenomenological Accounts

Phenomenological accounts are used by researchers when they want to understand how an individual makes his or her own personal meaning of a situation or experience. Building upon the work of Alfred Schutz, Thomas Luckmann, and Jurgen Habermas, these accounts see the participant as the one who deciphers meaning and assigns cause and effect to events, using his or her own worldview. The participants give the researchers access to their life-worlds, how they give conscious meaning to or interpret their lived experiences, how they organize thoughts and feelings, and how they interpret all the encounters in their daily social world. It is of particular importance in these accounts that researchers are aware of their own assumptions and do not apply their views to the individual(s) studied; participants must interpret and assign their own meaning to events.

While data may be collected from a combination of interviews, individuals' own accounts, the researcher's own observations, etc., Max van Manen (1997, 2011) suggests the goal is "borrowing other experiences" to help the researcher understand the phenomenon at hand—not having a "subject" and analyzing participants from a distance.

When writing about gerontological applications using a phenomenological approach, A. Edmund Sherman (1984) provides the example of Joseph Kuypers and Vern Bengtson's social reconstruction model (as an alternative to the social-breakdown model), which links an older person's sense of self, identity, and role to interaction between environment, social worlds, and self-evaluation. James Holstein and Jaber Gubrium (1995) encourage researchers not to dismiss daily life as normal or routinized but to see the potential for understanding an older person's views and way of making sense of the lived experience.

Though previously less explored in gerontology, phenomenological studies can include topics such as self-care and aging (Söderhamn, 2013) or older women's sexuality (Drummond et al., 2013). Phenomenology was used to study African-American caregivers' accounts of dementia and impact on self-identity and role (Lindauer, Harvath, Berry & Wros, 2016) and how society bio-medicalizes the aging body (Powell, 2014). Other researchers looked at older persons' thoughts and feelings about using safety sensory devices in their home (Pol, van Nes, van Hartingsveldt, Buurman, de Rooij & Kröse, 2016), choosing to leave home for a preferred residential setting (Minney, Hons & Ranzijn, 2015), or living with an illness or chronic condition, such as Parkinson's (Haahr, Kirkevold, Hall & Østergaard, 2013). These methods have been suggested as being less positivistic and more decolonized (not generated from those in power over those with less power) for use with indigenous older populations (Braun, Browne, Ka'opua, Kim & Mokuau, 2014).

Developing Qualitative Research Designs

Choosing a Method

While all qualitative methodological choices (narrative analysis, ethnography, grounded theory, case studies, and phenomenological accounts) have similarities, each may be more suited to a particular application. Factors to consider when choosing a design include a project's or topic's scope or magnitude, intention of the work, availability of existing theory, time available for the project, existing resources and materials, access to the field setting, researcher's level of comfort with being in the field in immersive work, and comfort with older persons as co-researchers. Table 4.2 provides a comparison of features of each qualitative design for a planned research project.

Collecting Data

In qualitative analysis, data collection and analysis often occur together, with the lines and distinctions between collection and analysis being more dynamic and flexible. While the two processes are divided here (for explanation), the ordering may differ according to the individual study. This process of data collection and analysis is interactive, cyclical, and reciprocal, while still based on systematic analysis processes.

Generally, qualitative analysis is seen as looking for summaries or **themes** (as ways to represent the data). But, when I present these analysis strategies, I do not want to imply a static or one-directional process that would synthesize or reduce the qualitative data back into rigid, fixed, or purely quantitative models. While we look for themes in the data, we also look at **counternarratives** or differing, discrepant voices. There is an acknowledgement of two views (the researcher and the person studied) and ways to assess that the researcher's description is authentic.

Sampling and Selecting Cases

There are several approaches to sampling in qualitative research. First, keep in mind that the focus is to provide vivid, deep, rich description of events, and the ultimate goal is not to be representative (that is a quantitative construct). Qualitative researchers need to release the idea of needing to generalize results. There is no need to apologize for "not being a representation or generalizable" in the quantitative sense. Rigor and publication both play a role in this **concern over sample size**. Secondly, think about the needed number of cases being driven by the research question and approach and not an "n" or predetermined sample size. While researchers have tried to generate sample-size guidelines to address an often-asked question ("So, how many cases do I need?"), these golden numbers do not exist. For example, a report by the National Center for Research Methods at the University of Southampton—*How many*

Table. 4.2 Comparison of Features of Each Qualitative Design

	Narrative Analysis	Ethnography	Grounded Theory	Case Studies	Phenomenological Accounts
Intention of the Work/ Project	Analysis of story and teller's point of view	Fieldwork and participant observation in a field setting	Theory development where none/ limited exits	Study of a bounded entity or system	Understanding of how older individuals attach meaning to their experience, self, and social worlds
Project's Scope or Magnitude	Varies by narrative type—printed, collected via written, oral interview	Requires more time than other methods to gain access, acceptance, and immersion in the group	Requires more time in analysis—since goal is new theory construction	Varies by how a case is defined and number of cases sought	Varies by how a case is defined and number of cases sought
Availability of Existing Theory	Account builds on/adds to existing theory	Account builds on/adds to existing theory	Little to none	Account builds on/adds to existing theory	Account builds on/adds to existing theory
Time Available for the Work/ Project	Varies by project's scope	Varies by project's scope	Varies by project's scope	Varies by project's scope	Varies by project's scope
Planning, Resources, and Existing Materials	Planning differs if seeking discussion/ interview/ conversation with individual(s) or printed materials collection	Extensive fieldwork and observation requires time and support	Time needs to be allocated to capture counter-narratives (discrepant cases when aspects of a theory emerges)	Time and resources depend upon length of time exploring the case(s) and number of cases included	In-depth accounts require substantial time to collect and discuss with individual
Access to the Field/Setting	Assessing printed materials and seeking discussion/ interview/ conversation with individual(s) or pose different access issues; trust of interviewee(s) is key for authentic narrative	Gatekeepers (helping gain access to field settings) and people's trust are key	Repeated interviews/ field access are needed to explore/flesh out stages of theory development	Number of cases and level of depth sought determine time spent in the field	Number of cases and level of depth sought determine time spent in the field
Researcher's Level of Comfort with Immersive Fieldwork	Important for discussion/ interview/ conversation with individual(s); lesser if using printed materials	Essential	Essential	Important for discussion/ interview/ conversation with individual(s)	Self-reflexivity of researcher and level of comfort are key for this method
Researcher's Level of Comfort with Older Persons as Co-researchers	Lesser if using printed materials	Needed for members to review the authenticity of the study	Members help construct and assess theory's relatability	Depends upon approach and use of members as part of study	Essential; key element of the philosophical approach of this method

qualitative interviews is enough?—consulted 14 experts and five newer researchers about appropriate qualitative sample sizes. The report concluded "it depends" on a multitude of factors (Baker, Edwards & Doidge, 2012, p. 1).

General, wide-ranging estimates say the "right" sample size for your study can be one person (in the case of a phenomenological or case study), four or five people for case studies, six to nine persons for focus groups, and range up to 30 or more (for grounded theory creation) or 30 to 50 or more (for an ethnographic study) (see Creswell, 2013, pp. 156–157; Onwuegbuzie & Leech, 2007). If there is a need to create "qualitative power analyses," authors suggest the analysis must be based on several descriptive factors: the appropriateness of participants selected, location, and other aspects related to the sample (Onwuegbuzie & Leech, 2007, p. 105). Others suggest that several factors either increase or decrease qualitative sample size: the nature of the topic (known topics can have smaller samples than unknown ones), quality of the data (more surface data requires more participants), study design (longitudinal or repeated interviews indicate lesser participants), and the possibility to gather shadow data (meaning that participants will also comment about the experiences of others, then less cases would be needed). For a full discussion, see Janice Morse (2000).

In terms of how participants are selected, sampling can be **purposive** (also called criterion based) where the researcher chooses participants for a particular reason—for example, long-term residents of an assisted-living facility or older persons leading an advocacy-training program. Sampling can be **convenience based**, where participants are selected based on ease of accessibility or availability. Following the purposive example, participants in convenience sampling could be any resident of the assisted-living facility found in a common area when the researcher visits and any elder participating in an advocacy program at a particular rally or event. **Key informants**, those knowledgeable about the topic of the study, may aid as "gatekeepers" in getting the researcher access to the field or participants. In these situations, an Activities Director or Advocacy Trainer could make the initial introductions. Once research is underway, one participant may often recommend another (a process called snowball sampling).

Yvonne Lincoln and Egon Guba suggest **theoretical sampling** for those researchers grounding theory. As the term's name suggests, cases or participants are selected to aid in the development of theory because they represent a category or element of the theory. In theoretical sampling, cases can be selected throughout the course of the study and need not be completed prior to the study or pre-arranged ahead of time. Sampling stops when **saturation** occurs (or no new data, ideas, themes emerge). For example, in the case of grounding theory about the role of language in Latino grandparents-raising-grandchildren service usage, if all grandparent's interviews presented the need for bilingual services for their grandchildren, the researcher may then sample, or choose, grandparents that use existing services in English to see how these views fit into the emergent theory the researcher is actively constructing. But, when addressing sampling transparency in the qualitative-sampling processes, a researcher must describe how saturation is reached and carefully explain why he or she feels no additional cases are needed (see O'Reilly & Parker, 2012).

Generating and Managing Data

Field Notes and Memos

A researcher's personal reflections and observations of people, actions, and events, as participant or participant observer in the field, are key data and may include direct narrative and quotes of participants. These should be written (by hand or electronically) or audio recorded throughout the course of your study while the experiences are fresh in your mind. **Memos**, on the other hand, may include some of your field-note data but serve several other functions. Memos are extremely versatile in style and function; they can be analytical, methodological, or theoretical in nature (Charmaz, 2006; Marshall & Rossman, 2011). As a way to reflect, organize, and categorize data, **analytical memos** go beyond description and include examination of the materials and your observations. **Methodological memos** provide an opportunity to record thoughts and any ongoing issues with your methodology—e.g., difficulties with questions or the interview script, locating participants, etc. **Theoretical memos** (often associated with Grounded Theory development) are a place to explore relationships between concepts you are uncovering and how they may relate to each other to form a theory or conceptual framework.

Transcription

In qualitative work, recorded verbal data from interviews, focus groups, and other aspects of the field are foundational elements of analysis. To conduct analysis, the researcher must be extremely familiar with his or her data. That said, while software programs and transcription services exist, most researchers will transcribe their own audiotapes or digitally recorded files. This process increases familiarity, assists analysis, and allows names, places, and other identifiers to be replaced with pseudonyms (fake names). The researcher as transcriber also maintains Institutional Review Board (IRB) confidentiality concerns.

Analytic Approach to Data Analysis

A general practice for qualitative data analysis is to create categories or themes from commonalities in data and also to note discrepant or counternarrative cases (those differing from other cases in some way or offering an alternative explanation or description of events). Codes can be generated from participants' direct expressions or as a concept from the researcher's own interpretation of the data. In some cases, pre-existing codes may be used. In cases where theory creation (grounded theory) is the goal, all analysis is driven from themes or ideas arising from the data in the data-collection and analysis processes.

Qualitative data analysis can take on several forms, including thematic analysis (as in qualitative content analysis or grounded-theory construction) or narrative analyses (as in conversation, discourse, and critical-discourse analysis). Narrative-analysis designs can be holistic or embedded, thematic or structural, interactional, character and plot based, or viewed for how they create the teller's identity (see Gubrium & Sankar, 1994; Tekle & Vermunt, 2012).

As noted above, in the "Collecting Data" section, while analytical approaches may combine and summarize the data, a qualitative analytical approach recognizes the differences between common, emergent views and accepts diverse and divergent views of a situation in all its complexities (Phoenix, Smith & Sparkes, 2010). In the following sections, I will describe some of the traditional coding practices and also some alternative approaches to coding that vary from the more commonly used ones.

Thematic Analysis

Traditional Coding Practices for Researchers: Types of Codes and Coding Themes

Codes are ways of organizing the data we gather from a variety of sources, including interview transcripts, field notes, participant observation, documents, etc. While codes are used to generate themes, they are not necessarily themes in and of themselves (Saldaña, 2009).

Inductive vs. deductive approach to coding. As part of the **deductive approach** (also called top-coding), categories of analysis (called codes) are planned before the analysis begins. For example, in a study using crowding-in and crowding-out theory to evaluate the role of senior centers in the North American aging network in literature, researchers began with deductive coding (see Weil & Moore, 2015). As part of the deductive-coding process, four codes, based on crowding-in and crowding-out theory, were established before data analysis began. Was the article an example of each of the following four categories or codes? Crowding out—substitution; crowding out—compensation; crowding in—stimulate; and crowding in—complement—yes or no? Then, for each "yes" classification, the researchers highlighted text within the article that described the center's relationship to the aging network to justify that code.

As part of an **inductive approach** (also called bottom-up coding), concepts and ideas that arose while analyzing data in each article (as opposed to those pre-determined categories) were also added to the overall analytical framework. Some examples of emergent, inductive codes from the study used as an example include codes about center members as powerful, portrayal of members as needy, and the importance of center-based social networks. Codes also emerged about the tension between traditional vs. new center models, the need for marketing/outreach, viewing centers as a setting for new consumerism, and attracting potential center members while keeping existing ones.

Grounded theory coding practices. In a grounded-theory approach, several types of coding practices are used to, ultimately, generate a theory. The sequence is often thought of as open/*in vivo* coding → axial coding → selective coding. Coding to ground theory is iterative—meaning the transcripts and data are read and reviewed. **Open codes** arise from the data and are not predetermined by the researcher. While reviewing the data many times, the researcher begins to see patterns, and categories arise in the data. These categories are recorded or noted as open codes. Open codes are often based on ***in vivo* codes** that arise from exact words or phrases uttered by a participant. **Axial codes** take the open codes and *in vivo* codes and suggest relationships (e.g., hierarchies or categories and subcategories) between these codes to create larger elements or ideas. **Selective codes** (also called substantive codes) build axial codes into elements of theory.

Weston Verlaine Donaldson's (2014) dissertation is an example of the grounded theory method to form a framework about long-term-care staff's existing knowledge and need for additional training in working with LGBT residents. The researcher used *in vivo* text from staff to create open codes. The direct quote "Oh yeah well I worked in a hospital back in New York in the early '90s, and with the AIDS when that was just all coming about, and we had quite a few gay patients and I didn't notice that anyone treated them any different" was made into an open code (renamed: "participant's previous experience working with gay patients in AIDS crisis"). This open code became a broader axial code, "past experience caring for LGBT patients." In selective coding, this axial code was grouped in with other axial codes that had similar ideas referring to staff's prior knowledge/work with the LGBT community. The overarching selective code became "experience with LGBT people." Lastly, the researcher used the selective codes (including "experience with LGBT people") to create a visual diagram that depicted a conceptual framework about the staff's existing knowledge and training needs for competency to work with LGBT residents (pp. 20–22).

Emergent, less-traditional, alternative coding practices. In a special issue of *Qualitative Inquiry* devoted to "Qualitative data analysis after coding," the editors brought together authors to describe their alternative coding strategies (St. Pierre & Jackson, 2014). Several of these new coding treatments as options to explore are abduction, coding narrative absent in the data, coding by one's own writing and photographs, acknowledging the limits of codes to capture reality, coding without marginalizing groups, and sensory-based coding.

While deductive and inductive approaches are more common in coding, an abductive approach is another way to code qualitative data. **Abduction** represents the way we solve ordinary, daily life problems, the "qualitative inquiry in everyday life" (Brinkmann, 2014, p. 723). It "presents research as part of the life process, as what we do in situations of breakdown that inevitably arise in life's situations, big or small. There is no talk here of collecting data or framing them theoretically but rather of navigating existential, moral, and political situations as individual and collectives. . . . Abduction is not driven by data or theory but by astonishment, mystery, and breakdowns in one's understanding" (Brinkmann, 2014, p. 722). For example, you are studying social networking among older women in neighborhoods and notice a situation: the women start to avoid a particular once-favored restaurant now under new ownership. You think the cause is that the new management team rush the women out of their establishment, allowing less time for socializing. You abduct using your own intuition, as a point to begin the study. You can address this as a possible theme to explore but continue on with rigorous qualitative practices.

Researchers suggest we look for absences and gaps in the narratives or text we are analyzing (Rosiek & Heffernan, 2014). There is a need to focus on omissions and missing data or items absent from discussion. Codes are then created about these "**silences in the data**." For example, you are interviewing a 75-year-old dating couple and their adult children about moving to a new state, and the children never mention their mother's partner during the interview, though he or she is right there. Their omission becomes a code. A researcher's personal writing and photos can also be alternative coding devices. Instead of using memos and audit trails to mark the data-analysis process, by being embedded and listening to the interview or narratives over and over again, the researcher can write his or her thoughts about the data and use photos after the interviews as a different form of memoing and analysis (Augustine, 2014).

A researcher may have difficulty capturing data and reducing experiences to codes. The use of words to capture, create, order, and explain data and relationships may be limited (Holmes, 2014). Alternatively, researcher may seek to **omit narratives** from coding that marginalize groups further or oppresse groups—because reproducing the text may perpetuate the oppression. Instead, researchers can place blanks or stricken-through text in their place. Or they can actively include resistance narratives in the data analysis, exploring the reasons behind the participants' refusal to participate (Tuck & Yang, 2014).

Lastly, **somatographic analysis** suggests using body-based or arts-based work to record and critically analyze data. Coding "involve[s] mobilizing body-based and arts-informed technique that help researchers follow, trace, ride, or otherwise come into deep relation with the palpating forces of the data themselves. . . . [Traditional coding is replaced with] a relationship with data grounded in its immanent, co-implicative, communal qualities, moving through analysis with the question 'what do these data do?'" (Clark/Keefe, 2014, p. 790). Clark/Keefe describes her process of coding as using two columns. In the first, she records the details of the setting or facts—such as demographic, location, etc. In the second, she draws a visual depiction of what she is seeing and what is occurring.

Narrative Analysis

General Narrative Analysis

Narrative analysis can encompass many designs. This analysis style allows the researcher great flexibility and options. One can perform content or thematic analysis (with coding strategies mentioned above) or use elements of case studies, discourse, or conversations as data for analysis (which will be discussed below). Narrative analysis utilizes parts of the entire narrative or uses a holistic approach to review the text as a whole (Gubrium & Sankar, 1994; Tekle & Vermunt, 2012).

The narrative-analysis approach has several options, such as the holistic or categorical choice and the content- or form-analysis options about how the story is put together (Riessman, 1993; Tuval-Mashiach, Zilber & Lieblich, 1998). The **holistic approach** examines the whole text, while the categorical reviews parts of it. A **content-analysis approach** generates themes from the text, while a **form-based analysis** examines the story's structure and way it is told. One can also look at the story, in its entirety, for the self-assigned role of the storyteller in the story, the story in relation to the larger culture, ways the story may be retold, the storyteller's interpretation of the story and its structure, and unique features of a story (Kenyon & Mader, 1999). For example, researchers looking at accounts of resilience among older persons reviewed interview text for "grammar of resilience," including story tone (optimistic, pessimistic, etc.), autobiographical reasoning (how tellers make meaning of events), and use of master cultural narratives (the story linked to a greater reality or larger societal events).

Analysis topologies have been created to review stories from the point of view of the storyteller and the listener (or "story analysis"). Cassandra Phoenix, Brett Smith, and Andrew Sparkes's (2010) Typology of Narrative Analyses proposes we analyze the "whats" and "hows" from either (or both) the story analyst's or the storyteller's perspective. The analysts may use structural analysis, content analysis, or holistic-based analyses to get at the "what" of the story while using performative analysis, interactive analysis, or rhetorical analysis to answer the "how" or way the story was told to them. Storytellers combine the "what" and "how" of the story by using creative analytical practices (auto-ethnography, biography, ethnodrama, visual narratives, and fiction; see Randall, Baldwin, McKenzie-Mohr, McKim & Furlong, 2015).

The **interactive effect** upon the telling of the narrative is explored in William Randall, Suzanne Prior and Marianne Skarborn's (2006) "How listeners shape what tellers tell." The interviewer's roles (being a "local, friendly minister," "affirming, naïve, cheerleader," or "formal respectful outsider") each elicited different stories from the same teller (pp. 385–386). Auto-ethnographical analysis includes the reflections of the researchers in the process, as their way of interpreting the story (Holt, 2008; Kidd & Finlayson, 2009; Phoenix, Smith & Sparkes, 2010). The researcher's presence and effect upon the narrative process can be described as the **"investigator's imprint"** (Andrews, Squire & Tamboukou, 2013, p. 258).

Case Study Analysis

In *Case study research: Design and methods* (2014), Robert Yin describes his analytical process for case studies with steps: relying on theoretical propositions to form the initial research question, thinking about rival explanations, developing a way to describe the case, describing what the researcher learns, and summarizing the findings of all steps. He offers several analytical strategies. **Pattern-matching** compares what is found in data to the researcher's expectations and explanation-building, or looking for alternative explanations and listing any problems encountered. A researcher can perform a **time-series analysis** for cases, looking for changes over time, or employ **logic models** to examine the relationship of different types of outcomes that are defined and tested. Researchers may explore **cross-case synthesis**, comparing the case of interest to other cases, including those in literature. While this is used in qualitative case analysis, some suggest that Yin's approach may too-closely mirror quantitative analysis (Evers & Van Staa, 2010).

Discourse Analysis and Critical Discourse Analysis

While linked, discourse analysis and critical discourse analysis both focus on the use of language in settings, where "talk constitutes reality" and benefits studies with older people (Wood & Kroger, 1995). Discourse analysis follows earlier ethnomethodological work, by Harold Garfinkel and Alfred Schultz, examining language use as a form of the person's self-expression and how he or she sees and interacts with the social world, including the role of the listener.

Discourse analysis (of many varieties, including Foucauldian) is a process of interpreting conversation and content of language with critical reflection upon the analysis (Hjelm, 2013). Discourse analysis examines a person's expression of ideas through words, voice, intention, activeness or passiveness of language, and use of pronouns. As people talk, they may also be creating their identity of sense of "self" that they use to "recognize themselves" in relationship to others—"struggling with or resisting forms of power or self-understanding" (Yates & Hiles, 2010, pp. 63–64). This analysis can focus on the form, structure, and meaning of the conversation or take a more linguistic approach, focusing on syntax, argument cohesion, changes in the tone of the voice, etc.

The researcher reads the text many times and describes how the speaker uses words and phrases to communicate. These items are noted as quotes to show how an individual uses language choice, expression, and conversational structure to make sense of the world and express his or her knowledge of the world. For example, in a study about how death is treated in skilled-care facilities, researchers found a thread of "fear of death" expressed by staff using direct quotes (for example: "[F]or the first week I found death very tangible. . . . I believe one distances oneself and concentrates on the daily care"). The corresponding code was seen as "dying is silent and silences" and the theme defined as "avoidance of death." (For complete analysis, see Österlind, Hansebo, Andersson, Ternestedt & Hellström, 2011, p. 534, Table 1.)

Linda Wood and Rolf Kroger (1995) suggest that an adapted version of Johnathan Potter and Margaret Wetherell's Stages of Discourse Analysis would work well in aging studies. The **steps in this discourse-analysis** approach are research-question development, sample selection, collection of documents and records, interviewing, transcription, coding (organizing data), analysis of the functions of talk, validation and collective agreement in analysis, and reporting and application of the data (pp. 87–90). They offer several studies as examples of discourse analysis used with older people, such as an older woman speaking more positively about herself with her peers yet speaking more about frailty with a younger person (Coupland, Coupland & Giles, 1991); changing priorities of health and social types of talk among older patients and staff (Coupland, Robinson & Coupland, 1994); the use of personal pronouns (I, me, my, mine) in the speech of persons with Alzheimer's disease (Sabat & Harre, 1992); the use of a first or surname for older persons by medical personnel (Grainger, 1993); a caseworker's language against reminiscence among those in her care (Middleton & Buchanan, 1993); and the use of speech, in the form of humor, to discuss old age in the *Golden Girls* television show (Harwood & Giles, 1992).

Critical discourse analysis examines **power dynamics** and the role of age, race, class, and gender of the speaker and the relationship of the speaker to hegemonic (dominant) societal norms (van Dijk, 1994). Researchers used a form of critical-discourse analysis, called **dispositive analysis**, to analyze middle age as discussed in comedic films' actions, objects, and **linguistic practices** of speech and text. Using the film *Lost in Translation*, the researchers found that the younger female character references the age of her 50-year-old male friend through several aspects of her speech. She describes his actions (having a mid-life crisis, being in a long-term marriage), uses objects to make age-related jokes (a bad wardrobe choice, driving a Porsche, etc.), and uses linguistic practices to denote his "old age" ("You're probably having a midlife crisis," or, referring to another woman, "She is close to your age, you can talk about things you have in common . . . growing up in the 50s"; Gatling, Mills & Lindsay, 2014, Tables 2 & 3).

Quality in Qualitative Research

Trustworthiness as Rigor

In qualitative studies, rigor is called **trustworthiness**. Yvonne Lincoln and Egon Guba have developed four elements (or ways) to ensure trustworthiness. The first is **credibility** or confirmation of findings through the use of multiple data sources, multiple methods, and/or several researchers. As a comparison for those more familiar with only a quantitative approach, credibility can be thought of as similar to internal validity in quantitative models. Second, when addressing **transferability**, the researcher describes in which instances the findings of his or her study are applicable or relatable to other studies. The closest quantitative comparison is external validity. Third, qualitative researchers must address **dependability**, that findings are based only on the data—even if the field setting or study direction change. Dependability is similar to reliability in quantitative models. **Confirmability**, the fourth element of trustworthiness, maintains that researchers include their own self-reflection about their role as data collectors and interpreters, including any potential biases. Adding discrepant cases or counternarratives that challenge the existing findings may be part of this step. Confirmability can be generally related to the concept of objectivity in quantitative analysis.

Researchers' Role as Part of an Analysis Team

Qualitative researchers may work on a data-collection and analysis team. When this is the case, they must provide details about the process the team used to assign codes to analyze data. This process is called **inter-coder reliability** or **inter-coder agreement** (MacPhail, Khoza, Abler & Ranganathan, 2015). To establish inter-coder reliability, two or more coders code independently and then compare the matching or sameness of coding. This approach is better because it employs simpler and more direct coding plans. The percentage of code matching by the team is reported. For example, the same codes were applied to the data by the team of three coders 90% of the time. Differences in coding were discussed, and a consensus was reached about coding those cases.

An **Inter-Coding Reliability (ICR) statistic**, such as Klaus Krippendorff's alpha, can calculate inter-coder reliability while removing the possibility that the matching codes were made by chance (Krippendorff, 2012). Calculating these statistics may be difficult in qualitative coding because a researcher may choose different lengths of text to correspond to a code. Researchers suggest providing the pre-highlighted text blocks selected by one researcher to other researchers, and then having the second researcher or group assign codes. Another option is to have coding matched on deductive (pre-determined) codes only, which may work better than assessing matching on inductive or emergent coding (MacPhail, Khoza, Abler & Ranganathan, 2015). In inter-coder agreement, two or more coders code data, reconciling differences in coding through discussion and agreement. If a different code or value was assigned by a researcher, both researchers discuss the case and resolve the issue through consensus and refined coding strategies moving forward in analysis. Table 4.3 provides real examples of issues that occurred when each qualitative design was used in an applied setting.

Table 4.3 Qualitative Research Methods Live

Research Design	Case	Common Problems	Examples	Insight/Strategies	Solutions
Narrative research	Life stories and reminiscence	Style of interviewer/ guide impacts reminiscence type	While interviewing older persons as part of an introductory gerontology course, undergraduate students often recorded narratives of "active aging," "active retirement," "happy grandparenting" (see Ramsey, Mendoza & Weil, 2014). (Narrative)	Storyline of the older storyteller may reflect perceived ageism revealed on the part of the listener or dominant cultural aged script (De Medeiros, 2014; Lundgren, 2013). The interview can be seen as a confessional mode or life-script mode. Listening types can create the following matched reminiscence types: the local minister persona (integrative reminiscence); the affirming naïve cheerleader type (transmissive reminiscence); and the formal, respectful outsider (narrative reminiscence; Randall, Prior & Skarborn, 2006).	The role of the researcher and recognition of his or her own social position, or self-reflexivity, are key. In work with older adults, researchers need to take into account differences in social position and ignore the possible effect of age differences between themselves and those they interview. There is also a false assumption that older persons are more self-reflexive than their younger counterparts when participating in field research (Biggs, 2005). Further probing and questioning can move a respondent past more general master scripts and beyond expected behaviors or answers.
Grounded theory	General interview script with intergenerational Latino grandfamilies about service and program usage	Intergenerational interviewing conflicts	While meeting with grandparents in their homes with their children and grandchildren present, adult children were often confused by the open interview script and informal questions (see Mendoza, A., *Grandparents raising grandchildren: A look at Latino cultural influences on needs and service usage*, 2012).	Older persons, as grandparents, may not have had legal rights over their grandchildren—and, in the case of this study, may not have had legal status. Grandparents may feel pressure to provide culturally normative scripts about being a "good grandparent" or to avoid offending children and losing contact with the grandchildren they are raising.	Literature suggests—along with benefits—grandparents may feel stigma/stress due to their new parental roles. This uncertainty may be coupled with dynamics of family members present during part of the interview. In some regions, legal status and custody issues influence answers and power dynamics as well as age/other social characteristics of the interviewee. Separate interviews, varied interviewers, and Certificates of Confidentiality from the National Institutes of Health can provide more opportunities for open discussion.

Ethnography	Ethnographic work at a senior center	Marginalized or blurred researcher's role	The social position of the interviewer affects responses given by those interviewed (e.g., older women believed the ethnographer was a reporter for a local newspaper—moving the tone toward the politics of keeping their center open in difficult financial times). Roles between center-goers and researcher blurred with attendees "teaching [the researcher] something about being old." Other times, center-goers would ask, "Is this what you wanted to know?" or state, "I'm taking too much of" or "wasting" "too much of your time."	Van den Hoonaard (2005) suggests that sometimes the researcher may be perceived as a "hybrid, half researcher, half guest and acquaintance" (p. 402). Older female interviewees feel there is a definite right answer the researcher seeks, or are less talkative due to the perceived marginalization of their roles. Researchers may not take into account social position differences and lessen, or ignore, the possible effect differences between themselves and those they study. Individual characteristics such as age, race, ethnicity, gender, social class, and perceived health status will affect the way researchers are received by the sample of older persons studied.	Periodic checks to see how the group sees your role to address any misperceptions. Biggs (2005) suggests that often the interviewer is guilty of "forgetting to look behind the mask" (p. 124), not examining his or her own motivation behind the work, and failing to account for social-position differences and incompatibilities between interviewer and interviewee. Researchers should guard against projecting their own field's view upon those they study. Including peer/older research team members to collect data might be warranted. Bindels, Baur, Cox, Heijing, and Abma (2014) found older co-researchers added insight into interviews with frail older persons ("bridging the gap" between the academic and older interviewee). The older co-researcher lends experiential knowledge and stories, but the relationship of the two researchers takes time to develop and must be fit to the study at hand.
		Expectations of those interviewed: a social desirability effect	Participants might be motivated to offer overly positive self-presentation.	Knowing the study is about social activities, participants could focus on the positive role of the center in their lives—e.g., "It's like a drug" or "We're unhappy when we can't get here."	Counternarrative (of differing opinions/characteristics) can address older participants' desire to please the interviewer. After interviewing the first wave of active volunteers, the sample was varied to include less-frequent attendees and those never attending the center. Each group provided different viewpoints.

Adapted from: Weil, J. (2015). Applying research methods to a gerontological population: Matching data collection to characteristics of older persons. *Educational Gerontology, 41*(10), 723–742.

Computer-Assisted/Aided Qualitative Data Analysis Software (CAQDAS)

While software may assist in the data-analysis process, it should never drive analysis. There are several software packages and advantages and disadvantages of their use. The advantages include managing large amounts of textual, audio, and visual data; assistance with organizing codes and categories; and ways to graphically/visually represent the data. Limitations include being more removed from the data, the software learning curve, and the risk of overreliance on technical (and not methodological) design. The goal of software in analysis is never to be used to sanitize or quantify qualitative work (Rowles & Schoenberg, 2002). See Chapter 9 for a discussion of software options such as ATLAS.ti and NVivo. See the blog post https://atlastiblog.wordpress.com/2014/09/26/using-atlas-ti-for-coding-ethnographic-and-policy-data/#comments, for an example of ATLAS.ti software use.

Combining with Other Methods

Qualitative research is often combined with quantitative work in a mixed-methods approach. The mixed-methods designs have **nomenclature** with the prioritized method in all capital letters and the lesser prioritized methods in lowercase letters. A plus sign is used for convergent methods, and arrows are used for sequential methods. For example, a mostly qualitative study—with some quantitative aspects—in which the qualitative work leads to the quantitative would be noted: QUAL → quant. Chapter 7 provides a full discussion of mixed-methods design.

Challenges and Ethical Issues

Some general issues related to the qualitative method might be witnessing illegal/illicit/dangerous events in a field setting; the researcher losing his or her perspective/stance as a researcher (negatively labeled in the past as **"going native"**); and the researcher missing the real experience (where participants tell the researcher what they believe he or she wants to hear). Some believe that qualitative studies raise additional IRB issues—in part, due to their iterative nature and more flexible interview schedules than, say, a structured survey. Additionally, the fluid nature and adaptability to conditions encountered in the field setting can raise concerns.

Qualitative gerontological work can have its own ethical issues, including vulnerability due to emotional status or physical condition. In interviewing older persons about the impact of social isolation, Cherry Russell found she also encountered the "social intrusion into lonely lives" (1999, p. 404). She reported concerns about how much post-study or non-study contact she should have because, at times, participants did not want to end the interview. They may have been grieving a recent loss or just lonely and welcomed the companionship. Other researchers investigating whether or not studies with dying people require additional ethical safeguards found that these studies did not, but dying people do bring unique issues to research. Near-death participants may have different motivations for study participation, varying capability to consent to participation, differing views of their roles and rights in the study (having "nothing to lose" or participate as a benefit or duty), and different end-of-life practices based on their ethical/cultural groups (Phipps, 2002, p. 108).

The Assisting family Carers, through the use of Telematics Interventions to meet Older Persons' Needs (ACTION) study, examined the use of videophones for caregivers and frail older people in their homes in five countries. The researchers found being mindful and addressing particular concerns (e.g., the use of the camera when the study was not going on and the way the study would impact healthcare access) allowed them to maintain the ethical standards outlined in their study (Magnusson & Hanson, 2003).

For those with impaired cognitive status (such as dementia), qualitative researchers have found some ethical concerns about the person with dementia being silent, answering in shorter phrases or the affirmative, or echoing the answers of caregivers (Sugarman, Roter, Cain, Wallace, Schmechel & Welsh-Bohmer, 2007). Researchers suggest a "revisionist person-centered inclusionary consent" process—meaning that the consent process be an ongoing process rather than a one-time event (Dewing, 2002, p. 157). Researchers also warn that gatekeepers can exclude participation when the person with dementia may wish to consent (Hellström, Nolan, Nordenfelt & Lundh, 2007). Residents living in care settings may also be subject to gatekeepers making their own decisions about consent and possible inclusion in a study for their residents without including the resident in the process.

Older persons, particularly older women, may exhibit marginalized or blurred roles in a study. For example, as reported in my own ethnographic work at a senior center, some women saw my role in different forms at different times. Some wondered if they were "teaching [me] something about being old" or asked me, "Is this what you wanted to know?" or stated, "I'm taking too much of" or "wasting" "too much of your time" (Weil, 2015). This changing role of the researcher as a "hybrid, half researcher, half guest and acquaintance" may happen in the field (Van den Hoonaard, 2005, p. 402). Older women (and older men, as well) may also express social desirability in their answers by telling the researcher what they believe he or she wants to hear or being more silent due to the marginalization of the older woman's role in society. These can be "remedied" by the researcher's awareness and not "forgetting to look behind the mask" (Biggs, 2005, p. 124). Researchers can be self-reflexive about their own role, motivations, and differences between themselves and those they study. Adding older persons as equal co-researchers can help bridge the gap between the researcher and older-person roles (Bindels, Baur, Cox, Heijing & Abma, 2014). For example, in a grounded-theory approach with several generations of Latino grandparents raising grandchildren's families and speaking about their service and program needs, there were ethical issues of interviewing grandparents with their adult children and grandchildren, perhaps initially giving "appropriate" answers (Mendoza, 2012). Also, legal status may hamper participation in qualitative studies, since a multitude of data are collected from many people in a family. **Certificates of Confidentiality** from the National Institutes of Health (NIH, 2016) can be a safeguard. Certificates of Confidentiality (CoC) are another option if the researcher is working with a "sensitive health-related topic that collects names or other identifying characteristics of subjects, and that has been approved by an IRB"; they "allow researchers to refuse to disclose names or other identifying characteristics of research subjects in response to legal demands" (NIH, Certificates of Confidentiality, CoC Kiosk, para 1). Separating interviewees can also provide more opportunities for open discussion and be an effective strategy.

The researchers, themselves, can also face ethical issues when leaving the field and analyzing data. In *The Craft of life course research*, Glen Elder, Jr. and Janet Giele warn about the secondary traumatic effects of the ethnographic process on the researcher and team. For example, if a researcher or team witnesses abuse or loss or hears about it in the field, the impact may also be felt throughout the data-analysis process—not only at the time of the initial experience. Professional organizations each have general codes of ethics; for a full discussion of ethics for all research approaches, see Chapter 10.

Reporting and Evaluating Qualitative Work

To close this chapter, several strategies aid in the process of writing up your findings, whether you are evaluating qualitative methods, writing up a qualitative proposal or report, or preparing a formal academic manuscript. These include the following:

- Provide a detailed description of your process: from research question to sample selection and data collection.
- Be explicit about your coding or other data analysis process.
- Include your own self-reflection about your role in the work.
- Adhere to trustworthiness and transparent reporting to show rigor.
- Do not feel that you have to make the report of your findings fit cookie-cutter or narrow reporting approaches.
- Use the deep, thick, rich text descriptions that are an essential feature of the work.
- Report ethical and gerontology-specific issues you encounter and how you addressed them.

Providing a Detailed Description of Your Process: From Research Question to Sample Selection and Data Collection

Gerontological literature, overwhelmingly, calls for more methodological explanation in all aspects of qualitative work. When writing up your own work or evaluating that of others, explain how you arrived at your research question and how that question was matched to a philosophical/epistemological perspective or worldview (objectivist, constructionist, subjectivist, transformative or pragmatic, or a mixture). Explain how these choices related to your research approach (quantitative, qualitative, mixed methods) and research design (specific types of quantitative, qualitative, mixed methods; Schoenberg, Shenk & Kart, 2007; Weil, 2015). While you should be descriptive in the body of your writing, some editors suggest you do not need to explicitly use language that states "this is a qualitative study" in the title (Schoenberg, Shenk & Kart, 2007). Others suggest that since sampling may differ from what some quantitative researchers are used to reading, you need to take some time to explain how you gained access to the field and gained rapport with participants, and how your data were collected—interviewing, observation, participant writing, etc. (Warren-Findlow, 2013). These "smaller" or "specialized subsamples" of unique populations or data are of increasing interest in gerontological journals (Carr, 2015, p. 267). Journals and other publications are becoming more receptive to including poetry and visual images as part of data analysis and accepting of expanding word counts (Kivnick & Pruchno, 2011).

Be Explicit about Your Coding or Other Data-Analysis Processes

The reader wants to know how you developed codes (deductive, inductive coding, etc.) and who did the coding. Often, in reports of qualitative work, there is not enough information about how the researcher or team developed a coding process and coded throughout the study. What was each person's role, and how was conflict in coding addressed? (Warren-Findlow, 2013). The write-up of analysis needs to be more than one sentence, such as "thematic content analysis was used to code data." A full description of the technique used is warranted as some might be less familiar with qualitative analytical designs (Schoenberg, Shenk & Kart, 2007; Weil, 2015).

Include Your Own Self-Reflection about Your Role in the Work

Just as you have to explain your coding process as a researcher, you also have to explain your role in the study, since, in qualitative research, the researcher is the instrument or data-collection and analysis tool, as well. Granted, this is easier to do in a book, thesis, or dissertation than in research-article format. But it is essential to offer the reader the views and experiences of the researcher in the study. You may have to decide the level, or amount, of information you want to share, but beginning with an explanation of how and why you selected the topic along with your relationship to the field setting can be a good starting point.

As far as reflexivity, some suggest keeping research diaries, taking frequent/daily personal notes, creating visual representations, and talking about your role with others (peers and participants) on and off your project as being helpful in understanding and relaying your role (see Probst & Berenson, 2014).

Adhere to Trustworthiness and Transparent Reporting to Show Rigor

Several options can be employed to describe the way you achieved rigor. Of course, address the four elements of Yvonne Lincoln and Egon Guba's (1985) concept of trustworthiness (credibility, transferability, dependability, and confirmability). And do not feel that you have to address quantitative terminology for reliability and validity in your own qualitative research (Warren-Findlow, 2013). Also, consider older persons as co-researchers, and member-checkers, of your process and findings (Bindels, Baur, Cox, Heijing & Abma, 2014; Tanner, 2012).

Do Not Feel You Have to Make the Report of Your Findings Fit Cookie-Cutter or Narrow Reporting Approaches

Ground your writing in theory, and show the place of your work in the existing body of literature. State the implications of your findings without under- or over-statement of them (Schoenberg, Shenk & Kart, 2007). See Table 1 in Schoenberg and McAuley's (2007) "Promoting qualitative research": "A guide for use by authors and reviewers to thoroughly and appropriately evaluate qualitative research articles." This table provides specific directions about writing up all sections of your work—overall presentation, title, background, research questions or purpose, methods, design and procedure, finding/results, and discussion (Schoenberg & McAuley, 2007; Schoenberg, Miller & Pruchno, 2011).

Use the Deep, Thick, Rich Text Descriptions that Are an Essential Feature of the Work

While space and page length may be issues, blocks of direct quotation of participants are the hallmark of good qualitative writing. Providing these rich, thick descriptions allows readers to review the participants' own words along with the interpretation of the researcher. Participants' own voices and a detailed description of the research setting are key in qualitative reporting to reach the exploratory and explanatory goal of the work (Warren-Findlow, 2013). Keep in mind confidentiality concerns about items that may reveal the identity or status of your participants, and use pseudonyms. For example, I ask my participants to select their own pseudonyms and am careful to make sure that the names they choose are not too closely related, or similar sounding, to their own real names.

Report Ethical and Gerontology-Specific Issues You Encounter and How You Addressed Them

Rather than see ethical issues as a failing or sheer difficulties, reframe them as experiences the researcher has because of the length of time in the field setting and level of acceptance found with participants. Understanding the experience of aging and new issues to address in research (e.g., entering and leaving the field, personal and professional boundaries in research, issues of frailty and changing cognitive status) as well as witnessing abuse or fraud or caregiver stress can provide vehicles for participatory designs and participant safeguards. Lessons learned in the field can enrich and improve future research designs that maintain the quality of life and dignity of participants.

This chapter introduced the wide range of qualitative designs used in gerontology under five major categories (narrative analysis, ethnography, grounded theory, case studies, and phenomenological accounts). It described the structure and techniques needed to conduct studies using each of the designs and how to report findings by design to an academic audience. Unique data collection and analysis issues, ways to select a design type, and a comparison of all design types were provided. The chapter presented both past examples of qualitative method used in the gerontological literature and contemporary examples of issues that arise when using each design type in an applied setting. The discussion of ethical issues that can arise in qualitative research and use of analysis software and mixing qualitative methods with other types was begun. The next chapter provides the same overview of the next method, using quantitative research designs.

Discussion Questions

- Some common elements of qualitative research designs include rich, thick data; access to the field; sampling methods; saturation; coding; trustworthiness; decision to use software; and the role of the interviewer. Define each of these terms and any benefits or barriers associated with each term.
- When would a gerontological researcher choose to use grounded theory? How does it differ from the other designs—narrative analysis, ethnography, grounded theory, case studies, and phenomenological accounts?
- You are a journal reviewer asked to review a qualitative report. What specific elements would you look for to assure the study's rigor?
- As a qualitative researcher, you will undoubtedly be asked about your sample size—especially in case studies and phenomenological work. How will you explain your sample size to others who might be more familiar with the larger sample sized used in quantitative research? How will you address their concerns about "generalizability"?
- The chapter discussed how characteristics of the listener shape what he or she is told. How does the style of the interviewer impact the information that an interviewee provides? What is the power in storytelling for the person telling it?
- Imagine you are the interviewer and are told the following narrative. What is the message that the teller wanted you to hear and learn about from his story? What is a master narrative? What is the master narrative of this interview?

Jack, 76, divorced after 40 years from "Madame X," is a self-described "ex-transit worker" "with a good income and pension." He states: "I am busy; I am always on my feet. I ran track in high school; I dance with the ladies here—they love it—they need someone to dance with. . . . I was a martial artist and taught discipline. I like to give back because people have it worse off than me. I help cook in the kitchen. The girls that get assistance are not here today, but they need help and I help them. I am always on the go."

- You have decided to do some ethnographic work about the topic of intergenerational service learning on your campus or at your organization. No work has been done at your campus or institution before, and you feel embedded in the community. Choose one of the ethnographic options (critical ethnography, autoethnography, digital ethnography, participatory ethnography, and performance ethnography), and frame a study around a general research question about this topic.
- Qualitative researchers may encounter ethical issues during their studies (such as mixing roles in the field, learning about and recording illegal and/or illicit behaviors, witnessing changes in participants' cognitive status, experiencing secondary trauma, working with marginalized groups, etc.). Choose a couple of these ethical issues, and state your own plan for addressing them. Discuss some potential ethical safeguards mentioned in this chapter.

Bibliography

Abdulrahim, S., Ajrouch, K., Jammal, A., & Antonucci, T. (2012). Survey methods and aging research in an Arab sociocultural context: A case study from Beirut, Lebanon. *Journals of Gerontology: Social Sciences, 67*(6), 775–782.

Allen, R. E., & Wiles, J. L. (2014). Receiving support when older: What makes it ok? *The Gerontologist, 54*, 670–682.

Andrews, M., Squire, C., & Tamboukou, M. (2013). *Doing narrative research* (2nd ed.). Los Angeles, CA: Sage Publications.

Anthony, S., & Jack, S. (2009). Qualitative case study methodology in nursing research: An integrative review. *Journal of Advanced Nursing, 65*(6), 1171–1181.

Augustine, S. M. (2014). Living in a post-coding world: Analysis as assemblage. *Qualitative Inquiry, 20*(6), 747–753.

Babbie, E. (2013). *The basics of social research.* New York: Cengage Learning.

Baker, S. E., Edwards, R., & Doidge, M. (2012). *How many qualitative interviews is enough? Expert voices and early career reflections on sampling and cases in qualitative research.* National Center for Research Methods. Retrieved from http://eprints.ncrm.ac.uk/2273

Biggs, S. (2005). Beyond appearance: Perspectives on identity in later life and some implications for method. *Journal of Gerontology: Social Sciences, 60B*, S118–128.

Bindels, J., Baur, V., Cox, K., Heijing, S., & Abma, T. (2014). Older people as co-researchers: A collaborative journey. *Ageing and Society, 34*(6), 951–973.

Birren, J. E., & Cochran, K. (2001). *Telling the stories of life through guided autobiography groups.* Baltimore, MD: Johns Hopkins Press.

Black, H. K., & Rubinstein, R. L. (2005). Direct care workers' response to dying and death in the nursing home: A case study. *The Journals of Gerontology Series B: Psychological Sciences and Social Sciences, 60*(1), S3–S10.

Bowers, B., Fibich, B., & Jacobson, N. (2001). Care-as-service, care-as-relating, care-as-comfort: Understanding nursing home residents' definitions of quality. *Gerontologist, 41*(4), 539–545.

Bowker, L. H. (1982). *Humanizing institutions for the aged.* Lexington, MA: Lexington Books.

Braun, K. L., Browne, C. V., Ka'opua, L. S., Kim, B. J., & Mokuau, N. (2014). Research on indigenous elders: From positivistic to decolonizing methodologies. *The Gerontologist, 54*(1), 117–126.

Brinkmann, S. (2014). Doing without data. *Qualitative Inquiry, 20*(6), 720–725.

Brown, P. A. (2008). A review of the literature on case study research. *CJNSE/RCJCÉ, 1*(1), 1–13.

Butler, R. N. (1963). The life review: An interpretation of reminiscence in the aged. *Psychiatry, 26*, 65–75.

Campbell, J. L., Quincy, C., Osserman, J., & Pedersen, O. K. (2013). Coding in-depth semistructured interviews: Problems of unitization and intercoder reliability and agreement. *Sociological Methods & Research, 42*(3), 294–320. doi:10.1177/0049124113500475

Carr, D. (2015). Editorial. *The Journals of Gerontology, Series B: Psychological Sciences and Social Sciences, 70*(2), 179.

Charmaz, K. (2006). *Constructing grounded theory: A practical guide through qualitative analysis.* London and Thousand Oaks, CA: Sage Publications.

Cheung, C. K., & Kam, P. K. (2012). Resiliency in older Hong Kong Chinese: Using the grounded theory approach to reveal social and spiritual conditions. *Journal of Aging Studies, 26*(3), 355–367.

Clark, P. G. (2002). Values and voices in teaching gerontology and geriatrics case studies as stories. *The Gerontologist, 42*(3), 297–303.

Clark/Keefe, K. (2014). Suspended animation attuning to material-discursive data and attending via poesis during somatographic inquiry. *Qualitative Inquiry, 20*(6), 790–800.

Clark-McGhee, K., & Castro, M. (2015). A narrative analysis of poetry written from the words of people given a diagnosis of dementia. *Dementia, 14*(1), 9–26.

Corcoran, M. A. (2011). Caregiving styles: A cognitive and behavioral typology associated with dementia family caregiving. *The Gerontologist, 51*(4), 463–472.

Counts, D., & Counts, D. (1996). *Over the next hill: An ethnography of RVing seniors in North America.* Peterborough, Ontario: Broadview Press.

Coupland, J., Robinson, J. D., & Coupland, N. (1994). Frame negotiation in doctor-elderly patient consultations. *Discourse & Society, 5*(1), 89–124.

Coupland, N., Coupland, J., & Giles, H. (1991). *Language, society and the elderly: Discourse, identity and ageing.* Oxford, UK: Blackwell.

Creswell, J. W. (2013). *Qualitative inquiry and research design: Choosing among five approaches.* Thousand Oaks, CA: Sage Publications.

de Medeiros, K. (2014). *Narrative gerontology in research and practice.* New York: Springer.

de Medeiros, K., & Rubinstein, R. L. (2015). "Shadow stories" in oral interviews: Narrative care through careful listening. *Journal of Aging Studies, 34*, 162–168. doi:10.1016/j.jaging.2015.02.009

Denzin, N. K. (1996). *Interpretive ethnography: Ethnographic practices for the 21st century.* Thousand Oaks, CA: Sage Publications.

Denzin, N. K. (2003). *Performance ethnography: Critical pedagogy and the politics of culture.* Thousand Oaks, CA: Sage Publications.

Denzin, N. K., & Lincoln, Y. S. (2005). *The Sage handbook of qualitative research.* New York: Sage Publications.

Dewing, J. (2002). From ritual to relationship: A person-centered approach to consent in qualitative research with older people who have dementia. *Dementia, 1*(2), 157–171.

Donaldson, W. (2014). *Exploring staff clinical knowledge and practice with LGBT residents in long-term care: A grounded theory of cultural competency and training needs.* Dissertation, Department of Psychology, Colorado State University, Fort Collins, Colorado.

Davisson, D. (2015). Times Change & Tapestry, poems [personal correspondence].

Drummond, J. D., Brotman, S., Silverman, M., Sussman, T., Orzeck, P., Barylak, L., & Wallach, I. (2013). The impact of caregiving: Older women's experiences of sexuality and intimacy. *Affilia, Journal of Women and Social Work, 28*(4), 415–428.

Eckert, J. K. (1980). *The unseen elderly: A study of marginally subsistent hotel dwellers.* San Diego, CA: Campanile Press/San Diego State University.

Eckert, J. K. (1988). "Ethnographic research on aging." In S. Reinhartz, & G. D. Rowles (Eds.), *Qualitative gerontology* (pp. 241–255). New York: Springer.

Eckert, J. K. (2009). *Inside assisted living: The search for home.* Baltimore, MD: Johns Hopkins University Press.

Elder, Jr., G. H., & Giele, J. Z. (2009). *The craft of life course research.* New York: Guilford Press.

Ellis, C. (1999). Heartful autoethnography. *Qualitative Health Research, 9*(5), 669–683.

Evers, J. C., & Van Staa, A. (2010). "Qualitative analysis in case study." In A. J. Mills, G. Durepos, & E. Wiebe (Eds.), *Encyclopedia of case study research* (Vol. 2). Thousand Oaks, CA: Sage Publications.

Flatt, M. A., Settersten, R. A., Ponsaran, R., & Fishman, J. R. (2013). Are "anti-aging medicine" and "successful aging" two sides of the same coin? Views of anti-aging practitioners. *The Journals of Gerontology Series B: Psychological Sciences and Social Sciences, 68*(6), 944–955.

Furman, F. (1997). *Facing the mirror: Older women and beauty shop culture.* New York: Routledge.

Garfinkel, H. (1967). *Studies in ethnomethodology.* Englewood Cliffs, NJ: Prentice-Hall.

Gatling, M., Mills, J., & Lindsay, D. (2014). Representations of middle age in comedy film: A critical discourse analysis. *The Qualitative Report, 19*(23), 1–15. Retrieved from http://www.nova.edu/ssss/QR/QR19/gatling23.pdf

Geertz, C. (1973). *The Interpretation of cultures*. New York: Basic Books.
George, L. K. (2013). Matching corporate interests with older adults' needs: A case study. *Public Policy and Aging Report, 23*(1), 23–26.
Glaser, B. G., & Strauss, A. L. (1965). Discovery of substantive theory: A basic strategy underlying qualitative research. *American Behavioral Scientist, 8*(6), 5–12.
Glaser, B. G., & Strauss, A. L. (1966). *Awareness of dying*. Piscataway, NJ: Transaction Publishers.
Glaser, B. G., & Strauss, A. L. (1967). *The discovery of grounded theory: Strategies for qualitative research*. Chicago, IL: Aldine.
González, A., Ramírez, M. P., & Viadel, V. (2012). Attitudes of the elderly toward information and communications technologies. *Educational Gerontology, 38*(9), 585–594.
Grainger, K. (1993). "That's a lovely bath dear": Reality construction in the discourse of elderly care. *Journal of Aging Studies, 7*(3), 247–262.
Greenfield, E. A. (2013). The longevity of community aging initiatives: A framework for describing NORC programs' sustainability goals and strategies. *Journal of Housing for the Elderly, 27*(1–2), 120–145.
Gubrium, J. (1975). *Living and dying at Murray Manor*. New York: St. Martin's Press.
Gubrium, J. (1986). *Oldtimers and Alzheimer's: The descriptive organization of senility*. Greenwich, CT: JAI Press.
Gubrium, J. (1991). *The Mosaic of care: Frail elderly and their families in the real world*. New York: Springer.
Gubrium, J. F., & Buckholdt, D. (1982). *Describing care: Image and practice in rehabilitation*. Cambridge, MA: Oelgeschlager, Gunn & Hain.
Gubrium, J. F., Holstein, J., Marvasti, A., & McKinney, K. (2012). *The Sage handbook of interview research: The complexity of the craft*. Thousand Oaks, CA: Sage Publications.
Gubrium, J. F., Puddephatt, A., Shaffir, W., & Kleinknecht, S. (2009). "How Murray Manor became an ethnography." In A. Puddephatt, W. Shaffir & S. Kleinknecht (Eds.), *Ethnographies revisited: Constructing theory in the field* (pp. 121–134). New York: Routledge.
Gubrium, J. F., & Sankar, A. (1990). *The home care experience: Ethnography and policy*. Newbury Park, CA: Sage Publications.
Gubrium, J. F., & Sankar, A. (1994). *Qualitative methods in aging research*. Thousand Oaks, CA: Sage Publications.
Haahr, A., Kirkevold, M., Hall, E. O., & Østergaard, K. (2013). "Being in it together": Living with a partner receiving deep brain stimulation for advanced Parkinson's disease–A hermeneutic phenomenological study. *Journal of Advanced Nursing, 69*(2), 338–347.
Harwood, J., & Giles, H. (1992). "Don't make me laugh": Age representations in a humorous context. *Discourse & Society, 3*(4), 403–436.
Hellström, I., Nolan, M., Nordenfelt, L., & Lundh, U. (2007). Ethical and methodological issues in interviewing persons with dementia. *Nursing Ethics, 14*(5), 608–619.
Hjelm, T. (2013). Empowering discourse: Discourse analysis as method and practice in the sociology classroom. *Teaching in Higher Education, 18*(8), 871–882.
Hochschild, A. R. (1978). *The unexpected community: Portrait of an old age subculture*. Berkeley, CA: University of California Press.
Holmes, R. (2014). Fresh kills: The spectacle of (de) composing data. *Qualitative Inquiry, 20*(6), 781–789.
Holstein, J. A., & Gubrium, J. F. (1995). *The Active Interview*. Thousand Oaks: Sage.
Holt, N. L. (2008). Representation, legitimation, and autoethnography: An autoethnographic writing story. *International Journal of Qualitative Methods, 2*(1), 18–28.
Humble, A. (2014). *Qualitative research trends in gerontology: An 18-year analysis of 7 journals (1995–2012)*. Gerontology Society of America Annual Scientific Meeting, November 6th, 2014, Washington, DC.
Jacobs, J. (1974). *Fun city: An ethnographic study of a retirement community*. New York: Holt, Rinehart and Winston.
Kemp, C. L., Ball, M. M., Hollingsworth, C., & Perkins, M. (2012). Strangers and friends: Residents' social careers in assisted living. *Journals of Gerontology Series B: Psychological Sciences And Social Sciences, 67*(4), 491–502.
Kemp, C. L., Ball, M. M., & Perkins, M. M. (2016). Couples' social careers in assisted living: Reconciling individual and shared situations. *The Gerontologist, 56*(5), 841–854. doi:10.1093/geront/gnv025
Kenyon, G., Ruth, J.-E., & Mader, W. (1999). "Elements of a narrative gerontology." In V. L. Bengston, & K. W. Schaie (Eds.), *Handbook of theories of aging* (pp. 40–58). New York: Springer.
Kidd, J., & Finlayson, M. (2009). When needs must: Interpreting autoethnographical stories. *Qualitative Inquiry, 15*(6), 980–998.
Kivnick, H. Q., & Pruchno, R. (2011). Bridges and boundaries: Humanities and arts enhance gerontology. *The Gerontologist, 51*(2), 142–144.
Klinenberg, E. (2002). *Heat wave: A social autopsy of disaster in Chicago*. Chicago, IL: University of Chicago Press.
Kontos, P. (2010). "Embodied selfhood: Ethnographic reflections, performing ethnography, and humanizing dementia care." In Graham, J. E., & Stephenson, P. H. (Eds.) *Contesting aging & loss*. Toronto, Canada: University of Toronto Press.

Krippendorff, K. (2012). *Content analysis: An introduction to its methodology*. New York: Sage Publications.
Kuypers, J. A. (1973). Social breakdown and competence. *Human Development, 16*(3), 181–201.
Lincoln, Y., & Guba, E. (1985). *Naturalistic inquiry*. Newbury Park, CA: Sage Publications.
Lindauer, A., Harvath, T. A., Berry, P. H., & Wros, P. (2016). The meanings African American caregivers ascribe to dementia-related changes: The paradox of hanging on to loss. *The Gerontologist, 56*(4), 733–742. doi:10.1093/geront/gnv023
Loe, M. (2011). *Aging our way: Lessons for living from 85 and beyond*. New York: Oxford University Press.
Lundgren, A. (2013). Doing age: Methodological reflections on interviewing. *Qualitative Research, 13*(6), 668–684. doi:10.1177/1468794112459670
MacPhail, C., Khoza, N., Abler, L., & Ranganathan, M. (2016). Process guidelines for establishing Intercoder Reliability in qualitative studies. *Qualitative Research, 16*(2), 198–212. doi:10.1177/1468794115577012
Magnusson, L., & Hanson, E. J. (2003). Ethical issues arising from a research, technology and development project to support frail older people and their family carers at home. *Health & Social Care in the Community, 11*(5), 431–439.
Marshall, C., & Rossman, G. B. (2011). *Designing qualitative research* (5th ed.). Los Angeles, CA: Sage Publications.
Marshall, L. (2014). Thinking differently about aging: Changing attitudes through the humanities. *The Gerontologist*, (2014), 1–7. doi:10.1093/geront/gnu069
McMillan, L., Booth, J., Currie, K., & Howe, T. (2012). A grounded theory of taking control after fall-induced hip fracture. *Disability and Rehabilitation, 34*(26), 2234–2241.
Mendoza, A. (2012). *Grandparents raising grandchildren: A look at Latino cultural influences on needs and service usage*. Thesis.
Merriam, S. B. (2009). *Qualitative research: A guide to design and implementation* (2nd ed.). San Francisco, CA: Jossey-Bass.
Middleton, D., & Buchanan, K. (1993). Is reminiscence working?: Accounting for the therapeutic benefits of reminiscence work with older people. *Journal of Aging Studies, 7*(3), 321–333.
Milligan, C. (2009). *There's no place like home: Place and care in an ageing society*. Ashgate, UK: Farnham.
Minney, M. J., Hons, B. A., & Ranzijn, R. (2015). "We had a beautiful home . . . but I think I'm happier here": A good or better life in residential aged care. *The Gerontologist, 55*(4), 519–525. doi:10.1093/geront/gnu069
Morse, J. M. (2000). Determining sample size. *Qualitative Health Research, 10*(1), 3–5.
Mundle, R. (2015). A narrative analysis of spiritual distress in geriatric physical rehabilitation. *Journal of Health Psychology, 20*(3), 273–285. doi:10.1177/1359105314566609
Myerhoff, B. (1979). *Number our days*. New York: Dutton.
National Institutes of Health (NIH). (2015). *Certificates of confidentiality contacts at NIH and other DHHS agencies that issue certificates*. Retrieved from http://grants.nih.gov/grants/policy/coc/contacts.htm
National Institutes of Health (NIH). (2016). *Certificates of Confidentiality (CoC) kiosk*. Retrieved from https://humansubjects.nih.gov/coc/index
O'Donnell, L., Carson, L., Forciea, M. A., Kinosian, B., Shea, J., Yudin, J., & Miller, R. K. (2013). What students experienced: A narrative analysis of essays written by first-year medical students participating in a geriatrics home visit. *Journal of the American Geriatrics Society, 61*(9), 1592–1597.
Onwuegbuzie, A. J., & Leech, N. L. (2007). A call for qualitative power analyses. *Quality & Quantity, 41*(1), 105–121.
O'Reilly, M., & Parker, N. (2012). "Unsatisfactory saturation": A critical exploration of the notion of saturated sample sizes in qualitative research. *Qualitative Research, 13*(2), 190–197. doi:10.1177/1468794112446106
Österlind, J., Hansebo, G., Andersson, J., Ternestedt, B., & Hellström, I., (2011). A discourse of silence: Professional carers reasoning about death and dying in nursing homes. *Ageing & Society, 31*(4), 529.
Perkinson, M. A., & Solimeo, S. L. (2013). Aging in cultural context and as narrative process: Conceptual foundations of the anthropology of aging as reflected in the works of Margaret Clark and Sharon Kaufman. *The Gerontologist, 54*(1), 101–107. doi:10.1093/geront/gnt128
Phipps, E. J. (2002). What's end of life got to do with it? Research ethics with populations at life's end. *The Gerontologist, 42*(3), 104–108.
Phoenix, C., & Smith, B. (2011). Telling a (good?) counterstory of aging: Natural bodybuilding meets the narrative of decline. *The Journals of Gerontology Series B: Psychological Sciences and Social Sciences, 66*(5), 628–639. doi:10.1093/geronb/gbr077
Phoenix, C., Smith, B., & Sparkes, A. C. (2010). Narrative analysis in aging studies: A typology for consideration. *Journal of Aging Studies, 24*(1), 1–11.
Pol, M., van Nes, F., van Hartingsveldt, M., Buurman, B., de Rooij, S., & Kröse, B. (2016). Older people's perspectives regarding the use of sensor monitoring in their home. *The Gerontologist, 56*(3), 485–493. doi:10.1093/geront/gnu104
Pope, N. D., Kolomer, S., & Glass, A. P. (2012). How women in late midlife become caregivers for their aging parents. *Journal of Women & Aging, 24*(3), 242–261.

Potter, J., & Wetherell, M. (1987). *Discourse and social psychology: Beyond attitudes and behaviour*. London, UK: Sage Publications.
Powell, J. L. (2014). "You'll never walk alone": Phenomenology and ageing in contemporary culture. *International Letters of Social and Humanistic Sciences, 16*, 19–30.
Probst, B., & Berenson, L. (2014). The double arrow: How qualitative social work researchers use reflexivity. *Qualitative Social Work, 13*(6), 813–827.
Pruchno, R., Bowers, B. J., Kivnick, H., Schoenberg, N., Van Haitsma, K., Whittington, F. J., & Williamson, J. B. (2014). Editorial: Science or fishing? *Gerontologist, 54*(2), 145–146.
Ramsey, A., Mendoza, A. N., & Weil, J. (2014). Using experiential and collaborative methods with undergraduates and older persons as part of an introduction to gerontology course. *PRISM: A Journal of Regional Engagement, 3*(1), 1–21.
Randall, W. L. (2013). The importance of being ironic: Narrative openness and personal resilience in later life. *The Gerontologist, 53*(1), 9–16. doi:10.1093/geront/gns048
Randall, W. L., Baldwin, C., McKenzie-Mohr, S., McKim, E., & Furlong, D. (2015). Narrative and resilience: A comparative analysis of how older adults story their lives. *Journal of Aging Studies, 34*, 155–161.
Randall, W. L., Prior, S., & Skarborn, M. (2006). How listeners shape what tellers tell: Patterns of interaction in lifestory interviews and their impact on reminiscence by elderly interviewees. *Journal of Aging Studies, 20*(4), 381–396.
Riessman, C. K. (1993). *Narrative analysis*. Newbury Park, CA: Sage Publications.
Romo, R. D., Wallhagen, M. I., Yourman, L., Yeung, C. C., Eng, C., Micco, G., & Smith, A. K. (2013). Perceptions of successful aging among diverse elders with late-life disability. *The Gerontologist, 53*(6), 939–949.
Rosiek, J. L., & Heffernan, J. (2014). Can't code what the community can't see: A case of the erasure of heteronormative harassment. *Qualitative Inquiry, 20*(6), 726–733.
Roth, E. G., Eckert, J. K., & Morgan, L. A. (2015). Stigma and discontinuity in multilevel senior housing's continuum of care. *The Gerontologist, 56*(5), 868. doi:10.1093/geront/gnv055
Rowan, N. L., Giunta, N., Grudowski, E. S., & Anderson, K. A. (2013). Aging well and gay in rural America: A case study. *Journal of Gerontological Social Work, 56*(3), 185–200.
Rowles, G. D. (1978). *Prisoners of space?: Exploring the geographical experience of older people*. Boulder, CO: Westview Press.
Rowles, G. D., & Schoenberg, N. E. (2002). *Qualitative gerontology: A contemporary perspective*. New York: Springer.
Russell, C. (1999). Interviewing vulnerable old people: Ethical and methodological implications of imaging our subjects. *Journal of Aging Studies, 13*, 303–417.
Sabat, S. R., & Harré, R. (1992). The construction and deconstruction of self in Alzheimer's disease. *Ageing and Society, 12*, 443–443.
Saldaña, J. (2009). *The coding manual for qualitative researchers*. Los Angeles, CA: Sage Publications.
Saunders, P. A., Saunders, P. A., & Amaechi, M. (2013). Intergenerational co-construction of narrative gerontology in theory and in practice. *The Gerontologist, 53*(3), 520–523.
Schensul, J., & LeCompte, M. (2013). *Specialized ethnographic methods: A mixed methods approach*. Lanham, MD: AltaMira.
Schoenberg, N., & McAuley, W. (2007). Promoting qualitative research. *Gerontologist, 47*(5), 576–577.
Schoenberg, N., Miller, E., & Pruchno, R. (2011). The qualitative portfolio at the *Gerontologist:* Strong and getting stronger. *The Gerontologist, 51*(3), 281–284.
Schoenberg, N., Shenk, D., & Kart, C. (2007). Food for thought: The publication of qualitative research. *The Journal of Applied Gerontology, 26*, 4–16.
Sheehan, S. (1984). *Kate Quinton's days*. Boston, MA: Houghton Mifflin.
Sherman, E. A. (1984). *Working with older persons: Cognitive and phenomenological methods*. Boston, MA: Kluwer-Nijhoff.
Sixsmith, J., Sixsmith, A., Fänge, A. M., Naumann, D., Kucsera, C. S. A. B. A., Tomsone, S., & Woolrych, R. (2014). Healthy ageing and home: The perspectives of very old people in five European countries. *Social Science & Medicine, 106*, 1–9.
Smithers, J. (1985). *Determined survivors: Community life among the urban elderly*. New Brunswick, NJ: Rutgers University Press.
Söderhamn, O. (2013). Phenomenological perspectives on self-care in aging. *Clinical Interventions in Aging, 8*, 605–608.
Solimeo, S. (2009). *With shaking hands*. New Brunswick, NJ: Rutgers University Press.
Stafford, P. (2001). Teaching the ethnography of aging. *Educational Gerontology, 27*(7), 557–567.
Stafford, P. (2009). *Elderburbia: Aging with a sense of place in America*. Santa Barbara, CA: Praeger.
Stake, R. E. (2008). "Qualitative case studies." In N. K. Denzin, & Lincoln, Y. S. (Eds.), *Strategies of qualitative inquiry* (pp. 119–149). Los Angeles, CA: Sage Publications.

St. Pierre, E. A., & Jackson, A. Y. (2014). Qualitative data analysis after coding. *Qualitative Inquiry, 20*(6), 715–719.
Sugarman, J., Roter, D., Cain, C., Wallace, R., Schmechel, D., & Welsh-Bohmer, K. A. (2007). Proxies and consent discussions for dementia research. *Journal of the American Geriatrics Society, 55*(4), 556–561.
Tanner, D. (2012). Co-research with older people with dementia: Experience and reflections. *Journal of Mental Health, 21*(3), 296–306.
Tekle, F. B., & Vermunt, J. K. (2012). *APA handbook of research methods in psychology.* Washington, DC: American Psychological Association.
Tira, C., Jackson, A., & Tomnay, J. (2014). Pathways to late-life problematic gambling in seniors: A grounded theory approach. *The Gerontologist, 54*(6), 1035–1048.
Tuck, E., & Yang, K. W. (2014). Unbecoming claims pedagogies of refusal in qualitative research. *Qualitative Inquiry, 20*(6), 811–818. doi:10.1177/1077800414530265
Tuval-Mashiach, R., Zilber, T., & Lieblich, A. (1998). *Narrative research: Reading, analysis, and interpretation.* Thousand Oaks, CA: Sage Publications.
Van den Hoonaard, D. (2005). Am I doing it right? Older widows as interview participants in qualitative research. *Journal of Aging Studies, 19*, 393–406.
van Dijk, T. A. (1994). Critical discourse analysis. *Discourse & Society, 5*(4), 435–436.
van Manen, M. (1997). From meaning to method. *Qualitative Health Research, 7*(3), 345–369.
van Manen, M. (2011). *Phenomenology online: Empirical methods.* Retrieved from http://www.phenomenologyonline.com/
Van Wagenen, A., Driskell, J., & Bradford, J. (2013). "I'm still raring to go": Successful aging among lesbian, gay, bisexual, and transgender older adults. *Journal of Aging Studies, 27*(1), 1–14.
Vesperi, M. (1985). *City of green benches: Growing old in a new downtown.* Ithaca, NY: Cornell University Press.
Wallhagen, M. (2010). The stigma of hearing loss. *The Gerontologist, 50*(1), 66–75.
Warren-Findlow, J. (2013). Qualitative research in JG: SS: "I'll take a side of coleslaw with that". *The Journals of Gerontology Series B: Psychological Sciences and Social Sciences, 68*(3), 407–408. doi:10.1093/geronb/gbt017
Weil, J. (2014). *The new neighborhood senior center: Redefining social and service roles for the Baby Boom generation.* New Brunswick, NJ: Rutgers University Press.
Weil, J. (2015). Applying research methods to a gerontological population: Matching data collection to characteristics of older persons. *Educational Gerontology, 41*(10), 723–742. doi:10.1080/03601277.2015.1048172
Weil, J., & Moore, N. (2015). *North American's senior centers' role in the aging network: A literature review using adapted crowding in and crowding out theories.* Unpublished manuscript.
Wilmoth, J., Skytthe, A., Friou, D., & Jeune, B. (1996). The oldest man ever? A case study of exceptional longevity. *The Gerontologist, 36*(6), 783–788. doi:10.1093/geront/36.6.783
Wood, L. A., & Kroger, R. O. (1995). Discourse analysis in research on aging. *Canadian Journal on Aging, 14*(S1), 82–99.
Yates, S., & Hiles, D. (2010). Towards a "critical ontology of ourselves"?: Foucault, subjectivity and discourse analysis. *Theory & Psychology, 20*(1), 52–75.
Yin, R. K. (2014). *Case study research: Design and methods* (5th ed.). Los Angeles, CA: Sage Publications.

5
Quantitative Methods

Coverage of quantitative methods is divided between the next two chapters. This chapter covers the introductory elements of the major quantitative research designs (the causal comparative method, correlation, pre-testing/post-testing and experimental designs, structured observation, and single-case research). Features of each design and advantages and disadvantages of using each method are presented. This chapter begins to suggest ways to select a quantitative design option best suited to a study's research question, goals, and purpose. A step-by-step approach is provided to create a quantitative design—from choosing a method, sampling and participant selection, variable creation, data collection, reliability and validity testing, and establishing causality to considerations when conducting secondary data analysis. Questions to ask when working with secondary data and an applied example of secondary data analysis use are included. Online data resources for datasets focused around older populations are included at the end of the chapter. Age-period-cohort issues in aging studies are revisited from their initial discussion in Chapter 2. Extra features include examples of ways to improve survey-question wording and responses for use with older respondents along with a guide to reviewing existing survey data. Real-life issues are discussed—from applying quantitative designs with older people in the field to ways normal age-related changes impact quantitative designs.

As in many other fields, the quantitative-qualitative debate presents itself as a constant in the study of aging. Traditionally, the quantitative approach was equated with being more scientific and systematic than other approaches, but this is no longer the case. The dominance of quantitative research was tied to elite statistical knowledge or power (Desrosières, 1998). Now, qualitative, mixed-methods, and emergent research approaches are gaining equal weight in the field and are more common. Research is becoming more interdisciplinary and is moving past "paradigm wars" or "politics of method," numbers vs. words, positivist models, and constructed dichotomies of objective vs. subjective approaches (Cooper, Glaesser, Gomm & Hammersley, 2012, p. 8).

Quantitative Aging Research in Print and Academic Journals

The historical dominance of quantitative methods in gerontological publication is expressed by an exchange of letters and editorials by Charles Longino and Ingrid Arnet Connidis. Longino reminds researchers not to "lose sight of the humanity behind the numbers" (2005, p. S117). In his 2005 editorial in the *Journal of Gerontology: Social Sciences*, "Putting a human face on gerontological research: Identity issues," Longino reflects upon why the journal puts a photo of an older person on every issue's cover when most other journals do not to imply the humanity behind the numbers. He writes about the abundance of quantitative articles published by the journal during his time as editor "drawn from analyses of large data sets, often panel studies, conducted by others. The authors never looked in the eyes of research subjects and asked a question. The respondents . . . are faceless abstractions. . . . [W]e lose sight of the person and instead manipulate categories and levels" (2005, p. S117).

Connidis, Social Science Editor of the *Canadian Journal of Gerontology*, responded, thanking Longino for his "poetic and compelling call to remember the humanity behind the numbers and to see the faces of our subjects as a very useful start for class discussions of research on aging." She called for "more pieces in the *Journals on Gerontology* that challenge us to consider how we approach the study of aging" as a way to address the methodological gap (2005, p. 342).

Recently, the journal *Science* published an article that noted concerns about the lack of reproducibility in psychology studies. This article brought the role of quantitative research and replicability in gerontology back to light. Editors of a gerontology journal questioned, "Is gerontology in crisis?" And they responded to the replication call: "Like other top-tier journals, we are guilty of favoring novel studies over replication studies. We agree, however, with the *Science* article's conclusion that 'Innovation points out paths that are possible; replication points out paths that are likely; progress relies on both.' To that end, we will strive for a better balance" (Pruchno et al., 2015, p. 893). So, the role of quantitative studies in social gerontology continues.

Deciding How to Choose a Research Method and Design Selection: Quantitative Options

Purpose of Quantitative Options

Quantitative studies have four main functions: description, explanation, exploration, and/or prediction. **Descriptive** studies do not seek to test a hypothesis. They describe or paint a picture of the phenomena you are studying with numerical data. **Exploratory studies** seek to begin to research an issue of interest via a pilot or smaller-scale study. **Explanatory studies** (also called "confirmatory") seek to find a relationship for a phenomenon or events being studied to generate more research. **Predictive** studies seek to establish cause and effect among variables in a study.

Before you begin a quantitative project, you need to decide the purpose of the study you are beginning. Do you seek to describe a phenomenon? This would mean your study would produce descriptive statistics such as counts or frequency distributions—for example, the characteristics (age, ethnicity, race, gender, and socioeconomic status) of older adults attending a retirement-planning workshop. Or your goal may be to collect data about a topic that has little data to date. In this exploratory design, you could look at the use of time and activities for older persons living in a small-home, skilled-care model, such as those in the new Green House project. An explanatory study would describe the relationship or causal order of events in your study. For example, increased attendance at grandparenting workshops might lead to reduced anxiety about resources for grandparents raising grandchildren. Evaluative designs seek to test or measure the impact of a program or intervention. Programs can range from an evidence-based exercise program, such as a Matter of Balance, to a statewide policy, such as Colorado Choice Transitions (CCT) that seeks to move those in skilled-care settings to community-based settings. A predictive study, like a hypothesis, has a goal of predicting/forecasting the change in one event upon another.

Overview of Quantitative Design Choices

Quantitative research in social gerontology offers the researcher several design choices. Surveys are probably the most common/familiar option, but researchers can also choose from a causal comparative method, correlation, pre-testing/post-testing, experimental designs, structured observation, and single-case research designs. Each method will be reviewed, followed by a process to compare and make a choice.

Surveys

Survey construction. **Surveys** measure attitudes, behaviors, and beliefs and also collect demographic information. Survey questions can be **closed** (with fixed responses) or **open ended** (with space for narrative comments). Demographic and other factual data are collected using closed-ended questions. This type of question has fixed or preformatted response categories. Open-ended questions generally begin with a prompt, and the respondent can then answer in his or her own words.

Many feel that the **Likert scale**, a five-point scale with non-dichotomous answers (i.e., 1 = strongly disagree to 5 = strongly agree), is synonymous with the survey method. When using scales, it is important to address fence-sitters, those who cling to the middle or neutral value of a scale with an odd number of responses. For example, those choosing a "3" on a scale of 1 to 5. This middle value choice does not reflect an opinion of either agreement or disagreement. Eliminating the neutral/middle value by using a second **prompt** is a good option. This prompt lets the respondent provide a non-neutral opinion—for example, "If you had to choose a non-neutral value, would you say you: strongly agree, agree, disagree, or strongly disagree?" Good closed-ended survey questions also include an "Other, specify" category (in case the responses provided are not exhaustive) and "Don't know" and "Not applicable" responses. Scales, as with other measures, also need to be culturally appropriate or relevant. For example, a loneliness scale was translated and validated from its original Dutch for use with Turkish and Surinamese older migrants in different country settings (Uysal-Bozkir, Fokkema, MacNeil-Vroomen, van Tilburg & de Rooij, 2015). The researchers employed cognitive interviewing to see how respondents thought through questions and worked to make sure Dutch terms and concepts were relevant and culturally appropriate in the Turkish and Surinamese language options.

A well-constructed survey must have clear **question wording**—if questions are not clearly worded, there is more room for different interpretations and misinterpretations among respondents. See Box 5.1 below for examples of good wording for survey questions. In terms of question order, begin with questions that ask most directly about the survey's topic to gather data about the topic of interest and cue the respondent in to the survey's main focus. Keep these questions straightforward and interesting. It is best to keep any sensitive questions to the end of the instrument. Much like the flow of a literature review, more general questions are followed by ones that are more specific (i.e., asking for details about that line of

Box 5.1 Best Practices in Question Wording and Response Categories

All surveys must be evaluated in terms of the way the questions and response categories are worded. "Bad" wording leads to "bad" statistical data. There are many titles or ways to label such errors. Here, I compiled many of the most common question-writing flaws related to aging and older populations.

Question issues

Question wording must be clear, jargon-free, not include two questions in one, and avoid leading the respondent to a particular answer or asking for items that the respondent would not be able to recall or remember. All language must, of course, be free from bias and ageist language.

Biased Statements or Terms

Problematic Wording

As an elderly person, on a scale of 1 to 5 (with 1 = very dissatisfied and 5 = very satisfied), please rate your level of satisfaction with your retirement savings.

Better Wording

As a person 75 years of age and older, on a scale of 1 to 5 (with 1 = very dissatisfied and 5 = very satisfied), please rate your level of satisfaction with your retirement savings.

Problematic Wording

How does it feel to have early stage dementia?

Better Wording

How does it feel to have changes in memory?

Ambiguous, Unclear, or Unclear Wording

Problematic Wording

Have you had contact with the aging network in your community in the last week?

Better Wording

Have you attended a senior center in the last week?

Asking Several Questions in One

Problematic Wording

Do you support the changes in Medicare policy, the reauthorization of the Older Americans' Act, and new hospice legislation?

Better Wording

Do you support the changes in Medicare policy?
Do you support the reauthorization of the Older Americans' Act?
Do you support the new hospice legislation?

Leading Questions

Problematic Wording

Given the unusually high crime rate in your neighborhood, do you feel safe walking alone there at night as a vulnerable older person?

Better Wording

Do you feel safe walking alone in your neighborhood at night as someone 65 and older with mobility issues?

Double Negatives

Problematic Wording

Do you disagree with those who do not want to build more affordable housing for those 65 and over?

Better Option

Some people do not want to build more affordable housing for those 65 and over. Do you agree or disagree that we should build more affordable housing for those 65 and over?

Unbalanced Responses

Problematic Wording

Is your health excellent, very good, or good?

Better Option

Is your health excellent, very good, good, fair, or poor?

Problematic Wording

What was your income for the past year, 2016? Please choose from one of the following categories:

Less than $10,000
$10,000 to $40,000
$40,000 to $50,000
$50,000 to $75,000
$75,000 or more

Better Option

What was your income for the past year, 2016? Please choose from one of the following categories:

Less than $10,000
$10,000 to $39,999
$40,000 to $69,999
$70,000 to $99,999
$100,000 or more

False Premises

Problematic Wording

When did you stop financially abusing your parent?

Better Option

Has there been an occasion when you have taken or used a parent's money without his or her permission?

Problematic Wording

How much loneliness do you experience on a daily basis?

Better Option

Do you experience loneliness on a daily basis?

Issues of Recall or Memory (Varies by Baseline Cognitive Status)

Problematic Wording

What did you eat for breakfast last Thursday?

Better Option

What do you typically eat for breakfast on weekdays?

questioning). Questions should also have a time frame of reference for the item being measured. Is the time interval the last week, a typical week, yesterday, or two weeks ago?

Remember to include filter questions, those that assess eligibility or appropriateness of other questions that follow. For example, ask the respondent about his or her lifetime marital status before asking questions related to widowhood or loss of a partner. There is always a chance of **idiosyncratic variation** (a question reading differently to someone because of the way the question is constructed). To prevent getting an answer to something other than the question asked, surveys will often break down complex concepts into several questions or **sub-scales/measures** (e.g., the Cornell Depression Scale with subcategories of depressive symptoms: mood related, behavioral, cyclic, and changes in ideas/thinking). **Non-response reasons** are important to note. Did the respondent refuse the survey? Complete only a part of it? Or was the researcher unable to contact the respondent? If the survey is administered face-to-face, the interviewer's characteristics may affect respondents' answers. The following interviewer's approach or behaviors can impact responses given:

- Appearance: race, class, gender, sexuality, age . . .
- Tone: gruff, professional, rushed . . .
- Ability: well or less trained . . .
- Place where interview is conducted: in the community in the continuum of care
- Others present during the interview: adult children, grandchildren, caregivers, facility staff

There is much debate over whether the interviewers need to be matched on characteristics to those they interview—and in which situations it might it be helpful to match the respondent and interviewer. **Issues of identity-politics**, or basing decisions and actions on sharing common characteristics with a person or group, are addressed for all methods in Chapter 10.

Mode of Administration

Surveys can be delivered in a variety of ways: self-administered, telephone, and face-to-face interview. Surveys can be sent by mail or via the Internet/online. Some examples of self-administered and printed survey use include a **"leave-behind"** questionnaire—for example, one examining the relationship between older adults (50+) about debt and psychological well-being (Zurlo, Yoon & Kim, 2014). These surveys are left with the respondent and can be completed and returned at his or her convenience. Researchers have used follow-up mailed surveys to assess midlife influences on an older person's view of "aging well" (Pruchno & Wilson-Genderson, 2015). Mailed surveys have been used to investigate persons 60 years of age, older persons' personality factors, and attitudes toward aging (Bryant, Bei, Gilson, Komiti, Jackson & Judd, 2014). Face-to-face surveys have been used to examine cultural beliefs related to Alzheimer's disease (Sun, Gao & Coon, 2015). Online surveys have gathered information about persons at nursing homes that have adopted culture-change models (Elliot, Cohen, Reed, Nolet & Zimmerman, 2014). Web-based surveys assessed caregivers' desire to pay for technological monitoring of loved ones (Schulz, Beach, Matthews, Courtney, De Vito Dabbs & Mecca, 2015), and experts were surveyed via the web about what we know and need to learn about exercise programs for older adults (Hughes, Marquez, Moni, Nguyen, Desai & Jones, 2011). In addition, many researchers use nursing-home data from Medicare's Online Survey and Certification Reporting System databases originally collected by field reviewers.

Causal Comparative

Unlike experimental designs that look at prospective causality, the **causal comparative** approach tests causal relationships after they have occurred or after the fact (*ex post facto*) (Brewer & Kuhn, 2010). A causal comparative design can test how changes in the independent variable effect changes in a dependent variable. This design can also test how two preexisting, naturally occurring groups differ in a dependent variable. This design is a good choice when data already exists to address a research question at hand and the researcher seeks to assign cause and effect. While this design is more commonly used in education research, gerontological examples exist. Researchers tested the cause and effect of two variables, examining the effect of older age upon empathy scores (O'Brien, Konrath, Grühn & Hagen, 2013). Others examined the way naturally existing groups differed in an outcome. For example, researchers compared nursing homes in different states in terms of their own state-specific policies and staff requirements. They examined how these polices and requirements affected each state's nursing-home quality (Walsh, Lane & Troyer, 2014).

Correlation

Correlation designs examine the association between variables. This approach cannot impose causal order—stating which instance or variable affected the other—but can describe co-occurring changes and strength and magnitude of the association. There are several correlational types. **Bivariate correlation**, also called zero-order correlation, tests a relationship between two variables. This approach produces a coefficient for bivariate association such as **Pearson's correlation coefficient** (r) with a range from -1 to +1, indicating the strength of the relationship between the variables. Values closer to zero indicate a weak relationship, and ±1 is a strong relationship. Researchers have looked at correlations between gratitude and wisdom in older persons (König & Glück, 2014) and nursing staff's absenteeism and nursing-home-quality scores (Castle & Ferguson-Rome, 2014).

Partial correlational designs introduce a third variable and look at the association between the two original variables in the presence of the third variable. This third variable is also called a control variable.

Tests for correlation of association are available based on variables' level of measurement. For **nominal/categorical-level** variables that differ only by name or label, we can use x^2, Phi, Cramer's V, or lambda (as a Proportional Reduction of Error, PRE, measure). For **ordinal-level** variables that can be ranked or ordered, we can use gamma, Kendall's tau, Somers'd, or Spearman's rho. For **interval-ratio level** variables, true numerical values, we can use Pearson's correlation coefficient (r), the coefficient of determination (r^2), or regression. Correlation can also be used to test the reliability of items in instruments or agreement among raters, inter-rater reliability.

Single-Case Research Design

While **single-case studies** are often thought of as a qualitative design, a quantitative single-case design does exist. This design has its origin and application in experimental design. Quantitative single-case research design can have one participant or subject or a naturally occurring group as a subject (e.g., residents in an independent living or a village model). Since there are no comparison groups, this design focuses on the impact of interventions (independent variables) upon outcomes (dependent variable) for an individual or individual group over time. The goal of this design is to establish causal order "within-subject rather than a between-subjects" during baseline and experimental phases (Boyer, 2010; Smith, 2012, p. 2). Researchers state that three conditions must be met in this single-case study design: (1) the unit of analysis is one case (an individual or group), (2) there are repeated baseline and post-intervention measurements, and (3) comparisons are made between baseline, treatment, and post-treatment phases (Kratochwill et al., 2010; Moeyaert, Ugille, Ferron, Beretvas & Van den Noortgate, 2014). This design is often referred to as an AB design with A as the conditions at baseline and B as the intervention. However, these steps (and lettering) can be made into many combinations (Graham, Karmarkar & Ottenbacher, 2012).

A single-case example is the scenario of an 86-year-old woman, Mrs. Robinson, who lives in skilled care and is a fall risk. Staff tell her to remain in her wheelchair instead of trying to rise and walk unstably. Each time she raises herself from her wheelchair, staff run to her, tell her to remain seated, and get her the item she is seeking. Due to these behavioral interventions, Mrs. Robinson remains seated and then becomes less apt to rise from her wheelchair and walk (Thomas & Hersen, 2011). In another example, three men with Alzheimer's disease were provided with both indirect (reframing and restating utterances, reinforcement) and direct (more corrective, punishing, sentence completion) interventions to encourage greater amounts of speaking. This design, called ABAC, consisted of a baseline, an intervention, a second baseline, and a second intervention. Researchers found more words and coherent speech were used with the indirect, restating approach than the more corrective one (Gentry & Fisher, 2007).

The single-case research design is not commonly used, and its method of analysis is questioned and being improved (Boyer, 2010; Kratochwill & Levin, 2010). It has greater application in the fields of psychology, medicine, rehabilitation, and clinical health and as a precursor to theory creation (Boyer, 2010). Due to small sample size, generalizability is an issue, and internal validity concerns (about other causal factors) can exist. Ethical concerns include a researcher conducting the study and also measuring the results without recognition of any potential bias in design (see Boyer, 2010). For ways to improve validity, see Kratochwill et al. [2010]). For ways to review a single-case design, see Andrew Egel and Christine Barthold's (2010) "Single subject design and analysis," in *The reviewer's guide to quantitative methods in the social sciences* (New York: Routledge).

Pre-testing/Post-testing and Experimental Design

The *Chronicle of Higher Education Review* published a commentary by Brian Earp and Jim Everett about "How to fix psychology's replication crisis" and the lessening use of repeated experimental design. Earp and Everett (2015), the original authors, pointed out that the findings from many studies using experimental methods could not be replicated or repeated in other lab settings—and that findings were more a feature of design than real difference. As mentioned at the beginning of this chapter, gerontological journals are responding. Early on, gerontological studies found that stereotyping of older participants caused slower gait (Bargh, Chen & Burrows, 1996). Others re-conducted this experiment and found differing results for stereotyping effects—when conducted in other languages (Doyen, Klein, Pichon & Cleeremans, 2012; Ramscar, Shaoul, Baayen & Tbingen, 2015). Recently, the work about the impact of stereotypes upon older persons has been expanded. Researchers looking at the effect of stereotypes upon memory found that extremely positive portrayals of aging negatively impacted memory functioning and attention span of older people (Fung, Li, Zhang, Sit, Cheng & Isaacowitz, 2015).

Despite issues of reproducibility, **pre- and post-test designs** in social gerontology have their roots in experimental methods and use many of the same elements: control groups, experimental groups, intervention, and matching. The two groups are either the group receiving the intervention (experimental) or the group that is not (control). Often, the researcher will choose naturally existing groups. He or she may also match persons in each group based on similar characteristics (such as age, race, ethnicity, gender, socioeconomic status, etc.) so that these other aspects of one's social position do not impact the study. **Matching**, however, can also defeat the purpose of random group assignment because participants are matched on several characteristics but may have great differences in other non-matched characteristics. These non-matched characteristics may introduce difference and bias.

Social experiments are also subject to risks such as selection bias, exogenous change, contamination, placebo, and Hawthorne Effects. **Selection bias** refers to the composition of participants or the way they have been chosen to participate in the study. If participants are not randomly chosen, they may not represent the population about which you wish to make statements. **Exogenous change** can occur when other events not part of the study itself happen during the study. These outside events, then, can impact your findings. In social experiments, many things that we cannot control happen in the lives and world of those we study. For example, during a study of the attitude of persons near retirement age toward retirement, new stringent policies are passed to cut Social Security benefits. The new policies may generate a spike of increased uncertainty about retirement in a way not present when the study began. **Contamination** occurs when the lines between the two groups (the experimental and control) are crossed and the knowledge or treatment (designed to affect only the experimental group) begins to affect both groups. The **placebo effect** is when positive effects are seen without administering a treatment or intervention. The **Hawthorne Effect** refers to the impact of a researcher, or the effect of the experience of being studied, upon the behaviors of those studied. People in a study may modify their behaviors because they are being studied and want to be seen a certain way or live up to the researcher's expectations. Some suggest this concept needs more research and testing itself (McCambridge, Witton & Elbourne, 2014).

Examples of quasi-experiments and modified experimental gerontological designs include a musical and singing intervention to improve cognitive, emotional, and social functioning of dyads of caregivers and persons with early stage dementia (Särkämö et al., 2014). A quasi-experimental, layered memory program (health, lifestyle, stress, etc.) was tested as an intervention to improve health-help-seeking behavior (Wiegand, Troyer, Gojmerac & Murphy, 2013). A tele-health intervention was tested as a way to improve health outcomes of those with chronic disease; the intervention was shown to improve health, social functioning, and depression scores (Gellis, Kenaley, McGinty, Bardelli, Davitt, & Ten Have, 2012). Researchers also tested a physical-activity protocol with cognitively impaired residents of a skilled-care facility to improve overlap functioning and time and intensity of physical activity (Galik, Resnick, Hammersla & Brightwater, 2014). Another modified social gerontological experiment tested two interventions (one mindfulness based and the other community-caregiver-education based) to improve caregiver mental health and social support and to ease anxiety, stress, depression, anxiety, and burden (Whitebird, Kreitzer, Crain, Lewis, Hanson, & Enstad, 2013). The researchers found that each intervention was linked to improvement in different outcomes.

Researchers suggest that more needs to be done to include older adults in clinical, experimental trials—since older adults would be the target group of tested interventions. Future trials must have more age-friendly communication, embrace concurrent medical conditions, and focus efforts on retention and benefits over merely a recruitment push (Herrera, Snipes, King, Torres-Vigil, Goldberg & Weinberg, 2010). Some existing examples of experimental designs are public health's use of clinical trials. Vitamin D has been proposed for testing in community-dwelling persons 65 years and older as a preventative measure against falls and fractures (Hidalgo, 2011). Several clinical trials examined the effects of lowering cholesterol upon the health of those 80 years of age and older (Petersen, Christensen & Kragstrup, 2010). Clinical trials tested the impact of folic acid and other treatments in improving memory and cognitive function in persons 65 and older in China, finding folic acid to have short-term efficacy (Ma et al., 2015).

Structured Observation

While observation is often thought of as a qualitative design, quantitative work has a long history of using pre-determined categories to collect data through observational approaches. Researchers describe **observational studies** as experimental design without random assignment to groups. In biomedical or pharmaceutical research, an observational study is often defined as one where "participants are not randomized or otherwise preassigned to an exposure. The choice of treatments is up to patients and their physicians." An observational study may be prospective or "longitudinal in nature, where the consequential outcomes of interest occur after study commencement" (Berger, Dreyer, Anderson, Towse, Sedrakyan & Normand, 2012, p. 219). Performance-based tests and assessments of functional abilities are an example of quantitative structured observation (see Applegate, Blass & Williams, 1990; Simonsick, Maffeo, Rogers, Skinner, Davis & Guralnik, 1997).

Table 5.1 Advantages and Disadvantages of Each Quantitative Design

Design	Features	Advantages	Disadvantages
Survey, Self-Administered (often done by mail or via the Internet/online)	*Length* Less than 30 minutes to complete No more than six pages	Can be done by one researcher Covers a large geographic area Reaches a large number of respondents Respondent can complete it when they wish Respondents are less identifiable than in other types Avoids interviewer bias Least costly of the three survey methods	Low response rates Multiple follow-up mailings are needed to increase response rates Never know who is actually answering the questions Interviewer cannot clarify questions Interviewer cannot observe the accuracy of responses (e.g., intended 90-year-old female respondent could be a 56-year-old male) Requires a level of comfort with technology
Survey, Telephone	Best kept short; Closed-ended questions only	Few interviewers can reach many respondents Covers a wide geographic area Can use Computer Assisted Telephone Interviewing (CATI) to decrease interviewer error—e.g., a 65-year-old woman who states she has had no children is then later asked about her number of grandchildren	Credibility issues: telemarketing and telephone fraud alerts have negatively impacted trust in telephone surveys Response rates can be low: due to repeated call backs, hang-ups, unlisted numbers, cell-phone-only users Anyone can answer the phone and survey No use of visual aids, reliance upon hearing
Survey, Face-to-Face Interview	Best response rates, since it is more difficult for respondents to refuse in person	Best response rate since refusal is more difficult Interviewer can probe and explain questions Can be longer than mailed or phone surveys Included observation of non-verbal communication Can use visual aids	Very costly Skill and training of the interviewer are crucial Interviewer bias can occur
Single-Case Study	An adaptation of more experimental design with one person/group and baseline, multiple pre- and post-measurements	Can give insight into cause/effect for the group studied and lead to larger studies/investigation	Small sample-size limits generalizability, and, since researcher does intervention and collects/analyzes data, bias can exist
Pre-testing/ Post-Testing (Experimental Design)	In social gerontology, these are more quasi than "real" experiments	Can help to show cause and effect and behavioral change to treatment or behavioral intervention	Threats to internal validity (design of the experiment) or external validity (generalizing result to larger groups)
Causal Comparative	Compares one or more independent variables after the event or phenomena has occurred; uses characteristics of naturally occurring groups	Allows the research to test causal ordering	Issues of controlling for possible other causal variables exist

(*Continued*)

Table 5.1 (Continued)

Design	Features	Advantages	Disadvantages
Correlation	Looks at changes in a couple/several variables at once	Measures association between events/variables	Only assesses changes but cannot assign temporal order
Structured Observation	Uses observational methods to collect data	Provides descriptive statistics/frequencies of observed events	Cannot assign causal order and is subject to observers' skill, training, and/or bias

Choosing a Method

While all quantitative methodological choices (survey [all types], single-case study, pre-testing/post-testing or experimental design, causal comparative, correlation, and structured observation) have similarities, each may be more suited to a particular application. Factors to consider when choosing a design include the purpose of your research design, population and sample option (design, size), availability of data, time needed for the project and time-constraint issues, planning, resources, existing materials, access to data, researcher's level of comfort with quantitative work, and comfort with older persons as co-researchers. Table 5.2 provides a comparison of features of each quantitative design with your planned research project. By plotting the purpose of your study with other criteria—the sample, availability of data, time needed for the project, time constraints, issues of planning, resources, and existing materials, access to data or population, researcher's level of comfort with quantitative work, and the researcher's level of comfort with older persons as co-researchers—you can narrow down the most suitable design types. Table 5.3 provides real-life issues from application of surveys and secondary analysis of data as quantitative research methods.

Collecting Data

Sampling

You can either collect a sample or analyze an existing dataset. If you choose to collect your own data, you should consider a few things when deciding upon your **sampling design.** You will need to consider how readily variable a sampling frame is for the population you wish to study. Note how generalizable (which groups you want to generalize to) and representative (having the sample characteristics as your population) your sample needs to be. You will need to keep in mind ways your sample may differ from the population's characteristics and introduce error if you want to generalize findings back to the population the sample is drawn from. It is rare that a researcher will study an **entire population**—or conduct a census—like the U.S. Decennial Census. If drawn systematically from the entire population, sampling is a good way to conduct studies with smaller groups and infer/refer back to the entire population. Some key issues in sampling are selecting cases, random/non-random or probability-based/non-probability-based designs, sampling frame and unit of analysis selection, and sample power.

Selecting Cases/Sampling Frame and Unit of Analysis Selection

Each sample consists of elements referred to as **units of analysis (UOA)**. These units can range from individuals to entire settings such as an organization or country. For example, when studying quality of life in skilled care, a unit of analysis could be at the level of resident,

Table 5.2 Comparison of Features of Each Quantitative Design

	Survey (All Types)	Single-Case Study	Pre-testing/Post-testing (Experimental Design)	Causal Comparative	Correlation	Structured Observation
Purpose of Design	Could be any: descriptive, exploratory, explanatory, evaluative	Mostly descriptive, exploratory	Mostly causal, explanatory, evaluative, predictive	Mostly causal, explanatory, evaluative, predictive	Mostly explanatory	Mostly descriptive, explanatory, or exploratory for larger studies
Population and Sample Options (Design, Size)	Varies by type—self-administered, telephone, face-to-face	Case can be one person or a group as a unit	Depending upon analysis plan, power calculations are needed, and larger samples may be required	Depending upon analysis plan, power calculations are needed, and larger samples may be required	Depending upon analysis plan, power calculations are needed, and larger samples may be required	Due to observational nature, sample sizes may be smaller than other quantitative methods
Availability of Data	Must be collected by researcher	Must be collected by researcher	Can be collected by researcher or be a secondary analysis of existing data	Can be collected by researcher or be a secondary analysis of existing data	Must be collected by researcher	Must be collected by researcher
Time Needed for the Project/ Timeframe/Time constraint/ Issues	Varies by project's scope; can include multiple launches	Varies by project's scope and amount of interventions in design	Varies by project's scope; less time if secondary analysis of existing data	Varies by project's scope; less time if secondary analysis of existing data	Varies by project's scope and intricacy of behaviors/ phenomenon measured	Varies by project's scope and intricacy of behaviors/ phenomenon measured
Planning, Resources, and Existing Materials	Planning differs by mode of delivery. Self-administered (often done by mail, or via the Internet/online). If mailed, take resources/costs and online survey design ability. Telephone interviews are costly and require trained callers and software. Face-to-face interviews require trained personnel and travel costs.	Recruitment of cases and trained personnel	Experience needed matching subjects and assigning to groups; of statistical analysis ability for pre-test/ post-test data	Experience needed in statistical analysis	Experience needed in statistical analysis	Trained personnel and pre-conceived data collection categories

(Continued)

Table 5.2 (Continued)

	Survey (All Types)	Single-Case Study	Pre-testing/Post-testing (Experimental Design)	Causal Comparative	Correlation	Structured Observation
Access to Data or Population Requirements	All data must be collected, and response rates vary by mode of delivery (highest for face-to-face; lowest for self-administered—all types interviewee[s])	Difficulty of access to cases depends on commonality of condition or behavior studied	Persons may not complete both assessments	Access to population depends on primary/ secondary data use—number of cases related to power	Access to population depends on primary/ secondary data use—number of cases related to power	Varies by project's scope and intricacy of behaviors/ phenomenon measured
Researcher's Level of Comfort with Quantitative Work	Necessary for the design and analysis	Although quantitative analysis can be qualitative-like and on a smaller scale	Essential	Essential	Essential	Mostly descriptive statistics
Researcher's Level of Comfort with Older Persons as Co-researchers	Lesser if using printed/online materials—more crucial for telephone and for most face-to-face	Crucial, since researcher is closely involved in the study	Depends upon how tests are administered—face-to-face or written	Less person contact, if secondary analysis	Less person contact, if secondary analysis	Crucial since researcher is closely involved in the study

Table 5.3 Issues from Application of Quantitative Research Methods

Research Design	Case	Common Problems	Examples	Insight/Strategies	Solutions
Surveys	Two-to-three-month and six-month follow-up. Telephone Calls on a Hip Fracture Project: demographics, assistive device use, physical therapy, FIM, pain assessment, re-hospitalization, and social activities.	Unfamiliarity with structured scales or scales not being conversational	Closed-ended questions not seen as "natural" or conversational. Respondents did not care for the format and wanted to "chat."	Chatting at the end of the interview produced great insight into the respondent's quality of life. Respondents talked about what they valued in their recovery process: e.g., writing a husband's memoir or attending a ceremony honoring their accomplishments in their hometown, attending a family celebration, shopping at a local supermarket, better maneuvering around his/her apartment, or being less in pain. Functional abilities were not primary. Probes with questions to re-direct to stay on the interview script with prompts—"We can talk about this at the end of the survey; now, let's go back to the question . . ."—work.	When administering scales (i.e., the FIM), triangulation (multiple methods or sources) allows for collection of respondent's answer in two forms—coded numerical answers (dictated by FIM guidelines) and open-ended respondent narrative. These two items can be compared to assess fit of the measure to capture lived experience. Since self-rating of abilities differs from algorithmic coding of a structured scale, keep a formal place in the data collection for the older person's self-assessment of ability. Add in some pre-survey informal chatting time. Peel and Wilson (2008) suggest this pre-interview "small talk" is used to build rapport and trust. It helps establish a reciprocal relationship while storytelling elements work in answers.

(*Continued*)

Table 5.3 (Continued)

Research Design	Case	Common Problems	Examples	Insight/Strategies	Solutions
		Scales not capturing individuals' own assessment of their experiences	The FIM, rating functional independence and recording lowest level of functional ability, created issues for older respondents with varying abilities. E.g., an older woman with multiple sclerosis scored a 1 on the FIM—since she was unable to get out of bed. She insisted since her abilities ranged from a 1 to a 7 within the time period, her score should be averaged to more accurately reflect her true ability. She became angry and frustrated that the measure would reflect her performance in what she perceived as such a negative, inaccurate way.	Wenger, when asking open-ended versions of closed-ended questions, found different ideas emerged. When "asked about needs for and receipt of help with personal care . . . most people struggled against enormous odds to maintain independence and often gave up on a task rather than ask for help" (1999, p. 371). This information would have been lost or miscoded in closed-ended questions with frequency-based responses. Porter (2007) compared the discrepancy between closed-ended difficulty scales and open-ended ADL and IADL responses given by individuals. When no fixed-response options were provided, older women thought "difficulty" was not the best word for what they were experiencing; other aspects of completing the task were more important than difficulty; and that difficulty is not a constant but varies from time to time. Women had difficulty rating "difficulty" and suggested better phrasing be used such as my "biggest" or "hardest" job; some wondered what exactly "difficulty" really means. Morgan and Kunkel (2006) suggest researchers reconsider the value of a slightly higher score on an ADL disability scale. Does a 3 versus a 5 directly translate into meaningful differences for those tested?	An explanatory design in which the qualitative open-ended measures could capture intra-individual variation over a period of time rather than sum functioning to a single lowest score. The unexpected respondents' reactions to the FIM as being punitive could have been investigated/probed further.

Translation of scales into other languages and the use of "medical-ese" or jargon.	FIM translation into other languages (Spanish, Yiddish, Turkish) was problematic. Difficulty using these terms was compounded when being explained by non-medically trained translators. Non-native English speakers asked about difficulty "washing, rinsing or drying the body," "adjusting clothing before/ after toilet use and cleansing," or with "bowel/ bladder management" saw these questions as too clinical, sensitive, or awkward. Medical terminology was seen as different from ordinary speech patterns.	Greenwood (2009) suggests the vocabulary used by researchers for people and activities differs from the vocabulary used by older people in everyday life. For example, would care providers see themselves as a "carer," or would someone post-stroke call themselves a "stroke survivor"?	Exploratory work could have been done. Although the FIM was standard with psychometric testing done, and the instrument piloted, a disconnect between the terminology and the respondent's comprehension remained in this sample. An exploratory design would have allowed for the respondents' own language and idioms to become part of the quantitative instrument or be used to develop a taxonomy of terminology for this sample. Measures that are more conversational and use everyday terminology and simpler language aid both in comprehension and in validity.
Proxy (non-older person) respondents	Less than half the time, in the two-to-three-month follow-up phone calls, the respondent was actually the older individual enrolled in the study.	Choice of respondent was most often influenced by cognitive ability or preference of the individual. Not having the original person enrolled in the study responding introduces the potential for over- or underestimation of the individual's ability based on who is actually responding to the question. Gerontological literature debates the difference and appropriateness of self- vs. other-rated health data and whose assessment more accurately predicts an individual's true ability (Albert, Bear-Lehman, Burkhardt, Merete-Roa, Noboa-Lemonier & Teresi, 2006). Van Herk, van Dijk, Biemold, Tibboel, Baar, and de Wit (2009) found caregivers generally rate an individual's abilities much lower than the individual would rate himself or herself.	Victor, Westerhof, and Bond (2007) found reasons for non-response and proxy use differ for younger and older populations. Illness or physical and cognitive impairments accounted for 21% of non-response and proxy use in the 70–85 age range but only 3% in those aged 40–54. For both proxy and missing data issues with frail older people, Peel and Wilson (2008) suggest dividing an interview up into sections to prevent fatigue or boredom; they found common causes for both proxy use and missing data—using this strategy they had only 1.3% of proxy data and 7.2% of missing data due to older respondents' memory loss, hearing loss, agitation, or inappropriate interview behaviors.

(*Continued*)

Table 5.3 (Continued)

Research Design	Case	Common Problems	Examples	Insight/Strategies	Solutions
		Missing data	The two-to-three-month call had 15% of data missing for walking and 17% for stair climbing; 15% of FIM items had missing data. The six-month call had missing data for questions about pain, hospitalization, and social activities.	Missing data was often due to proxy respondents who were unable to assess questions relating to an older person's self-ratings of health or medical and social activities.	Researchers need to reconsider the value of adding questions that produce large amounts of missing data to the instrument or ways to collect the data via an alternate methodology such as direct observation, performance-based tasks, or another data source. Options include chart review or a pain or social-activity journal. These methods can be successful even for those with varying levels of cognitive ability.
Secondary Analysis of Data	Women's Health and Aging Study (WHAS)	Performance-based measures with missing data	Strenuous performance-based tasks can produce a large portion of the sample with a substantial amount of missing data on key indicators. Screening for pre-existing conditions (paralysis, being bed-bound, limb amputations, recent joint or hip surgery, or an active cardiac condition) excluded many of the older women from attempting a majority of performance-based tasks. Missing data existed for important performance-based items: hip flexion test (22%), knee-extension tests (18%), and Perdue pegboard (14%).	Researchers can opt for more age-appropriate tests instead of applying tests for general populations to older ones without adaptation—resulting in tests that capture the heartiest elders. Performance-based tests should be devised that allow for more of those 65 and over being included in the sample. This means not necessarily less-rigorous testing but population-appropriate tests. Tests can be modified from elders' feedback and concerns about the tests to improve comprehension.	Cueing scripts can be developed from explanatory design with those excluded or not able to complete the performance-based testing providing insight on the narrative needed to create good cues to design other testing strategies (e.g., the Timed Up & Go Test [TUG]). Christensen et al. (2013) found that providing post-hip fracture opportunity to practice the tasks before formally being tested increased the percentage of older individuals able to complete all tests.
		Uniqueness of sample and/or heterogeneity of the sample on individual items.	The sample is chosen for their difficulty with at least one task in two or more of four functional domains—mobility, upper-extremity strength, ADL tasks, and IADL tasks—and living in a community setting. African-American women and those 85 years of age or more were oversampled. Commonly used social-class variables showed great variability within each cohort—65 to 74, 75 to 84, and 85+.	Samples of older persons can be selected from rare populations, hampering generalizability. For additional information, see Morgan and Kunkel (2006).	Weighting the sample by strata needs to be a part of the data-analysis process (Weil, Hutchinson & Traxler, 2014).

Adapted from: Weil, J. (2015). Applying research methods to a gerontological population: Matching data collection to characteristics of older persons. *Educational Gerontology, 41*(10), 723–742.

all staff, the nursing home itself, skilled-care corporations, skilled care in an entire state, or even a country. This UOA selection is crucial since errors of inference or application can result. If you are studying individuals and make statements about groups, that is called **ecological fallacy**. On the other hand, if you are studying groups but then apply your findings to individuals, that is a **reductionist fallacy**. Stating the unit of analysis helps make reference to appropriate groups.

Random/Non-Random or Probability-Based/Non-Probability-Based Designs

Another major decision is whether you will use a probability-based sampling or non-probability-based sampling—each choice having its own benefits and limitations. The strength of a well-designed, **probability-based random sample** is that, when the sample is selected, it closely represents the underlying population from which it is drawn. Therefore, findings can be generalized back to the population from which the sample was selected. The researcher determines the probability of participants' selection, which lends itself to representativeness. **Probability-based, random designs** include simple random sampling (with/without replacement), systematic sampling, cluster sampling, and stratified sampling.

Simple random sample chooses elements from a **sampling frame** or a list of all possible participants, using random selection, sometimes in the form of a random numbers table, to create this type of sample. This process ensures that each element has the same chance/probability of being selected. **Systematic random sampling** builds upon a simple random sample, selecting cases using a sampling interval. The first case is randomly selected, as is every nth case thereafter. This process requires a complete sampling frame and, unfortunately, is subject to periodicity, or patterns in the sample frame or list. (For example, you are sampling every 10th case, and every 10th case is the name of a centenarian. Your final sample would be all persons in their 100s and not represent the entire age composition of the group.) **Stratified random sample** involved random sampling within several classes or strata. After strata are determined, cases are randomly selected from within each stratum. Either each stratum can have the same characteristics as the population from which it is drawn, or each stratum can differ in how its characteristics are represented in the population. For example, a stratified random sample for three age groups as strata (65–74, 75–84, and 85 and over) may oversample the last stratum of those 85 and over to have equal numbers of participants, as would the other to younger age groups (those 65–74, 75–84). **Cluster sampling** is similar to stratified sampling, except the units are naturally occurring clusters or groups. The sampling occurs in a series of each cluster. Each cluster becomes a sampling frame from which cases are drawn. Selecting different types of clusters may help the sample from becoming too homogenous. For example, if you were conducting a study of Area Agency on Aging's (AAA) staff satisfaction, each AAA would be its own cluster with staff sampled from each cluster.

Non-probability-based sampling techniques are used when a random sample cannot be drawn. For example, a sampling frame, or list of all persons or entities in the population, is needed to draw a random sample. Non-probability-based samples are used in this case. Non-probability, non-random sampling options include availability (or convenience) sampling, quota sampling, purposive sampling, and snowball sampling. **Availability or convenience samples** are based on selecting readily available cases and are often used for pilot testing. **Quota sampling** selects a sample based on a characteristic of note, but these selection items are not matched to their representation in the population. **Purposive sampling** selects each element of the sample for a specific reason or purpose, such as knowledge about an issue or expertise. **Snowball sampling** begins with one participant, who then recommends another, who recommends another; it is used with populations or groups that do not have a sampling frame or are tough to reach/locate.

Sampling Error, Sample Size, and Power

Since sampling units are being selected from the population, if the sample statistics differ from the population's parameters, some error can exist. There is some error expected in probability sampling from the general design, but other errors can be introduced if other situations occur. **Error**, arising from incomplete sampling frames that do not represent the entire population or systematic patterns in the cases, defeats the random selection process.

Sample size is often equated with the question "What is your N?" N refers to the total number of persons in your sample, if your study has only one sample. If your study has multiple samples or you are referring to a smaller part of the total, use the smaller case "n" (Acheson, 2010; American Psychological Association, 2010). Some style guides require that each N be italicized. Having an adequate sample size is important because it gives the researcher more confidence that he or she can conduct certain statistical tests with his or her data or that he or she is reaching parameter estimates (Hutchinson, 2015). Some very general sample-size adages are as follows: a larger size can decrease error; the more complex the design, the larger the sample; and weaker relationships need larger samples. Many online programs and apps can calculate sample size—such as G*Power (http://www.gpower.hhu.de/en.html). Unfortunately, sample-size and power calculations are not so simple or cut and dry. A warning from an Applied Statistical Research Methods colleague, Susan Hutchinson, notes:

- When conducting multiple tests with data, researchers must consider sample size required for each test and each variable type (nominal, dichotomous, or interaction terms).
- In survey research, in addition to having adequate sample size for statistical power and accurate parameter estimates, sample size needs to be large enough for representativeness.

(November 27, 2015, personal correspondence).

Some ways to maintain sample size during waves of a longitudinal study are to collect data from others in the household or living situation and also to contact those who refused to participate at earlier waves to see if they wish to participate in later waves (see O'Muircheartaigh, English, Pedlow & Kwok, 2014).

Operationalizing Variables/Indicators

The concepts in your study need to be carefully defined, or conceptualized and **operationalized**, into variables that can be measured. Conceptualization is simply specifying what we mean by a term. "Older people" (a concept) can have a whole range of meanings. Operationalization, then, lets us explains how we will measure the concept—those 65 and older, 75 and older, or 85 and older?

We define variables as **discrete** (if it is the smallest unit of analysis and we cannot divide it further, such as residents of cohousing) or **continuous** (if it can be infinitely divided, such as age). Another classification, **the level of measurement of a variable** (as nominal/categorical, ordinal, or interval-ratio in the social sciences), lets us choose appropriate tests and analysis. Variables in the **nominal level of measurement** (also called categorical or qualitative) differ in kind, not amount. They have no ranking or ordering and might be **dichotomous variables** (Y/N)—for example, nationality, race, ethnicity, or gender. Variables in the **ordinal**

level of measurement have categories that can be ranked relative to one another. They can be thought of in terms of being "greater than/less than" or "higher/lower" or "low, medium, high" comparisons. For example, level of cognitive impairment can be ranked as mild, moderate, or severe. Since social research has few true interval-level variables, we combine interval and ratio into one category, **interval-ratio level variables**. This group includes variables with categories that have the same distance between them and either do or do not have a fixed-zero value—for example, age or income that can be divided into smaller and smaller units.

Establishing Causality

Quantitative designs can establish causality among independent variables as cause and among dependent variables as effect. Several elements are needed to establish basic causality (Mulaik, 2009). First, there must be appropriate time ordering with the independent variable occurring before the dependent. Second, there needs to be an association between the independent and dependent variables—so that if the independent changes, it brings about a change in the dependent variable. Third, the relationship between the independent and dependent variables must not be caused by another variable (spuriousness). Fourth, the direction of variables must be in proper causal order, so that the independent causes the dependent (and not the reverse or reciprocal relationship). Last, a change in the independent variable effects change across the dependent variable. We often note independent (X) variables, dependent (Y) variables, and the direction of the relationship between X & Y (as positive, negative/inverse) in what we state as a general hypothesis statement.

Meditating variables are a causal link or those that the independent variables operate through to impact the dependent variable. Mediator variables connect (or intervene) the independent and dependent variable's relationship. Mediator variables are sought when there is an unexpectedly low relationship between an independent and dependent variable (Baron & Kenny, 1986). Four criteria must be established for a mediation. First, the independent variable predicts the dependent variable. Second, the independent variable predicts the mediator variable. Third, the mediator variable predicts the dependent variable. Last, the mediation is complete when, after the mediator is introduced, the relationship between the independent and dependent variables no longer exists. Once the mediator is controlled for, there is no relationship between the independent and dependent variables (see Baron & Kenny, 1986; Judd & Kenny, 1981). David Kenny's "mediation" homepage offers a wealth of resources (http://davidakenny.net/cm/mediate.htm).

Gerontological research often tests for mediation in relationships between variables. One study examined the relationship between personality traits and ego integrity. The authors tested well-being as a mediator, or variable by which personality traits impact ego integrity (Westerhof, Bohlmeijer & McAdams, 2015). Another study proposed several health indicators—perceived physical difficulties and social support—as mediators in the relationship between social class and depression. For mediation to be found present, each potential mediator needs to be related to social class (the independent variable), and each mediator must also predict depression (the dependent variable). Then, when social class and potential mediators are entered into regression together, the relationship between social class (X) and depression (Y) should no longer exist. Testing showed that perceived physical difficulties do not mediate the relationship between social class and depression. The mediation was incomplete since social class still independently affects depression (Weil, 2007).

Moderating variables are those that interact with the independent variables to produce different outcomes in the dependent variables. In moderation, the relationship between the independent and dependent variables changes across levels of the moderator. Age was tested as a moderator in a study of the relationship of neuroticism (anxiety or distress) and physical functioning in older persons (Canada, Stephan, Jaconelli & Duberstein, 2014). Initially, neuroticism was found to be significantly and negatively associated with physical functioning, meaning that the more that anxiety was reported, the worse that physical functioning was reported. The roles of three age groups (young age group, middle age group, and old age group) were tested as moderators in this neuroticism → physical-functioning relationship. The neuroticism → physical-functioning relationship varied with the interactions, across each age group, by level of age in each of the two samples. In both samples, the neuroticism → physical-functioning relationship was only significant for the interaction with older age groups.

Longitudinal designs, fixing the ordering of variables in time, are one way to address causal ordering in research design. A (fixed) panel design follows the same group of people throughout time periods (or waves), best establishing causal changes within those studied. The Longitudinal Studies of Aging (LSOAs) is an example because it is a "collaborative project of National Center for Health Statistics and the National Institute on Aging . . . a multi-cohort study of persons 70+ designed to measure changes in the health, functional status, living arrangements, and health services utilization of two cohorts of Americans as they move into and through the oldest ages" (http://www.cdc.gov/nchs/lsoa.htm). For a list of additional age-based datasets, see this book's companion website.

Gerontological longitudinal studies have examined older women's falls and fall-related effects in a 12-year, fixed-panel design using three-year intervals (Peeters, Geeske, Jones, Byles & Dobson, 2015). Other researchers used longitudinal designs to examine older persons' self-perceived health after a health crisis at six-month and 2.5-year time periods (Wolff, Schüz, Ziegelmann, Warner & Wurm, 2015). Using the National Social Life, Health, and Aging Project, researchers looked at mental-health changes over two waves (Payne, Hedberg, Kozloski, Dale & McClintock, 2014). Researchers examined two waves of the National Comorbidity Survey (over 10 years) to see the effects of military war service earlier in life to predict later-life post-traumatic stress disorder (Sachs-Ericsson, Joiner, Cougle, Stanley & Sheffler, 2015). Other researchers examined seven waves of the Health and Retirement Study to create ADL trajectories (Martin, Zimmer & Lee, 2015).

While **repeated cross-sectional designs** (with different people at each study interval) mimic longitudinal approaches, they do not track the same people over time, which impacts causality. Some call repeated cross-sectionality "not-quite-longitudinal designs" (Menard, 2002).

However, repeated cross-sectional designs may have higher response rates than longitudinal studies and reflect trends over time. Repeated cohort design includes those using multiple General Social Survey (GSS) waves to examine older persons' views of cohabitation (Brown & Wright, 2016). Researchers have conducted cross-sectional studies of GLBT elders and self-rated quality of life (Fredriksen-Goldsen, Kim, Shiu, Goldsen & Emlet, 2015) and active identity profiles of older persons (Morrow-Howell, Putnam, Lee, Greenfield, Inoue & Chen, 2014). Cross-sectional design was used to examine activity levels and related well-being for those 50 years of age and older (Matz-Costa, Besen, James & Pitt-Catsouphes, 2014). But researchers using both cross-sectional and longitudinal approaches found differing results when studying age-related changes in the older persons' brain functioning (Pfefferbaum & Sullivan, 2015).

Generating and Managing Data: Primary Data and Secondary Data

To collect or not to collect one's own data—that is the question. Sometimes a researcher uses an existing dataset rather than collecting his or her own data. **Secondary data analysis** is a form of research in which the data collected and processed by one researcher are reanalyzed—often for a different purpose—by another. This is especially appropriate in the case of survey data. Data archives are repositories or libraries for the storage and distribution of data for secondary analysis. This method of analysis extracts knowledge that was not the original focus of the survey and uses new research questions and novel interpretation of existing data. Advantages of secondary analysis of data include low cost, less time spent on data collection, expertise of original data collectors, reinterpretation of the data, and exploration of missed opportunities in the existing data. Disadvantages of secondary analysis of data include the availability or accessibility of the data, a need to be able to read and recode the data from its original form, and differences in coding of the data from what is stated in its documentation. There are larger issues of validity (does the data match your research question?) and amounts and ways the original investigators handled missing data. Examples of secondary data analysis include Ageing and Retirement in Europe and the Organisation for Economic Co-operation and Development analysis of the Survey of Health that collected older persons' preferences in health care from 14 countries (Mair, Quiñones & Pasha, 2015). See Box 5.2 for some questions to ask when working with secondary data and Box 5.3 for an example of issues in secondary analysis of the Women's Health and Aging Study. For data-warehouse options for existing datasets about older persons, see online resources in this book's companion website.

Box 5.2 Questions to Ask When Working with Secondary Data

Who collected the data?
Why were they collected?
Where were they collected?
When were they collected? Were they timely?
What was the sampling strategy (probability, non-probability)?
What was the unit of analysis?
What was the major research question? Hypothesis(es)?
How were they collected?
What was the response rate?
Was the respondent the older adult, or was a proxy/other person providing answers for the older person?
Which questions did the respondents refuse to answer? Which respondents did not answer? Any trends in refused questions?
What types of questions were asked?
What were the actual questions asked? (See the codebook or measures document.)
Were the data cleaned? Are there synthetic data?
How did they handle missing data?
Are the data relevant to your research questions?
Do the variables match?
What about conceptualization and operationalization?
What is the data format (SAS, SPSS, ASCII)? What is the data structure?
What are your resources for data retrieval? And your technical skill?
What about ethical considerations, such as confidentiality?
Who paid for it (e.g., government, individual, group, Older Americans Act [OAA], Area Agency on Aging [AAA], Association for the Advancement of Retired Persons [AARP] etc.)?

Box 5.3 The Use of Data in Secondary Analysis: The Women's Health and Aging Study

The Women's Health and Aging Study: Health and Social Characteristics of Older Women with Disability

- A random, age-stratified sample of 1,002 women, 65 years of age and older, living in a community setting
- Conducted by the Epidemiology, Demography, and Biometry Program of the National Institutes of Health and Aging at the Johns Hopkins Medical Center
- From the Health Care Financing Administration's (HCFA) Medicare files from 1992 to 1995, Baltimore, MD

Participants:

- Women: stratified in three groups (65–74, 75–84, 85+)
- Score of 18 or higher on the Mini-Mental State Exam (MMSE)
- Functional limitations as defined by the WHAS researchers: difficulty with at least one or more tasks in two or more of four functional domains used in the screening—mobility/exercise tolerance, upper extremity ability, ADLs, and IADLs
- Completed 39 separate performance-based tests and physical exams conducted by a study nurse or interviewer

Reasons for selection and major WHAS-1 advantages:

- Distinctive in use of 39 performance-based measures
- Performance-based tests used commonly used measures and standard instruments with trained observers
- Performance-based measures can be compared to self-rated measures (more typically available in the past)
- Addresses the ongoing debate within the field of gerontology about performance-based measures as the "gold standard"
- Oversampled by race
- Stratified by age group
- Used an age-based measure for depression

Getting the data:

- WHAS Data Acquisition System differed in projected timelines and receipt of data
- Once the data were received: re-conceptualization of helpers/social networks, and coding and tracking measures over time was noted

WHAS-1 disadvantages:

- Missing data on key variables of interest, such as exclusion criteria for performance-based tests
- Pre-existing conditions in the study protocols included paralysis, being bed-bound, having limb amputations, having major joint/hip surgery within the prior three months, and having an active cardiac condition
- The tests affected by pre-existing conditions: hip flexion test (22%), knee-extension tests (18%), the Perdue pegboard (14%)

- Income: codebook, ordinal categories; data as actual dollar amounts, in original sample; 38% missing
- Rare population with heterogeneity
- Women are included because they have difficulty with at least one task in two or more of four possible functional domains—exercise tolerance/mobility, upper-extremity strength, ADL tasks (self-care), and IADL tasks (higher functioning)—yet are functional enough to remain in a community setting
- The sample consists of all women and contains an oversampling of African-American women and those 85+ as compared to the general 65+ population
- The distributions of income and education also have increased heterogeneity present in sample by age cohort
- The general use of the performance-based data is difficult for others to reproduce
- Latter waves were collected with varying sample sizes
- Missing data coded in many differing ways
- Questionnaire, codebook, and journal articles differ in variables' response choices

Note: Based on my presentation in the Applied Statistics and Research Methods (ASRM) Colloquium Series, University of Northern Colorado, March 23, 2011.

This chapter, the first of two quantitative chapters, was designed to provide an overview of the quantitative design options. The chapter reviewed a brief history of the role of quantitative studies in gerontological journals and the key elements needed in setting up a solid foundation for a quantitative research study. Each quantitative design type (surveys, the causal comparative method, correlation, pre-testing/post-testing and experimental designs, structured observation, and single-case research) was described and critiqued. Sections took the reader through the steps of study design: defining the study's purpose (to describe, predict, evaluate, or explore) and matching it to one of the quantitative design types (surveys, the causal comparative method, correlation, pre-testing/post-testing and experimental designs, structured observation, and single-case research). Examples of published peer-reviewed journal articles were provided to illustrate how each design has been used in gerontology. The chapter included ways to decide upon units of analysis and probability-based and non-probability-based sampling methods. Decision-making suggestions for defining variables, establishing reliability and validity, and establishing causality were provided for the researcher. Revisiting issues of age-period-cohort, this chapter included the role of longitudinal design in addressing these issues. Extra features about concerns when writing good survey questions and how to explore secondary analysis of data as options were outlined with applied examples included. Tables were provided so the reader can see how sensory and cognitive age-related changes related to the use of quantitative methods. The chapter concluded with data collection and management, which will be picked up in the next chapter.

Discussion Questions

- Discuss an example of a research question, project, or setting when each of the quantitative designs would be most appropriate: self-administered survey (often done by mail, or via the Internet/online), telephone survey, face-to-face interview-style survey, single-case study, pre-testing/post-testing (experimental design), causal comparative, correlation, and structured observation.

- Using Tables 5.3 and 5.4, discuss some issues that arise from the application of quantitative research methods with older persons in the real world. Provide some examples about how normative age-related changes impact administration of specific quantitative methods.
- How do age-related sensory changes impact each mode of survey delivery (mail/online, face-to-face, and telephone)?
- How viable are social media and online options for research with persons 65 years of age and older? What factors should a researcher consider when using these methods with this population?
- Why would a gerontological researcher choose to use a secondary analysis of data approach?
- Design a study that seeks to establish causality of social support and happiness for persons 85 years of age and over. What steps are needed to establish causal order of social support and happiness? Then, discuss ways you would test for size and quality of social networks as mediators or moderating variables.
- Explain why age-period-cohort is an issue in gerontology. Which type of design best addresses age? Period? Cohort concerns?
- Researchers using both cross-sectional and longitudinal approaches found differing results when studying age-related changes in older persons' brain functioning. Cross-sectional studies showed greater rates of decline than longitudinal studies. Explain some possible reasons for these different findings by design type.

Bibliography

Acheson, A. (2010). "Sample size." In N. J. Salkind (Ed.), *Encyclopedia of research design* (Vol. 3, pp. 1299–1301). Thousand Oaks, CA: Sage Reference.

Albert, S. M., Bear-Lehman, J., Burkhardt, A., Merete-Roa, B., Noboa-Lemonier, R., & Teresi, J. (2006). Variation in sources of clinician-rated and self-rated instrumental activities of daily living disability. *Journals of Gerontology, 61A*, 826–831.

American Psychological Association. (2010). *Publication manual of the American Psychological Association* (6th ed., 2nd printing [corr. rev.] ed.). Washington, DC: American Psychological Association.

Applegate, W. B., Blass, J. P., & Williams, T. F. (1990). Instruments for the functional assessment of older patients. *New England Journal of Medicine, 322*(17), 1207–1214.

Babbie, E. R. (1992). *The practice of social research* (6th ed.). Belmont, CA: Wadsworth.

Bargh, J. A., Chen, M., & Burrows, L. (1996). Automaticity of social behavior: Direct effects of trait construct and stereotype activation on action. *Journal of Personality and Social Psychology, 71*(2), 230.

Baron, R. M., & Kenny, D. A. (1986). The moderator-mediator variable distinction in social psychological research: Conceptual, strategic and statistical considerations. *Journal of Personality and Social Psychology, 51*, 1173–1182.

Berger, M. L., Dreyer, N., Anderson, F., Towse, A., Sedrakyan, A., & Normand, S. L. (2012). Prospective observational studies to assess comparative effectiveness: The ISPOR good research practices task force report. *Value in Health, 15*(2), 217–230.

Boyer, W. (2010). "Quantitative single-case research design." In A. J. Mills, G. Durepos, & E. Wiebe (Eds.), *Encyclopedia of case study research* (pp. 765–767). Thousand Oaks, CA: Sage Publications Inc.

Brewer, E. W., & Kuhn, J. (2010). "Causal-comparative design." In N. J. Salkind (Ed.), *Encyclopedia of research design* (Vol. 1, pp. 124–131). Thousand Oaks, CA: Sage Reference.

Brown, S. L., & Wright, M. R. (2016). Older adults' attitudes toward cohabitation: Two decades of change. *The Journals of Gerontology Series B: Psychological Sciences and Social Sciences, 71*(4), 755–764. doi:10.1093/geronb/gbv053.

Bryant, C., Bei, B., Gilson, K. M., Komiti, A., Jackson, H., & Judd, F. (2016). Antecedents of attitudes to aging: A study of the roles of personality and well-being. *The Gerontologist, 56*(2), 256–265. doi:10.1093/geront/gnu041.

Canada, B., Stephan, Y., Jaconelli, A., & Duberstein, P. R. (2016). The moderating effect of chronological age on the relation between neuroticism and physical functioning: Cross-sectional evidence from two French samples.

The Journals of Gerontology Series B: Psychological Sciences and Social Sciences, 71(1), 35–40. doi:10.1093/geronb/gbu083

Carlson, E. (2008). *The lucky few: Between the greatest generation and the Baby Boom.* Dordrecht and London: Springer.

Castle, N. G., & Ferguson-Rome, J. C. (2015). Influence of nurse aide absenteeism on nursing home quality. *The Gerontologist, 55*(4), 605–615. doi:10.1093/geront/gnt167.

Christensen, K., Thinggaard, M., Oksuzyan, A., Steenstrup, T., Andersen-Ranberg, K., Jeune, B., & Vaupel, J. W. (2013). Physical and cognitive functioning of people older than 90 years: A comparison of two Danish cohorts born 10 years apart. *The Lancet, 382*, 1507–1513.

Connidis, I. A. (2005). Letter to the editor: Qualitative and quantitative research methods. *The Journals of Gerontology Series B: Psychological Sciences and Social Sciences, 60*(6), S342.

Cooper, B., Glaesser, J., Gomm, R., & Hammersley, M. (2012). *Challenging the qualitative-quantitative divide: Explorations in case-focused causal analysis.* New York and London: Bloomsbury Publishing.

Cotten, S., Ford, G., Ford, S., & Hale, T. (2014). Internet use and depression among retired older adults in the United States: A longitudinal analysis. *Journals of Gerontology Series B: Psychological Sciences and Social Sciences, 69*(5), 763–771. doi:10.1093/geronb/gbu018

Creswell, J. W. (2014). *Research design: Qualitative, quantitative, and mixed methods approaches* (4th ed.). Thousand Oaks, CA: Sage Publications.

Dale, A., Arber, S., & Procter, M. (2004). "A sociological perspective on secondary analysis." In C. Seale (Ed.), *Social research methods* (pp. 137–159). New York: Routledge.

Desrosières, A. (1998). *The politics of large numbers: A history of statistical reasoning.* Cambridge, MA: Harvard University Press.

Doyen, S., Klein, O., Pichon, C. L., & Cleeremans, A. (2012). Behavioral priming: It's all in the mind, but whose mind. *PLoS ONE, 7*(1), e29081

Earp, B., & Everett, J. (October 25, 2015). How to fix psychology's replication crisis. *The Chronicle Review.* Retrieved from http://chronicle.com/article/How-to-Fix-Psychology-s/233857

Egel, A. L., & Barthold, C. H. (2010). Single subject design and analysis. In G. R. Hancock & R. O. Mueller (Eds.), *The reviewer's guide to quantitative methods in the social sciences* (pp. 357–370). New York: Routledge.

Elder Jr, G. H., & Giele, J. Z. (Eds.). (2009). *The craft of life course research.* New York: Guilford Press.

Elliot, A., Cohen, L. W., Reed, D., Nolet, K., & Zimmerman, S. (2014). A "recipe" for culture change? Findings from the THRIVE survey of culture change adopters. *The Gerontologist, 54*(Suppl 1), S17–S24.

Fredriksen-Goldsen, K. I., Kim, H., Shiu, C., Goldsen, J., & Emlet, C. A. (2015). Successful aging among LGBT older adults: Physical and mental health-related quality of life by age group. *The Gerontologist, 55*(1), 154–168. doi:10.1093/geront/gnu081

Fung, H. H., Li, T., Zhang, X., Sit, I. M. I., Cheng, S., & Isaacowitz, D. M. (2015). Positive portrayals of old age do not always have positive consequences. *The Journals of Gerontology Series B: Psychological Sciences and Social Sciences, 70*(6), 913.

Galik, E., Resnick, B., Hammersla, M., & Brightwater, J. (2014). Optimizing function and physical activity among nursing home residents with dementia: Testing the impact of function-focused care. *The Gerontologist, 54*(6), 930–943.

Gellis, Z. D., Kenaley, B., McGinty, J., Bardelli, E., Davitt, J., & Ten Have, T. (2012). Outcomes of a telehealth intervention for homebound older adults with heart or chronic respiratory failure: A randomized controlled trial. *The Gerontologist, 52*(4), 541–552.

Gentry, R. A., & Fisher, J. E. (2007). Facilitating conversation in elderly persons with Alzheimer's disease. *Clinical Gerontologist, 31*(2), 77–98.

Graham, J. E., Karmarkar, A. M., & Ottenbacher, K. J. (2012). Small sample research designs for evidence-based rehabilitation: Issues and methods. *Archives of Physical Medicine and Rehabilitation, 93*(Suppl 8), S111–S116. Retrieved from http://doi.org/10.1016/j.apmr.2011.12.017

Greenwood, N. (2009). Reflections of a researcher interviewing older people. *Nursing Older People, 21*(7), 30–31.

Guralnik, J. M., Fried, L. P., Simonsick, E. M., Kasper, J. D., & Lafferty, M. E. (Eds.). (1995). *The women's health and aging study: Health and social characteristics of older women with disability.* Bethesda, MD: National Institute on Aging, NIH Pub. No. 95–4009.

Hawkley, L., Kocherginsky, M., Wong, J., Kim, J., & Cagney, K. (2014). Missing data in wave 2 of NSHAP: Prevalence, predictors, and recommended treatment. *Journals of Gerontology Series B: Psychological Sciences and Social Sciences, 69*(Suppl 2), S38–S50. doi:10.1093/geronb/gbu044

Herrera, A. P., Snipes, S. A., King, D. W., Torres-Vigil, I., Goldberg, D. S., & Weinberg, A. D. (2010). Disparate inclusion of older adults in clinical trials: Priorities and opportunities for policy and practice change. *American Journal of Public Health, 100*(S1), S105–S112. doi:10.2105/AJPH.2009.162982

Hidalgo, J., & ANVITAD Group. (2011). Prevention of falls and fractures in old people by administration of calcium and vitamin D: A randomized clinical trial. *BMC Public Health, 11*(1), 910–910. doi:10.1186/1471–2458–11–910
Hutchinson, S. (2015). Sample size recommendations email. Personal correspondence.
Judd, C. M., & Kenny, D. A. (1981). Process analysis: Estimating mediation in treatment evaluations. *Evaluation Review, 5*, 602–619.
Kang, Y., Meng, H., & Miller, N. A. (2011). Rurality and nursing home quality: Evidence from the 2004 national nursing home survey. *The Gerontologist, 51*(6), 761–773. doi:10.1093/geront/gnr065
Kiecolt, K. J., & Nathan, L. E. (1985). *Secondary analysis of survey data*. Beverly Hills, CA: Sage Publications.
König, S., & Glück, J. (2014). "Gratitude is with me all the time": How gratitude relates to wisdom. *The Journals of Gerontology Series B: Psychological Sciences and Social Sciences, 69*(5), 655–666.
Kratochwill, T. R., Hitchcock, J., Horner, R. H., Levin, J. R., Odom, S. L., Rindskopf, D. M., & Shadish, W. R. (2010). *Single-case designs technical documentation*. What Works Clearinghouse. Retrieved from http://ies.ed.gov/ncee/wwc/documentsum.aspx?sid=229
Kratochwill, T. R., & Levin, J. R. (2010). Enhancing the scientific credibility of single-case intervention research: Randomization to the rescue. *Psychological Methods, 15*(2), 124–144. doi:10.1037/a0017736
Longino, C. F. (2005). Putting a human face on gerontological research: Identity issues. *Journals of Gerontology: Series B, 60*(3), 117–117. doi:10.1093/geronb/60.3.S117
Ma, F., Wu, T., Zhao, J., Han, F., Marseglia, A., Liu, H., & Huang, G. (2016). Effects of 6-month folic acid supplementation on cognitive function and blood biomarkers in mild cognitive impairment: A randomized controlled trial in China. *The Journals of Gerontology Series A: Biological Sciences and Medical Sciences, 71*(10), 1376–1383. doi:10.1093/gerona/glv183
Mahato, R. K., Narayan, A., & Kumar, P. S. (2013). Efficacy of balance and mobility exercises on gait speed and energy expenditure in ageing adults: A quasi-experimental interventional clinical trial. *Indian Journal of Physiotherapy and Occupational Therapy, 7*(4), 172.
Mair, C. A., Quiñones, A. R., & Pasha, M. A. (2016). Care preferences among middle-aged and older adults with chronic disease in Europe: Individual health care needs and national health care infrastructure. *The Gerontologist, 56*(4), 687–701. doi:10.1093/geront/gnu119
Hughes, S. L., Marquez, D. X., Moni, G., Nguyen, H. Q., Desai, P., & Jones, D. L. (2011). Physical activity and older adults: Expert consensus for a new research agenda. *The Gerontologist, 51*(6), 822–832.
Martin, L. G., Zimmer, Z., & Lee, J. (2015). Foundations of activity of daily living trajectories of older Americans. *The Journals of Gerontology Series B: Psychological Sciences and Social Sciences*. doi:10.1093/geronb/gbv074.
Matthew, D., & Sutton, C. (2004). *Social research*. Thousand Oaks, CA: Sage Publications Inc.
Matz-Costa, C., Besen, E., James, J., & Pitt-Catsouphes, M. (2014). Differential impact of multiple levels of productive activity engagement on psychological well-being in middle and later life. *Gerontologist, 54*, 277–289.
McCambridge, J., Witton, J., & Elbourne, D. (2014). Systematic review of the Hawthorne effect: New concepts are needed to study research participation effects. *Journal of Clinical Epidemiology, 67*(3), 267–277. doi:10.1016/j.jclinepi.2013.08.015
Menard, S. (2002). *Longitudinal research* (2nd ed.). Thousand Oaks, CA: Sage Publications Inc.
Moeyaert, M., Ugille, M., Ferron, J. M., Beretvas, S. N., & Van den Noortgate, W. (2014). The influence of the design matrix on treatment effect estimates in the quantitative analyses of single-subject experimental design research. *Behavior Modification, 38*(5), 665–704.
Morgan, L., & Kunkel, S. (2006). *Aging, society, and the life course*. New York: Springer.
Morrow-Howell, N., Putnam, M., Lee, Y., Greenfield, J., Inoue, M., & Chen, H. (2014). An investigation of activity profiles of older adults. *Journals of Gerontology Series B: Psychological Sciences and Social Sciences, 69*(5), 809–821. doi:10.1093/geronb/gbu002
Mulaik, S. A. (2009). *Linear causal modeling with structural equations*. Hoboken: CRC Press.
Neuman, L. (2007). *Basics of social research: Qualitative and quantitative approaches*. Boston: Pearson.
O'Brien, E., Konrath, S. H., Grühn, D., & Hagen, A. L. (2013). Empathic concern and perspective taking: Linear and quadratic effects of age across the adult life span. *The Journals of Gerontology Series B: Psychological Sciences and Social Sciences, 68*(2), 168–175.
O'Muircheartaigh, C., English, N., Pedlow, S., & Kwok, P. (2014). Sample design, sample augmentation, and estimation for wave 2 of the NSHAP. *Journals of Gerontology Series B: Psychological Sciences and Social Sciences, 69*(Suppl 2), S15–S26. doi:10.1093/geronb/gbu053
Open Science Collaboration. (2015). Estimating the reproducibility of psychological science. *Science, 349*(6251), 943–953. doi:10.1126/science.aac4716
Payne, C., Hedberg, E., Kozloski, M., Dale, W., & McClintock, M. (2014). Using and interpreting mental health measures in the national social life, health, and aging project. *Journals of Gerontology Series B: Psychological Sciences and Social Sciences, 69*(Suppl 2), S99–S116.

Peel, N., & Wilson, C. (2008). Frail older people as participants in research. *Educational Gerontology, 34*(5), 407–417.

Peeters, G. M. E. E. Geeske, Jones, M., Byles, J., & Dobson, A. J. (2015). Long-term consequences of noninjurious and injurious falls on well-being in older women. *The Journals of Gerontology: Series A, Biological Sciences and Medical Sciences, 70*(12), 1519.

Petersen, L., Christensen, K., & Kragstrup, J. (2010). Lipid-lowering treatment to the end? A review of observational studies and RCTs on cholesterol and mortality in 80+-year olds. *Age and Ageing, 39*(6), 674–680. doi:10.1093/ageing/afq129

Pfefferbaum, A., & Sullivan, E. (2015). Cross-sectional versus longitudinal estimates of age-related changes in the adult brain: Overlaps and discrepancies. *Neurobiology of Aging, 36*(9), 2563–2567. doi:10.1016/j.neurobiolaging.2015.05.005

Porter, E. (2007). Scales and tales: Older women's difficulty with daily tasks. *Journal of Gerontology: Social Sciences, 62B*, S153–S159.

Pruchno, R. A., Bowers, B. J., Castle, N. G., Gonyea, J. G., Kivnick, H., Meeks, S., & Williamson, J. B. (2015). Is gerontology in crisis? *The Gerontologist, 55*(6), 893. doi:10.1093/geront/gnv141

Pruchno, R. A., & Wilson-Genderson, M. (2015). A longitudinal examination of the effects of early influences and midlife characteristics on successful aging. *The Journals of Gerontology Series B: Psychological Sciences and Social Sciences, 70*(6), 850–859. doi:10.1093/geronb/gbu046

Ramscar, M., Shaoul, C., Baayen, R. H., & Tbingen, E. K. U. (2015). *Why many priming results don't (and won't) replicate: A quantitative analysis.* Manuscript, University of Tübingen.

Randall, W. L., Prior, S. M., & Skarborn, M. (2006). How listeners shape what tellers tell: Patterns of interaction in lifestory interviews and their impact on reminiscence by elderly interviewees. *Journal of Aging Studies, 20*(4), 381–396.

Sachs-Ericsson, N., Joiner, T. E., Cougle, J. R., Stanley, I. H., & Sheffler, J. L. (2016). Combat exposure in early adulthood interacts with recent stressors to predict PTSD in aging male veterans. *The Gerontologist, 56*(1), 82. doi:10.1093/geront/gnv036

Särkämö, T., Tervaniemi, M., Laitinen, S., Numminen, A., Kurki, M., Johnson, J. K., & Rantanen, P. (2014). Cognitive, emotional, and social benefits of regular musical activities in early dementia: Randomized controlled study. *The Gerontologist, 54*(4), 634–650.

Schulz, R., Beach, S. R., Matthews, J. T., Courtney, K., Dabbs, A. D. V., & Mecca, L. P. (2016). Caregivers' willingness to pay for technologies to support caregiving. *The Gerontologist, 56*(1), 82. doi:10.1093/geront/gnv036

Schutt, R. K. (2011). *Investigating the social world: The process and practice of research.* Thousand Oaks, CA: Pine Forge Press.

Simonsick, E., Maffeo, C., Rogers, S., Skinner, E., Davis, D., Guralnik, J., Fried, Linda P., & WHAS Research Group. (1997). Methodology and feasibility of a home-based examination in disabled older women: The women's health and aging study. *Journals of Gerontology Series A: Biological Sciences and Medical Sciences, 52*(5), M264–M274. doi:10.1093/gerona/52A.5.M264

Smith, E. (2008). *Using secondary data in educational and social research.* New York: Open University Press.

Smith, J. (2012). Single-case experimental designs: A systematic review of published research and current standards. *Psychological Methods, 17*(4), 510–550. doi:10.1037/a0029312

Sun, F., Gao, X., & Coon, D. W. (2015). Perceived threat of Alzheimer's disease among Chinese American older adults: The role of Alzheimer's disease literacy. *The Journals of Gerontology Series B: Psychological Sciences and Social Sciences, 70*(2), 245–255. doi:10.1093/geronb/gbt095

Thomas, J. C., & Hersen, M. (2011). *Understanding research in clinical and counseling psychology* (2nd ed.). (pp. 479–480). New York: Routledge Ltd. doi:10.4324/9780203831700

Tourangeau, R., & Plewes, T. J. (Eds.). (2013). *Nonresponse in social science surveys: A research agenda.* Retrieved from http://www.nap.edu/openbook.php?record_id=18293

Trzesniewski, K., & Lucas, R. (2008). *Secondary data analysis: An introduction for psychologists.* Washington, DC: American Psychological Association.

Uysal-Bozkir, O., Fokkema, T. MacNeil-Vroomen, J., van Tilburg, T., & Rooij, S. (2015). Translation and validation of the De Jong Gierveld Loneliness Scale among older migrants living in the Netherlands, *The Journals of Gerontology Series B: Psychological Sciences and Social Science, 70*(2), 245–255. doi:10.1093/geronb/gbt095

van Herk, R., van Dijk, M., Biemold, N., Tibboel, D., Baar, F., & de Wit, R. (2009). Assessment of pain: Can caregivers or relatives rate pain in nursing home residents? *Journal of Clinical Nursing, 18*, 2478–2485.

Victor, C., Westerhof, G., & Bond, J. (2007). "Researching ageing." In J. Bond, P. Coleman, & S. Peace (Eds.), *Ageing in society* (pp. 83–112). London, UK: Sage Publications.

Walsh, J. E., Lane, S. J., & Troyer, J. L. (2014). Impact of medication aide use on skilled nursing facility quality. *The Gerontologist, 54*(6), 976–988.

Weil, J. (2007). *Social class and depression: A study of older women with functional limitations living in the community.* ProQuest Dissertations Publishing.

Weil, J. (2015). Applying research methods to a gerontological population: Matching data collection to characteristics of older persons. *Educational Gerontology, 41*(10), 723–742. doi:10.1080/03601277.2015.1048172

Weil, J., Hutchinson, S., & Traxler, K. (2014). Exploring the relationships among performance- based functional ability, self-rated disability, perceived instrumental support, and depression: A structural equation model analysis. *Research on Aging, 36*(6), 683–706.

Wenger, C. (1999). Advantages gained by combining qualitative and quantitative data in a longitudinal study. *Journal of Aging Studies, 13*, 369–376.

Westerhof, G. J., Bohlmeijer, E. T., & McAdams, D. P. (2015). The relation of ego integrity and despair to personality traits and mental health. *The Journals of Gerontology Series B: Psychological Sciences and Social Sciences, 2015*, 1–9. doi:10.1093/geronb/gbv062

Whitebird, R. R., Kreitzer, M., Crain, A. L., Lewis, B. A., Hanson, L. R., & Enstad, C. J. (2013). Mindfulness-based stress reduction for family caregivers: A randomized controlled trial. *The Gerontologist, 53*(4), 676–686.

Wiegand, M. A., Troyer, A. K., Gojmerac, C., & Murphy, K. J. (2013). Facilitating change in health-related behaviors and intentions: A randomized controlled trial of a multidimensional memory program for older adults. *Aging & Mental Health, 17*(7), 806–815.

Wolff, J. K., Schüz, B., Ziegelmann, J. P., Warner, L. M., & Wurm, S. (2015). Short-term buffers, but long-term suffers? Differential effects of negative self-perceptions of aging following serious health events. *The Journals of Gerontology Series B: Psychological Sciences and Social Sciences, 2015*, 1–7. doi: 10.1093/geronb/gbv058

Wunsch, K., Weigelt, M., & Stöckel, T. (2015). Anticipatory motor planning in older adults. *The Journals of Gerontology Series B: Psychological Sciences and Social Sciences, 2015*, 1–11. doi:10.1093/geronb/gbv078

Zurlo, K. A., Yoon, W., & Kim, H. (2014). Unsecured consumer debt and mental health outcomes in middle-aged and older Americans. *The Journals of Gerontology Series B: Psychological Sciences and Social Sciences, 69*(3), 461–469.

6
Quantitative Data Analysis and Evaluation

This chapter follows the preceding quantitative chapter, which served as a guide to the creation of quantitative research design for a study and ended with ways to collect data. This chapter begins with decisions about data-analysis approaches. It includes descriptive and inferential options. It offers researchers ways to visually depict data and describe one variable in a study with measures of central tendency and variation. Ways to use bivariate measures of association and statistical analysis for multiple variables in a study are covered. Gerontological examples from published studies are provided to illustrate all analysis methods discussed. Flowcharts assist in choosing appropriate quantitative statistical tests. Ways of ensuring quality and reliability and validity in analysis are discussed with an age-based depression example. The chapter includes a section about how to develop new measures for use with older populations. The role of a researcher as part of a quantitative research team and unique ethical considerations of quantitative designs with older persons are presented. The chapter concludes with detailed steps in the process of writing up and evaluating quantitative work. Steps include stating a clear research question and/or hypotheses; operationalizing variables; setting significance levels as part of statistical testing; and describing sampling method and participants, issues that occur in data collection, aspects of data cleaning and management, and presentation of findings.

Analytic Approach to Data Analysis

Deciding how to present data is one of the first steps in the data-analysis process. A **descriptive approach**, or descriptive research, seeks to describe, or summarize, the sample's characteristics using variables. **Variables** are the way concepts are operationalized or discussed in a study. Variables must have values that vary. If a researcher is interested in examining a variable in great detail—but does not want to test for relationships with other variables or identify a cause-and-effect relationship with that variable—descriptive statistics are best. **Descriptive statistics** can depict one variable (**univariate**) in a **frequency distribution** (or table that summarized counts in each category of a variable). Box 6.1 is an example of a frequency distribution for the number of siblings for a sample of rural persons who are 65 years of age and older—by each number of sibling. Box 6.2 presents the frequency of siblings—this time grouped in categories.

Box 6.1 Ungrouped Frequency Distribution of Number of Siblings for Rural Persons 65 Years of Age and Older

Number of Children, Reported	Frequency	Percent	Valid Percent	Cumulative Percent
0	1	4.2	4.2	4.2
1	6	25.0	25.0	29.2
2	5	20.8	20.8	50.0
3	1	4.2	4.2	54.2
4	3	12.5	12.5	66.7
5	2	8.3	8.3	75.0
6	1	4.2	4.2	79.2
7	2	8.3	8.3	87.5
9	1	4.2	4.2	91.7
12	1	4.2	4.2	95.8
14	1	4.2	4.2	100.0
Total	24	100.0	100.0	

Box 6.2 Grouped Frequency Distribution of Number of Siblings for Rural Persons 65 Years of Age and Older

Category	Frequency	Percent	Valid Percent	Cumulative Percent
None	1	4.2	4.2	4.2
1 or 2 siblings	11	45.8	45.8	50.0
3 to 5 siblings	6	25.0	25.0	75.0
6 or more siblings	6	25.0	25.0	100.0
Total	24	100.0	100.0	

Visual displays or depictions of data (such as bar charts or histograms) are also common in descriptive statistics. Figures 6.1 and 6.2 present the number-of-siblings data as a bar chart and then a pie chart.

A variable can also be summarized using **measures of central tendency** (such as the arithmetic mean, median, or mode) or measures of **variation** (such as range and standard deviation). The **arithmetic mean** is the average of all values of the variable. The **median** is the value that divides the distribution in half, and the **mode** is the value, or values, that occur most frequently. The **standard deviation** is used to tell how far values are from the mean, and the **range** shows the spread of scores from lowest to highest. Assigning a measure of central tendency and variations is determined by **level of measurement.** To recap Chapter 5, **nominal variables** are those that are names or labels (e.g., gender, race, ethnicity, geographic location). **Ordinal variables** are those that can be ranked or ordered (e.g., ratings of skilled-care facilities' treatment of residents—low, medium, high—or health as excellent, good, fair,

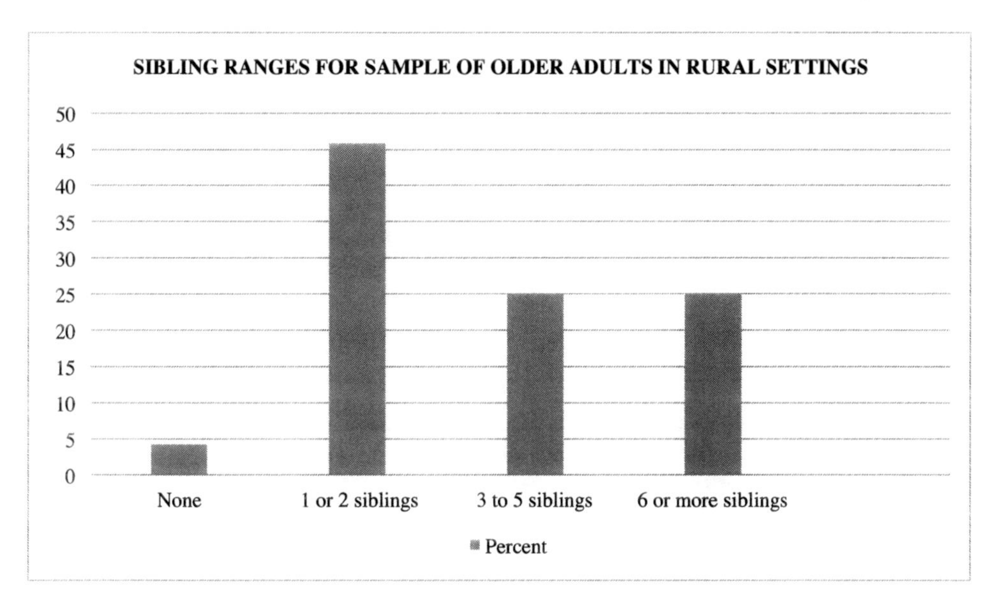

Figure 6.1 Rural Siblings Bar Chart

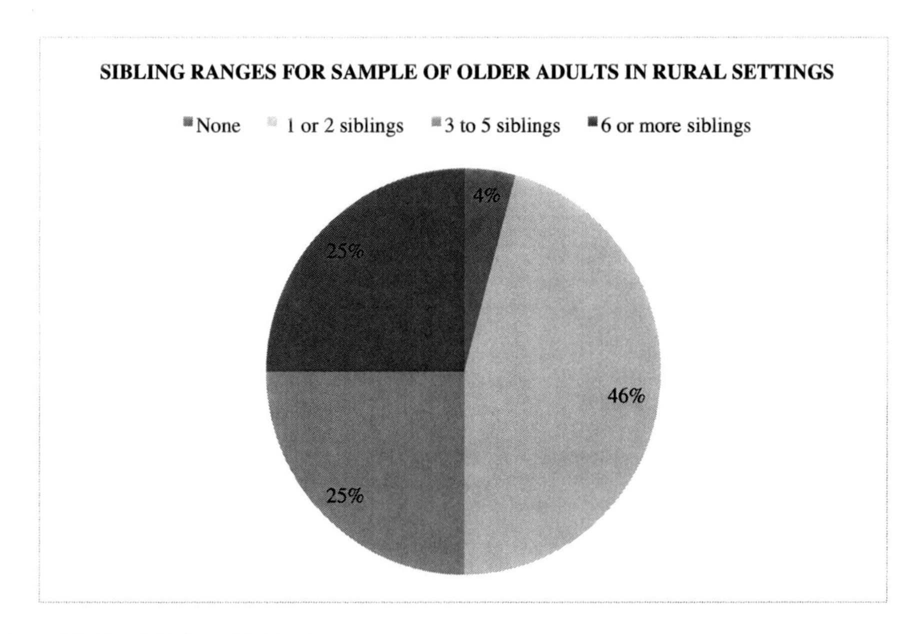

Figure 6.2 Rural Siblings Pie Chart

poor), and **interval-ratio** refers to items with a true zero and equal or fixed distance between items (e.g., age in number of years).

Researchers often want to explore relationships or patterns between two variables. **Cross tabulations** (also called crosstabs) is a **bivariate** approach to look at the relationships between two variables. **Bivariate measures of association** provide a number quantifying the relationship between the two variables for the researcher, and, in some cases, that number provides the strength of the relationship. Like measures of central tendency and variation, bivariate measures of association are based on variables' level of measurement.

Fully understating measures of association is the subject for another book. Table 6.1 is intended to provide an overview for researchers who may want to explore this topic further. Table 6.1 also provides examples of central tendency and variation choices by level of measurement.

In an **inferential** approach, findings from a sample or samples are used to generalize back to the larger population. The most commonly selected type of inferential statistics process is hypothesis testing. A basic, typical **hypothesis statement** with two variables (one independent and one dependent) would be: "If the independent variable increases (or decreases or

Table 6.1 Level of Measurement and Appropriate Bivariate Measures of Association

Level of Measurement	Univariate		Bivariate	
	Measure of Central Tendency	**Measures of Variation**	**Measures of Association**	**Notes**
Nominal	Mode	Index of Qualitative Variation	Phi (Φ) Cramer's *V* Lambda (λ) for Proportional Reduction in Error (PRE) Based	Phi: based Chi-Square (χ^2) Easy to compute appropriate for 2 × 2 bivariate / crosstab tables Values range: 0 (no association) to 1 (perfect association) Cramer's V like Phi but used for larger tables; > than 2 × 2 tables Values range: 0 (no association) to 1 (perfect association) Lambda reduces error by using the independent variable to predict the dependent variable Limitations: Absence of a direct or meaningful interpretation for values between the extremes of 0.00 and 1.00. A Phi of .18 is less than a Phi of .36 but cannot perform mathematical functions with the values
Ordinal	Mode *Median*	Range	Gamma (G) Spearman's rho (r_s)	Gamma (G) can be used for 1 ordinal + 1 interval-ratio level variables Spearman's rho (rs) works best for ordinal-level variables that are "continuous" in form, for tables that have many more than six rows/columns, ranging from 0 (no association) to +/–1.00 (perfect association), uses t-test to interpret
Interval Ratio	Mode Median Arithmetic Mean *Symmetric Distribution:* Mean *Skewed Distribution:* Median or Outliers	Range Standard Deviation	Pearson's *r*, Coefficient of Determination (r^2) Regression, All Types	Pearson's r and the Coefficient of Determination (r^2) indicate strength of the relationship between two variables; a value of 0.0 indicates no linear relationship, and a value of +/–1.00 indicates a perfect linear relationship Regression allows for more than three variables at once

changes), then the dependent variable will increase (or decrease or change)." Hypothesis testing, however, offers two hypotheses. The **null hypothesis** states that there is "no difference" between the groups being tested. The **alternate hypothesis** is where the real relationship between groups is stated. Hypotheses can also predict differences only (with a **two-tailed test**) or direction (with a **one-tailed**). In a two-tailed hypothesis test, the researcher seeks only to find difference between groups tested. In a one-tailed hypothesis test, the alternate hypothesis is making a directional statement about the relationship between the groups tested (e.g., with greater-than or less-than statements; see Banerjee, Chitnis, Jadhav, Bhawalkar & Chaudhury, 2009).

Hypotheses are used to find results within a certain predefined degree of error, or willingness to accept that findings are not based on chance, which is called **a P-value.** Researchers can set P-values (from lowest to highest significance level) at $p \leq 0.10$ (marginal significance), $p \leq 0.05$ (*), $p \leq 0.01$ (**), or $p \leq 0.01$ (***). The lower the P-value, the less likely a relationship is found by chance—or, conversely, the more confident a researcher can be that the relationship he or she finds is not due to chance. P-values are affected by both large and small sample sizes. Larger samples have increased sensitivity to noting differences and may indicate "overstated" significance or find significance that may not exist. Smaller samples, lacking the sensitivity to pick up small differences, may "miss" significant relationships due to smaller size and be unable to distinguish significance that is present.

Type 1 and Type 2 Errors

P-values relate to the chance of making a Type I error. Errors can occur when a researcher makes decisions during hypothesis testing. An **alpha (α) or Type I error** occurs if a researcher rejects the null hypothesis (of "no difference") when it is true. In other words, the researcher finds differences between the sample and populations he or she is testing or two samples he or she is testing—when there is no difference. On the other hand, if a researcher accepts the null hypothesis (of "no difference") when it is false, he or she is making a **beta (β) or Type II error.** Here, researchers find no difference in the sample and populations or two samples they are testing—when there is a difference.

Types of Statistical Tests Using Hypothesis Testing

Chi-square, x^2, tests are widely used to test for significant differences in observed vs. expected values for two groups, since they can be used by variables of all levels of measurement. In aging research, Chi-square, x^2, has been used to test if differences exist in the way syllabi of sociology of aging and syllabi of social-gerontology courses cover the same concepts (Dossey-Newby & Krull, 2005). Chapter 9 includes an interpretation of the quantitative software output for a chi-square test.

Independent t-tests (or two sample t-tests) test hypotheses and look at significant differences in means of two groups or interventions on a dependent variable. Independent t-tests were used to compare groups of older persons on individual dependent variables of gait scores in cognitive, motor, behavioral, and clinical domains (Lord, Galna, Verghese, Coleman, Burn & Rochester, 2013). Independent t-tests examined differences between the groups in individual dependent variables of variety of services recommended, compliance, and service use (Kwak, Montgomery, Kosloski & Lang, 2011). A **paired t-test** uses repeated measure to look for significant differences in a mean for the same group at two different times. A paired t-test is often used for pre- and post-test comparisons. Paired t-tests were used to test gender differences for several health-status indicators (Gold et al., 2002) and caregiver and elder scores on several elements of caregiving at several points in time (Horowitz, Goodman & Reinhardt, 2004).

Basic **analysis of variance (ANOVA)** is like t-testing in its use of group comparisons for hypothesis testing. ANOVA, however, expands the number of groups used in t-testing. ANOVA tests for significant difference in the means of *two or more groups* upon a dependent variable. ANOVA lets a researcher test for "between group" and "within group" differences, or variation, in the samples. ANOVA has been used to test personal characteristics and setting-based elements for several age groups and reading for pleasure (Shake, Shulley & Soto-Freita, 2015). A researcher can choose from different types of ANOVA. For example, a one-way ANOVA has one independent and one dependent variable. Factorial ANOVA focuses on the independent variables with the number before the word as a way to reference the number of independent variables (e.g., a two-way factorial ANOVA has two independent variables). Repeated measures of ANOVA can assess changes between two or more groups over time. Repeated ANOVA was used to test pre- and post-interview moods in groups of older and younger adults (Cheng & Grühn, 2014). **Analysis of covariance (ANCOVA)** is ANOVA controlling for other independent variable as covariate, removing the influence of that variable. ANCOVA designs have been used to control for education when testing factors related to memory impairment (Rosa, Deason, Budson & Gutchess, 2016) and to control for baseline differences in social, emotional, and cognitive effects when testing the relationship of music and dementia (Sarkamo et al., 2014). Table 6.2 offers additional examples of each inferential approach.

Multivariate analysis of variance (MANOVA) is like ANOVA but tests for significant difference in two or more groups upon *two or more/multiple outcome or dependent variables*. **Multivariate analysis of covariance (MANCOVA)** is MANOVA but adds in control or other covariates that might impact the dependent variable. MANOVA was used to test several outcomes (cognition, well-being, and dysfunctional caregiving thoughts) after an intervention for caregivers and care recipients (Rodriguez-Sanchez et al., 2014). MANCOVA tested the impact of psychosocial interventions on emotional and behavioral dementia symptoms for those in skilled care using three covariates (ADLs, mental status, and level of social isolation; Van Haitsma, Curyto, Abbott, Towsley, Spector & Kleban, 2015).

Multiple regression tests for the significant effect of multiple independent variables in predicting variation on a dependent variable. The procedure tests how much each independent variable and, also, how much all independent variables combined contribute to variance in the dependent variable. Multiple regression has been used to identify predictors of loneliness risk in lesbian, gay, and bisexual older adults (Kim & Fredriksen-Goldsen, 2014). In **logistic regression** tests, independent variables significantly predict variation in a *dichotomous* dependent variable. Logistic regression has been used to examine the impact of many independent variables (gender, activities of daily living, living situation, social contact country's view of parent-child relationship, level of social support) and interactions of these independent variables upon the presence of depression in older persons (Djundeva, Mills, Wittek & Steverink, 2015). Logistic regression has been used to identify which nursing-home characteristics are more likely to indicate an environment that has undergone culture change (Grabowski, Elliot, Leitzell, Cohen & Zimmerman, 2014). Logistic regression has also been used to predict short-term mortality risk (risk or no risk) for those in long-term care (Heppenstall, Broad, Boyd, Gott & Connolly, 2015). Logistic designs have tested which features of an older person's social network predict abuse (Schafer & Koltai, 2015) and which characteristics of a widow's life predicted if she would live with her children (Seltzer & Friedman, 2014).

Table 6.2 Choosing Statistical Tests

What do you plan to do?	Predict outcomes:	Tests	Coefficients	Considerations	Example
	x^2	Relationship between variables	x^2, *df*, significance level	Typically thought of as 2×2, but can be expanded to include more variables. Can be performed with variables at all levels of measurement.	Is there a relationship between age (those less than 65 and those 65+) and happiness?
	t-test	Independent t-test tests significant differences of means from two separate groups Paired t-test difference in the means for the same group over time	*F* statistic, *df*, t-value	Typically used in hypothesis testing. Can also be combined with other tests.	Do those less than 65 and those 65+ differ in level of happiness? Does level of happiness differ for those 65+ before and after a meaningful living intervention?
	ANOVA	Basic ANOVA tests for significant differences in two or more means from the same or different groups	*F* statistic or F ratio, *df*	Many design choices, including one-way, factorial, repeated measures, etc. To control for variables (as covariates), use ANCOVA	Do happiness scores (0–100) vary for those for age categories (ages 60–64, 65–74, 75–84, and 85+)?
	MANOVA	MANOVA tests two or more groups on two or more dependent variables	*F* statistic, *df*	Like ANOVA but increases the number of outcomes / dependent variables options To control for variables (as covariates), use MANCOVA	Do happiness scores (0–100) and resilience scores (1–25) vary for those for age categories (ages 60–64, 65–74, 75–84, and 85+)?

(*Continued*)

Table 6.2 (Continued)

What do you plan to do?	Predict outcomes:	Tests	Coefficients	Considerations	Example
	Multiple regression	Tests the impact of multiple independent variables in predicting one dependent variable	R^2, Adjusted R^2, R^2 Change Unstandardized coefficients, standardized coefficients (*Beta*) values	Independent variable can be varied levels of measurement. Variables can be entered in steps or in a hierarchical manner.	Do age, demographic, socio-economic, physical health, mental health, social support, living arrangements, and personality factors predict happiness score?
	Logistic regression	Tests the impact of multiple independent variables in predicting one dichotomous, dependent variable	Log likelihood, odds ratios	The dependent variable must be dichotomous Provides odds ratios of how changes in an independent variable will affect the dependent variable	Do age, demographic, socio-economic, physical health, mental health, social support, living arrangements, and personality factors predict being happy (or not happy)?
	Path analysis	Tests for direct and indirect relationships of continuous variables in a model	Standardized path coefficient	Provides a visual, causal model of relationships tested	What is the relationship between physical functional ability and happiness—testing the relationship of physical health status, mental health status, and social support, as indirect or variables?
Is a visual representation of variables' relationships needed? Is error a risk?	Structural equation modeling	Tests the relationship of independent variables with a dependent variable (direct paths) as well as relationships of variables in the model (indirect) A model of latent variables is created to represent observed/actual variables	Comparative Fit Index (CFI), Root Mean Square Error of Approximation (RMSEA), Tucker-Lewis Index (TLI)	Reduces risk of measurement error in relationships Many/several variables are needed to construct latent variables or main concepts Provides a visual, causal model	What is the relationship between physical functional ability and happiness—testing the relationship of physical health status, mental health status, and social support, as indirect or spurious variables?

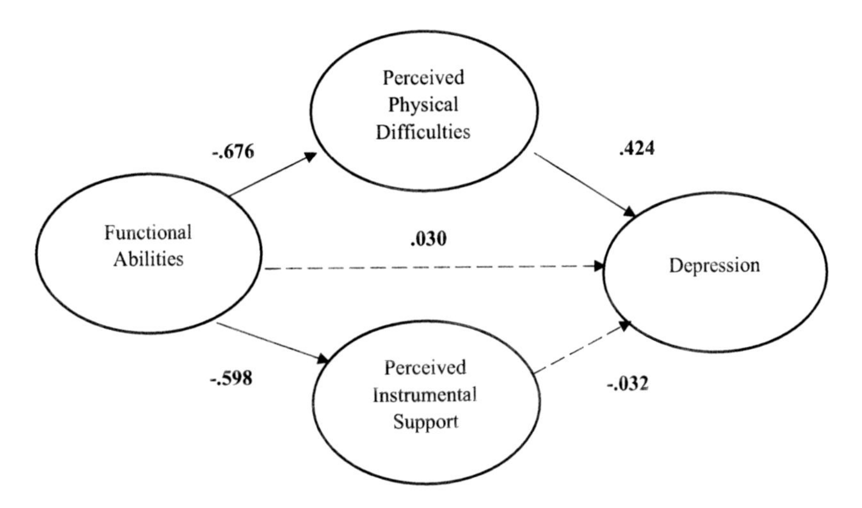

Note: Path coefficients are standardized. Solid lines indicate statistically significant path coefficients, p < .01, and dashed lines indicate nonsignificant path coefficients.

Figure 6.3 Example of an SEM Model

Reprinted from: Weil, J., Hutchinson, S. R. and Traxler, K. (2014). Exploring the relationships among performance-based functional ability, self-rated disability, perceived instrumental support, and depression: A structural equation model analysis. *Research on Aging, 36*(6), 683–706.

Path analysis examines significant indirect and direct relationships between variables and upon the dependent variable. Independent variables are called exogenous, and dependent variables are call endogenous. Path analysis examined the direct relationship between step reaction time in adults 62 years of age and older in relationship to repeated falls, as well as strength, balance ability, and cognition as mediators (Delbaere, Sturnieks, Pijnappels & Lord, 2010). **Structural equation modeling** (SEM) uses several statistical techniques to take many observed variables to create latent variables and test their relationships while reducing measurement error. Researchers have used structural equation modeling to examine the relationship of well-being with older persons who are HIV positive (Porter, Brennan-Ing, Burr, Dugan & Karpiak, 2015). Researchers also used SEM to examine self-rated and performance-based factors associated with depressive symptomology in older women (Weil, Hutchinson & Traxler, 2014). Figure 6.3 provides the relationship of latent variables associated with depression in older women.

Quality in Quantitative Research

Reliability and validity are two key elements of quality in quantitative research. While both are needed for rigor, they are not the same concepts. **Validity** questions whether the right concept is being measured. In other words, is the researcher really measuring the concept that he or she intends to measure? **Reliability** is concerned with whether the measure provides the same results over time.

Accuracy of Measures: Reliability

Reliability refers to stability or consistency of a measure over a brief time interval. One of the most common types of reliability is **test-retest reliability**—that if a researcher administers/

applies the measure a second time, those results will be the same as the first assessment. For example, if you administer the Lawton Instrumental Activities of Daily Living Scale and measure tasks twice in two days with no major changes in the older respondent's lifestyle, the scores should be similar if not the same. In **intra-observer, or intra-rater reliability**, the observations by the same observer would be in agreement. Would the same observer give the same report at two points in time? Inter-observer reliability or inter-rater reliability implies agreement between many observers. Similarly, if two researchers use the Lawton Instrumental Activities of Daily Living Scale on the same day with the same older adults, those scores should be the same or very close.

Some reliability indicators show how the concepts one measures relate to each other. **Inter-item reliability** (also called internal consistency) means that the researcher has included enough items or questions to measure all aspects of the concept being measured. Lawton's measure does not have sub-scales, but—if IADLs were grouped by home-based tasks, shopping and outside-the-home tasks, and transportation—each of these sub-scales would measure a different component of the IADL concept. **Cronbach's alpha (α)** can be used to report the strength of relationships (with a range of 0–1) between scales/sub-scales at the ordinal level of measurement. "Typically, a 'high' reliability coefficient is considered to be .90 or above, 'very good' is .80 to .89, and 'good' or 'adequate' is .70 to .79" (Multon & Coleman, 2010, p. 162; Tavakol & Dennick, 2011). **Alternate-form reliability** compares individuals' answers to slightly different versions of survey questions (i.e., slightly reworded questions) to make sure answers are consistent across questions about the same concept.

Accuracy of Measures: Validity

A **measure** must capture the concept a researcher intends to measure/evaluate in his or her study. The most basic type of validity a study must meet is face validity. **Face validity** asks this question: on its face, or by general reading, does the question or instrument relate to the concept the researcher is claiming to study? Here is an example of bad face validity: a study's goal is to investigate the role of staff in quality of life for residents in memory care and the leading questions staff ask about residents' financial and medical insurance status. Face validity could be achieved by questions that ask about the staff's views of memory-care residents, staff-run activities in memory care, or staff's views/evaluation of memory care residents' quality of life. **Construct validity** "proves" soundness of a measure by grounding the measure in a theory or model and defining the concept you are measuring. If we use the example above, the quality-of-life term (in the role of staff in quality of life for residents in memory care) needs to be more carefully defined to be based in theory—since theoretical work about quality of life in care would list factors such as meaningful activities or staff using memory-supporting techniques before financial and medical coverage.

Content validity assures that the measure captures all dimensions of the concept the researcher is measuring. Here, the quality-of-life measures would need to be expanded—including meaningful activities or staff using memory-supporting techniques and more items representing this concept. **Criterion validity** is achieved when the item you are measuring (or its variables) is similar to another separate, established indicator that measures the same concept. In the example, if a previously valid and reliable measure for resident satisfaction in memory care existed, you could compare the score on that measure to yours. In another example, you develop a new depression scale of older adults. If an older person is rated as depressed on your scale, and he or she is also scored as having depressive symptomology on the Geriatric Depression Scale (GDS) or the Center for Epidemiological Studies Depression (CES-D), then your measure would have criterion validity (see Box 6.3). If you

Box 6.3 Comparison of Assessment Instruments for Depression in Older Adults

	Geriatric Depression Scale (GDS)	**Center for Epidemiological Studies of Depression Scale (CES-D)**
Long Form	Are you basically satisfied with your life? Have you dropped many of your activities and interests? Do you feel that your life is empty? Do you often get bored? Are you hopeful about the future? Are you bothered by thoughts you can't get out of your head? Are you in good spirits most of the time? Are you afraid that something bad is going to happen to you? Do you feel happy most of the time? Do you often feel helpless? Do you often get restless and fidgety? Do you prefer to stay at home, rather than going out and doing new things? Do you frequently worry about the future? Do you feel you have more problems with memory than most? Do you think it is wonderful to be alive now? Do you often feel downhearted and blue? Do you feel pretty worthless the way you are now? Do you worry a lot about the past? Do you find life very exciting? Is it hard for you to get started on new projects? Do you feel full of energy? Do you feel that your situation is hopeless? Do you think that most people are better off than you are? Do you frequently get upset over little things? Do you frequently feel like crying? Do you have trouble concentrating? Do you enjoy getting up in the morning? Do you prefer to avoid social gatherings? Is it easy for you to make decisions? Is your mind as clear as it used to be? This is the original scoring for the scale: one point for each of these answers with some reverse coded. *Scoring:* Not depressed: 0–9 Mild depression:10–19 Severe depression: 20–30	I was bothered by things that don't usually bother me. I did not feel like eating; my appetite was poor. I felt that I could not shake off the blues even with the help of my family or friends. I felt that I was just as good as other people. I had trouble keeping my mind on what I was doing. I felt depressed. I felt everything I did was an effort. I felt hopeful about the future. I thought my life had been a failure. I felt fearful. My sleep was restless. I was happy. I talked less than usual. I felt lonely. People were unfriendly. I enjoyed life. I had crying spells. I felt sad. I felt that people disliked me. I could not get "going." *Scoring:* 0 = Rarely or none of the time (less than one day) 1 = Some or little of the time (one to two days) 2 = Occasionally or a moderate amount of time (three to four days) 3 = Most or all of the time (five to seven days) 16 to 26 = mild depression; ≥ 27 = major depression
Short Form	Are you basically satisfied with your life? Have you dropped many of your activities and interests? Do you feel that your life is empty? Do you often get bored? Are you in good spirits most of the time? Are you afraid that something bad is going to happen to you? Do you feel happy most of the time? Do you often feel helpless? Do you prefer to stay at home, rather than going out and doing new things? Do you feel you have more problems with memory than most? Do you think it is wonderful to be alive now? Do you feel pretty worthless the way you are now? Do you feel full of energy? Do you feel that your situation is hopeless? Do you think that most people are better off than you are?	I was bothered by things that usually don't bother me. I had trouble keeping my mind on what I was doing. I felt depressed. I felt that everything I did was an effort. I felt hopeful about the future. I felt fearful. My sleep was restless. I was happy. I felt lonely. I could not "get going."

(http://www.stanford.edu/~yesavage/Testing.htm)

use two measures for depression, and they produce similar results, this is also a form of **concurrent validity**. If a score on a measure predicts another, such as a score on a depressing measure predicting future cognitive impairment, that is called predictive validity.

New Measurement Development

The quality of quantitative research is based on the quality of measurement tools. An existing measure may be revised to reduce administration time, improve ease of use, or have the measure's wording updated. When instruments are changed, the new versions must be carefully reviewed. For example, researchers used factor analysis to create a shorter 12-item version of the 33-item Computer Proficiency Questionnaire (CPQ) to evaluate an older person's computer proficiency across several domains of a computer use (Boot et al., 2015).

Another research team sought to create a measure to capture the concept of wisdom. They used a two-step Delhi process to define properties of wisdom. This process combined over 50 Likert measures on a survey with over 50 experts. In Phase 1, experts were given a survey to rate concepts they associated with wisdom. In Phase 2, concepts in agreement were removed, and 12 items that did not receive agreement were re-ranked, with agreement on 9 final attributes of wisdom. The researchers found "wisdom is a uniquely human but rare personal quality, which can be learned and measured, and increases with age through advanced cognitive and emotional development that is experience driven. At the same time, wisdom is not expected to increase by taking medication" (Jeste, Ardelt, Blazer, Kraemer, Vaillant & Meeks, 2010, p. 10).

Some suggest that quality measures be expanded/operationalized to include application in different settings. Researchers evaluated the efficacy of a person-centered care (PCC) measure when used within the Veterans Health Administration. Cognitive interviews (that ask the respondent about the process of answering questions: What was the question's intent and meaning? What helped with recall? What information was needed to answer question?), questionnaire revision, and psychometric testing of measures led to the creation of a shorter, also reliable and valid, version of the measure (Sullivan et al., 2013). Other research teams tested how consistently nursing-home-related concepts were understood by Nursing Home Directors and Directors of Nursing. Cognitive interviewing revealed each group had a different interpretation of commonly used terms, such as "direct care worker" or "palliative care" (Tyler, Shield, Rosenthal, Miller, Wetle & Clark, 2011)—illustrating the importance of clearly defining measures and concepts.

Researchers' Role as Part of an Analysis Team

Quantitative researchers on a team face several issues. Initially, if each member is coding data, the team must have established a high interrater reliability in data collection, coding, and analysis. Some **interrater coefficients** to consider would be percent of agreement (70%), Cohen's kappa (0.5), odds ratios (1), Cronbach's alpha (0.7), or Pearson's correlation coefficient (0.7) that tests the strength of the relationship between two variables (Kellow & Willson, 2008, pp. 15–28.) Increasingly, academic, peer-reviewed journals are also asking the author-members of a team to delineate their individual roles in the project. Tasks completed by the author are published along with the article. Quantitative researchers in medical and health-based teams may also need to be able to work as part of a varied, interdisciplinary team (e.g., geriatricians, orthopedists, palliative care, etc.). For example, large teams and an ongoing training requirement might be needed for conducting performance-based tests or in-person interviewing, or if the project is multi-disciplinary, inter-disciplinary, or longitudinal or has a large sample size.

Combining Quantitative Designs with Other Methods

It is increasingly common to combine some quantitative designs with qualitative ones—since each offers complementary data. See Chapter 7, "Mixed Methods," for a discussion of mixed-methods designs that include quantitative methods.

Challenges and Ethical Issues in Quantitative Research

Quantitative research requires statistical skill or access to software to conduct analysis. Jason Osborne (2008) mentions several ways that quantitative research can pose challenges due to expertise needed. They include over-relying on a consultant's expertise and being less familiar with other statistical analysis choices. Joel Best (2013) created several books addressing problems in interpretation of quantitative data, and he covers other issues, such as misinterpretation of statistics and unclear use of terminology and concepts.

Additionally, ethical issues can emerge, owing to the nature of the study design, such as performance-based or intervention-based designs. Research can conflict with clinical treatment in some designs. In reviewing medical studies with older participants, researchers have had difficulty separating out medical treatment from study-related interventions. Researchers have found time limitations when assessing capacity to consent in studies. There has been exposure to extra/non-study data without the older participant's permission and increased pain and discomfort for vulnerable participants. Researchers have reported feeling ambivalence or difficulty in discussing health or ethical concerns when they are in a purely research (and not a practitioner) role (Gladman et al., 2015).

Quantitative studies can place considerable time demands on dying patients in clinical trials, while end-of-life professionals may not encourage their patients to be in such trials (Bruera, Higginson, Von Gunten & Morita, 2014). Others suggest that professionals may not make older patients fully aware of risk in clinical studies (Daugherty, Banik, Janish & Ratain, 2000). (See Chapter 10 for a discussion of issues of cognitive status and consent ability.)

There is the potential for **data linking**, or merging older persons' records with other data sources and across studies, or lack of interaction with people enrolled in the study. Dennis Hogan and Carrie Spearin (2009) express concerns about possibilities for data linkage and identification of older individuals by linking large national datasets of Social Security, Medicare, and Medicaid data. Soazig Clifton (2012) suggests that "in large-scale surveys researcher will not have contact with participants" (paragraph 1). Themes of humanizing quantitative research and putting a face on data open this chapter and will be addressed in Chapter 7.

Writing Up and Evaluating Quantitative Work

Several components go into writing up, and also being able to evaluate, quantitative studies. A researcher needs to provide a detailed description of your process: from research question to findings.

Stating a Clear Research Question

Whether the researcher is writing up findings or evaluating an existing study, the research question or questions must be clearly stated and easily comprehended by the reader. If the

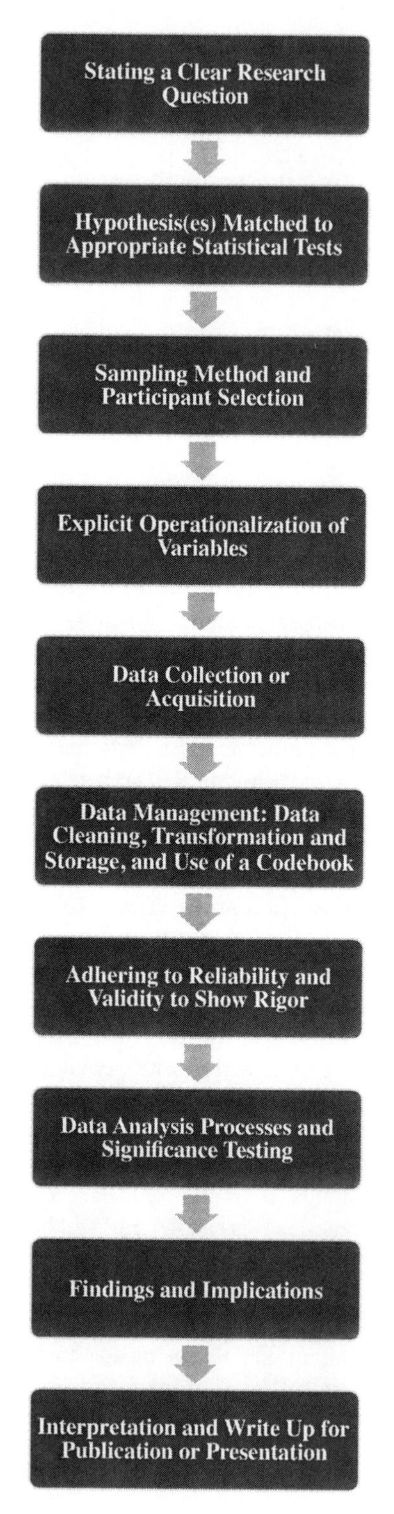

Figure 6.4 Steps in Quantitative Research Write Up or Evaluation

study's focus is on description, the research question states the goal of the study. If the design is inferential, the research question will lead to the statement of hypothesis(es). When writing or reading quantitative research, ask yourself: Is the research question self-evident? Are the hypotheses (if included) in line with the research question?

Hypothesis(es) Matched to Appropriate Statistical Tests

In inferential studies that go beyond describing a sample, hypotheses must state the full relationship of variables being tested. They must have direction (with the exception of those including nominal-level data) and degree of change. For example, will an increase in the independent variable increase or decrease the dependent variable? A basic hypothesis statement must include direction of the change. How much will the independent variable cause a change in the dependent variable?

Sampling Method and Participant Selection

A quantitative study needs to describe, in great detail, how a sample was defined and collected. What were the eligibility criteria for inclusion in the sample? Was the sample probability or non-probability based? How was sample size calculated/determined? Are there weights attached to the sample? What was the response rate among respondents? If applicable—as in the case of a longitudinal or repeated measure—what were the attrition rates or amounts of missing data? Did those who left the sample have similar characteristics—such as being frail or living in a particular setting? For pre- and post-tests or quasi-experimental designs, was any cross-contamination between groups present?

Once the sampling methods are described, participants' descriptive characteristics (of central tendency and variation along demographic and other key variables) should be noted. The text should also note the reason a particular sampling method was selected and the advantages and disadvantages of this particular method.

Explicit Operationalization of Variables

Initially, the researcher should define all concepts in the study with unambiguous, operationalized definitions. Measures of reliability for scales should be included that show the measure is appropriate/applicable for the population of interest. For example, you are measuring depression for women 90 years of age and older living in skilled care and have chosen to use the Center for Epidemiologic Studies Depression Scale (CES-D). Is using the CES-D test reliable and valid for this group? Or would other measures have been more appropriate for this group, such as the Beck Depression Inventory (BDI), the Geriatric Depression Scale (GDS), or the Cornell Scale for Depression in Dementia (CSDD), for example? Suitability of measures is not universal but specific to group, language, and place.

Data Collection or Acquisition

Primary data collection and secondary data acquisition, although different, have some commonalities/common approaches. Primary data collection should include a description of the entire data-collection process. During what time interval were the data collected? Who collected the data (an individual or team of data collectors)? What instruments or tools were used to collect the data? What problems arose? How were these addressed (or not addressed) during the study?

Secondary data require a description of the original use and intention behind the first data collection, along with the source of data collection and funder, if applicable. Often, secondary data analysis requires using variables that are a close match to concepts in the present study or variables that may arrive differently than stated in documentation included with the original data. Discussing differences in the present study's original concept, and how that concept is later operationalized with the secondary data, is key.

Data Management: Data Cleaning, Transformation and Storage, and Use of a Codebook

Self- and other-collected data require both cleaning and transformation (called **recoding**) to prepare them for data analysis. Most often, data-analysis software—such as the Statistical Package for the Social Science (SPSS), Statistical Analysis System (SAS), or R Data Analysis Software—is used to assist with both data management and analysis of the data. Choice of software may impact the significance of findings based on the formulas and algorithms used by the software's programmers (Hutchinson, Olmos & Teman, 2013). Chapter 9 includes examples of software and program use in greater detail.

Data cleaning examines raw data to check for values or answers that are out of range or are outliers (e.g., a study examining widowhood in women 75 and older, where a respondent's gender is listed, mistakenly, as male, or age of a respondent is listed as 45). Patterns are examined, so if a widow states she has three adult children, data about each child is collected/listed. If she states she has no children, the set of questions about adult children's information is skipped with no information about children recorded. After cleaning, the data may be transformed or recoded. Good recoding practice mandates that a copy of the original dataset be kept and that all variables (both recoded and original), along with their operationalized definitions, be kept in a **codebook** (see example in Table 6.3).

Table 6.3 Sample Codebook

Variable Group/Variable	Variable Definition/ Label Recoding	Variable Name in SPSS	Response Values and Labels*
Family Relationships			
Siblings	All siblings of respondent, birth, step, and adopted	siblings	0.00 No 1.00 Yes
Number of Siblings		sibnumber	Interval-ratio value
Sibling ranges		Sibrange	1.00 only child/none 2.00 1 or 2 siblings 3.00 3 to 5 siblings 4.00 6 or more siblings
Socioeconomic Status			
Education	Number of years of education completed to date	educ	Interval-ratio value; range 1–14 years
Educational Categories		educats	1.000 less than grammar 2.000 grammar 3.00 some h.s. 4.00 h.s. grad 5.00 some college 6.00 college grad plus

Variable Group/Variable	Variable Definition/ Label Recoding	Variable Name in SPSS	Response Values and Labels*
Performance-Based Physical Health Measures			
Performance-Based ADL Tasks	Mean index score for 9 tasks	pbadl9	Index; Range 0–1
Performance-Based IADL Tasks	Mean index score for 6 tasks, no missing data	pbiadl6	Index; Range 0–1
Recent Stressors			
Role Change Dichotomy	1 = experiencing 1 or more events	dmajorle	Dummy variable: 0.00 no major role change 1.00 experienced major role change
Acute Behavioral Adjustment Dichotomy	1 = experiencing 1 or more events	dminorle	Dummy variable: 0.00 no minor role change 1.00 experienced minor role change
Self-Reported Perceived Difficulties			
Perceived ADL Difficulties Summed Measure	Count of how many of 8 ADL tasks a person received help	sradldf8	Range: 0 to 8
Perceived IADL Difficulties Summed Measure	Count of how many of 6 IADL tasks a person received help	sriadl6	Range: 0 to 6
Self-Reported Social Support Received			
Social Support Received with ADL Tasks Dichotomy	1 = usually receives help with one activity	dsuppadl	0 no help 1.000 gets help
Social Support Received with IADL Tasks	Dichotomy, 1 = usually receives help with one activity	dsuppiadl	0 no help 1.000 gets help
Depression			
Depression Summary Score	Summary of 30 indicators for depressive symptomology; greater scores = more depressive symptoms	gdsmn25	Range: 0 to 30
Depression Dichotomies	Dichotomy based on mean, 1 = above the mean Dichotomy based on median, 1 = above the median	meandep meddep	Dichotomous variable: 0.00 below the mean 1.00 at the mean or above Dichotomous variable: 0.00 below the median 1.00 at the median or above
Interaction Terms			
Interaction Terms for Social Support Received with ADLs	Social Support Received with ADLs* Perceived ADL Difficulty	isspdadls	Does the effect of support received with ADLs depend upon the level of ADL difficulty?
Interaction Terms for Social Support Received with IADLs	Social Support Received with IADLs* Perceived IADL Difficulty	isspdiadls	Does the effect of support received with IADLs depend upon the level of IADL difficulty?

Note: *See text below for discussion of how to code different types of missing values.

Researchers need to discuss how to handle **missing data**. For example, in survey data-collection practices, 7, 77, or 777 means the respondent refused to answer a question; 8, 88, or 888 means the respondent said "don't know"; and 9, 99, or 999 indicates the question was "non-applicable" to that particular respondent.

Adhering to Reliability and Validity to Show Rigor

Researchers generally cover the basics of reliability and validity in reporting, such as Cronbach's alpha to show Likert scale reliability or interrater reliability if there is a research-data collection team. Face validity is often assumed through the explicit operationalization or definition of variables. In addition, content or criterion validity, as well as other forms of both validity and reliability, should be discussed because they directly impact the researchers' choice of measures.

Data Analysis Processes and Significance Testing

Data analysis consists of taking cleaned/recoded data and applying them to the statistical test or tests chosen as part of the design of the project. It is important to recheck that the data meet the requirements and assumptions of the test. Any variation should be stated. Steps in the process must be clearly stated. Significance levels of results must be reported as they detail the level by which results are real and not by chance. The lower the P-value, the lesser the probability findings are by chance. Yet it must be noted that significant results do not necessarily mean meaningful or important results, that is, where the researcher's interpretation comes into play.

Findings and Implications

Findings need to be linked back to the research questions and hypotheses. Were they "proven" or supported via statistical testing? Were these findings interpreted beyond statistical significance and applied back to the original goals of the study? Were the findings tied back to either theoretical premises or a conceptual model? Were plausible explanations given as to why the proposed relationship was not found? Did the authors provide both implications of their findings to practice and to the field and future directions for additional research?

Researcher's Role in the Work: Self-Reflection and Gerontology-Specific Issues Encountered

The quantitative researcher, like the qualitative one, is present throughout the work from conception of the initial design to operationalization of variables, data collection, choice of test for the analysis, and writing of the report. The researcher's choice of design/method, crossover with medical or other roles, protection of participants' information, and sensory and cognitive changes can impact quantitative work. Part of self-reflection should be an assessment of the researcher's role in the project. When conducting face-to-face surveys, how was the researcher experienced by the older respondents? If collecting observed data and having dual roles as researcher and clinician, how did these two roles intersect and work together in the study? Was there role confusion on the participants' part—seeing the researcher more as a clinician or friend? Each perceived role would produce different interactions and answers. Participants' comments about the researcher's role should be mentioned. If recruitment and retention of older persons, caregivers, or aging network staff were issues, how were they addressed and remedied during the study? If one design was chosen over another based on researchers' familiarity or lack of familiarity with a better method, that choice should be recognized and noted. Changes in cognitive status or any impact of changing status upon the study should be addressed and assessed.

This chapter takes the quantitative design selected by guidelines in the prior chapter and moves the analytical process for the data forward. Appropriate ways to visually display data and statistical tests for one, and more than one, variables are outlined. Each test is tied to a gerontological journal article that employs that analysis method. The chapter reviews key elements of quality in quantitative work, such as reliability and validity, and level of significance and error. The development of new measures as a way to improve rigor of design is discussed. The researcher's active roles in the work, as well as ethical challenges unique to quantitative designs, are explained with questions for the researcher to consider about each. A series of ten steps offers the researcher ways to write up his or her quantitative work for publication, presentation, or grant-proposal submission. These steps can also be applied when a researcher is evaluating existing quantitative reports.

Discussion Questions

- Discuss when a descriptive approach is best and when an inferential one is preferred for data from older persons. What analysis can you do with one variable, two, or three or more? How does level of measure impact your choice of test or analysis?
- Review the ethical issues associated with quantitative studies. List those related to recruiting or co-researching with older participants, to the different study designs, and to the researcher's role. Which do you think pose the greatest ethical threat? Explain your choice.
- A researcher is using two measures of depression in a study to address issues of reliability and validity. Explain how the Geriatric Depression Scale (GDS) and the Center for Epidemiological Studies of Depression Scale (CES-D) can be used to demonstrate specific types of reliability and validity concepts.
- A researcher is using two measures of mental-status assessment in a study to address issues of reliability and validity. Explain how the Mini Mental State Examination (MMSE) and the Montreal Cognitive Assessment (MoCA) can be used to demonstrate specific types of reliability and validity concepts.
- Choose a commonly used assessment instrument used with older persons. Then prepare a brief outline of the instrument selected, explaining the following: what it was created to measure, what elements the measure contains (e.g., survey questions, exercises to perform, etc.), a brief overview of any relevant literature on use, strengths and weaknesses of the instrument, and how it was found to be reliable and valid.
- Several types of reminiscence have been found to boost self-esteem, decrease depression, improve coping with loss and grief, enhance memory, provide a setting for life review, and improve overall well-being. You are designing a variable to measure reminiscence and have begun to investigate ways to operationalize reminiscence types. Some types of reminiscence are integrative (recollection of past plans, goal-directed activities, and the attainment of goals; using past

attempts to overcome difficulties, and drawing from past experience to solve present problems; and using problem-focused coping strategies to buffer against emotional distress) and instrumental reminiscence (encouraging recall of experiences, providing a sense of meaning or purpose in life; coming to terms with or accepting past negative experiences; positively evaluating how one measures up to one's ideals; and demonstrating continuity between the participant's sense of self in the past and his or her self-beliefs now). There is also the Reminiscence Functions Scale (RFS). Discuss the ways to improve reliability and validity by using the RFS scale. When would it be better to create your own definitions for reminiscence terms?

- You turn on the television and see a news story about how a large pharmaceutical company decided to test its "new and improved memory-enhancing drug" at a local senior activity center. The representatives are approaching members at the local senior center with senior center staff and asking the members if they want to participate in the study. Those that participate will receive a gift card to a local store and have free, ongoing health screenings by registered nurses. What are some ethical dilemmas here? What can be done to fix them?

Bibliography

Banerjee, A., Chitnis, U. B., Jadhav, S. L., Bhawalkar, J. S., & Chaudhury, S. (2009). Hypothesis testing, type I and type II errors. *Industrial Psychiatry Journal, 18*(2), 127–131. doi:10.4103/0972–6748.62274

Best, J. (2013). *Stat-spotting: A field guide to identifying dubious data*. Berkeley: University of California Press.

Boot, W., Charness, N., Czaja, S., Sharit, J., Rogers, W., Fisk, A., & Nair, S. (2015). Computer proficiency questionnaire: Assessing low and high computer proficient seniors. *Gerontologist, 55*(3), 404–411. doi:10.1093/geront/gnt117

Bruera, E., Higginson, I., Von Gunten, C. F., & Morita, T. (Eds.). (2014). *Textbook of palliative medicine and supportive care*. Boca Raton, FL: CRC Press.

Cheng, Y., & Grühn, D. (2015). Age differences in reactions to social rejection: The role of cognitive resources and appraisals. *The Journals of Gerontology Series B: Psychological Sciences and Social Sciences, 70*(6), 830–839. doi:10.1093/geronb/gbu054

Clifton, S. (2012). *Ethical issues in quantitative research*. NIHR School for Social Care Research (SSCR). Ethics workshop. King's College London. Retrieved from http://www.lse.ac.uk/LSEHealthAndSocialCare/events/PastEvents/2012/SSCR-Ethics-Workshop.aspx

Daugherty, C. K., Banik, D. M., Janish, L., & Ratain, M. J. (2000). Quantitative analysis of ethical issues in phase I trials: A survey interview study of 144 advanced cancer patients. *IRB, 22*(3), 6–14.

Delbaere, K., Sturnieks, D. L., Pijnappels, M. A. G. M., & Lord, S. R. (2010). The association between choice stepping reaction time and falls in older adults—A path analysis model. *Age and Ageing, 39*(1), 99–104. doi:10.1093/ageing/afp200

Djundeva, M., Mills, M., Wittek, R., & Steverink, N. (2015). Receiving instrumental support in late parent–child relationships and parental depression. *The Journals of Gerontology Series B: Psychological Sciences and Social Sciences, 70*(6), 981–994. doi:10.1093/geronb/gbu136

Dossey-Newby, P., & Krull, A. C. (2005). What's in a name? An examination of sociology of aging versus social gerontology course content. *Educational Gerontology, 31*(3), 225–233. doi:10.1080/03601270590900954

Gladman, J., Harwood, R., Conroy, S., Logan, P., Elliott, R., Jones, R., & Frowd, N. (2015). Medical crises in older people: Cohort study of older people attending acute medical units, developmental work and randomised controlled trial of a specialist geriatric medical intervention for high-risk older people; cohort study of older people with men. *Programme Grants for Applied Research (PGfAR), 3*(4), 37–61.

Gold, C., Malmberg, B., McClearn, G., Pedersen, N., Berg, S., Hälsohögskolan, & Åldrande—livsvillkor och hälsa, H. (2002). Gender and health: A study of older unlike-sex twins. *Journals of Gerontology Series B: Psychological Sciences and Social Sciences, 57*(3), S168–S176. doi:10.1093/geronb/57.3.S168

Grabowski, D., Elliot, A., Leitzell, B., Cohen, L., & Zimmerman, S. (2014). Who are the innovators? Nursing homes implementing culture change. *Gerontologist, 54*(Suppl 1), S65–S75. doi:10.1093/geront/gnt144

Hancock, G. R., & Mueller, R. O. (2010). *The reviewer's guide to quantitative methods in the social sciences*. New York: Routledge.

Heppenstall, C., Broad, J., Boyd, M., Gott, M., & Connolly, M. (2015). Progress towards predicting 1-year mortality in older people living in residential long-term care. *Age and Ageing, 44*(3), 497–501. doi:10.1093/ageing/afu206

Hogan, D. P., & Spearin, C. E. (2009). "Collecting and interpreting life records." In G. H. Elder Jr., & J. Z. Giele (Eds.), *The craft of life course research* (pp. 51–69). New York: Guilford.

Horowitz, A., Goodman, C., & Reinhardt, J. (2004). Congruence between disabled elders and their primary caregivers. *Gerontologist, 44*(4), 532–542. doi:10.1093/geront/44.4.532

Hutchinson, S., Olmos, A., & Teman, E. (2013). *Adequacy of model fit in confirmatory factor. Analysis and structural equation models: It depends on what software you use.* Paper presented at the 2013 annual meeting of the American Evaluation Association in Washington, DC.

Jeste, D., Ardelt, M., Blazer, D., Kraemer, H., Vaillant, G., & Meeks, T. (2010). Expert consensus on characteristics of wisdom: A Delphi method study. *Gerontologist, 50*(5), 668–680.

Kane, R. (2003). Definition, measurement, and correlates of quality of life in nursing homes: Toward a reasonable practice, research, and policy agenda. *Gerontologist, 43*(2), 28–36. doi:10.1093/geront/43.suppl_2.28

Kellow, J. T., & Willson, V. L. (2008). "Setting standards and establishing cut scores on criterion-referenced assessments: Some technical and practical considerations." In J. W. Osborne (Ed.), *Best practices in quantitative methods* (pp. 15–28). Thousand Oaks: Sage.

Kim, H., & Fredriksen-Goldsen, K. I. (2016). Living arrangement and loneliness among lesbian, gay, and bisexual older adults. *The Gerontologist, 6*(3), 548–558. doi:10.1093/geront/gnu083

Kwak, J., Montgomery, R. J. V., Kosloski, K., & Lang, J. (2011). The impact of TCARE® on service recommendation, use, and caregiver well-being. *The Gerontologist, 51*(5), 704–713. doi:10.1093/geront/gnr047

Lord, S., Galna, B., Verghese, J., Coleman, S., Burn, D., & Rochester, L. (2013). Independent domains of gait in older adults and associated motor and nonmotor attributes: Validation of a factor analysis approach. *Journals of Gerontology Series A: Biological Sciences and Medical Sciences, 68*(7), 820–827. doi:10.1093/gerona/gls255

Martin, J. (2015). *Organizational strategies for addressing disparities among marginalized older adults*. Executive summary, no. June.

Multon, K. D., & Coleman, J. S. M. (2010). "Coefficient alpha." In N. J. Salkind (Ed.), *Encyclopedia of research design* (Vol. 1, pp. 159–163). Thousand Oaks, CA: Sage Reference.

National Institutes of Health (NIH). (2015). *Peer review process*. Retrieved December 26, 2015, from http://grants.nih.gov/grants/peer_review_process.htm

National Institutes of Health (NIH). (2015). *Scoring system and procedure*. Retrieved December 26, 2015, from https://grants.nih.gov/grants/peer/guidelines_general/scoring_system_and_procedure.pdf

Noble, R. B., Bailer, A. J., Kunkel, S. R., & Straker, J. K. (2006). Sample size requirements for studying small populations in gerontology research. *Health Services and Outcomes Research Methodology, 6*(1), 59–67. doi:10.1007/s10742-006-0001-4

Osborne, J. W. (2008). *Best practices in quantitative methods*. Thousand Oaks, CA: Sage Publications.

Porter, K. E., Brennan-Ing, M., Burr, J. A., Dugan, E., & Karpiak, S. E. (2015). Stigma and psychological well-being among older adults with HIV: The impact of spirituality and integrative health approaches. *The Gerontologist*, 2015, 1–10. doi:10.1093/geront/gnv128

Rodriguez-Sánchez, E., Criado-Gutiérrez, J. M., Mora-Simón, S., Muriel-Diaz, M. P., Gómez-Marcos, M. A., Recio-Rodríguez, J., Patino-Alonso, C., Valero-Juan, L., Maderuelo-Fernandez, J., García-Ortiz, L., & the DERIVA Group. (2014). Physical activity program for patients with dementia and their relative caregivers: Randomized clinical trial in primary health care (AFISDEMyF study). *BMC Neurology, 14*(63),1–10. doi:10.1186/1471-2377-14-63.

Rodriguez-Sanchez, E., Patino-Alonso, M., Mora-Simon, S., Gomez-Marcos, M., Perez-Penaranda, A., Losada-Baltar, A., & Garcia-Ortiz, L. (2013). Effects of a psychological intervention in a primary health care center for caregivers of dependent relatives: A randomized trial. *Gerontologist, 53*(3), 397–406. doi:10.1093/geront/gns086

Rosa, N. M., Deason, R. G., Budson, A. E., & Gutchess, A. H. (2016). Source memory for self and other in patients with mild cognitive impairment due to Alzheimer's disease. *The Journals of Gerontology. Series B, Psychological Sciences and Social Sciences, 71*(1), 59.

Salkind, N. J. (2010). *Encyclopedia of research design*. Thousand Oaks, CA: Sage Publications.

Sarkamo, T., Tervaniemi, M., Laitinen, S., Numminen, A., Kurki, M., Johnson, J., & Rantanen, P. (2014). Cognitive, emotional, and social benefits of regular musical activities in early dementia: Randomized controlled study. *Gerontologist, 54*(4), 634–650. doi:10.1093/geront/gnt100

Schafer, M., & Koltai, J. (2015). Does embeddedness protect? Personal network density and vulnerability to mistreatment among older American adults. *Journals of Gerontology Series B: Psychological Sciences and Social Sciences, 70*(4), 597–606. doi:10.1093/geronb/gbu071

Seltzer, J. A., & Friedman, E. M. (2014). Widowed mothers' coresidence with adult children. *The Journals of Gerontology Series B: Psychological Sciences and Social Sciences, 69*(1), 63–74.

Shake, M. C., Shulley, L. J., & Soto-Freita, A. M. (2016). Effects of individual differences and situational features on age differences in mindless reading. *The Journals of Gerontology Series B: Psychological Sciences and Social Sciences, 71*(5), 808–820. doi:10.1093/geronb/gbv012

Sullivan, J., Meterko, M., Baker, E., Stolzmann, K., Adjognon, O., Ballah, K., & Parker, V. (2013; 2012). Reliability and validity of a person-centered care staff survey in Veterans' health administration community living centers. *Gerontologist, 53*(4), 596–607.

Tavakol, M., & Dennick, R. (2011). Making sense of Cronbach's alpha. *International Journal of Medical Education, 2*, 53.

Tyler, D., Shield, R., Rosenthal, M., Miller, S., Wetle, T., & Clark, M. (2011). How valid are the responses to nursing home survey questions? Some issues and concerns. *Gerontologist, 51*(2), 201–211. doi:10.1093/geront/gnq095

Van Haitsma, K., Curyto, K., Abbott, K., Towsley, G., Spector, A., & Kleban, M. (2015). A randomized controlled trial for an individualized positive psychosocial intervention for the affective and behavioral symptoms of dementia in nursing home residents. *Journals of Gerontology Series B: Psychological Sciences and Social Sciences, 70*(1), 35–45. doi:10.1093/geronb/gbt102

Weil, J., Hutchinson, S. R., & Traxler, K. (2014). Exploring the relationships among performance-based functional ability, self-rated disability, perceived instrumental support, and depression: A structural equation model analysis. *Research on Aging, 36*(6), 683–706.

7
Mixed Methods

This chapter provides the terminology and design types for mixed-methods studies. Benefits and barriers of mixed-methods approaches are covered. Gerontological applications and examples of designs using this "third method" in the real world are provided. True mixed-methods designs are defined along with designs that approximate mixed methods but are not true mixed-methods designs. Characteristics of good mixed-methods design are detailed. Each design type (explanatory sequential, exploratory sequential, convergent parallel, embedded, transformative, and multi-level) is reviewed along with a decision-making process for selecting each design. Nomenclature and sampling options are explained. Steps are provided for general data analysis methods and design-specific data analysis designs. The chapter concludes with ways to integrate findings from the quantitative and qualitative aspects of a mixed-methods design. Unique mixed-methods terminology for reliability and validity (legitimization and inference transferability, or applying results to other settings) is covered.

Integrating Mixed-Methods Research Further into Gerontological Practice

Mixed-methods-approach designs are used in the field of aging. The emergence of **mixed methods**, combining quantitative and qualitative designs, began in the 1980s as mixed methods were seen as a "third methodological movement" (Tashakkori, 2009). Use of mixed-methods designs continues to grow with increasingly diverse application. The *Journal of Mixed Methods Research* was even created in 2007 as a place to publish and promote mixed-methods work (Greene, 2015). Mary Beth Happ (2009) reviewed the history and types of published gerontological mixed-methods work from the early studies of Kayser-Jones and colleagues (1989) to those that have one dominant design (Bishop, Weinberg, Leutz, Dossa, Pfefferle & Zincavage, 2008; Chapin, Reed & Dobbs, 2004; Liang, Kasman, Wang, Yuan & Mandelblatt, 2006). She pointed out examples of sequential designs (Barg, Huss-Ashmore, Wittink, Murray, Bogner & Gallo, 2006; Bishop, Weinberg, Leutz, Dossa, Pfefferle, & Zincavage, 2008; Cox, Green, Seo, Inaba & Quillen, 2006; Hildon, Smith, Netuveli & Blane, 2008; Howes, 2008; Hwalek, Straub & Kosniewski, 2008; Ingersoll-Dayton, Saengtienchai, Kespichayawattana & Aungsuroch, 2004) and concurrent mixed methods (Emlet, 2007). Happ found studies quantifying qualitative interviews (Schroepfer, 2008) and frameworks for combining data (Caracelli & Green, 1993; Driscoll, Appiah-Yeboah, Salib & Rupert, 2007; Onwuegbuzie & Teddlie, 2003; Sandelowski, 2003). She described early studies that have provided ways to integrate findings in mixed-methods analysis (Berglund & Ericsson, 2003; Chapin, Reed & Dobbs, 2004; Cohen-Mansfield, Creedon, Malone, Parpura-Gill, Dakheel-Ali & Heasly, 2006; Pillemer et al., 2008; Yeatts & Cready, 2007; Morgan & Konrad, 2008). Happ (2009) has adapted Creswell and Plano Clark's stage model of mixed-methods design types into a four-level model to encourage mixed-methods work to become more fully incorporated into gerontological work.

Benefits of Mixed-Methods Designs in Gerontology

There are clear benefits in applying mixed-methods designs to studies on aging. Researchers found adding focus groups to telephone surveys for those 60 and older provided additional differing health data that was "invaluable for increasing confidence in results" (Jensen, Finifter, Wilson & Koenig, 2007, p. 32). Using a mixed-method design was seen to capture the multi-dimensionality of elders' loneliness and depression and the meaning behind associated stereotypes (Barg, Huss-Ashmore, Wittink, Murray, Bogner & Gallo, 2006). A meta-review of studies focusing on stroke recovery found the combination of falsely divided quantitative/qualitative methodological paradigms could fill gaps in stroke research (Clarke, 2009). Integrating mixed-methods strategies into a longitudinal clinical study of aging led to recognition of the broad spectrum of what the aging process is, in terms of changes in multiple layers of psychosocial development and spirituality (Van Ness, Fried & Gill, 2011). Mixed methods offered a complementary process of highlighting differences in studies of cancer recovery and independence (Esbensen, Thome & Thomsen, 2012). Mixed methods also provided synergistic insights about programs focusing on cognitive abilities and problem solving with elders (Stine-Morrow, Parisi, Morrow, Greene & Park, 2007).

Studies have called for future mixed or qualitative work to help understand quantitative-based findings. Some suggest that qualitative work is useful in explaining non-significant quantitative findings (see Schroepfer, 2008). See Box 7.1 and Figures 7.1 and 7.2 for ways mixed methods can better address a research question than a one-method approach.

Box 7.1 Potential for Mixing Methods in the Field: "Live" Examples

Understanding Life Post–Hip Facture

In the past, I worked on a federal health study of persons 62 and older who had hip-fracture surgery. The study used a structured survey and follow-up calls three and six months after surgery to measure health and social outcomes. The older adult was the person contacted less than half the time due to the person's choice or changes in cognitive or health status.

We know there is a concern when the person answering the question is someone other than the older person (Weil, 2015). Proxy and self-rating differ, and another person cannot assess certain factors about the older person's experience—such as level of pain or satisfaction rating. Older persons also rate items higher/better than when reported by a proxy.

Missing data were a cause for concern since answers could help predict post-surgical outcomes. Adding additional data collection points and types (as a true mixed-methods study) would have provided complementary data to fill the gaps or thoroughly examine the reasons for the gaps/missing data. See Figure 7.1 for an example of mixed-methods design that would have been better suited this project.

Transition to Care

After doing experiential work with my undergraduate classes in an assisted-living facility, I was approached to create a study about the effects of the transition from home to care upon older persons as they became residents. The initial proposition was to interview new residents face-to-face within the first week or two after their arrival in the care setting. This design would have worked and has been reported in the literature. But also formally surveying all levels of staff at the assisted living facility at the same time of the resident interviews would provide richer data and a more complete picture of the transition-to-care experience. See Figure 7.2 for an example of a mixed-methods design that could be better suited to this project.

Lack of Use of Mixed-Methods Designs in Gerontology

Researchers continue to cite several reasons why mixed methods, although gaining usage, remain underutilized in gerontology. Reasons include the lack of knowledge of mixed-methods terminology. Though mixed-methods designs use quantitative and qualitative terms, there are also sampling and reliability and validity terms unique to mixed-methods designs.

Mixed-methods studies can suffer from a lack of true integration of methodological design. Sometimes mixing multiple methods, mixed statistical modeling, and true mixed-methods designs can be confused or mistaken for each other (Teddlie & Tashakkori, 2012).

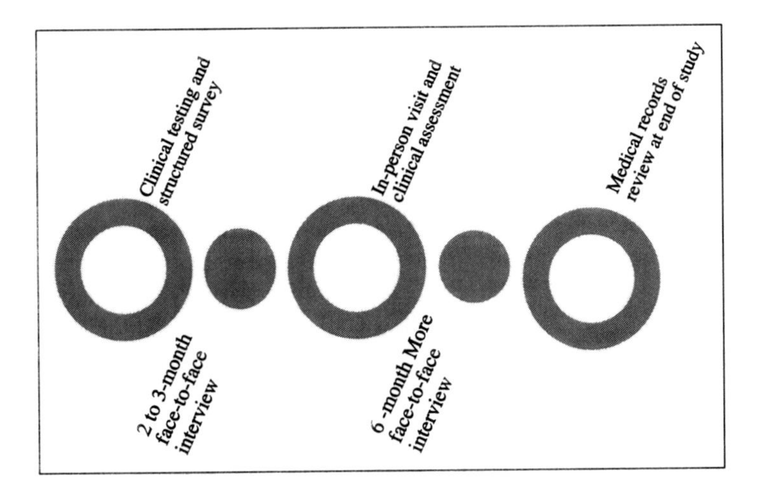

Figure 7.1 Mixing Methods in a Hip-Fracture Study

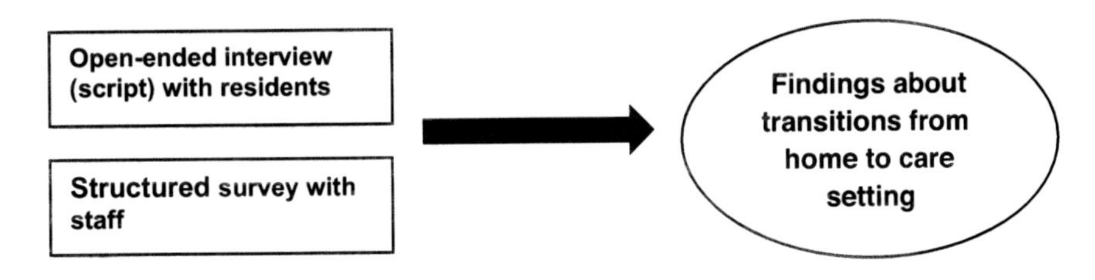

Figure 7.2 A Mixed-Methods Study of Care Transitions

Multiple methods have been "mixed" over time. For example, a qualitative multi-method study describing the experience of rural gay older men used biographic narrative, visual ethnography, and focus groups to make a film/screenplay as a way of empowering lesbian and gay rural older persons (Fenge & Jones, 2012). Two studies—one a qualitative data collection of married couples in assisted living, and the second a separate, distinct, quantitative study—examined residents' social networks (Kemp, Ball & Perkins, 2016). While both examples are multi-method designs, they are not formal mixed-methods designs. Additionally, there can be varied applications or modification of the same mixed methods designs.

Mixed methods have design complexity. Clark, Anderson, Wertz, Zhou, Schumacher, and Miaskowski (2014) conducted a meta-analysis of mixed-method longitudinal studies in the health sciences and found several issues in the published studies. There was a lack of discussion of how probability and non-probability-based samples were combined and how participants were selected. Discussion of time in mixed longitudinal designs was hard to describe with authors sometimes counting contact points with participants.

Data analysis and integration of quantitative and qualitative can be difficult. Designs used different levels of measurement and units of analysis. Quantitative elements can use inferential analysis, and qualitative items are themed. Integration across the methods is minimal—mostly one set of data used to describe/explain the other. The decision-making process in choosing a mixed-methods design is not sufficiently discussed (Vrkljan, 2009).

There is also the paucity of training and guides for gerontologists, cost, and lack of interdisciplinary collaboration (Clarke, 2009; Happ, 2009). Issues of power, leadership, and control can arise in a two-team mixed quantitative and qualitative study. In a knee-rehabilitation study, the quantitative group looked at post-surgical functional ability, and the qualitative team looked at how rehabilitation and exercise are interpreted. Issues arose as to which team was the leader and which was the better science. These debates left some negative relationships between researchers and left no real standout leadership for the groups (Lunde, Heggen & Strand, 2013).

Mixed-methods experts summarized common **barriers to mixing methods** (Apesoa-Varano & Hinton, 2013; Johnson, Onwuegbuzie & Turner, 2007; Lunde, Heggen & Strand, 2013). Researchers conducting mixed-methods studies may have methodological preferences, focusing on one aspect of the study over another, or find one type of data is more interesting. There might be difficulty getting over ideological differences in approaches and the lack of prior mixed-methods experience. Conflicting timelines for designs and a lack of ways to really integrate results may present barriers. Mixed-methods authors may find themselves writing for different audiences and for journals with differing publication structures and limited recognition of mixed-methods designs.

Defining True Mixed-Methods Designs and Benefits

Mixed methods are often associated with pragmatist paradigm orientation, but, since they are complementary in combining both quantitative and qualitative designs, several paradigms can be used to achieve this goal. Real mixed-methods designs can use any philosophical paradigm. All paradigms or orientation are discussed in Chapter 1. To recap paradigms, **pragmatism** avoids construction of reality debates and lets the researcher apply methods in the real world. The researcher is not interested in getting at a universal truth or being linked to only one philosophy—the real goal is problem solving, or how the data and outcomes can help solve real-world problems. **Objectivism** is defined as the belief in the existence of an objective, external reality that can be measured and tested. **Positivism** is associated with the traditional quantitative "scientific approach" to study people. A positivist approach argues that studies are objective and generalizable; post-positivists use the scientific method with variables, hypotheses, and theory to quantify and explain reality. **Constructionism** seeks to capture the way individuals construct or create reality. Research is centered upon participants' views and ways of constructing meaning in their daily worlds. Interpretivism acknowledges there are multiple views of reality (including those of the researcher and those "studied"), so the "participant" is the best at describing experience, events, etc., in his or her own life. **Symbolic interactionism** explores how people attach meaning to their experiences in the world based on their interaction with society. **Subjectivism** posits that our views of reality are filtered or seen throughout subjective viewpoints or vantage points. A **critical or transformative** worldview includes power and political dynamics of oppressed/marginalized groups and societal influences upon these groups. **Feminism** is an inclusive approach to account for women's voices and intersectionality statuses—reflecting society's role in creating gender-based social problems.

Seeking a common definition by mixed-methods experts, researchers suggested that mixed-methods designs contain elements found in an acronym for the word "mixed." Tony Onwuegbuzie (2012) offers that a mixed-methods approach should include:

M (be a *m*ethodological thinker of multiple approaches)
I (use *i*ntegrated, integral approaches and be competent in both quantitative and qualitative approaches)
X (be *x*enophilous as a researcher drawn to the new or unknown)
E (*e*mpower universal knowledge)
D (push for the *d*evelopment of new applications and procedures)

Types of Mixed-Methods Designs

Mixed-methods research designs are classified according to two major dimensions: **time order** (do quantitative and qualitative parts occur at the same time, or does one follow the other?) and **paradigm emphasis** (do quantitative and qualitative parts have equal status, or does one part having a dominant status?). Six common **types of mixed-methods designs** have been identified. They are sequential explanatory, sequential exploratory, convergent parallel, embedded, transformative, and multi-level (Creswell & Plano Clark, 2010).

A **sequential explanatory** design begins with a quantitative method and then is followed by a qualitative method to further explain the findings of the first quantitative approach.

Gerontologists have used a sequential explanatory design to examine the relationship between health resources and well-being for those ages 40–85. A quantitative start examined the hypothesized relationship of health and wellness variables through secondary analysis in a national survey. The quantitative analysis was followed by a qualitative interview (with those from another sample but similar group; Craciun, Gellert & Flick, 2015). Researchers who were interested in studying the culture change movement (from hospital-like to home-like skilled care environment) used a quantitative survey of over 4,000 skilled care facilities followed by an independent in-depth interview with 65 nursing home administrators (Shield, Looze, Tyler, Lepore & Miller, 2014). Other researchers examined why older persons dropped out of a walking study. The quantitative first part was a baseline survey followed by a face-to-face or telephone interview to gather information about reasons why older persons dropped out of the study (Rogers et al., 2014). A sequential explanatory design examined

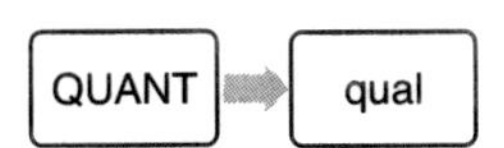

Figure 7.3 Sequential Explanatory Design

how city planners adapt communities to become age-friendly. In this study, an online quantitative survey of city planners was followed by a more in-depth, open-ended telephone survey of a smaller group of the same city planners (Lehning, 2012).

A **sequential exploratory** mixed-methods design first uses a qualitative approach to explore a phenomenon and then uses knowledge gained in testing by quantitative designs. This sequential exploratory design is often used in survey/instrument development. Researchers used a modified version of this design to examine how perceived and received support from family impacted African-American older men's level of stress. The qualitative data were themed and used to create variables tested in the latter quantitative analysis (Watkins, Wharton, Mitchell, Matusko & Kales, 2015). Researchers used a sequential exploratory design to see how leisure related to definitions of successful aging for Australian persons in a Third Age group. Information from the qualitative interviews informed the construction of the quantitative survey (Boyes, 2013).

Convergent parallel designs do not have one dominant method; instead, this design uses each method (quantitative or qualitative), equally taking the findings from each to explain the research question at hand. Researchers have used this concurrent design to collect fall experience data from older persons (via semi-structured interviews) and biomedical data (from medical records' chart review; Leavy et al., 2015). Others used a convergent parallel design to test a new online caregiver resource for those caring for an elder with dementia. The methods included a quantitative structured survey and a more in-depth, short qualitative interview (Gaugler, Reese & Tanler, 2015). Researchers looking at supportive housing for those with mental illness (for those less than 50 years of age and 50 and older) used a convergent parallel design. They mixed quantitative data from a statewide database and qualitative interviews, observations, and focus groups with persons in local supportive housing programs (Henwood, Katz & Gilmer, 2015).

Embedded mixed-methods design includes both quantitative and qualitative elements together with one element enhancing ("supplementing") another. Embedded designs can be both sequential and concurrent. Think of this design as "qualitative embedded within an experiment" or "qualitative interviews in long-term data collection" (Creswell & Plano Clark, 2010, p. 72). A sequential embedded study was used to assess a management process for rural age home staff in Australia. A quantitative management tool was piloted by use of a qualitative study. The qualitative work gathered key concepts for the tool. Qualitative work done after the quantitative tool added context for the quantitative interpretation (Hodgkin, Warburton &

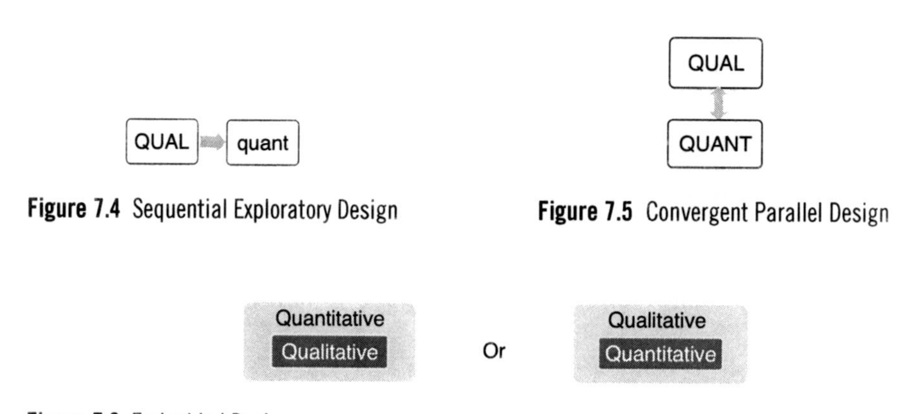

Figure 7.4 Sequential Exploratory Design

Figure 7.5 Convergent Parallel Design

Figure 7.6 Embedded Design

Savy, 2012). A sequential embedded design was also used to add qualitative interview data to an 11-year multi-wave longitudinal study about how the oldest Swedish persons made decisions to relocate to facility-based housing, or, as it was called, shelter in care (Nygren & Iwarsson, 2009).

Transformative mixed-methods designs are chosen when the researcher is using theory to guide his or her design. This design addresses issues of injustice or marginalization (Creswell & Plano Clark, 2010; Mertens, 2010). A transformative paradigm addresses social problems using a social justice and ethics-based approach. It includes an acceptance of multiple realties of those in the study (e.g., researchers, participants) instead of assuming one view or a universal reality. Power differentials for those in the study due to each person's social position are recognized. This design investigates the "experience of discrimination and oppression on whatever basis, including but not limited to, race and ethnicity, disability, immigrant status, political conflicts, sexual orientation, poverty, gender, age, or the multitude of other characteristics . . . with less access to social justice." Investigation of the "power structures that perpetuate social inequities" is an integral part of the research from the start (Mertens, 2010, p. 62). Transformative mixed-methods designs can be sequential or concurrent and can resemble the layout of other mixed-methods designs. Walker, Hennessy, and ESRC Growing Older Programme (2004) cite work by Victor, Scambler, Bond, and Bowling (2000) about theory-based and grounding of loneliness in old age as a sequential transformative design.

Multiphase designs, as the name implies, refer to mixed-methods studies done in more than two phases. Typical multiphase mixed-methods designs are used in program evaluation or in large-scale healthcare settings evaluation (Creswell & Plano Clark, 2010, p. 162). Multiphase designs can be sequential or concurrent over several periods of time. Figure 7.7 is an example of a sequential multiphase design.

Apesoa-Varano and Hinton's (2013) Men's Health and Aging study can be seen as a sequential multiphase design. It is part of a large heath project examining older men and depression. The first quantitative phase of clinic-based surveys was followed by a two-approach second phase. Phase 2 employed both qualitative in-depth interviews and quantitative surveys with depressed older men and qualitative interviews with treating physicians.

Researchers used a three-phase approach to study senior athletes' views about the "successful aging" concept. The first wave included a quantitative questionnaire with biomedical and screening data; then, in a second wave, qualitative focus groups were used to see how athletes define health activities. The third quantitative phase consisted of follow-up questions with some of the same athletes (Ostlund-Lagerstrom et al., 2015). Researchers used an intervention mixed-method design resembling clinical trial interventions (Fetters, Curry & Creswell, 2013).

In another sequential multiphase design, researchers proposed an iterative model about the role of loneliness and depression where each part of the design had equal weight. The study included a wave of structured surveys, follow-up telephone interviews, and open-ended

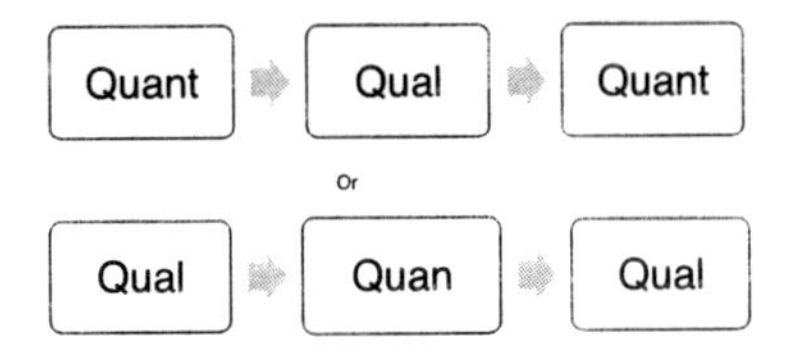

Figure 7.7 Sequential Multiphase Design

Table. 7.1 Comparison of Features of Each Mixed-Methods Design

	Explanatory sequential	Exploratory sequential	Convergent parallel	Embedded	Transformative	Multi-level
Goal	Use qualitative to explain quantitative	Use qualitative to create quantitative instruments	Synergy between qualitative and quantitative	One design occurs within/as a part of another design	To address injustice or marginalization	Evaluation of long-term programs
Which phase is first?	QUANT	QUAL	Concurrent	Either	Either	Either
Which phase is second?	Qual	quant	Concurrent	Either	Either	Either
Which phase has more weight?	QUANT	QUAL	Equal	The dominant method/the one in which the second one is embedded	Either, depending upon the design (convergent/ concurrent or sequential)	Either, depending upon the design (convergent/ concurrent or sequential)
Sampling options	All available	All available	All available	All available	All available	All available
Assurance of reliability/ validity	All available	All available	All available	All available	All available	All available
How is analysis run?	*Explanatory:* Determine who will be the follow-up group Explain how qualitative will further the quantitative Use quantitative as demographics and qualitative to explain quantitative	*Exploratory:* Determine which quantitative data are the follow-up Decide on the instruments psychometrics Explain how quantitative explains the qualitative Codes become variables and how to make qualitative quantitative	*Convergent:* Decide how to compare the qualitative and quantitative data Quantify the qualitative data Decide the stats that will link datasets Use a joint display with qualitative columns and quantitative rows Side-by-side quantitative and qualitative analysis combine codes and statistical outcomes in a figure and transform qualitative to quantitative	*Embedded:* Plan the relationship of primary and secondary datasets How qualitative themes relate to phases of the study	*Transformative:* Decide on the best analysis for the question Which designs work best How results can show inequality How quantitative and qualitative express the theme	*Multiphase:* Decide how data analysis applies to all phases Decide how to combine data at all phases and compare to evaluative goal

Adapted from Creswell & Plano Clark, 2010, Tables 7.2 and 7.5

interviews about definitions of loneliness and depression with the same people from the original sample (Barg, Huss-Ashmore, Wittink, Murray, Bogner & Gallo, 2006).

Sampling Design in Mixed Methods

The previous quantitative and qualitative chapters discussed specific types of probability-based and non-probability-based sampling methods. All these sampling options apply to mixed-methods designs. Mixed methods involve selecting the sample around criteria suggested by Charles Teddlie and Yu (2007). **Mixed-methods sampling** should be based on the research question or hypotheses. Sampling should be true to each sampling protocol and should create "good" data. A well-selected sample allows inferences from all designs, which can lend to generalizability, if appropriate. Sampling methods need to be based on ethical practices; be feasible and efficient; and provide, for future studies, details about how samples were collected.

Sampling design options in mixed methods are based upon the relationships of participants in each of the quantitative or qualitative sampling parts of the design. In **identical sampling**, the same sample of participants is in all parts of the design (Collins, Onwuegbuzie & Jiao, 2007). **Parallel sampling** involves different samples or participants in each part of the design, but all participants are selected from the same underlying population. **Nested sampling** means that the entire study uses the same sample of participants. One part of the nested design uses the whole sample, and another part of the design uses only a smaller part of that same sample of participants. **Multilevel sampling** takes multiple samples from different populations.

Nomenclature

Traditional mixed-methods designs use a **nomenclature** involving capitalization and arrows or plus signs. The prioritized method is in all capital letters; the lesser prioritized methods are in lowercase letters. A plus sign is used for methods occurring at the same time. Arrows are used to indicate the order of designs that follow each other in time order. For example, a sequential explanatory design beginning with a quantitative design and followed by a qualitative one would be noted as this: QUANT → qual. See Figure 7.8 for more examples. Researchers use this method (Morse & Niehaus, 2009; Greene, 2007), though some are calling for extension of this notation system (Cameron, 2011).

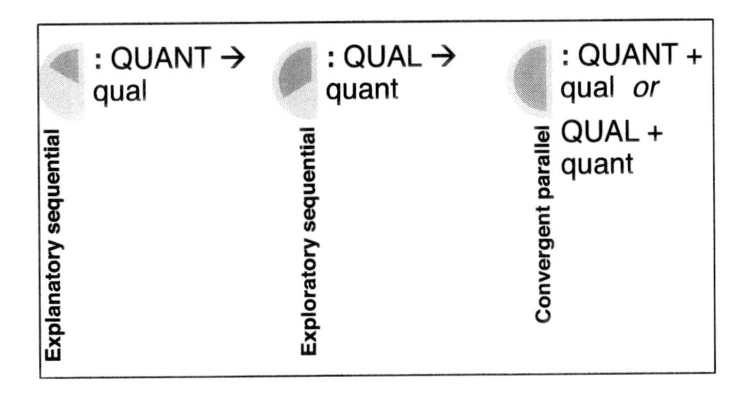

Figure 7.8 Three Basic Mixed-Methods Designs by Notation

Data Analysis in Mixed-Methods Design

Mixed-methods data analysis depends upon the types of quantitative and qualitative elements included. With this said, there are some general analysis strategies that apply to all designs (Greene, 2009; Onwuegbuzie & Teddlie, 2003). See Table 7.1 for specific analytical strategies by type of specific mixed-method design as suggested by John Creswell and Vicki Plano Clark (2010, Tables 7.2 and 7.5).

Methods Justification and Sampling Design

Since the options in mixed-methods designs vary, a researcher needs to justify the need for the design she or he chooses and offer a rationale for the ordering of these elements in the design. Sampling is then conducted according to the method (for qualitative, non-probability-based options and for quantitative, non-probability-based options). The sampling procedures used in each element must be described in detail. An added mixed-methods sampling dimension is the need to mention if the samples have the same or different participants in each.

Individual Integrity in Elements

A mixed-methods study needs to maintain the individual integrity of each part of the design. Quantitative and qualitative standards and vocabulary need to be used and matched to that element. For quantitative parts, discuss reliability and validity; and, for qualitative parts, address rigor. Issues of representativeness (in the quantitative part) and saturation (in the qualitative design) should be addressed.

Data Cleaning, Reduction, and Consolidation or Transformation

All data must be cleaned before any analysis can begin. For quantitative data, frequency distributions and descriptive statistics can be used to review data and identify outlying values. Variables can be recoded or collapsed. Qualitative data can be pooled with coding criteria established. Codes are created and made into larger code groups, or families, and discrepant cases or codes are noted. Statistical testing can be planned if qualitative data is made into quantitative data.

Data Comparison/Data Analysis/Data Integration

Mixed-method designs include constant comparative design and triangulation (Apesoa-Varano & Hinton, 2013). Post-cleaning and condensing of data, qualitative data's themes can be compared and combined or synthesized. Descriptive (frequency distribution, summary statistics) and inferential analysis can occur (cluster analysis, correlation, ANOVA, multivariate, SEM, path) for quantitative data. Qualitative themes and quantitative variables for the same constructs can be compared. The "creation of blended variables" in this "matching process . . . facilitates further analysis" (Bazeley, 2009, p. 205). See Figure 7.9 for a comparison of variables and themes.

Integration of quantitative and qualitative elements of data and findings is the goal of mixed-methods designs. True integration in mixed methods happens when "quantitative and qualitative components can be considered 'integrated' to the extent that these components are explicitly related to each other within a single study and in such a way as to be mutually illuminating, thereby producing findings that are greater than the sum of the parts" (Bazeley, 2009, p. 7). Integration can happen in three ways: Data are integrated by building through sequential integration. Data are integrated by merging or bringing the quantitative and qualitative elements together. Integration can also be embedded and happen repeatedly throughout the ongoing data analysis (Fetters, Curry & Creswell, 2013).

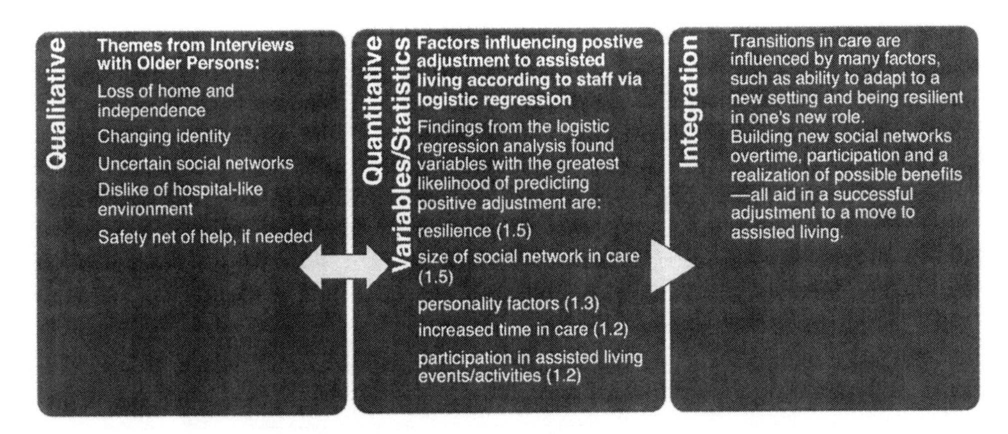

Figure 7.9 Integration of Qualitative and Quantitative Findings of a Transitions of Care Study

Visualize Results

Images, visual displays, and/or matrices help the reader see how the data from each design have been integrated and work together. Some data display qualitative and quantitative data together. See Figure 7.9 for a matrix.

Applying Reliability and Validity and Rigor in Mixed-Methods Designs

In mixed-methods designs, **legitimization** addresses validity, while **inference transferability** allows researchers to apply findings of one study to other settings. Researchers have developed "a framework for assessing legitimation in mixed research" (Onwuegbuzie, Johnson & Collins, 2010) that includes several legitimation (validity) markers and advances the work of earlier mixed-methods theorists (Greene, 2009, 2015). Onwuegbuzie, Johnson, and Collins (2010) offer the following concepts:

Table 7.2 Mixed-Methods Legitimization Terminology

Inside-outside legitimization:	both researcher's and respondents' views are present
Paradigmatic validity:	see the viewpoints of quantitative and qualitative designs as a continuum, not a dualism with correct orientation and philosophy
Commensurability legitimization:	accept two methods as compatible
Weakness minimization legitimization:	assess how well one method can compensate for missing elements of another and how each approach balances the other
Sequential legitimization:	interpret how the time ordering of one phase impacts another
Conversion legitimization:	once data are converted to another form, check for misinterpretation of data from their original form
Sample integration legitimization:	the relationship between the samples impacts inference; to make best inferences, quantitative and qualitative samples should be the same people
Political legitimization:	write about the conflict and difficulty to get third method accepted; why it is necessary to use mixed methods and advantages to studies and researchers conducting the studies
Multiple validities legitimization:	address both qualitative and quantitative aspects of validity

Inference transferability refers to how well and in what settings a mixed-methods study's results can be applied more broadly. Inference transferability depends upon design quality and interpretive rigor. Quality and rigor can be attained if: inferences made from the data match both the data and the theory (**conceptual consistency**); the inferences make sense for all groups being studied (**interpretative agreement**); other ideas/interpretations/explanations for the data interpretation are ruled out (**interpretive distinctness**; Tashakkori & Teddlie, 2003). Mixed-methods theorists suggest **meta-inferences** are analogous to a conclusion or summary of all mixed-methods write up (Creswell & Plano Clark, 2010). For a guide to reading mixed methods, see Morse and Niehaus's Appendix for a Worksheet for analyzing (2009) mixed-methods research articles.

This chapter illustrated the uniqueness of mixed-methods designs and how quantitative and qualitative elements are used to create true mixed-methods designs. Examples of pseudo–mixed methods were discussed. Advantages of mixed-methods design in the field of gerontology were discussed with examples of how to select and design each of six mixed-methods design types. New mixed-methods sampling, reliability, and validity terminology were defined. Ways to integrate and assure rigor, or legitimation, of mixed-methods designs and steps for data analysis and integration of quantitative and qualitative findings elements (including visual elements) were outlined.

Discussion Questions

- You meet a friend who cannot see the advantage of mixed-methods designs in aging research. Provide the friend with several advantages and disadvantages of this method for use in the field.
- What are some specific advantages in using mixed methods with older persons? To study aging-related issues?
- Use the following premise (what is the meaning of growing older?) for a mixed-methods study and apply it/create a design for it—using each of the possible mixed-methods designs: explanatory sequential, exploratory sequential, convergent parallel, embedded, transformative, and multi-level.
- How does mixed-methods sampling differ from quantitative and qualitative sampling designs? What role do quantitative and qualitative sampling designs play in a mixed-methods study?
- Explain how reliability and validity and rigor (inference transferability and legitimization) work in mixed-methods designs.

Bibliography

Apesoa-Varano, E. C., & Hinton, L. (2013). The promise of mixed-methods for advancing Latino health research. *Journal of Cross-Cultural Gerontology, 28*(3), 267–282. doi:10.1007/s10823–013–9209–2

Barg, F., Huss-Ashmore, R., Wittink, M., Murray, G., Bogner, H., & Gallo, J. (2006). A mixed-methods approach to understanding loneliness and depression in older adults. *Journals of Gerontology Series B: Psychological Sciences and Social Sciences, 61*(6), S329–S339.

Bazeley, P. (2009). Editorial: Integrating data analyses in mixed methods research. *Journal of Mixed Methods Research, 3*(3), 203–207.

Behar-Horenstein, L. S. (2010). "Mixed methods research." In Craig Kridel (Ed.), *Encyclopedia of curriculum studies* (Vol. 2, pp. 575–579). Thousand Oaks, CA: Sage Reference.

Berglund, A., & Ericsson, K. (2003). Different meanings of quality of life: A comparison between what elderly persons and geriatric staff believe is of importance. *International Journal of Nursing Practice, 9*, 112–119.

Biggs, S. (2005). Beyond appearance: Perspectives on identity in later life and some implications for method. *Journal of Gerontology: Social Sciences, 60B*, S118–S128.

Bishop, C., Weinberg, D., Leutz, W., Dossa, A., Pfefferle, S., & Zincavage, R. (2008). Nursing assistants' job commitment: Effects of nursing home organizational factors and impact on resident well-being. *The Gerontologist, 48*, 36–45.

Boyes, M. (2013). Outdoor adventure and successful ageing. *Ageing & Society, 33*(4), 644–665. doi:10.1017/S0144686X12000165

Cameron, R. (2011). *Extending the Mixed Methods Research (MMR) notation system.* SSRN Working Paper Series.

Caracelli, V., & Greene, J. (1993). Data analysis strategies for mixed-method evaluation designs. *Educational Evaluation and Policy Analysis, 15*, 195–207.

Chapin, R., Reed, C., Dobbs, D. (2004). Mental health needs and service use of older adults in assisted living settings: A mixed methods study. *Journal of Mental Health & Aging, 10*, 351–365.

Clarke, P. (2009). Understanding the experience of stroke: A mixed-method research agenda. *The Gerontologist, 49*(3), 293–302.

Cohen-Mansfield, J., Creedon, M., Malone, T., Parpura-Gill, A., Dakheel-Ali, M., & Heasly, C. (2006). Dressing of cognitively impaired nursing home residents: Description and analysis. *The Gerontologist, 46*, 89–96.

Collins, K. M. T., Onwuegbuzie, A. J., & Jiao, Q. G. (2007). A mixed methods investigation of mixed methods sampling designs in social and health science research. *Journal of Mixed Methods Research, 1*(3), 267–294. doi:10.1177/1558689807299526

Collins, K. M. T., Onwuegbuzie, A. J., & Jiao, Q. G. (2009). *Toward a broader understanding of stress and coping.* Charlotte, NC: Information Age.

Cox, E., Green, K., Seo, H., Inaba, M., & Quillen, A. (2006). Coping with late-life challenges: Development and validation of the care-receiver efficacy scale. *The Gerontologist, 46*, 640–649.

Craciun, C., Gellert, P., & Flick, U. (2015). Aging in precarious circumstances: Do positive views on aging make a difference? *The Gerontologist, 40*(3), 201–218. doi:10.1007/s12126-015-9223-5

Creswell, J. W. (2009). *Research design: Qualitative, quantitative, and mixed methods approaches* (3rd ed.). Thousand Oaks, CA: Sage Publications.

Creswell, J. W. (2014). *Research design: Qualitative, quantitative, and mixed methods approaches* (4th ed.). Thousand Oaks, CA: Sage Publications.

Creswell, J. W., & Plano Clark, V. L. (2010). *Designing and conducting mixed methods research.* Thousand Oaks, CA: Sage Publications.

Creswell, J. W., & Plano Clark, V. L. (2011). *Designing and conducting mixed methods research.* New York: Sage.

Creswell, J. W., Fetters, M., & Ivankova, N. (2004). Designing a mixed methods study in primary care. *Annals of Family Medicine, 2*, 7–12.

Denzin, N. K., & Lincoln, Y. S. (2011). *The Sage handbook of qualitative research.* New York: Sage Publications.

Driscoll, D., Appiah-Yeboah, A., Salib, P., & Rupert, D. (2007). Merging qualitative and quantitative data in mixed methods research: How to and why not. *Ecological and Environmental Anthropology, 3*(1), 19–28.

Duggleby, W. D., Swindle, J., Peacock, S., & Ghosh, S. (2011). A mixed methods study of hope, transitions, and quality of life in family caregivers of persons with Alzheimer's disease. *BMC Geriatrics, 11*, 1–12.

Emlet, C. (2007). Experiences of stigma in older adults living with HIV/AIDS: A mixed methods analysis. *AIDS Patient Care and STDs, 21*, 740–752.

Esbensen, B. A., Thome, B., &Thomsen, T. (2012). Dependency in elderly people newly diagnosed with cancer—A mixed-method study. *European Journal of Oncology Nursing, 16*(2), 137–144.

Fenge, L., & Jones, K. (2012; 2011). Gay and pleasant land? Exploring sexuality, ageing and rurality in a multi-method, performative project. *British Journal of Social Work, 42*(2), 300–317. doi:10.1093/bjsw/bcr058

Fetters, M. D., Curry, L. A., & Creswell, J. W. (2013). Achieving integration in mixed methods designs: Principles and practices. *Health Services Research, 48*(6 pt 2), 2134–2156. doi:10.1111/1475–6773.12117

Fries, C. (2009). Bourdieu's reflexive sociology as a theoretical basis for mixed methods research. *Journal of Mixed Methods Research, 3*, 326–348.

Gaugler, J. E., Reese, M., & Tanler, R. (2016). Care to plan: An online tool that offers tailored support to dementia caregivers. *The Gerontologist, 56*(6): 1161–1174. doi:10.1093/geront/gnv150

Geist, M. R., & Lahman, M. K. E. (2008). "Mixed methodology research." In F. T. L. Leong, E. M. Altmaier, & B. D. Johnson (Eds.), *Encyclopedia of counseling*. Thousand Oaks, CA: Sage Publications.

Greene, J. C. (2007). *Mixed methods in social inquiry* (1st ed.). San Francisco, CA: Jossey-Bass.

Greene, J. C. (2015). The emergence of mixing methods in the field of evaluation. *Qualitative Health Research, 25*(6), 746–750. doi:10.1177/1049732315576499

Happ, M. B. (2009). Mixed methods in gerontological research. *Research in Gerontological Nursing, 2*(2), 122–127. doi:10.3928/19404921-20090401-06

Henwood, B. F., Katz, M. L., & Gilmer, T. P. (2015). Aging in place within permanent supportive housing. *International Journal of Geriatric Psychiatry, 30*(1), 80–87. doi:10.1002/gps.4120

Hildon, Z., Smith, G., Netueli, G., & Blane, D. (2008). Understanding adversity and resilience at older ages. *Sociology of Health & Illness, 30*, 726–740.

Hodgkin, S., Warburton, J., & Savy, P. (2012). Using mixed methods to develop and implement a work sampling tool in residential aged care. *International Journal of Multiple Research Approaches, 6*(1), 23–32. doi:10.5172/mra.2012.6.1.23

Howes, C. (2008). Love, money, or flexibility: What motivates people to work in consumer-directed home care? *The Gerontologist, 48*, 46–59.

Hwalek, M., Straub, V., & Kosniewski, K. (2008). Older workers: An opportunity to expand long-term care/direct care labor force. *The Gerontologist, 48*, 90–103.

Ingersoll-Dayton, B., Saengtienchai, C., Kespichayawattana, J., & Aungsuroch, Y. (2004). Measuring psychological wellbeing: Insights from Thai elders. *The Gerontologist, 44*, 596–604.

Jensen, C., Finifter, D. H., Wilson, C. E., & Koenig, B. L. (2007). Community assessment of senior health using a telephone survey and supplementary methods. *Journal of Applied Gerontology, 26*, 17–33.

Johnson, R. B., Onwuegbuzie, A. J., & Turner, L. A. (2007). Toward a definition of mixed methods research. *Journal of Mixed Methods Research, 1*(2), 112–133. doi:10.1177/1558689806298224

Kayser-Jones, J., Wiener, C., & Barbaccia, J. (1989). Factors contributing to the hospitalization of nursing home residents. *The Gerontologist, 29*, 502–510.

Kemp, C. L., Ball, M. M., & Perkins, M. M. (2016). Couples' social careers in assisted living: Reconciling individual and shared situations. *The Gerontologist, 56*(5), 841–854. doi:10.1093/geront/gnv025

Krause, N. (2002). Comprehensive strategy for developing close-ended survey items for use in studies of older adults. *Journal of Gerontology: Social Sciences, 57B*, S263–S274.

Krause, N. (2006). The use of qualitative methods to improve quantitative methods to improve quantitative measures of health-related constructs. *Medical Care, 44*, S34–S38.

Kristensen, T., Ekdahl, C., Kehlet, H., & Bandholm, T. (2010). How many trials are needed to achieve performance stability of the Timed Up & Go Test in patients with hip fracture? *Archives of Physical Medicine and Rehabilitation, 91*, 885–889.

Leavy, B., Byberg, L., Michaelsson, K., Melhus, H., & Aberg, A. The fall descriptions and health characteristics of older adults with hip fracture: A mixed methods study. *BMC Geriatrics, 15*(1), 40. doi:10.1186/s12877–015–0036-x

Lehning, A. (2012). City governments and aging in place: Community design, transportation and housing innovation adoption. *Gerontologist, 52*(3), 345–356. doi:10.1093/geront/gnr089

Liang, W., Kasman, D., Wang, J., Yuan, E., & Mandelblatt, J. (2006). Communication between older women and physicians: Preliminary implications for satisfaction and intention to have mammography. *Patient Education and Counseling, 64*, 387–392.

Lunde, Å., Heggen, K., & Strand, R. (2013). Knowledge and power: Exploring unproductive interplay between quantitative and qualitative researchers. *Journal of Mixed Methods Research, 7*(2), 197–210. doi:10.1177/1558689812471087

Mertens, D. M. (2010). Transformative mixed methods research. *Qualitative Inquiry, 16*(6), 469–474. doi:10.1177/1077800410364612

Morgan, J. C., & Konrad, T. R. (2008). A mixed-method evaluation of a workforce development intervention for nursing assistants in nursing homes: The case of WIN A step UP. *The Gerontologist, 48(S*-1), 71–79. doi:10.1093/geront/48.Supplement_1.71

Morgan, L., & Kunkel, S. (2006). "Why conduct research?" In L. Morgan & S. Kunkel (Eds.), *Aging, society, and the life course* (pp. 27–49). New York: Springer Publishing.

Morse, J. M., & Niehaus, L. (2009). *Mixed method design: Principles and procedures*. Walnut Creek, CA: Left Coast Press.

Nygren, C., & Iwarsson, S. (2009). Negotiating and effectuating relocation to sheltered housing in old age: A Swedish study over 11 years. *European Journal of Ageing, 6*(3), 177–189.

O'Cathain, A. (2011). Editorial: Mixed methods research in the health sciences: A quiet revolution. *Journal of Mixed Methods Research, 3*, 3–6.

Onwuegbuzie, A. J. (2012). Introduction: Putting the MIXED back into quantitative and qualitative research in educational research and beyond: Moving toward the radical middle. *International Journal of Multiple Research Approaches, 6*(3), 192–219. doi:10.5172/mra.2012.6.3.192

Onwuegbuzie, A. J., & Johnson, R. B. (2006). The validity issue in mixed research. *Research in the Schools, 13*(1), 48.

Onwuegbuzie, A. J., Johnson, R. B., & Collins, K. M. (2011). A framework for assessing legitimation in mixed research. *Quality & Quantity: International Journal of Methodology, 45*, 1253–1271. doi:10.1007/s1113500992899

Onwuegbuzie, A. J., & Teddlie, C. (2003). "Framework for analyzing data in mixed methods research." In A. Tashakkori, & C. Teddlie (Eds.), *Handbook of mixed methods in social and behavioral research* (pp. 351–384). Thousand Oaks, CA: Sage Publications.

Ostlund-Lagerstrom, L., Blomberg, K., Algilani, S., Schoultz, M., Kihlgren, A., Brummer, R., & Institutionen för hälsovetenskap och medicin. (2015). Senior orienteering athletes as a model of healthy aging: A mixed-method approach. *BMC Geriatrics, 15*, 76. doi:10.1186/s12877–015–0072–6

Pettersson, C., Löfqvist, C., & Malmgren Fänge, A. (2012). Clients' experiences of housing adaptations: A longitudinal mixed-methods study. *Disability and Rehabilitation, 34*(20), 1706–1715. doi:10.3109/09638288.2012.660596

Pillemer, K., Meador, R., Henderson, C., Robison, J., Hegeman, C., Graham, E., & Schultz, L. (2008). Facility specialist model for improving retention of nursing home staff: Results from a randomized, controlled study. *The Gerontologist, 48*, 80–89.

Plano Clark, V. L., Anderson, N., Wertz, J. A., Zhou, Y., Schumacher, K., & Miaskowski, C. (2014). Conceptualizing longitudinal mixed methods designs: A methodological review of health sciences research. *Journal of Mixed Methods Research, 9*(4), 297–319.

Rogers, A., Harris, T., Victor, C., Woodcock, A., Limb, E., Kerry, S., & Cook, D. (2014). Which older people decline participation in a primary care trial of physical activity and why: Insights from a mixed methods approach. *BMC Geriatrics, 14*(1), 1–9. doi:10.1186/1471–2318–14–46

Sandelowski, M. (2003). "Tables or tableaux? The challenges of writing and reading mixed methods studies." In A. Tashakkori, & C. Teddlie (Eds.), *Handbook of mixed methods in social and behavioral research* (pp. 321–350). Thousand Oaks, CA: Sage Publications.

Schroepfer, T. A. (2008). Social relationships and their role in the consideration to hasten death. *The Gerontologist, 48*, 612–621.

Shield, R. R., Looze, J., Tyler, D., Lepore, M., & Miller, S. C. (2014). Why and how do nursing homes implement culture change practices? Insights from qualitative interviews in a mixed methods study. *Journal of Applied Gerontology, 33*(6), 737–763. doi:10.1177/0733464813491141

Stine-Morrow, E., Parisi, J., Morrow, D., Greene, J., & Park, D. (2007). An engagement model of cognitive optimization through adulthood. *Journal of Gerontology: Social Sciences, 62*(Special Issue 1), 62–69.

Tashakkori, A. (2009). Are we there yet? The state of the mixed methods community. *Journal of Mixed Methods Research, 3*, 287–291.

Tashakkori, A., & Teddlie, C. (1998). *Mixed methodology: Combining qualitative and quantitative approaches*. Thousand Oaks, CA: Sage Publications.

Tashakkori, A., & Teddlie, C. (2003). *Handbook of mixed methods in social & behavioral research*. Thousand Oaks, CA: Sage Publications.

Tashakkori, A., & Teddlie, C. (2010). Putting the human back in "Human research methodology": The researcher in mixed methods research. *Journal of Mixed Methods Research, 4*(4), 271–277. doi:10.1177/1558689810382532

Tashakkori, A., & Teddlie, C. (Eds.). (2010). *Sage handbook of mixed methods in social & behavioral research* (2nd ed.). Thousand Oaks, CA: Sage Publications.

Teddlie, C., & Tashakkori, A. (2009). *Foundations of mixed methods research: Integrating quantitative and qualitative approaches in the social and behavioral sciences*. Los Angeles: Sage Publications.

Teddlie, C., & Tashakkori, A. (2010). "Overview of contemporary issues in mixed methods research." In A. Tashakkori, & C. Teddlie (Eds.), *Sage handbook of mixed methods in social & behavioral research* (2nd ed., pp. 1–41). Thousand Oaks, CA: Sage Publications.

Teddlie, C., & Tashakkori, A. (2012). Common "Core" characteristics of mixed methods research: A review of critical issues and call for greater convergence. *American Behavioral Scientist, 56*(6), 774–788. doi:10.1177/000276421143379

Teddlie, C., & Yu, F. (2007). Mixed methods sampling: A typology with examples. *Journal of Mixed Methods Research, 1*(1), 77–100. doi:10.1177/2345678906292430

Travis, S., Bernard, M., Dixon, S., McAuley, W., Loving, G., & McClanahan, L. (2002). Obstacles to palliation and end-of-life care in a long-term care facility. *Gerontologist, 42*(3), 342–349. doi:10.1093/geront/42.3.342

Van Ness, P., Fried, T., & Gill, T. (2011). Mixed methods for the interpretation of longitudinal gerontologic data: Insights from philosophical hermeneutics. *Journal of Mixed Methods Research, 5*(4), 293–308. doi:10.1177/1558689811412973

Victor, C. R., Scambler, S. J., Bond, J., Bowling, A. (2000). Being alone in later life: Loneliness, isolation and living alone in later life. *Reviews in Clinical Gerontology, 10*, 407–417. doi:10.1017/S0959259800104101

Vrkljan, B. (2009). Constructing a mixed methods design to explore the older driver-copilot relationship. *Journal of Mixed Methods Research, 3*, 371–385.

Walker, A., Hennessy, C. H., & ESRC Growing Older Programme. (2004). *Growing older: Quality of life in old age*. Maidenhead, Berkshire, UK: Open University Press.

Watkins, D. C., Wharton, T., Mitchell, J. A., Matusko, N., & Kales, H. C. (2015). Perceptions and receptivity of non-spousal family support a mixed methods study of psychological distress among older, church-going African American men. *Journal of Mixed Methods Research, 2015*, 1–23. doi: 10.1177/1558689815622707

Weil, J. (2015). Applying research methods to a gerontological population: Matching data collection to characteristics of older persons. *Educational Gerontology, 41*(10), 723–742. doi:10.1080/03601277.2015.1048172

Yeatts, D., & Cready, C. (2007). Consequences of empowered CNA teams in nursing home settings: A longitudinal assessment. *The Gerontologist, 20*, 323–339.

8
Emerging and Future Methods

This purpose of this chapter is to introduce new trends in research designs and methodological approaches in gerontology. The chapter outlines new qualitative, quantitative, and mixed-methods designs while acknowledging that the lines between these methods are continually becoming blurred and overlapping. Qualitative emergent methods are embracing the arts and humanities and include photography (photovoice), drawing, painting sculpture, film, performance, visual diaries, and a range of digital and technology-inclusive methods. These methods include persons of all cognitive statuses and call for even greater reflexivity on the part of the researcher. Emergent quantitative methods include a mixing of biological and performance-based data with person-based reports and the use of GIS and sensors. The bench and social sciences are mixed in studies, and data are standardized across datasets. More complex mathematical models are being developed to address the Age-Period-Cohort issue and to display individual and group data to truly reflect a lifecourse perspective. These methods are requiring more technical and software-based skills of the researcher. Mixed methods continue to evolve and gain use in practice and publication. Emergent mixed methods have requirements of both the new quantitative and qualitative methods.

Trends in Emergent Methods in Gerontology

Gerontology's interdisciplinary nature is a benefit in bringing new methodologic approaches from one field to another. This interdisciplinary nature also encourages combining/merging a diverse set of methods to best meet a research question's call. In broadly reading the contemporary gerontological literature, several themes exist. A discussion of current themes/trends in research approaches in the field is necessary to put these new and emergent methodologies in context.

The first trend is the **redefining of age** and old age. Researchers are redefining the boundaries or demarcation of what is "old" and "very old/oldest old" in terms of chronological age. With lifespan increasing and segments of the population aging (such as the Baby Boomers in the United States), markers of "being old" at age 65 or "oldest old" at 85 or 90 years of age are no longer the case. These age markers may have begun tied to eligibility for social programs, benefits (Social Security, Medicare), or retirement age, but they no longer reflect these age markers in contemporary society.

Other measures of aging have also gained status in the field. There is much work in defining age by cognition and cognitive status (Rabbitt, 2015), while some researchers seek to define biological age and disentangle aspects of health that are tied to the aging process (Wolf, Freedman, Ondrich, Seplaki & Spillman, 2015). Researchers are also looking within the older individual to see the intra-individual factors and differences associated with aging (Diehl, Hooker & Sliwinski, 2015; Schafer & Ferraro, 2013).

The focus of gerontology and studies of aging is also becoming both individual/person-based to show heterogeneity in the aging process. **Embodiment**, or using the body and its interaction with the social world in research, and being a co-researcher and not an object in a research study, shows the individual aging focus (Carney & Gray, 2015). Embodiment "signifies the body as a vehicle of social agency. Embodiment encompasses all those actions performed by the body or on the body which are inextricably oriented towards the social. It is subject to and made salient by the actions and interpretations of self and others" (Gilleard & Higgs, 2015, online). Other researchers call for anti-ageism and the real accounts of aging to continue to combat the "**elderly mystique**" (of Cohen [1988]) or "gap between lived experience of old age and societal expectations of older people which are based on 'the detritus of gerontophobic views,' whose origins have been attributed, variously, to modernisation, demography, and rising economic wealth" (Carney & Gray, 2015, p. 123).

At the same time, trends are also focusing on **macro-level forces**: society, culture, and country. On the macro level, connections are made to synch data across countries or harmonize data and populations to make etic statements (Gatz, Reynolds, Finkel, Hahn, Zhou & Zavala, 2015). Gerontology journals are creating "**international spotlights**." Editors creating this feature hope "these articles will not only enhance our understanding about global aging but also spark international collaborations that ultimately will lead to more sophisticated research and better public policies and practices supporting older people" (McCutcheon & Pruchno, 2011, p. 424). Countries featured in the "spotlight" to date are as follows (from earliest to latest): Japan, Australia, Israel (2011); Chile, China (2012); Canada, France, Korea, Hong Kong, Thailand, Turkey (2013); Romania, Netherlands, Sweden, Spain, Czech Republic (2014); and Lebanon, Poland, India (2015).

Global aging is also accompanied with revisiting **ethnogerontology**, renewed interest in cultural aging, and increased multiple identities and stances, called intersectionality. Researchers cite Jacqueline Johnson as creating the term "ethnogerontology" as "the study of the causes, processes, and consequences of race, national origin, and culture on individual and population aging in the three broad areas of biological, psychological, and social aging" (Johnson [1985] in Crewe, 2005, p. 48). Researchers now "look at the ways in which race, ethnicity, and the lifecourse work in tandem in shaping the lives of people. . . . [I]n a society where race, ethnicity, and age are important elements of social organization, the lives of individuals, from their birth to death, are going to be impacted by their experiences and expressions of racial or ethnic prejudice, stereotyping, and discrimination" (Mitra & Weil, 2014, p. ix).

Cultural gerontology is related to ethnogerontology. Julia Twigg and Wendy Martin (2015) suggests, "Cultural gerontology indeed seeks to identify and understand the specificities of cultural contexts, whether revealed in the literature, historical analysis, art, or ethnography" (2016, 19). She adds that "cultural gerontology with its emphasis on subjectivity and identity, foregrounds the perspectives of older people themselves, decentering dominant, often objectifying accounts" (p. 20). **Intersectionality** builds upon earlier concepts of multiple jeopardy (or the combination of marginalized statuses in society) and attempts to bring in all social positions and the role of society in viewing, constructing, and regulating aging into one model to research (King, 1988). Some mandate "researchers to reveal the underlying categorical boundaries (such as race, class, gender, and age) that are constructed as interlocking systems of oppression and must be negotiated as people (who are raced, classed, and gendered) navigate those boundaries as they move through the lifecourse" (Byfield, 2014, pp. 48–49). Gerontology researchers call for studies to include older men—as often older women are the focus. A study of five leading behavioral journals found that 69% of older participants were women (LaLonde, Zimmermann & Poling, 2015). Others tried online methods to increase older men's participation in studies of retirement (Leontowitsch, 2013).

Gerotechnology and the use of **online methodologies** are on the increase. Technology can refer to a smartphone or tablet or can extend to sensors and robots (Schulz, Wahl, Matthews, De Vito Dabbs, Beach & Czaja, 2015). Gerotechnology has mostly been geared toward increasing older persons' quality of life through biomedical interventions and/or monitoring. (Past understanding of gerotechnology was of its use as mostly a gatekeeper.) Social media, online communities, and gaming are also included (Vosner, Bobek, Kokol & Krecic, 2016). Yet research design in gerontology continues to evolve with more disciplines and approaches merging.

Choosing among Emerging and Future Research Methods

Qualitative Options

Humanities and arts have merged with gerontological approaches to produce **creative research methods** (Gauntlett, 2007; Kara, 2015). Creative research methods seek to "explore the ways in which researchers can embrace people's everyday creativity in order to understand social experience. Seeking an alternative to traditional interviews and focus groups . . . video, collage, and drawing—and then interpret them" (Gauntlett, 2007; Xenitidou & Gilbert, 2009). Creative methods are arts based and can incorporate technology or be solely online based. These methods can expand traditional methods by incorporating innovative applications of existing methods, adding in mixed methods, or producing transformative research frameworks (Kara, 2015). While new, there is concern about how these emergent qualitative methods can fit into the existing academic publishing outlets.

Self-Photography/Photovoice

Researchers using **self-photography, or photovoice**, with diabetic rural older persons describe the technique as "a community-based participatory action methodology that puts the tools of research in the hands of participants" (Yankeelov, Faul, D'Ambrosio, Collins & Gordon, 2015, p. 199). Photovoice research actively involves the older participant who sees, captures, and reflects upon his or her self-created pictures of his or her daily world. Photovoice methods offer several data approaches and analysis strategies. The photos themselves can be analyzed for the intention of the picture taker or the theme and content of the photo. Photos can also be analyzed for artistic content and merit (e.g., lighting, angle, color, positioning of items within the frame). In a photovoice study of older persons' perceptions of hearing loss, Kenneth Southall found the older persons did not simply want to capture stereotypical images of the world of hearing loss. The group decided to photograph the experiences and events they encountered, as persons, in everyday life. The group met and presented their images and discussed the content on both the visual and the interpretive levels (Southall, 2014). Southhall has created a Prezi video of aspects of this photovoice project (Southall, 2015, https://prezi.com/rftayq0pp4ab/authentic-portraits-of-acquired-hearing-loss-a-photovoice-s/).

Visual Diaries and Film/Self-Documentary

Traditionally, gerontology has embraced the use of film and digital media as teaching tools (Scheidt, Bosch, Kivnick & Pruchno, 2012). This use has been expanded. Researchers now use **video diaries** to study the impact of chronic health conditions upon daily life. A researcher, Charlotte Bates, has described steps in the process. First, participants can choose a video or written journal option. Those choosing the video option were given a camera that recorded to a memory card, a tripod, and instructions about what to shoot ("tell me about your body or condition") within a fixed time interval. Bates suggested that researchers reconcile the "ethics of recognition"—meaning, make sure that participants are aware that they can choose to shoot their image and reveal their identity or choose to capture objects and not reveal themselves directly (Bates, 2015, p. 12). After videos were recorded, Bates transcribed the film's dialogue, added in survey responses, and re-watched all the video footage. She then looked at split-screen video clips and produced a one-hour file of 16 of those clips that included zooming and other editing techniques.

Drawing, Painting, Sculpture, and Lego®

The arts of drawing, painting, or sculpture are done for their artistic value or as an expression of the artist's identity. The artist's work is a reflection of his or her identity or the message he or she hopes to convey. This creative process is different from art therapies that use art for its healing value with older persons. Creative methods have included Lego® building as an adapted form of sculpture. The goal of the exercises is to have the individual build models that represent the person's sense of self or identity, or who they are. While not designed specifically for older adults, Lego® building as a metaphor for identity construction has been used with those in their midlife and early 50s (Gauntlett, 2007).

Laura Hofstadter is a 65-year-old photographer who created "Stages: A set of self-portraits," where she photographs herself in the style of well-recognized paintings by artists such as Degas, Vermeer, Da Vinci, Rembrandt, and Magritte. She describes the intention of her work:

> I tried to express my feelings as a woman growing older in a youth-obsessed society. The portfolio is narrative reflecting my experience of facing breast cancer, whose treatment disfigured my body. My hope is viewers confront preconceptions about youth, age, beauty, and body image when looking at these pictures.
>
> (http://laurahofstadter.com/cgi-bin/gallery.cgi?gallery=StagesSelfPortraits&num=13)

Drawings have been used in an IRB-approved study of Latino grandfamilies. Grandchildren, living with or primarily cared for by their grandparents, were asked to draw a picture of their families (Mendoza, 2012). In each drawing, after given assent, children not only drew their family but commented on how they saw the roles of family members and others in relation to their own identities. See Figure 8.1 for examples of the children's art.

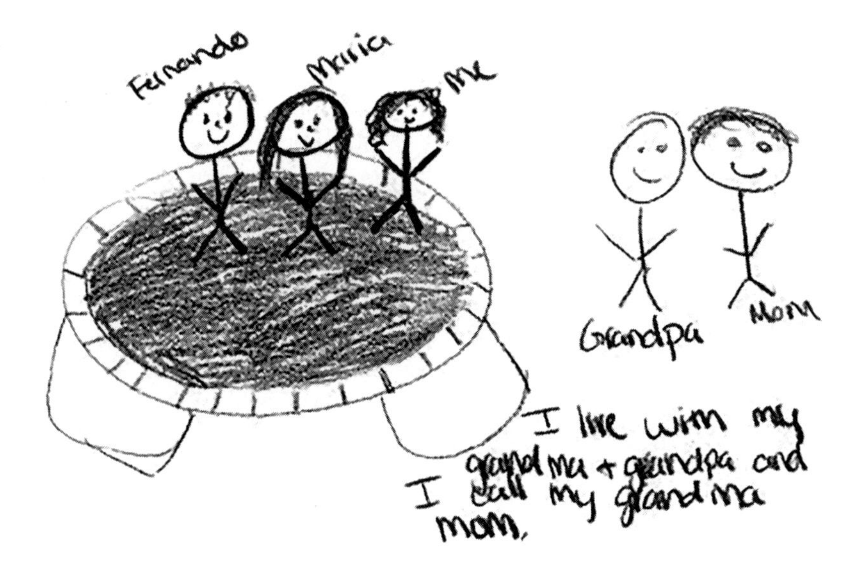

Figure 8.1 Children's Drawings of Their Grandfamilies

Source: Mendoza, A. N. (2012). *Grandparents raising grandchildren: A look at Latino cultural influences on needs and service usage* (Master's Thesis, University of Northern Colorado). Available from ProQuest (#839685528).

Technology and Virtual Methods

No longer in the "**grey digital divide**," or left out of technology use, older persons are active consumers of technology. Researchers are increasingly using technology in research design (Leontowitsch, 2013, p. 223). The digital divide is not the same for all persons 65 years of age and older. In fact, the likelihood of Internet/web usage has been found to decrease 8% each year after age 65, with those 85 years of age and older the least likely to use the Internet/web (Friemel, 2016). Online surveys, email questionnaires, and online groups have given rise to possibilities of using **web- or smartphone-based visual conversations** (via Skype, FaceTime, or Hangouts). There are **blogs** (for comment posting) and interactive webpages where users can co-create content (**wikis**). Data mining can occur from social media. Data can be drawn from posts on social media (**tweets**) or be created via **word clouds** (visual displays of words/content where greater emphasis is placed on more frequently used terms).

Online focus groups offer additional ways to interact and conduct research with older persons in an **online or virtual environment.** Synchronistic, "live," chat online has been found to produce longer responses than email in a study of older men and retirement. Since live chatting mimics real-time conversation more closely, additional questions and probing of ambiguous responses can be done (Leontowitsch, 2013). Some general cautions are warranted when using a digital method. Using the Internet, with any population, raises issues of rapport and trust. There are also issues of use of symbols to replace more complex written language and differing punctuation and interpretation of online text and narrative (Chan & Choi, 2013).

Digital Ethnographies

Digital ethnography (also called cyber ethnography, virtual ethnography, or netnography) expands the medium of traditional ethnographic practice. Digital ethnographies encompass the general practice and principles of non-digital ethnographic studies. But digital ethnography has unique issues: differences in the nature of the field or field setting, ways to address elements of time, and issues of the researcher's role, including deception in research.

In digital ethnography, the field is an online setting or virtual reality made up of social networks (Markham, 2016). Digital ethnography/netnography has been used with older persons as "observations of technologically mediated interactions in online networks and communities and the cyberculture shared between and among them" (Nimrod, 2011, p. 229; for an example of an online elder-based community, see http://coolgrandma.com/). Time in a traditional ethnography is **synchronous**, meaning the data collection, researcher, and participants are all interacting at the same period of time. Digital ethnography, however, can be **asynchronous**, or occurring at different periods in time. For example, a researcher could be chatting with a participant live online, or the researcher could be reading existing transcripts of texts posted in a chat room or blog.

Digital ethnography raises some issues about the researcher's stance. Some warn that digital technology should not trump technique (Atkinson, 2015). This method "leaves most of the specifics of the adaptation to the individual researcher. The researcher may choose to study the researched communities by utilizing a participative approach, which is closer to traditional ethnographic standards" (Nimrod, 2011, p. 229). Among ethical issues associated with the researcher's role in digital ethnography is deception: a researcher could pose as a member of a group and not identify himself or herself as a researcher to group members. For example, the researcher, posing as a caregiver but not one in reality, could enter a group of caregivers. Or a researcher can be a silent part of a group or a "lurker," or he or she might review email lists to locate potential participants (Beaulieu & Høybye, 2011). Others raise issues of what information is in the private vs. the public domain (Chan & Choi, 2013). For example, are tweets and blog entries that are posted openly really public access/open domain? Can they be directly quoted without the poster's consent?

Digital ethnography can also refer to the methods of **digital data collection or analysis**. Dhiraj Murthy (2011) suggests that digital pens recording field notes directly to a computer file can replace the traditional pen and paper approach. He describes **Ethno-Goggles**, eyeglasses worn that take video and photos of what the researchers is viewing. The goggles also include a microphone to capture the researcher's spoken reflections. There is software, called **Zing**, that lets several people use their keyboards simultaneously online to participate in online focus groups. Interactive polls and field notes can also be posted by the researcher as a blog.

Ethnopoetics and Narrative as Literature

Ethnopoetics is the use of poetry or the creation of poetry through participants' own words. These poems do not begin as true poems but are constructed by the researcher and older person to create "research poetry" (Miller & Brockie, 2015, p. 105). Researchers have used elder-themed open-ended interview data to create poems about their experiences surviving a flood. The created poems were then discussed with the elders to make sure the pieces resonated with them. Autobiographies are not just a source of data for content analysis; they are looked at as good stories. They are also about "intense experiences, crises, and major life events, linked with cultural location" (Kara, 2015, p. 25). Older persons can become digital storytellers recording their own narratives online (see Gubrium, 2009; and www.storycenter.org). Participants are active collaborators in the story-creation process.

Ethnodrama

Ethnodrama is the process of taking interview or written/recorded text from an individual one is studying and creating a dramatic interpretation or performance of that work. The performance can be filmed or audio recorded. For example, researchers created a theater performance (research-based theater) called *Advocating for Hilda*, from interviews about what it is like to care for a person with dementia. The video performance was then shown to caregivers as a target audience to help them recognize and discuss their care experiences (Speechley, DeForge, Ward-Griffin, Marlatt & Gutmanis, 2015).

Embodiment work, as mentioned in Chapter 4, includes using body-based or arts-based work to collect or represent data—"mobilizing body-based and arts-informed techniques that help researchers follow, trace, ride, or otherwise come into deep relation with the palpating forces of the data themselves . . . a relationship with data grounded in its immanent, co-implicative, communal qualities" (Clark/Keefe, 2014, p. 790).

Deep Mapping

Deep mapping is described as a mixture of social sciences, ethnography, and visual media to create a sense of what place, setting, or geography is like for a person. A team of filmmakers, researchers, and media/photography experts have conducted visual mapping to capture the sense of a rural place for elders in England (Bailey & Biggs, 2012). The data-mapping process "brings together a multiplicity of voices, information, impressions, and perspectives in a multimedia representation of a particular environment [including] creative arts practices, critical reflection and ethnography . . . [and] proceeds by interweaving a broad spectrum of distinct imaginally and conceptually-based material—threads of text, sound and image—into a provisional re-patterning" (Bailey & Biggs, 2012, p. 318; see some examples of data mapping at http://www.newdynamics.group.shef.ac.uk/ageingresearchprojects.html).

Gaming and Avatar Identities

Gaming is emerging as a research-design option. Game researchers found games designed for persons 60 years of age and older focus on depicting the negative characteristics of the older player, such as lack of physical or mental functioning. These games are offered as ways of "warding off aging by [their] consumption" (Iversen, 2016, p. 20). Most games market the perceived functional benefits of game playing. Game researchers took a different course of action and, in a two-year evaluation, studied which type of game appealed to those 60 years of age and older. After some initial reluctance, participants enjoyed increased concentration and preferred interactive games (such as trivia or map/treasure hunting). The persons 60 years of age and over in the study preferred to be co-creators of these games (Sayago, Rosales, Righi, Ferreira, Coleman & Blat, 2016). Older persons' choice in avatar images to represent them online followed common online identity practices. Avatars were selected based on favored individual characteristics, to resemble the person in real life, or to stress the player's expertise as a competitor in the game (Martey, 2014).

More Closely Examining Researchers' Roles and Designs Inclusive of All Cognitive Statuses

Self-reflexivity of the researcher and inclusion of older persons as co-researchers continues as a trend. Authors suggest that individual (qualitative) researchers look deeper within themselves and explore their conscious and unconscious issues in the selection of a sample and the related implications (Reybold, Lammert & Stribling, 2012). While researchers become more introspective, research designs evolve to include persons with a broader range of cognitive statuses. The Evaluation to Sign Consent (ESC) and other techniques have been developed to assure that a person with cognitive impairment understands the details of a research study and can fully participate (Artzer & Weil, 2016).

Diaries for people with dementia, in any form (photos, audio, written, or in combination), are used in research to include elders' own voices and as advocacy measures (Bartlett, 2014). **Dementia theater** is created by or about persons with cognitive impairment, with performances relaying the subjects' lived experiences. An example is the play *Cracked*. The playwright states that the title is drawn from a song lyric: "There is a crack in everything, that's how the light gets in" (Leonard Cohen). The script was created from words and experiences of people with dementia, their social networks, academic researchers work with dementia, and the guidance of a theater group. The play is based on the premise that:

> memory in all of its forms must be valorized, self-expression must be nurtured, and the humanity and full citizenship of persons who are living with dementia must be fully supported. This perspective is in contrast with the dehumanizing care practices that still prevail in many dementia care settings.
>
> (https://uwaterloo.ca/partnerships-in-dementia-care/re-imagining-dementia-through-arts/cracked-new-light-dementia; https://www.youtube.com/watch?v=v-hS2CnCmjs)

Quantitative Options

Elder-Computer Interaction, Body Sensors, Geographic Information Systems (GIS), and Paradata

Researchers reviewed 30 years of aging and **human-computer interaction (HCI)**. This revealed "aging as a problem, managed by technology" (Vines, Pritchard, Wright, Olivier & Brittain, 2015, p. 1). The literature focused on health concerns and physical and cognitive decline. It portrayed older persons as slow with technology but portrayed technology as a cure for social isolation and as helping with decreased independence. The researchers called for less biomedicalization of older people's technology use and HCI to embrace older persons' technological diversity in a "discourse of homogeneity" (Vines, Pritchard, Wright, Olivier & Brittain, 2015, p. 12). Otherwise, stereotypes will really limit design opportunities.

Independent living designs in gerontology have employed **sensor technology** for older persons' health measurements and tracking (Cisneros, Dyer-Chamberlain & Hickie, 2012). Digital homes that integrate the use of technology and the homeowner's preferences ("symbiotically") also offer data for research (Holoham, Chin, Callaghan & Mühlau, 2011, p. 647). Studies are beginning to explore body sensors and transmitter use in settings outside the home and into the older person's own community and local environment (de Haan, Choenni, Mulder, Kalidien & van Waart, 2011). Carnegie Mellon University and Google's Living Lab project is a present-day example of a "living lab for interconnected sensors [in the built environment] and gadgets" (Spice, 2015). Sensor-tracking mobile phone networks and tracking phone towers have been suggested as location-based study data (Eagle, 2011).

Geographic information systems (GIS) have been used to track and analyze older peoples' movement in their neighborhoods (Schwieger, 2010). Researchers used GIS to track neighborhood markers of leisure for persons 65 years of age and older. Leisure patterns (of time spent in parks, sport, sea, bus/transportation, and mountains), neighborhood social-class characteristics, and crime survey data were linked to GIS data. A supplementary GIS file for neighborhood crime data was also provided (Ribeiro, Pires, Carvalho & Pina, 2015).

With the use of technology as a method of data collection comes the ability to capture many aspects of the process of data collection, called **paradata**. Paradata consists of "keystroke files, capturing the navigation through a questionnaire, time stamps, reflecting the length of a question–answer sequence, and data from call records or contact attempts . . . [or] interviewer's observations about a sampled household or neighbourhood, and recordings of vocal properties of the interviewer and respondent. . . . [T]hey are a by-product of the data collection process capturing information about that process" (Durrant & Kreuter, 2013, p. 1).

Deeper Physical and Biological Measuring and Merging of "Hard" and "Soft" Sciences

The use, and mixing of, **biological, performance-based measures** is not new in gerontology. The level of biological investigation and linking of data is the new turn. Studies now combine self-rated and performance-based measures with biomarkers circulating in an older person's blood to define physical performance and disease risk across the lifespan (Peterson et al., 2016; George & Ferraro, 2016). Other studies have linked two of five examined genetic markers from blood samples of those 65 and over to predict 9% of variation in resilience of that group (Resnick, Klinedinst, Yerges-Armstrong, Choi & Dorsey, 2015).

The Geropathology Research Network (GRN) expands the use of biological markers in aging research. The GRN defines itself:

> We are introducing the term "geropathology" to designate the study of aging and age-related lesions and diseases in the form of whole necropsies/autopsies, surgical biopsies, histology, and molecular biomarkers, which encompasses multiple subspecialties including geriatrics, anatomic pathology, molecular pathology, clinical pathology, and gerontology.
>
> (Ladiges et al., 2016, p. 431)

There is a call for continued mixing of bench and social sciences' approaches. Authors have recently called for combining social gerontology with medical student training (Tinker, Hussain, D'Cruz, Tai & Zaidman, 2016). A special issue of the *Official Journal of the European Group for Research into Elderly and Physical Activity* exemplifies the mixing approach. The editors wrote: "Basic research and behavioral, practice-oriented considerations must be brought together for a successful acceptance and implementation of disease-specific physical activities in clinical and therapeutic situations" (Mechling, 2013, p. 2). Summing up the results of a workshop on health and aging, in "Preparing for an aging world: Engaging biogerontologists, geriatricians, and the society," the authors call for more interdisciplinary research and work combining biological science with age-based health interventions to improve outcomes (Nikolich-Žugich et al., 2015).

Data Harmonization and New Mathematical Models

Data harmonization is the process of standardizing variables and responses so that a concept can be tracked, linked, and followed in more than one dataset. The National Institutes of Health and Aging have called for more compatibility across datasets where variables currently have different response categories and levels of measurement. Findings from a National Institute on Aging's (2011) *Workshop on harmonization strategies for behavioral, social science, and genetic research* report suggest:

> Harmonization is not the same as homogenization; it's important for studies to maintain their unique focus and interests. . . . Harmonization should be viewed as an approach that provides insight into critical issues about existing measures, both in ways to facilitate cross-study analyses and to identify measures that can capture critical domains.
>
> (p. 3)

Gerontological researchers investigating ways to harmonize depression data for older persons found that differing response categories (Likert scales vs. dichotomous variables) made the harmonizing process more difficult. They suggest harmonization is a necessary, but slow-moving, process (Gatz, Reynolds, Finkel, Hahn, Zhou & Zavala, 2015). In the United States, the Inter-university Consortium for Political and Social Research (ICPSR) data warehouse has an online bibliography about good data stewardship practices for metadata (https://www.icpsr.umich.edu/icpsrweb/content/membership/data-stewardship.html#metadata). Internationally, researchers have recreated the Cross-National Equivalent file, of "equivalently defined variables" for eight international datasets (https://cnef.ehe.osu.edu/).

Gerontological research is becoming increasingly complex in design and analytical sophistication (George & Ferraro, 2016). Two examples are the interest and expansion of hierarchical **Age-Period-Cohort (APC)** designs and the application of latent class analysis at the individual and group levels. A recent work by Yang Yang and Keith Land, *Age-period-cohort analysis: New models, methods, and empirical applications*, offers researchers online syntax in STATA and R programmatic languages to increase the use of hierarchical APC models (see http://yangclaireyang.web.unc.edu/age-period-cohort-analysis-new-models-methods-and-empirical-applications/). Other researchers using APC models to examine risk of chronic disease employed the apcfit feature in STATA (Taylor, Campostrini, Gill, Carter, Dal Grande & Herriot, 2010). Details about the apcfit feature can be found in the *Stata Journal* (Rutherford, Lambert & Thompson, 2010).

Researchers are expanding the use of other descriptive and analytical methods. Some examine **latent class analysis predictors** for individual and group levels of disability. They question whether chronological age (or years lived) or time till death (TTD, years of life remaining until death) is a better predictor of disability trajectories, called a countdown model (Wolf, Freedman, Ondrich, Seplaki & Spillman, 2015). **The life history graph approach** plots multiple dimensions of life events and levels of population at once, like the true lifecourse approach, which places individual lives in a societal and temporal context. The researchers suggest that these:

> recent developments provide a foundation for social scientists to begin to incorporate multiple, simultaneous domains in their analyses. With these tools we can develop a more complete understanding of the life course, as opposed to studying lives as isolated, fragmented sequences of events.
>
> (Fitzhugh, Butts & Pixley, 2015, p. 34)

Mixed Methods

More Than Two Waves and Two Methodological Options

The multiphase mixed-methods design and other mixed designs are expanding and morphing to include more combinations and permutations of quantitative and qualitative methods. Published gerontological journal articles often talk about how the mixed-methods aspect was modified (e.g., "we are modifying the explanatory sequential design to include an additional two quantitative waves or two qualitative methods"). A researcher conducted a study of trends and next steps in mixed methods and wants more training in mixed-methods designs at all levels of education and new software packages or updates to existing ones to handle mixed data. Researchers need to develop a deposition embracing a mixed-methods approach, perhaps through more professional conferences and workshops promoting the method or offering mentorship. Ultimately, a mixed-methods skill set is needed that is adaptable to many types of mixed-methods designs (Guetterman, 2016).

This chapter has introduced new gerontological methods that have emergent use in the field. These methods closely match research questions and allow a researcher more flexibility in designing his or her study. As gerontology is an interdisciplinary field, emerging methods bring together the best practices of many research traditions and academic disciplines—from arts and humanities, to the digital and technological worlds, and biomedical markers or geographic tracking and sensors. Each of these emerging methods can be seen as additional tools in a researcher's toolkit.

Discussion Questions

- Provide some examples of differences in emergent quantitative and traditional quantitative methods. Then compare emergent qualitative and traditional qualitative methods and emergent mixed methods and traditional mixed-methods designs.
- What are some unique issues that arise when using emergent research methods in a study? Choose one of the designs described in each section of this chapter (quantitative, qualitative, and mixed methods) and consider the following: availability of prior examples, training, expertise and knowledge requirements, software use and capabilities, and potential ethical concerns.
- Review quantitative designs that include biosensors and GIS data and data harmonization. Then review qualitative ones that include producing images of participation and include persons with dementia. What are key things for researchers to consider if they choose to study older persons using each of these designs?
- Take some time to reflect about your own researcher's stance. How comfortable would you feel using each of the methods in this chapter? Which would you like to add/apply to your own current research? Which would you like to learn more about?

Bibliography

Artzer, R., & Weil, J. (2016). *Ethical practices in reminiscence with cognitively and non-cognitively impaired older adults*, Center for Honors, Scholars, and Leadership's Research Day, University of Northern Colorado, Greeley, CO: April 7, 2016.

Atkinson, P. (2015). *For ethnography*. London, UK: Sage Publications.

Bailey, J., & Biggs, I. (2012). "Either side of Delphy Bridge": A deep mapping project evoking and engaging the lives of older adults in rural North Cornwall. *Journal of Rural Studies, 28*(4), 318–328.

Bartlett, R. (2014). The emergent modes of dementia activism. *Ageing & Society, 34*(4), 623–644. doi:10.1017/S0144686X12001158

Bates, C. (2015). *Video methods: Social science research in motion.* New York: Routledge.

Beaulieu, A., & Høybye, M. (2011). "Studying mailing lists: Text, temporality, interaction and materiality at the intersection of email and the web." In S. Hesse-Bibe (Ed.), *The handbook of emergent technologies in social research* (pp. 257–274). Oxford: Oxford University Press.

Bengry-Howell, A., Wiles, R., Nind, M., & Crow, G. (2011). *A review of the academic impact of three methodological innovations: Netnography, child-led research and creative research methods.* NCRM Working Paper Series, University of Southampton.

Byfield, N. (2014). "Targets: The Existential Crisis of Black and Latino Male Youths." In D. Mitra, & J. Weil (Eds.), *Race and the lifecourse: Readings from the intersection of race, ethnicity, and age* (pp. 43–73). New York: Palgrave Macmillan.

Carney, G. M., & Gray, M. (2015). Unmasking the "elderly mystique": Why it is time to make the personal political in ageing research. *Journal of Aging Studies, 35*, 123–134.

Chan, K. B., & Choi, K. (2013). "Chapter 3: Methodology and internet research methods." In K.B. Chan & K. Choi (Eds.), *Online dating as a strategic game: Why and how men in Hong Kong use QQ to chase women in mainland China* (pp. 49–75). Berlin: Springer. doi:10.1007/978–3–642–39985–5

Cisneros, H., Dyer-Chamberlain, M., & Hickie, J. (2012). *Independent for life: Homes and neighborhoods for an aging America.* Austin, TX: University of Texas Press.

Clark/Keefe, K. (2014). Suspended animation: Attuning to material-discursive data and attending via poesis during somatographic inquiry, *Qualitative Inquiry, 20*(6), 790–800. doi:10.1177/1077800414530263

Cohen, E. S. (1988). The elderly mystique: Constraints on the autonomy of the elderly with disabilities. *The Gerontologist, 28*(Suppl), 24–31.

Conklin, J., Kothari, A., & Stolee, P. (2012). Finding the edges: Challenges of case study research in emergent social systems. *International Journal of Qualitative Methods, 11*(5), 727–727.

Crewe, S. E. (2005). Ethnogerontology: Preparing culturally competent social workers for the diverse facing of aging. *Journal of Gerontological Social Work, 43*(4), 45–58. doi:10.1300/J083v43n04_04

Diehl, M., Hooker, K., & Sliwinski, M. J. (2015). *Handbook of intraindividual variability across the life-span.* New York: Routledge.

Diehl, M., & Wahl, H. (2014). *Annual review of gerontology and geriatrics, 35, 2015: Subjective aging: New developments and future directions.* New York: Springer Publishing Company.

Durrant, G., & Kreuter, F. (2013). Editorial: The use of paradata in social survey research. *Journal of the Royal Statistical Society: Series A (Statistics in Society), 176*(1), 1–3.

Eagle, N. (2011). *Mobile phones as sensors for social research: Emergent technologies in social research* (pp. 492–521). New York: Oxford University Press.

Fitzhugh, S. M., Butts, C. T., & Pixley, J. E. (2015). A life history graph approach to the analysis and comparison of life histories. *Advances in Life Course Research, 25*, 16–34. doi:10.1016/j.alcr.2015.05.001

Foster, K., McAllister, M., & O'Brien, L. (2006). Extending the boundaries: Autoethnography as an emergent method in mental health nursing research. *International Journal of Mental Health Nursing, 15*(1), 44–53. doi:10.1111/j.1447–0349.2006.00402.x

Friemel, T. N. (2016). The digital divide has grown old: Determinants of a digital divide among seniors. *New Media & Society, 18*(2), 313–331.

Gatz, M., Reynolds, C. A., Finkel, D., Hahn, C. J., Zhou, Y., & Zavala, C. (2015). Data harmonization in aging research: Not so fast. *Experimental Aging Research, 41*(5), 475–495. doi:10.1080/0361073X.2015.1085748

Gauntlett, D. (2007). *Creative explorations: New approaches to identities and audiences.* New York: Routledge.

George, L. K., & Ferraro, K. F. (2016). "Aging and the social sciences: Progress and prospects." In L. K. George, K. F. Ferraro, D. S. Carr, J. M. Wilmoth, & D. Wolf (Eds.), *Handbook of aging and the social sciences* (pp. 3–22). London, UK: Elsevier Academic Press.

Gilleard, C., & Higgs, P. (2015). Aging, embodiment, and the somatic turn. *Age, Culture, Humanities: An Interdisciplinary Journal*, issue 2. Retrieved from http://ageculturehumanities.org/WP/aging-embodiment-and-the-somatic-turn/

Gubrium, A. (2009). Digital storytelling: An emergent method for health promotion research and practice. *Health Promotion Practice, 10*(2), 186–191.

Guetterman, T. C. (2016). What distinguishes a novice from an expert mixed methods researcher? *Quality & Quantity, 2016*, 1–22. doi:10.1007/s11135–016–0310–9

Haan, G. D., Choenni, S., Mulder, I., Kalidien, S., & van Waart, P. (2011). "Bringing the research lab into everyday life: Exploiting sensitive environments to acquire data for social research." In S. Hesse-Biber (Ed.), *The Oxford handbook of emergent technologies in social research* (pp. 522–541). New York: Oxford University Press.

Hesse-Biber, S. N. (2011). *The handbook of emergent technologies in social research*. New York: Oxford University Press.

Hesse-Biber, S. N., & Leavy, P. (2008). *Handbook of emergent methods*. New York: Guilford Press.

Holoham, A., Chin, J., Callaghan, V., & Mühlau, P. (2011). "The digital home: A new locus of social science research." In S.N. Hesse-Biber (Ed.), *The handbook of emergent technologies in social research* (pp. 647–666). New York: Oxford University Press.

Iversen, S. M. (2016). Play and productivity: The constitution of ageing adults in research on digital games. *Games and Culture, 11*(1–2), 7–27. doi:10.1177/1555412014557541

Jewitt, C., Xambo, A., & Price, S. (2016). Exploring methodological innovation in the social sciences: The body in digital environments and the arts. *International Journal of Social Research Methodology, 2016*, 1–16.

Kara, H. (2015). *Creative research methods in the social sciences: A practical guide*. Bristol: Policy Press.

King, D. K. (1988). Multiple jeopardy, multiple consciousness: The context of a Black feminist ideology. *Signs, 14*(1), 42–72.

Kozinets, R. V. (2015). *Netnography*. Chichester: John Wiley & Sons, Inc.

Ladiges, W., Ikeno, Y., Niedernhofer, L., McIndoe, R. A., Ciol, M. A., Ritchey, J., & Liggitt, D. (2016). The geropathology research network: An interdisciplinary approach for integrating pathology into research on aging. *The Journals of Gerontology. Series A, Biological Sciences and Medical Sciences, 71*(4), 431–434. doi:10.1093/gerona/glv079

LaLonde, K. B., Zimmermann, Z. J., & Poling, A. (2015). Behavioral gerontology research: Where are the male participants? *Behavioral Interventions, 30*(4), 378–385. doi:10.1002/bin.1416

Lamb, A., Anderson, T. R., & Daim, T. (2012). Research and development target-setting difficulties addressed through the emergent method: Technology forecasting using data envelopment analysis. *R&D Management, 42*(4), 327–341. doi:10.1111/j.1467–9310.2012.00687.x

Leontowitsch, M. (2013). "Interviewing older men online." In B. Pini & B. Pease (Eds.), *Men, masculinities and methodologies* (pp. 223–235). London: Palgrave Macmillan.

Lupton, E. (2011). *Graphic design thinking: Beyond brainstorming*. New York: Princeton Architectural Press.

Markham, A. N. (2016). "Ethnography in the digital era: From fields to flow, descriptions to interventions." In N. Denzin & Y. Lincoln (Eds.), *The Sage Handbook of Qualitative Research* (5th ed.). Thousand Oaks: Sage.

Martey, R. (2014). "Polite pigs and emotional elves: Age in digital worlds." In C. L. Harrington, D. D. Bielby, & A. R. Bardo (Eds.), *Aging, media, and culture* (pp. 193–203). Lanham: Lexington Books.

McCutcheon, M., & Pruchno, R. (2011). Introducing the international spotlight. *The Gerontologist, 51*(4), 423–424. doi:10.1093/geront/gnr070

Mechling, H. (2013). What we need to know, where we need to go. *European Review of Aging and Physical Activity, 10*(1), 1–4. doi:10.1007/s11556–013–0123-y

Mendoza, A. N. (2012). *Grandparents raising grandchildren: A look at Latino cultural influences on needs and service usage*. Master's Thesis, University of Northern Colorado. Available from ProQuest (#839685528).

Methven, L., Jimenez-Pranteda, M., & Ben Lawlor, J. (2016; 2015). Sensory and consumer science methods used with older adults: A review of current methods and recommendations for the future. *Food Quality and Preference, 48*, 333–344. doi:10.1016/j.foodqual.2015.07.001

Miller, E., & Brockie, L. (2015). The disaster flood experience: Older people's poetic voices of resilience. *Journal of Aging Studies, 34*, 103–112.

Mitra, D., & Weil, J. (2014). *Race and the lifecourse: Readings from the intersection of race, ethnicity, and age*. New York: Palgrave Macmillan.

Munn-Giddings, C., McVicar, A., Boyce, M., & O'Brien, N. (2016). Learning from older citizens' research groups. *Educational Gerontology, 42*(1), 58–69. doi:10.1080/03601277.2015.1065690

Murthy, D. (2011). "Emergent digital ethnographic methods for social research." In S. Hesse-Biber (Ed.), *Handbook of emergent technologies in social research* (pp. 158–179) Oxford: Oxford University Press.

National Institute on Aging. (November 29–30, 2011). *Workshop on harmonization strategies for behavioral, social science, and genetic research: Executive summary*. Washington, DC.

Nikolich-Žugich, J., Goldman, D. P., Cohen, P. R., Cortese, D., Fontana, L., Kennedy, B. K., & Richardson, A. (2016). Preparing for an aging world: Engaging biogerontologists, geriatricians, and the society. *The Journals of Gerontology Series A: Biological Sciences and Medical Sciences, 71*(4), 435–444. doi:10.1093/gerona/glv164

Nimrod, G. (2011). The fun culture in seniors' online communities. *The Gerontologist, 51*(2), 226–237. doi:10.1093/geront/gnq084

Nind, M., Wiles, R., Bengry-Howell, A., & Crow, G. (2013). Methodological innovation and research ethics: forces in tension or forces in harmony? *Qualitative Research, 13*(6), 650–667. doi:10.1177/1468794112455042

Peterson, M. J., Thompson, D. K., Pieper, C. F., Morey, M. C., Kraus, V. B., Kraus, W. E. & Cohen, H. J. (2016). A novel analytic technique to measure associations between circulating biomarkers and physical performance across the adult life span. *The Journals of Gerontology. Series A, Biological Sciences and Medical Sciences, 71*(2), 196.

Phillips, L. R., Salem, B. E., Jeffers, K. S., Kim, H., Ruiz, M. E., Salem, N., & Woods, D. L. (2015). Developing and proposing the ethno-cultural gerontological nursing model. *Journal of Transcultural Nursing, 26*(2), 118–128. doi:10.1177/1043659614563615

Rabbitt, P. (2015). *The aging mind: An owner's manual.* New York: Routledge.

Read, D. W. (2006). Kinship algebra expert system (KAES): A software implementation of a cultural theory. *Social Science Computer Review, 24*(1), 43–67. doi:10.1177/0894439305282372

Resnick, B., Klinedinst, N. J., Yerges-Armstrong, L., Choi, E. Y., & Dorsey, S. G. (2015). The impact of genetics on physical resilience and successful aging. *Journal of Aging and Health, 27*(6), 1084–1104. doi:10.1177/0898264315577586

Reybold, L. E., Lammert, J. D., & Stribling, S. M. (2012). Participant selection as a conscious research method: Thinking forward and the deliberation of "Emergent" findings. *Qualitative Research, 13*(6), 699–716. doi:10.1177/1468794112465634

Ribeiro, A. I., Pires, A., Carvalho, M. S., & Pina, M. F. (2015). Distance to parks and non-residential destinations influences physical activity of older people, but crime doesn't: A cross-sectional study in a southern European city. *BMC Public Health, 15*, 593–605. doi:10.1186/s12889–015–1879-y

Rutherford, M. J., Lambert, P. C., & Thompson, J. R. (2010). Age-period-cohort modeling. *Stata Journal, 10*(4), 606–627.

Sayago, S., Rosales, A., Righi, V., Ferreira, S., Coleman, G., & Blat, J. (2016). On the conceptualization, design, and evaluation of appealing, meaningful, and playable digital games for older people. *Games and Culture, 11*(1–2), 53–80. doi:10.1177/1555412015597108

Schafer, M. H., & Ferraro, K. F. (2013). Childhood misfortune and adult health: Enduring and cascadic effects on somatic and psychological symptoms? *Journal of Aging and Health, 25*(1), 3–28. doi:10.1177/0898264312464884

Scheidt, R. J., Bosch, J. V., Kivnick, H. Q., & Pruchno, R. (2012). Launching "on film and digital media". *The Gerontologist, 52*(4), 439–440. doi:10.1093/geront/gns087

Schulz, R., Wahl, H., Matthews, J. T., De Vito Dabbs, A., Beach, S. R., & Czaja, S. J. (2015). Advancing the aging and technology agenda in gerontology. *The Gerontologist, 55*(5), 724–734. doi:10.1093/geront/gnu071

Schwieger, A. (2010). For the analysis of mobility outside the home of older people: The potential of GPS technology and geographic information systems (GIS). *Zeitschrift Fur Gerontologie Und Geriatrie, 43*, 111–119.

Southall, K. (2014). Personal conversation and email, November 10.

Southall, K. (2015, August). *Authentic portraits of acquired hearing loss: A photovoice study.* Retrieved from https://prezi.com/rftayq0pp4ab/authentic-portraits-of-acquired-hearing-loss-a-photovoice-s/

Speechley, M., DeForge, R. T., Ward-Griffin, C., Marlatt, N. M., & Gutmanis, I. (2015). Creating an ethnodrama to catalyze dialogue in home-based dementia care. *Qualitative Health Research, 25*(11), 1551–1559.

Spice, B. (2015). *Carnegie Mellon University leads Google expedition to create technology for "Internet of things": Campus will be living lab for interconnected sensors, gadgets.* Retrieved from http://www.cmu.edu/news/stories/archives/2015/july/google-internet-of-things.html

Taylor, A. W., Campostrini, S., Gill, T. K., Carter, P., Dal Grande, E., & Herriot, M. (2010). The use of chronic disease risk factor surveillance systems for evidence-based decision-making: physical activity and nutrition as examples. *International Journal of Public Health, 55*(4), 243–249.

Tinker, A., Hussain, L., D'Cruz, J. L., Tai, W. Y. S., & Zaidman, S. (2016). Why should medical students study Social Gerontology? *Age and Ageing, 45*(2), 190–193. doi:10.1093/ageing/afw003

Twigg, J., & Martin, W. (Eds.). (2015). *Routledge handbook of cultural gerontology.* New York: Routledge.

Vines, J., Pritchard, G., Wright, P., Olivier, P., & Brittain, K. (2015). An age-old problem: Examining the discourses of ageing in HCI and strategies for future research. *ACM Transactions on Computer-Human Interaction (TOCHI), 22*(1), 1–27.

Vosner, H., Bobek, S., Kokol, P., & Krecic, M. (2016). Attitudes of active older internet users towards online social networking. *Computers in Human Behavior, 55*, 230–241. doi:10.1016/j.chb.2015.09.014

Wolf, D. A., Freedman, V. A., Ondrich, J. I., Seplaki, C. L., & Spillman, B. C. (2015). Disability trajectories at the end of life: A "countdown" model. *The Journals of Gerontology Series B: Psychological Sciences and Social Sciences, 70*(5), 745–752. doi:10.1093/geronb/gbu182

Xenitidou, M., & Gilbert, N. (2009). *Innovations in social science research methods project report.* NCRM E-Prints, United Kingdom.

Yang, Y., & Land, K. C. (2013). *Age-period-cohort analysis: New models, methods, and empirical applications.* Boca Raton, FL:CRC Press.

Yankeelov, P. A., Faul, A. C., D'Ambrosio, J. G., Collins, W. L., & Gordon, B. (2015). "Another day in paradise": A photovoice journey of rural older adults living with diabetes. *Journal of Applied Gerontology, 34*(2), 199–218. doi:10.1177/0733464813493136

Part III
Analyzing Results and Reporting Findings

9

Quantitative, Qualitative Software and Computer-Assisted Research

The selection and use of computerized data-analysis software (CDAS) programs are often discussed and debated. This chapter introduces the reader to the range of computerized software programs available for quantitative, qualitative, and mixed-methods data. The goal of the chapter is to describe common features of each type of computer software program (quantitative, qualitative, and mixed methods). The chapter gives an overview of instances/situations when each brand-name software program may have its best application and when to use each one. Screenshots of several brand-name programs are provided so the reader can become familiar with their look and format. This chapter will use the General Social Survey (GSS) data drawn from the GSS Data Explorer (beta version) from the University of Chicago to illustrate all concepts. The General Social Survey is an omnibus survey that covers a broad range of topics and is free to download from the GSS Data Explorer. It is designed for a general adult population and does not oversample older respondents but provides a vehicle to explore the same data discussed in this chapter. Sample output with interpretation of results/output is provided for crosstabs for quantitative data and the analogous co-occurrence tables in qualitative software. Aspects of data analysis will be addressed in terms of their relation to reading output, and a full discussion of types of data analysis techniques can be found in Chapters 4 through 8.

Overview of Software Options

Many **computerized data-analysis software** (CDAS) options are on the market. "Which software should I use?" is cited as one of the most commonly asked questions (Gibbs, 2014, p. 280). The software-selection process has been likened to "software wars" in online blogs (Data Camp Team, 2014). All quantitative software packages can perform the same basic group of statistical tests, such as descriptive statistics (frequency distributions, central tendency, and variation) and inferential tests (e.g., x^2, t-testing, ANOVA, and regression). Commonly used general quantitative software options include the **Statistical Package for the Social Sciences (SPSS)**, **Statistical Analysis Software (SAS)**,

Stata software by Stata Corp, and **R software** that offers options for statistical analysis. Also available are more specialized quantitative program options such as **MPlus**, a program for latent variable modeling, and **Lisrel,** which is commonly used for Structural Equation Modeling (SEM).

Researchers see the benefits of quantitative packages as reducing calculation errors, helping with data management with many users being more efficient, and offering visual data displays. While researchers do not question the use of software for quantitative analysis, there is more debate about the use of software in qualitative analysis (Charmaz, 2006). All computer-assisted qualitative data-analysis software (CAQDAS) programs do the same basic functions: importing multiple types of files (text files, PDFs, videos) and allowing the user to create codes, groups of codes, visual mapping of some type, frequency or groundedness of codes, and some cross tabulation or comparison of codes. Some offer autocoding and word counts. Commonly used qualitative options include **ATLAS.ti** and **Nvivo**. Some other qualitative software options include **HyperRESEARCH, QDA Miner, AnSWR, Qualrus, RQDA, and Ethnograph. MAXQDA** is suggested as a program for mixed-methods data analysis (Maietta, 2008).

Reviewers of quantitative and qualitative software stress that choice of software is often based on the preference and skill of the user but needs to match the user's task needs (Oliveira, Bitencourt, Teixeira & Santos, 2013). These software programs are analytical tools and should not be the driver or statistical tests or output produced just for the sake of it. For all software, one should look at the latest version because the version matters and may impact/change results produced (Hutchinson, Olmos & Teman, 2013). See Table 9.1 for a comparison of quantitative, qualitative, and mixed-methods software types with ideas about the best application for each type of software. Screenshots from SPSS are used to illustrate quantitative software, ATLAS.ti is used to show qualitative software, and MAXQDA is utilized for mixed-methods software.

Some key questions to ask when selecting software program include the following:

- Does it run natively on your computer?*
- How familiar are you with the software? What is your estimated learning curve?
- Does the software provide all the methods you need? If not, how extensible is it?*
- Does its extensibility use its own unique language or an external one that is commonly accessible from many packages?*
- Does it fully support the style (programming, or menus and dialog boxes, or workflow diagrams) that you like?*
- Are its visualization options (e.g., static vs. interactive) adequate for your problems?*
- Does it provide output in the form you prefer (e.g., cut and paste into a word processor vs. plain text)?*
- Does it handle large enough data sets?*
- Do your colleagues use it so you can easily share data and programs?*
- Are there colleagues who can help you troubleshoot problems along the way?
- What training options and online support exist?
- Is the software commonly used in your field? In journals and publication?
- Can you afford it?*
- How long does the license last? Are free updates included?

(* = The popularity of data analysis software, Muenchen, 2015)

Table 9.1 Computerized Data Analysis Software (CDAS) Options

Name	Data Type	Website	Best Application
SAS	Quantitative	http://www.sas.com/en_us/home.html	Handles a large number of variables and data; commonly used in government and businesses; code-heavy and a longer learning curve
SPSS	Quantitative	http://www-01.ibm.com/software/analytics/spss/	User-friendly; short learning curve; uses point-and-click syntax creation; common in social-science research methods courses; commonly available at universities; add-on packages such as SPSS AMOS add more statistical testing options (e.g., structural equation modeling [SEM] and Bayesian analysis)
STATA	Quantitative	http://www.stata.com/	Short learning curve; one-time license; active user community sharing knowledge and syntax
R	Quantitative	https://www.r-project.org/about.html	Free software; open-source; create data frames/sets; works on many platforms; users can add their own software; a dedicated group of users—Computer R Archive Network (CRAN)—works with SPSS and SAS (for example); longer learning curve and command based; needs more computer memory/capacity to run; need to define is missing; and output is less stylized
MPlus	Quantitative	https://www.statmodel.com/	For higher-level statistical testing (e.g., latent variable modeling, exploratory factor analysis, structural equation modeling, item response theory analysis, growth modeling, latent class analysis, latent transition analysis, latent class growth analysis, growth mixture analysis, survival analysis, multilevel analysis, complex survey data analysis, Bayesian analysis, Monte Carlo simulation); software creators are responsive to user questions
Lisrel	Quantitative	http://www.ssicentral.com/lisrel/	For higher-level statistical testing (e.g., structural equation modeling, hierarchical linear and non-linear modeling, generalized linear modeling, and generalized linear modeling for multilevel data)
ATLAS.ti	Qualitative	http://atlasti.com/	Supports multimedia files (documents, PDFs, and video) and Google Earth (for mapping); offers a side-by-side panel for transcription of video; coding style (as if in the margins) and groundedness of codes lets the user use grounded theory; has English, German, and Spanish as user interface languages—but all coding and files must be bundled in a Hermeneutic Unit grouping (that contains code, memos, primary documents, mapping, etc.)
NVivo	Qualitative	http://www.qsrinternational.com/what-is-nvivo	Supports multimedia files (documents, PDFs, and video) and social media (such as Twitter); has English, Chinese (Simplified Chinese), French, German, Japanese, Portuguese, or Spanish user-interface languages—Nvivo allows for survey data to be brought into the program as an Excel-like spreadsheet/table and coded—appears more tabular and less like traditional coding of text in the margins; includes social media and synchronistic team work
MAXQDA	Mixed methods	http://www.maxqda.com	Uses codes (themes) and variables (attributes); frequency of codes within and across cases; crosstabs of themes and variables; visually and statistically shows/measures relationships between variables and codes; tables of percentages, central tendency, and variation for codes; transformation of codes into variables into quantified variables, multiple levels of code hierarchy, allows longer memos, and has free reader (only)

Sources: Quantitative software: Data Camp Team blog (2014), Harvard Law School (2016), Ward (2013), Weil (2014); Qualitative software: Bassett (2010a, 2010b), Contreras (2015), Fielding (2012), Gibbs (2014), Lewis (2004); Mixed Methods: Hatani (2015), Humble (2010), Maietta (2008), Oliveira, Bitencourt, Teixeira and Santos (2013).

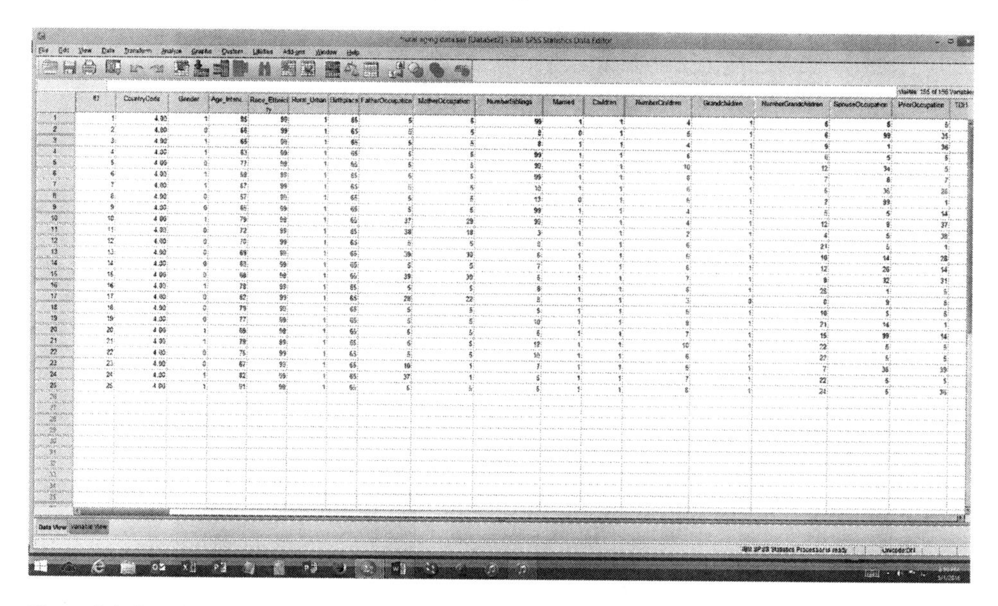

Figure 9.1 Data Views in SPSS

Quantitative Software Basics

Types of files. Quantitative software programs have three types of files: data, syntax, and output. The **data files** are the actual numerical values for the information you have collected. Each program assigns a different extension to these files, but they are the primary building blocks for your data analysis. Data in the data-editor window looks like an Excel spreadsheet, and they contain the actual coded responses from study participants.

The **syntax window** looks like a Word document. This area is the place where syntax/commands are typed that tell the quantitative software program which tests to do and which numbers to calculate. Syntax, or "Do File," windows are the direct programmatic language that specify the exact conditions of the tests or data transformation being conducted. Syntax, itself, can be written in program-specific codified language, but, in many cases, writing syntax or programmatic language has been augmented with drop-down or query menus and a point-and-click option making the analysis more widely applicable. Syntax statements can be pulled from the output files for future use or to doublecheck the conditions of the completed analysis.

Output, or results, windows display the result of tests and transformations dictated by syntax or point-and-click commands. In SPSS, the output window contains the results of all the calculations done for you by the quantitative software program and displays your results in tabular form. Log columns are included as a window within the output or results windows and provide an alert for errors that occur when running analysis. They also help navigate through the series of test results displayed in the output.

Variables, labeling, and data cleaning. Variables are the quantified or numeric values assigned response choices or categories of your data. **Variable names** may have character limits assigned by a particular software program, so adding variable labels allows the

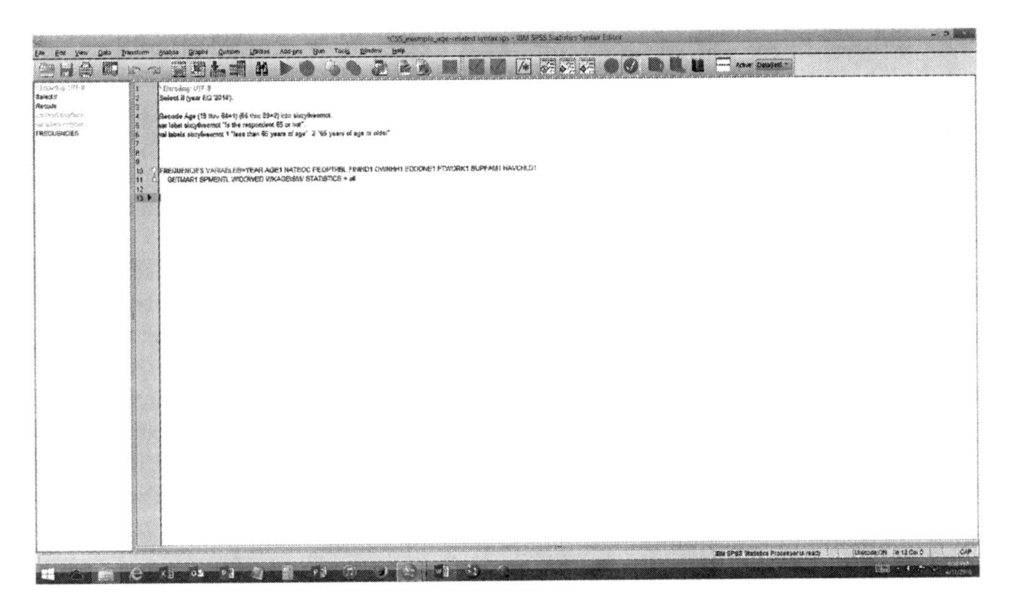

Figure 9.2 Syntax Window in SPSS

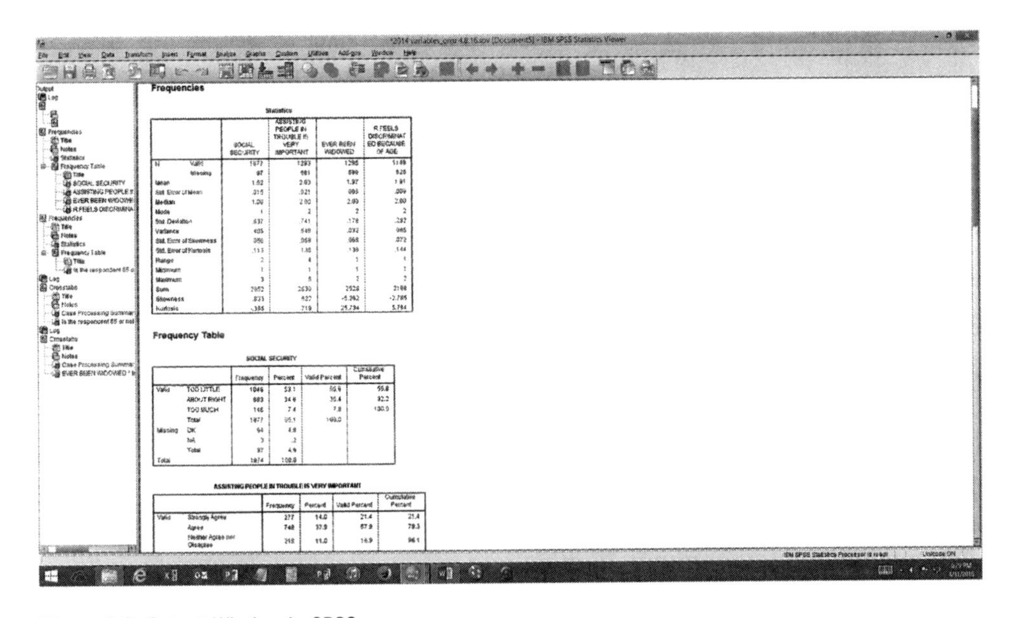

Figure 9.3 Output Window in SPSS

researcher to add a longer description to define what that variable is about. **Value labels** attach text or narrative to the variable itself and also words to each numerical response category.

For example, the General Social Survey (GSS) contains a variable called "wkageism." In the 2014 GSS, respondents were asked: "Do you feel in any way discriminated against on your job because of your age?" The response choices were (value, followed by value label): 1 = Yes, 2 = No, 8 = Don't know, 9 = No answer, and 0 = Not applicable.

The variable "famgen" recorded the number of family generations in household. The response choices were (value, followed by value label): 1 = 1 generation, 2 = 2 generations, children, 3 = 2 generation, parents, 4 = 2 generations, grandchildren, 5 = 3 generations, grandchildren, 6 = 3 generations, children, parents, 7 = 4 generations, and 0 = Not applicable.

The variable "natsoc" asks about views concerning national spending on social security: "We are faced with many problems in this country—none of which can be solved easily or inexpensively. I'm going to name some of these problems, and for each one, I'd like you to name some of these problems, and for each one I'd like you to tell me whether you think we're spending too much money on it, too little money, or about the right amount. Are we spending too much, too little, or about the right amount on Social Security?" The response choices are: (value, followed by value label) 1 = Too little, 2 = About right, 3 = Too much, 8 = Don't know, 9 = No answer, and 0 = Not applicable.

When entering numerical value choices into a data file, sometimes mistakes and errors can be made. For example, a value of "3" may be entered as a mistake or mistype for the wkageism variable (asking about job discrimination based upon age) when only values of 1 = Yes, 2 = No, 8 = Don't know, 9 = No answer, and 0 = Not applicable were valid. Data cleaning, or running frequency distributions for each variable to look for these outlying values, is a crucial step to do before any statistical testing. Doing so makes sure that outcomes are based on true data values. Digital data-collection tools, such as computerized data collection instruments and online surveys with dropdown menus and fixed-response choices, attempt to limit incorrect response-choice values in the data-entry process.

Recoding and Forming Scales, Summed Measures, Compute, Conditional Statements, Counting, Mean Index

Often the original form of a variable or data is not the only way in which a researcher uses that variable or data in analysis. Variables are **recoded**, or transformed, for a number of reasons, usually because the existing categories do not match our research question. So the raw data may be transformed or changed in a number of ways. Data transformation options include combining or collapsing variable responses into new ones or counting response types in a variable or across a couple/several variables and combining them into a summed measure or index. Recoding is simply the process of changing, combining, or collapsing the response categories of a variable.

Age can be used as an example of recoding to collapse variable categories. Age is generally collected as a number of chronological years. If a researcher is interested in studying those less than 65 years of age *and* those 65 years of age and over, he or she needs to divide all age responses into these two categories or groups. See Figure 9.4 for a visual depiction of this recoding process. See Box 9.1 and Figures 9.5 and 9.6 for both syntax and point-and-click recoding of age into two categories in SPSS. Other common recodes include collapsing number of years of school completed into several categories: grammar school, high school, college, and graduate school and beyond. Number of hours worked per week is also often recoded as part time (less than 40 hours) and full time (40 hours or more).

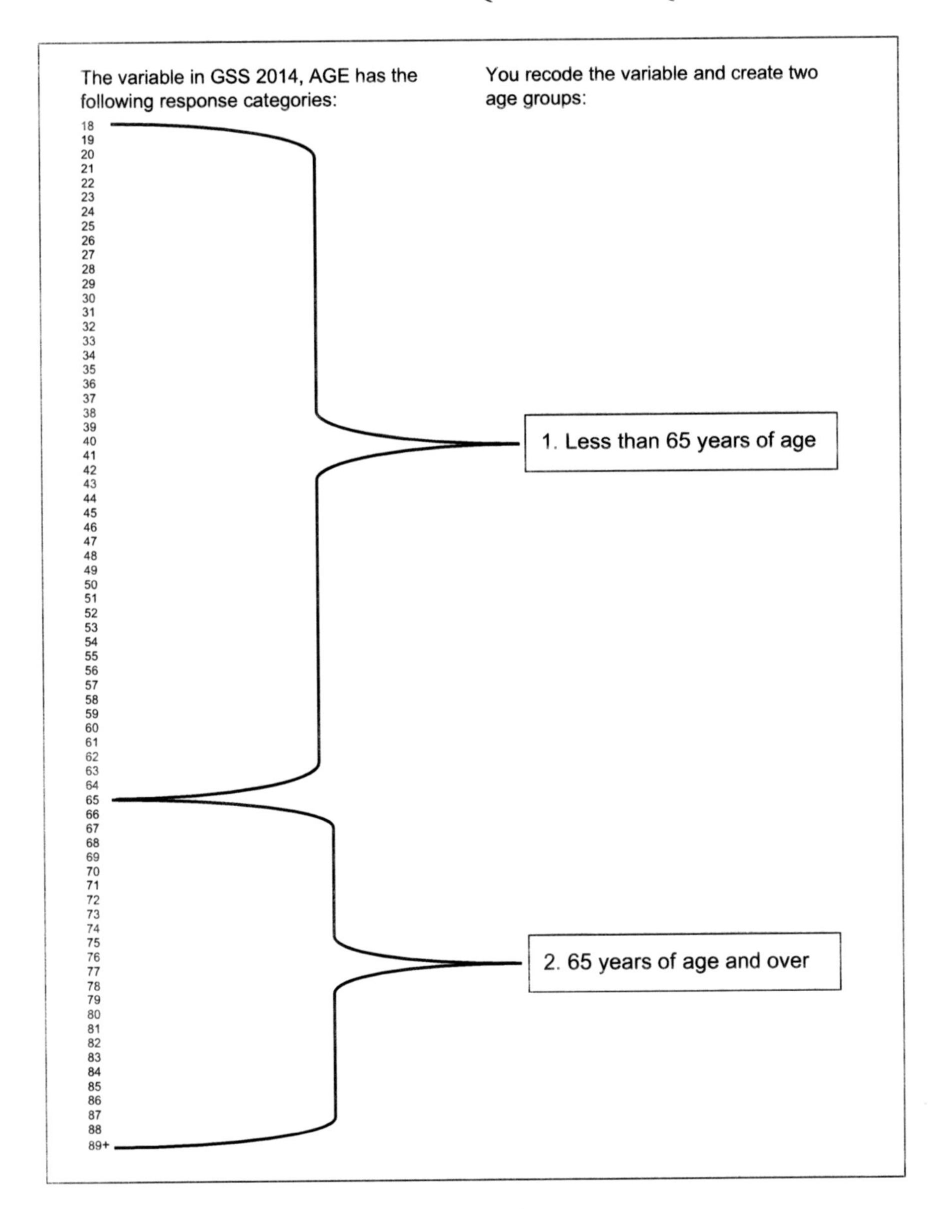

Figure 9.4 Age in Two Categories: 65 years of Age or Not?

Box 9.1 Recoding Age in Syntax in SPSS

Recode age (18 thru 64 = 1) (65 thru 89 = 2) into sixtyfiveornot.
var label sixtyfiveornot "Is the respondent 65 or not"
val labels sixtyfiveornot 1 "less than 65 years of age" 2 "65 years of age or older"
Frequencies variables = age sixtyfiveornot/stats = all.

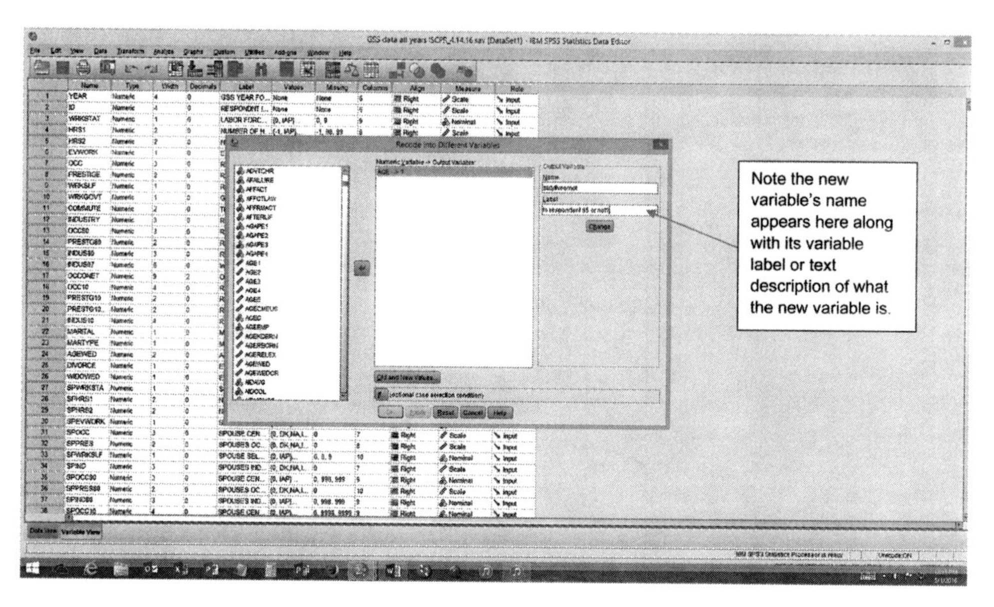

Figure 9.5 Recoding Age via Point and Click in SPSS

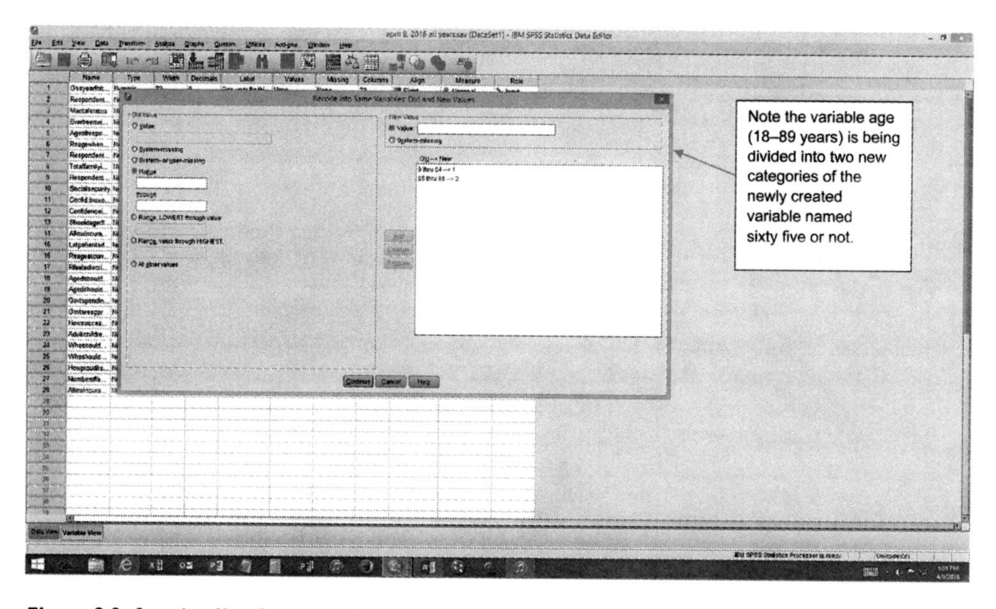

Figure 9.6 Creating New Response Categories

Often a survey has several questions asking about the same topic. Let's look at the following example about attitudes toward euthanasia based on some GSS questions and some created ones. The respondent is asked to rate his or her level of agreement (on a Likert scale) with five statements about the right to die. Likert scales are ordinal-response categories to a question, and they usually appear in five or seven categories. A typical/familiar five-response Likert scale is based on satisfaction rating, where: 1—Not at all satisfied, 2—Slightly satisfied, 3—Moderately satisfied, 4—Very satisfied, and 5—Extremely satisfied. The seven-point version of this satisfaction scale includes the following categories: 1—Completely dissatisfied, 2—Mostly dissatisfied, 3—Somewhat dissatisfied, 4—Neither satisfied or dissatisfied, 5—Somewhat satisfied, 6—Mostly satisfied, and 7—Completely satisfied. In this example, GSS respondents are asked: To what extent do you agree or disagree with the following statements? Do you strongly disagree, disagree, neither agree nor disagree, agree, or strongly agree?

a. Allow patients to die if doctors agree
b. Allow patients to die if the family agrees
c. Allow patients to die if they do not want treatment
d. Allow patients to die if their condition is incurable
e. Allow patients to die if their pain is not controllable

Scoring for the responses follows the five-response Likert scale pattern: 1 = Strongly disagree, 2 = Disagree, 3 = Neither agree or disagree, 4 = Agree, 5 = Strongly Agree.

A **scale** measures various aspects of a concept—in this case, attitudes toward euthanasia. If a researcher wants to create one numerical value or coefficient that represents the respondent's general attitude toward items in the scale, he or she may create a summed measure or index to summarize these data and give one overall score for all the items. There are two summary options. If respondents answer all questions asked in the set of questions, a summed measure provides a total sum of the respondents' answers for all questions in the group. But, more often, a respondent may not answer all questions. When a respondent may miss or refuse to answer a question, an **index** is a better choice. When creating an index score, the researcher can decide how many items must have valid answers for a score to be created. For example, a researcher may say that an index score can be created if a respondent answers three of the five questions asked. Following this rule above, if a respondent answers three of the five questions related to euthanasia (strongly disagree, disagree, neither agree nor disagree, agree, or strongly agree, if: doctor agrees, family agrees, person declines treatment, has an incurable condition, or has uncontrollable pain), an index score will be calculated. Figure 9.7 shows an index of the summary statistics for the created attitudes toward euthanasia.

A **Cronbach's alpha (α)** is calculated to see if the items measured in the index relate to the same concept reliably. In the social sciences, a 0.70 value or higher for Cronbach's alpha is considered acceptable. See Figure 9.8 for an example of Cronbach's alpha calculated for the euthanasia index that indicates the index has good reliability.

An **index's reliability** is affected by any individual item or items that differ in some way from the others in the scale; their inclusion can impact the Cronbach's alpha's value. Item-statistics for items in the scale can help you determine which items are closely related (correlated) and which, if removed, can improve your Cronbach's alpha's value.

As you can see in Figure 9.9, removing questions about treatment refusal and uncontrolled pain would raise the value of Cronbach's alpha and improve reliability for the index showing attitudes toward euthanasia. A researcher could speculate that these two questions might be different from the others—since they could be related to conditions that are not life threatening or seen as a refusal of aid on the part of the patient.

		Frequency	Percent	Valid Percent	Cumulative Percent
Valid	1.00	23	.5	2.4	2.4
	1.13	26	.6	2.7	5.0
	1.25	42	.9	4.3	9.3
	1.38	52	1.2	5.3	14.7
	1.50	74	1.6	7.6	22.2
	1.63	89	2.0	9.1	31.4
	1.75	109	2.4	11.2	42.5
	1.88	107	2.4	11.0	53.5
	2.00	94	2.1	9.6	63.1
	2.13	91	2.0	9.3	72.4
	2.25	69	1.5	7.1	79.5
	2.38	72	1.6	7.4	86.9
	2.50	41	.9	4.2	91.1
	2.63	31	.7	3.2	94.3
	2.75	22	.5	2.3	96.5
	2.88	13	.3	1.3	97.8
	3.00	4	.1	.4	98.3
	3.13	10	.2	1.0	99.3
	3.25	5	.1	.5	99.8
	3.75	1	.0	.1	99.9
	3.88	1	.0	.1	100.0
	Total	976	21.6	100.0	
Missing	System	13	78.4		
Total		989	100.0		

Here, for the 5 euthanasia-based items in the scale, respondents (63.1%) tend to lean towards the strongly disagree or disagree attitudes.

About 35.1% feel neutral about euthanasia for these 5 items.

Only 1.7% of respondents approach agreement on euthanasia for these 5 items.

Figure 9.7 Index of Average Let-Die Ratings for Five Conditions

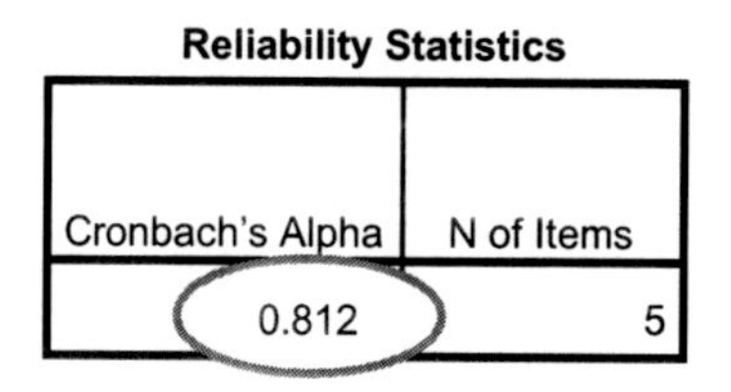

Reliability Statistics

Cronbach's Alpha	N of Items
0.812	5

Figure 9.8 Reliability Output for Cronbach's Alpha

Missing Cases or Data

Missing data are accepted as a usual part of the data-collection process in aging/gerontological research (Palmer, 2010). Missing data can cause problems in analysis if not handled correctly (Osborne, 2013). So understanding reasons for, and types of, missing data is crucial and can impact the way software handles the analysis of data (Graham, 2012; McKnight,

	Scale Mean if Item Deleted	Scale Variance if Item Deleted	Corrected Item - Total Correlation	Cronbach's Alpha if Item Deleted
Allow patients to die if doctors agree	7.68	4.529	.436	.810
Allow patients to die if the family agrees	7.67	4.348	.441	.799
Allow patients to die if they do not want treatment	7.32	4.200	.571	.824
Allow patients to die if their condition is incurable	7.99	4.675	.492	.749
Allow patients to die if their pain is not controllable	7.10	4.923	.578	.831

Figure 9.9 Item Reliability Output for Cronbach's Alpha

2007; Molenberghs, Fitzmaurice, Kenward, Tsiatis & Verbeke, 2015; Newman, 2014; Palmer, 2010; Sainani, 2015; Schlomer, Bauman & Card, 2010; Zhou, Zhou, Liu, Ding & Ebooks Corporation 2014).

Three aspects of missing data are important in deciding how to address the data with software programs. A researcher must further describe missing data by its being expected/ unexpected, the scope of the missing data, and possible patterns that exist in the data. **Expected missing data** can be appropriate if they are "missed" as part of an intended **skip pattern**—for example, asking a person 65 years of age and older if she or he is a homeowner. If the person says "no," missing data, coded as "Not applicable (NA)," would be expected on follow-up questions about type of home owners and length of homeownership. **Unexpected missing data** consists of questions mistakenly forgotten to be asked of a respondent or left unanswered by a respondent, and can include mistakes, such as data omissions, made when entering data. Following the homeownership example, if no answer was recorded for the initial homeownership question by a respondent or researcher and that information is left blank, then that datum is expectedly missing.

A researcher needs to understand the scope or level at which data are missing. **Item-level missing data** are data missing for a person from individual items on a survey. In the housing-survey example, a respondent does not answer a question about the cost of heating his or her home in the winter. **Construct-level missing data** are data that, when missed, eliminate an entire construct or set of variables from analysis. In this case, a respondent does not answer a series of questions related to renting space in his or her home to others (such as number of occupants, rent charged, length of occupancy, and shared expenses). Here, data for the entire rental concept would be missed for this respondent. **Person-level missing data** means that particular individuals did not respond to any questions; his or her responses are missing entirely. For the housing survey, this would mean the respondent refused the entire survey. Person-level missing data can also occur if a participant leaves the study—such as in the case of attrition, or participant loss, in a longitudinal study.

Exploring missing data for possible patterns is another crucial step. Datasets in the real world may have a mixture of three types of missing-data patterns (Sainani, 2015).

Missing-data patterns can be completely at random (MCAR), missing at random (MAR), or missing not random (MNAR). **Missing data completely at random (MCAR)** implies there is no pattern to the way data are missing and that the "missingness" does not follow a pattern. It is difficult to determine MCAR, but data in this category are thought to not greatly influence outcomes. For the example of homeownership, the one missed question asking about homeownership of the respondent or researcher, or the one missed question about utility expenses, would qualify as MCAR.

Missing at random (MAR) happens when data missed on one variable is related to answers on another question, variable, or event. So, it is missed due to a relationship with another data point. Let us say that in the housing study, the researcher wanted to follow up with only a part of the initial group for a second round of questions. The researcher wanted to focus only on homeowners 65 years of age that were female. In the second survey, data is missing for the other occupants in the home question. Since the missing-occupant data at round two is based on the participant's selection from the sample (being women), this missing-occupant data is based on being female homeowners who are 65 years of age and older and not independently missing. These data are MAR.

If data are **missing not random (MNAR**), the implication is that missing data are related to a question. In the housing example, if all those who failed to answer the cost-of-utilities questions were also in poor health, the missed-utilities questions were not missed at random. Rather, they were missed by a particular group: those with health concerns.

Software, such as SPSS, SAS, R, and MPlus have strategies to address missing data. There are also are free programs created to address missing data, such as Amelia and Norm (see Schlomer, Bauman & Card, 2010 for capabilities of each of these types of software and Newman, 2014, for syntax options). Osborne (2013) offers sample missing-data datasets and programming and syntax for working with missing data in SAS and SPSS.

Several computerized strategies assist with missing data. A researcher must decide if she or he wants to **delete** (remove) or **impute** (fill in) missing data. Deletions can be listwise or pairwise. **Listwise deletion** removes a case with any missing data from analysis. Some warn, though, that this is often a software default; the missing cases may differ from those remaining in the data and create issues of representativeness and bias (Schlomer, Bauman & Card, 2010). Some suggest that any deletion of data can remove data that are important to the study (Osborne, 2013). **Pairwise deletion** removes cases only if they have missing data on variables that are of key interest in the study's research questions, hypotheses, or analysis.

Instead of deleting cases based on missing data, researchers may impute or fill in the missing data. Data-imputation software techniques include single imputation, maximum likelihood, and multiple imputation. **Single imputation** means replacing one missing value in a dataset with a valid one. This can be done by using existing data to extrapolate a plausible data value. **Multiple imputation** creates a final version of the dataset by first creating several versions of the data as separate datasets with the missing values replaced, then averaging the results in the created data sets. Algorithms included in software do this process for the researcher. Full Information Maximum Likelihood technique uses existing information from other variables for that case to create data to fill in for the missing data in the existing dataset.

Daniel Newman (2014) offers three key considerations for missing data prior to data analysis. The first consideration, "Missing data are partly unavoidable, and partly avoidable," encourages researchers to acknowledge that some missing data can be expected because survey research is voluntary and the respondent may choose not to answer questions. But Newman suggests researchers must keep practices in place to collect as much complete data as possible—for example, as face-to-face data collection or including multiple questions to gather data about a concept of interest.

The second consideration, "Define the target population of interest," encourages researchers to carefully design questionnaires/surveys with the target group in mind, then collect data from a well-defined audience of interest. The well-constructed instruments reduce the amount of potential missing data.

The last consideration, "Abstinence is not an option," warns that a researcher cannot simply ignore the role of missing data in analysis. Newman states that choosing a way to treat missing data:

> involves choosing the lesser of evils. Avoiding missing data treatments is not an option. The data analyst must choose listwise deletion, pairwise deletion, single imputation/ad hoc technique, maximum likelihood technique, or multiple imputation—and then defend that choice. Missing data problems cannot be avoided by simply ignoring them.
>
> (Newman, 2014, p. 381–384)

Sampling, Case Selection

Quantitative software programs are a great sampling resource. Each software program (SPSS, SAS, and R) can draw simple random samples, cluster samples, and stratified samples. In addition to helping select a sample from a larger population of cases, quantitative software can also help apply sampling weights. **Sampling weights** help adjust the sample and its characteristics to match those of the population from which it is drawn. This reduces error when running statistical analyses from the sample.

Gerontological researchers often use sample weighting with national datasets. For example, researchers used National Health and Human Nutrition Examination Survey (NHANES) data to test the relationship of emotional support in midlife and later life. They reported using SAS 9.2 and its SURVEYMEANS and SURVEYFREQ procedures (Killian & Turner, 2014). After weighting the data so that the sample matched back to U.S. population characteristics, they provided tables of weighted descriptive and multivariate analysis. The researchers concluded:

> NHANES data are nationally representative of the U.S. noninstitutionalized population. Sample weights were used to correct for unequal probabilities of selection throughout the analyses, and clusters were used to compute standard errors. Therefore, the findings related to emotional support are representative of midlife and older adults in the U.S.
>
> (Killian & Turner, 2014, p. 104)

Other researchers weighted data from the Fifth National Survey of Older Americans Act to examine informal caregiver stressors (Longacre, Valdmanis, Handorf & Fang, 2016). These researchers justified their weighting process by saying: "Data were weighted specifically adjusting for nonresponse, followed by trimming of extreme weights" (2016, p. 2). They provided a link to a description of sampling weights and processes with this national dataset, so others could follow the researchers' processes (http://www.agid.acl.gov/DataFiles/NPS/Files.aspx?year=2009&serviceid=1). Another team of researchers used Stata's svy command to weight their three-country elder samples in their analyses (Rico-Uribe et al., 2016). They describe the weighting process:

> All data were weighted to account for the sampling design in each country and to generalize the study sample to the reference population. Post-stratification corrections

> were made to the weights to adjust for the population distribution obtained from the national census from each country, and for non-response.
>
> (Rico-Uribe et al., 2016, p. 5)

Another example of language used to describe the sample weighting process is seen in a study examining the relationship of care availability and care received using the National Health and Aging Trends Study (NHATS; Wolf, 2014). The researcher describes the weighting process:

> All analyses are weighted using analytic sample weights documented in [the dataset's technical paper], and standard errors reflect the complex sample design employed in NHATS.
>
> (p. S61)

Codebooks

Quantitative software programs generate codebooks that provide written accounts about aspects of your data and track any changes you made to the data. Software-produced **codebooks** generally include the variable name, its position in the dataset, the narrative or text variable labels (providing a longer description of what the variable is), the variable's level of measurement, and its technical aspects (type: string/numeric, number of characters, number of decimal places, etc.). The codebook also addresses how missing values for a variable are coded or noted.

Software producers' codebooks are a starting place, but adding more details to the generated codebook is of benefit to the researcher. Adding any variable recoding notes or reasons for recoding choices can aid when writing the analysis sections. The codebook entry for the previous example of recoding age from actual number of chronological years into two age groups could also include some reasoning as to why you made these changes and the variable's central tendency and variation values. See Figure 9.2 for an example of basic codebook items. Existing datasets also publish codebooks with details about the data. In this codebook example from the General Social Survey (Smith, Marsden & Hout, 2015), the years that the question was asked are added to the more traditionally included elements of question wording, variable name, response categories with values, and counts or percent of each response type.

Visual Displays: Pie Charts, Histograms, Boxplot, Quartiles

Quantitative software offers a wide array of ways to visually present data. For univariate data, **pie charts** allow responses to be displayed as portions or sections of a circle. Many other visual options can depict more than one variable. Bar charts, histograms, and boxplots can be the visual representation of the frequency distribution of one variable or of multiple variables. **Bar charts** are the most commonly used visual display. In Figure 9.11 you can see the SPSS point and click commands that help users choose how they wish to depict the data visually. Figure 9.12 shows a bar chart that depicts views about Social Security spending for two groups: those less than 65 years of age and those 65 years of age or older. **Histograms** can display the categories of one variable or the categories of one variable by another. **Boxplots** show the distribution of a variable or variables including a depiction of central tendency and variation. **Scatterplots** show the relationship between scale-level or higher variables and can be plotted against a regression line.

Statistical Analyses and Tests. The strength of quantitative software is its ability to run a wide range of uni- and multivariate statistical analyses on large amounts of data in a relatively short period of time. Each test can be identified by the user to account for missing data and run the user's preferences. Many guides exist to run specifically the statistical tests discussed in

Table 9.2 Codebook Items

Variable	Variable Name	Description	Level of Measurement	Percent (Total)	Central Tendency	Variation
Age, in number of years	Age	Age of respondent	Interval-ratio	(1969)	mean = 48.19	SD = 17.69
					median = 47	
65 or not?	Sixtyfiveornot	*Recoded variable:*	Nominal	80	mode = Less than 65 years of age	IQV = .08
Less than 65 years of age		Is Respondent older or younger than 65?		20		
65 years of age or older				(1969)		
Discrimination based on age	wkageism	"Do you feel in any way discriminated against on your job because of your age?"	Nominal	9.4	mode = (no)	IQV = .09
1 = Yes				90.6		
2 = No				(1148)		
Generations in one household	famgen	Records the number of family generations in household	Nominal	60.1	mode = (one generation)	IQV = .07
1 generation				37.5		
2 generations, children				1.0		
2 generations, parents				0.1		
2 generations, grandchildren				0.1		
3 generations, grandchildren				1.2		
3 generations, grandchildren, children and parents				(1974)		
Amount of Social Security spending	natsoc	Are we spending too much, too little, or about the right amount on Social Security?	Ordinal	55.8	median = (too little)	R = 2
1 = Too little				36.4		s.d. = 0.64
2 = About right				7.8		
3 = Too much				(1877)		

(Continued)

Table 9.2 (Continued)

Variable	Variable Name	Description	Level of Measurement	Percent (Total)	Central Tendency	Variation
Should aged live with their children?	aged	Should aged live with their children	Ordinal	51.8	median = (good idea)	R = 2
A good idea				32.2		s.d. = 0.75
A bad idea				16.0		
Depends				(1321)		
Adult children are important to help elderly parents	eldersup	Adult children are important to help elderly parents	Ordinal	20.9	median = (agree)	R = 4
1 (strongly agree)				65.2		s.d. = 0.50
2				7.7		
3				5.5		
4				0.7		
5 (strongly disagree)				(1276)		
Who should pay for help for elderly	eldcost	Who should pay for help for elderly?	Nominal	54.1	mode = (elderly people themselves or their family)	IQV = .9
The elderly people themselves or their family				45.9		
The government/public funds				(1049)		
Allow patients to die if incurable	letdie	Let patients die if doctors agree	Nominal	67.8	median = (yes)	IQV = .07
Yes				32.2		
No				(1250)		

733. When you retire, do you think Social Security benefits will be much better than those now paid of retirees, somewhat better, about the same, somewhat worse, or much worse?

[VAR: SOCSECRT]

Response	Punch	Year														
		1972–82	1982B	1983–87	1987B	1988–91	1993–98	2000	2002	2004	2006	2008	2010	2012	2014	All
Muchbetter	1	0	0	0	0	0	32	0	0	0	0	0	0	0	0	32
Somewhatbetter	2	0	0	0	0	0	86	0	0	0	0	0	0	0	0	86
Aboutthesame	3	0	0	0	0	0	318	0	0	0	0	0	0	0	0	318
Somewhatworse	4	0	0	0	0	0	360	0	0	0	0	0	0	0	0	360
Muchworse	5	0	0	0	0	0	420	0	0	0	0	0	0	0	0	420
Don'tknow	8	0	0	0	0	0	100	0	0	0	0	0	0	0	0	100
Noanswer	9	0	0	0	0	0	71	0	0	0	0	0	0	0	0	71
Notapplicable	IAP	13626	354	7542	353	5907	8947	2817	2765	2812	4510	2023	2044	1974	2538	58212

Figure 9.10 General Social Survey (GSS) Codebook Entry for Social Security Benefits Variable

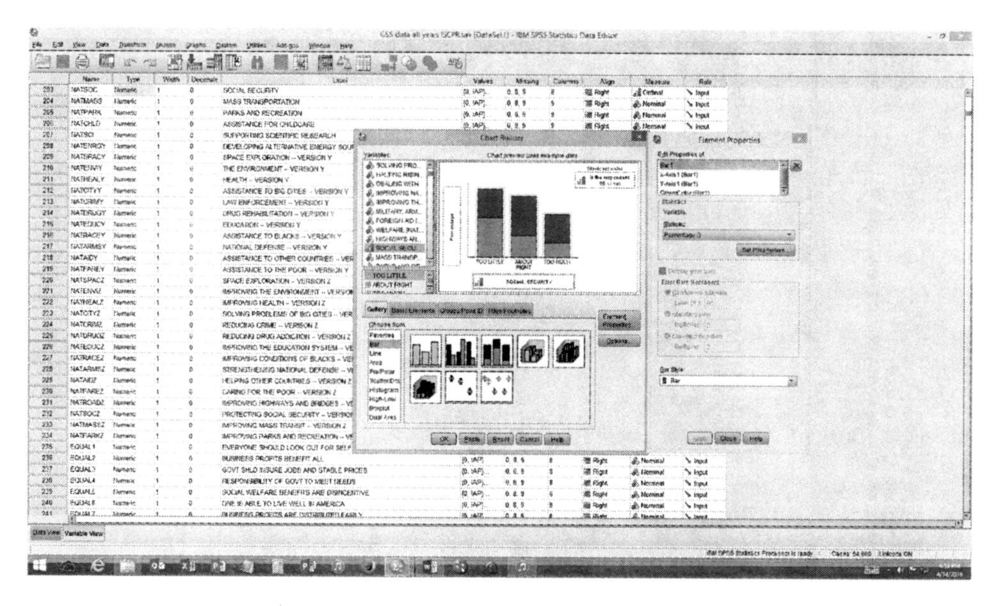

Figure 9.11 Chart Builder in SPSS

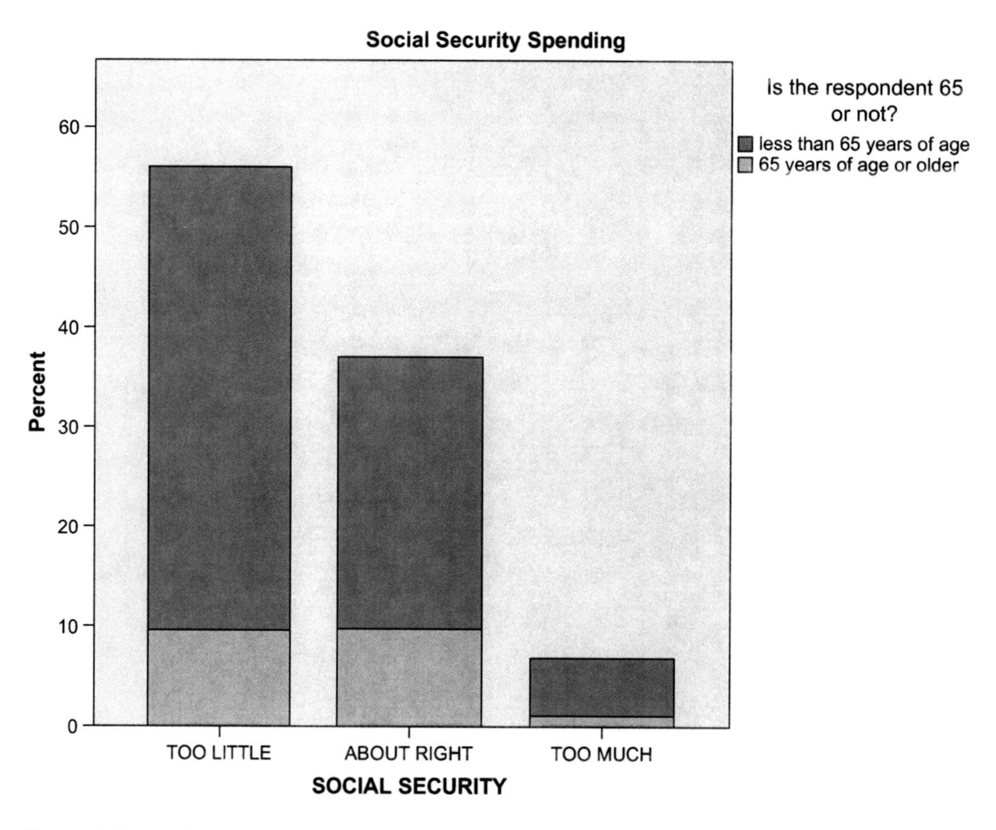

Figure 9.12 Bar Chart of Attitudes toward Social Security Spending for Two Groups

Chapters 5 and 6. Here, a crosstab will be used to demonstrate how to read quantitative software's output. **Crosstabs** are widely used to examine the relationships between two (or more) variables. Figure 9.13 is a crosstab of the relationship with age (those less than 65 years of age and those 65 years of age and over) with a rating of pride in the Social Security system (very proud, somewhat proud, not very proud, and not proud at all). Looking at the percentages in the column "less than 65 years of age," we see a pattern emerge. Those less than 65 years of age tend to cluster around the somewhat proud (36.9%) and not very proud (37.5%) opinions. When we look at the "65 years of age or older" column, a different pattern is evident. Those 65 years of age or older tend to feel more positively about the Social Security system—with the majority (45.7%) feeling somewhat proud, followed by those feeling very proud (29.1%).

Now that a relationship is seen for age group and pride in the Social Security system, a test for significance (that the relationship is not happening by chance) can be conducted. The **Chi-Square** (x^2), seen in Figure 9.14, tells us from the circled coefficient that this relationship is significant at the highest level (p≤.001). Note: while significance is interpretable, the Chi-Square coefficient (93.401) magnitude is less interpretable because it depends on a number of factors.

HOW PROUD OF ITS SOCIAL SECURITY SYSTEM * Is the respondent 65 or not Crosstabulation

			Is the respondent 65 or not		
			less than 65 years of age	65 years of age or older	Total
HOW PROUD OF ITS SOCIAL SECURITY SYSTEM	VERY PROUD	Count	88	72	160
		% within Is the respondent 65 or not	9.5%	29.1%	13.6%
	SOMEWHAT PROUD	Count	344	113	457
		% within Is the respondent 65 or not	36.9%	45.7%	38.8%
	NOT VERY PROUD	Count	349	40	389
		% within Is the respondent 65 or not	37.5%	16.2%	33.0%
	NOT PROUD AT ALL	Count	150	22	172
		% within Is the respondent 65 or not	16.1%	8.9%	14.6%
Total		Count	931	247	1178
		% within Is the respondent 65 or not	100.0%	100.0%	100.0%

Figure 9.13 Crosstab of Age and Pride in Social Security System

Chi-Square Tests

	Value	df	Asymptotic Significance (2-sided)
Pearson Chi-Square	93.401[a]	3	.000
Likelihood Ratio	89.204	3	.000
Linear-by-Linear Association	73.586	1	.000
N of Valid Cases	1178		

a. 0 cells (.0%) have expected count less than 5. The minimum expected count is 33.55.

Figure 9.14 Significance of the Relationship of Age and Pride in the Social Security System

Qualitative Software Basics

Types of Files

Qualitative data analysis programs accept a wide array of files as cases or individual pieces of data. These files include text documents (as in Word files), audio files, videos, and survey data (as from Excel). Some also incorporate data from Google Earth's geospatial data and social media. Each software program has a way of either saving program files as files directly with an extension or bundling them as a part of one Hermeneutic Unit (HU).

Memos and Annotations

Memos or annotations serve as a way for researchers to write their thoughts and reflections about experiences in the field. Once entered into qualitative software, they both become pieces of data and help researchers maintain and audit a trail of their work. Memos also track coding definitions and coding decisions. Memos in software can aid in recursive (repeated) coding or rethinking and examining the relationship between codes/concepts throughout the analysis (Friese, 2014).

Coding

Coding is the process of assigning labels to similar segments of text, video, or audio elements in the analysis. Codes can be predetermined before analysis or generated from the data, themselves. Qualitative software lets a researcher apply several types of codes (or nodes) to each case. Codes can exist alone or be based on/created from the direct quotes or text of documents to reflect the individuals' language (**in vivo**). Individual codes can be grouped together into hierarchical code groups (called **families or trees**). See Figure 9.15 for a list

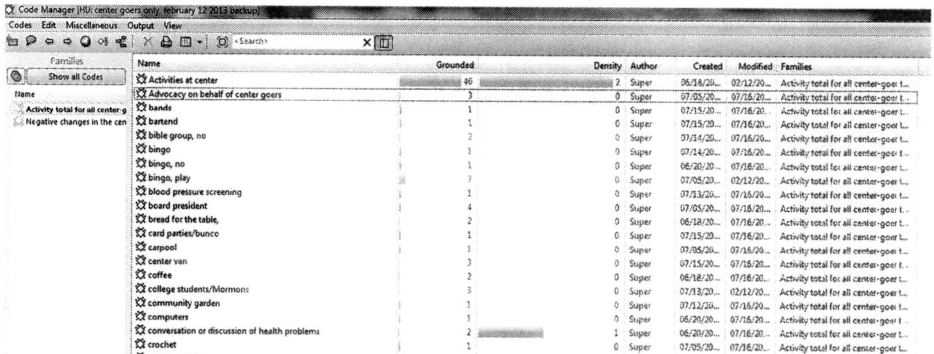

Figure 9.15 List of Codes in a Code Family

Source: http://atlasti.com/2014/09/26/using-atlas-ti-for-coding-ethnographic-and-policy-data/.

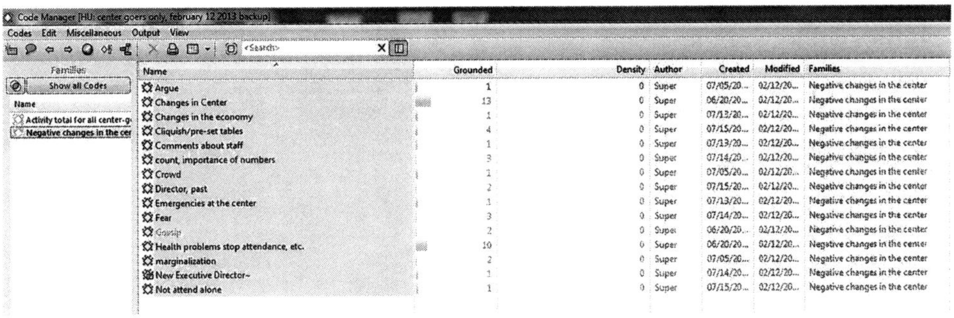

Code Manager [HU: center goers only, february 12 2013 backup]
Codes Edit Miscellaneous Output View

Families
Show all Codes
Name
Activity total for all center-g
Negative changes in the cer

Name	Grounded	Density	Author	Created	Modified	Families
Argue	1	0	Super	07/05/20...	02/12/20...	Negative changes in the center
Changes in Center	13	0	Super	06/20/20...	02/12/20...	Negative changes in the center
Changes in the economy	1	0	Super	07/13/20...	02/12/20...	Negative changes in the center
Cliquish/pre-set tables	4	0	Super	07/15/20...	02/12/20...	Negative changes in the center
Comments about staff	1	0	Super	07/13/20...	02/12/20...	Negative changes in the center
count, importance of numbers	3	0	Super	07/14/20...	02/12/20...	Negative changes in the center
Crowd	1	0	Super	07/05/20...	02/12/20...	Negative changes in the center
Director, past	2	0	Super	07/15/20...	02/12/20...	Negative changes in the center
Emergencies at the center	1	0	Super	07/13/20...	02/12/20...	Negative changes in the center
Fear	3	0	Super	07/14/20...	02/12/20...	Negative changes in the center
Gossip	2	0	Super	06/20/20...	02/12/20...	Negative changes in the center
Health problems stop attendance, etc.	10	0	Super	06/20/20...	02/12/20...	Negative changes in the center
marginalization	2	0	Super	07/05/20...	02/12/20...	Negative changes in the center
New Executive Director~	1	0	Super	07/14/20...	02/12/20...	Negative changes in the center
Not attend alone	1	0	Super	07/15/20...	02/12/20...	Negative changes in the center

Figure 9.16 Codes in a Family of Emergent Codes

of codes in a code family that I created for my senior-center book (Weil, 2014). Figure 9.16 shows how the individual activities codes (shown in Figure 9.15) for activities participated in at the center were grouped together into a larger positive "Activities for All Center-Goers" family. Another emergent "Negative Changes in the Center" family was created to include the more negative feelings about center activities.

Analyzing and Displaying Data

Frequencies, Groundedness, and Attributes

Qualitative programs provide users with counts of individual codes and code groups, called **frequencies or groundedness.** And, although thought of as more of a quantitative-feature software, some programs, such as Nvivo, allow for the creation of quantified variables, or attributes (MAXQDA does this as well; see the mixed-methods section, later in this chapter).

Crosstabs and Co-occurrence Table

Crosstabs and co-occurrence tables compare the amount of times that codes appear together just as would be done in a quantitative crosstab table. These tabular functions show patterns of codes appearing together. ATLAS.ti's co-occurrence table produces a C-Coefficient with values 0–1 indicating the strength of the co-occurring relationship between the codes. Ricardo Contreras of ATLAS.ti cautions users that the co-occurrence table, while quantifying data, is meant as a tool to further explore of the project's qualitative data. He suggests that the user ask himself or herself the following questions:

> What is this co-occurrence telling us about our research problem?
> How do these concepts relate to each other in the context of the study?
> How is this particular concept helping us understand this other particular concept?
> (Contreras, 2011)

Team Coding and Kappa

Multiple researchers on a project can code data, either simultaneously or individually, and the similarities of their coding can be assessed. In addition to the qualitative software options listed in Table 9.1, the free **Coding Analysis Toolkit (CAT)** can calculate inter-rater reliability.

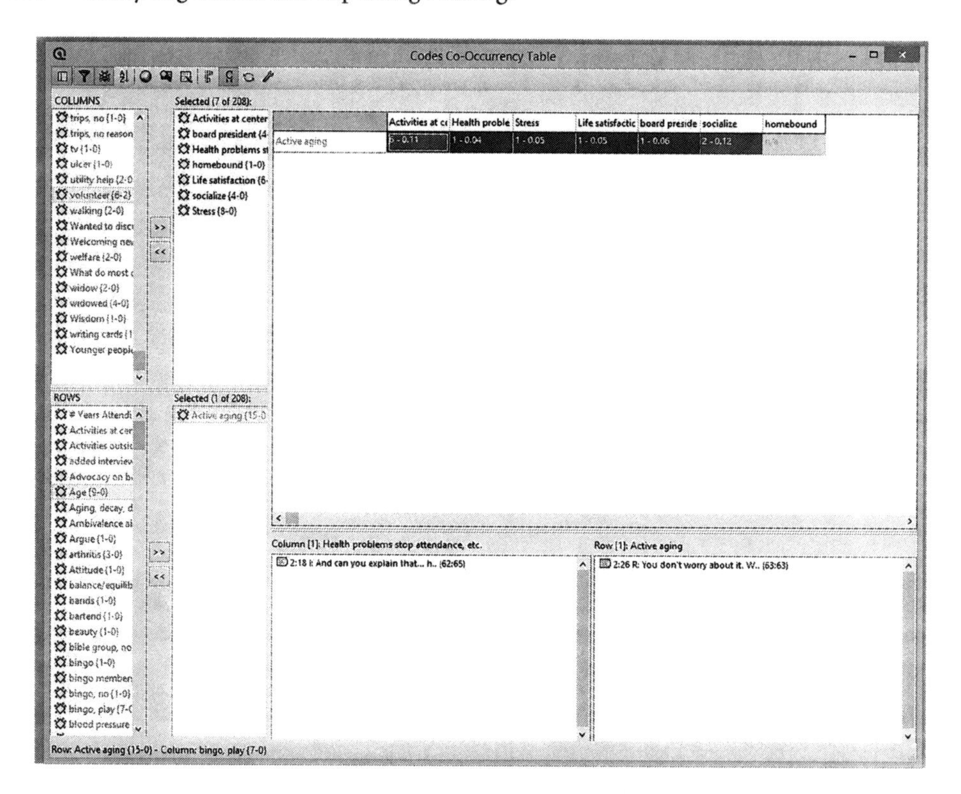

Figure 9.17 Co-occurrence Table for Activities at the Center and Active Aging, Health Problems, Life Satisfaction, Center Roles, Socialization, and Homebound Codes

The CAT is supported by the University of Pittsburgh and was created by its Qualitative Data Analysis Program (QDAP) group (see http://cat.texifter.com).

Visual Displays: Code Relationships, Word Clouds

Visual displays, whether visual word clouds of codes or maps of codes, produce a visual representation of the codes in the data. In a **word cloud**, the more frequently occurring codes appear in a larger font in the cloud. See Figure 9.18 for an example. **Maps**, such as the network map in Figure 9.19, illustrate codes and the relationships among them. Mapping helps a researcher understand that codes are related to each other as codes and subcodes or related codes at the same level.

Mixed-Methods Software Basics

While several software packages can be used for mixed-methods analysis, MAXQDA (named for sociologist Max Weber) has a set of functions that are specifically labeled "Mixed Methods." These functions allow users to create variables, divide codes by variable categories, create a crosstab with counts and percentages, and create a typology table (a bivariate table that includes calculation of measures of central tendency and variation).

Attributes

Also called variables, **attributes** can be created and added to each case or document. These variables attach different identifiers (age, gender, income, education, location) to

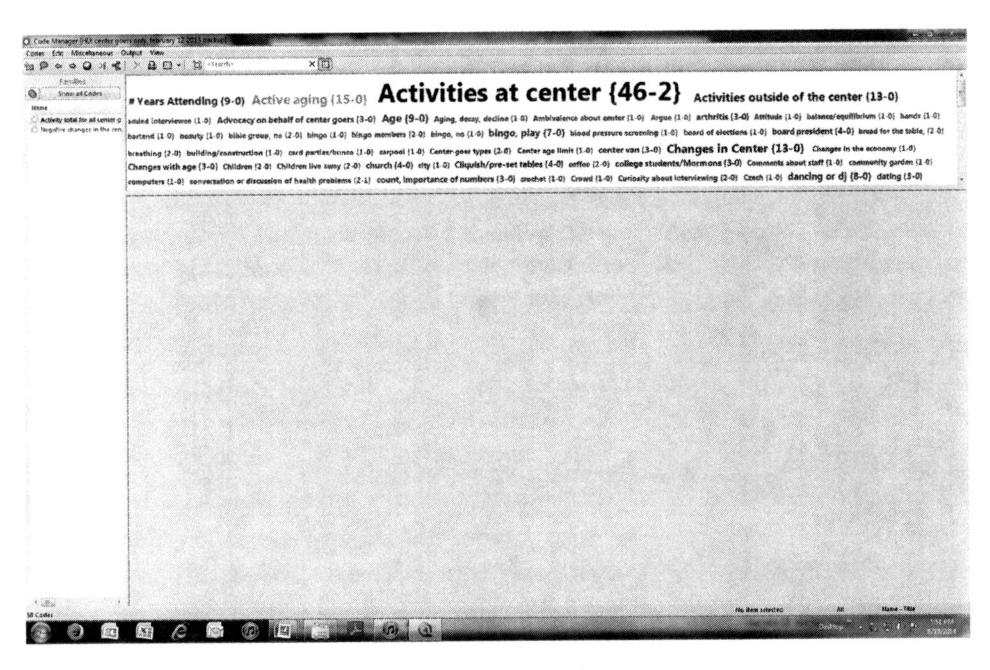

Figure 9.18 Word Cloud of All Activities at the Senior Center Codes

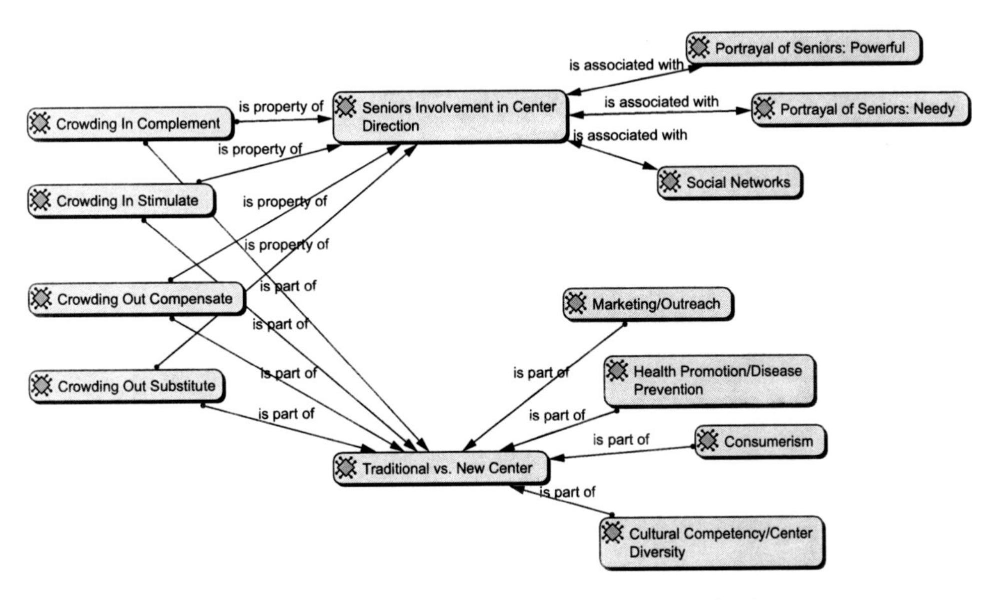

Figure 9.19 Code Network Map for Final Article Crowding In and Crowding Out Assessment

a case in addition to the codes also attached to documents or cases. The "activation by variable" function lets the user select cases that meet conditional statements for variables' values attached to the case. In the example in Figure 9.20, the codes of health and recreation are divided along the variable for location (with the categories Lyon, Berlin, and Vancouver).

	city=Lyon	city=Berlin	city=Vancouver
Health	Health: On a scale of 1-10, how satisfied are you with your health? Answer: _6_ I think I'm pretty okay. Just some minor aches in some areas, but I think I can live. I think I also, prevent myself in some ways. I see in movies, and family members dieing, and start to wonder. I never had major surgery, or even any problem, with my health. I'm also very paranoid, in that way. If I see someone in bad shape, and worry. What if? That is the question. What if it's me? I think that's all I'm really concerned with my health. Another thing is smoking and drinking. I don't do either of them. So I get really mad when people do it in front of me, because of second hand smoking. I don't want to die of cancer, because of some stupid person, wants to kill me too due to their cigarettes. Most of the time, I think I forget that I could. So I really don't make them stop. But I see on TV and movies, people dying of lung cancer, I really get upset. Another thing I feel bad is my own health, in keeping a good shape.	Health: On a scale of 1-10, how satisfied are you with your health? Answer: _8_ I am relatively happy with my current health. I feel that I have a decent looking physique but of course I would like it enhanced. I see all these guys in underwear ads and in clubs with these pumped up bodies and all I can think is "Damn I wish I looked like that!" If anything to make both myself and my girlfriend happier. But improving my health is something I know I can achieve. It is very easy to eat better and to work out more. You just have to do it and that's the hardest part of it all. Jon 9 - 12 (0) I dance my ass off every week and I play basketball whenever possible. I try and get out and do stuff whenever possible. I am relatively satisfied with my recreational\leisure activities. I am one of those people who feel guilty if I sit inside and watch TV on a beautiful day. I feel like I should be at	Relationships: I can definately say I am 100% happy with all my relationships in my life. My friends are always there for me and I would not give them up for the world. My boyfriend Joe is great. I can count on him for anything and I know he will never let me down. And my family and I are very close. Besides the usual parent-daughter fights, they live for me and I appreciate that so much. I have a very open relationship with my parents. I am able to talk to them about anything and I know I will always get good advice out of them..they always want the best for me. SECTION 2 - WORD TO STORY PROMPTS... Joanna 22 - 24 (0) HAPPINESS: Happiness does not remind me of one event. It makes me think of my life. Even though there are bad times, overall I am very happy with the way I turned out as a human being, and I like where my life is headed.
Recreation	Recreation: On a scale of 1-10, how satisfied are you with recreation and leisure in your life? Answer: _5_ Please list recreation\leisure events you	Recreation: On a scale of 1-10, how satisfied are you with recreation and leisure in your life? Answer: _9_ Please list recreation\leisure events you	Recreation: On a scale of 1-10, how satisfied are you with recreation and leisure in your life? Answer: _9_ Please list recreation\leisure events you

Figure 9.20 Quote Matrix of Location and Heath and Recreation

Source: http://www.maxqda.com/max12-tutorial/k-mixed-methods.

Crosstab and Typology Tables

The **crosstab feature** lets a user compare counts or percentages of codes by variable categories. In Figure 9.20, the code "parents" appears 25% of the time in documents of those with no siblings and, most often, in 75% of the documents of those with siblings. The **typology table** function takes the crosstab further. It quantifies codes and provides additional statistics for the relationship between the quantified codes and variable categories. The statistics are in either the form of numbers and percent or means and standard deviations based on variables' level of measurement. In Figure 9.22, several characteristics related to the depression level of those studies (e.g., average number of siblings, gender, and marital status) are compared. The analysis suggests depression is related to older age, having fewer siblings, being a woman, and not being married. See Barbour (2013) for additional MAXQDA details. Mixed-methods software provides basic analysis options; for more advanced quantitative tests and analysis, a purely quantitative program may be needed.

Crosstab

	Siblings = 0	Siblings > 0	SUM
People	9,1%	90,9%	100,0%
Friends	30,8%	69,2%	100,0%
Parents	27,3%	72,7%	100,0%
Partner	25,0%	75,0%	100,0%
Siblings	20,0%	80,0%	100,0%
∑ SUM	23,1%	76,9%	100,0%
# N (Documents)	28,6%	71,4%	100,0%

Figure 9.21 Crosstab with Percent

Typology Table

	Depressed = 1 (N=14)	Not depressed = 1 (N=12)
Age, Mean (SD)	42.1 (5.4)	39.8 (5.4)
Siblings, Mean (SD)	0.9 (0.6)	2.0 (1.5)
Gender: male, Number (%)	6 (42.9)	9 (75.0)
Married: yes, Number (%)	4 (28.6)	9 (75.0)

Figure 9.22 Typology Table

Each type of computerized data analysis software offers the user the ability to analyze datasets and produce tabular and visual output to represent the data. While each has unique advantages and disadvantages, it is up to the user and his or her ability to design and run each aspect of the analysis, set conditions, and address missing data. An overview of the basics of each type of software (quantitative, qualitative, and mixed methods) lets the user become an informed consumer and serves as a starting point for software selection. References at the end of this chapter are a guide for further and more detailed exploration of software options.

Discussion Questions

- When is software appropriate for quantitative analysis? Qualitative analysis? Mixed-methods analysis?
- Choose a project or study you are working on or planning to work on. Review the "key questions to ask when selecting software" in this chapter. What software characteristics are the most beneficial to your work?
- Explain what to look for in quantitative output.
- Discuss three reasons why missing data must be addressed by software programs.
- Why do we need to create a codebook? And why should we keep memos and an audit trail?
- Compare the following terms: groundedness vs. frequencies, codes vs. variables, code families vs. recoding variables, and crosstabs vs. co-occurrence tables.
- What additional features do mixed-methods software programs offer beyond those of quantitative and qualitative programs?

Bibliography

Barbour, R. (2013). *Introducing qualitative research: A student's guide*. New York: Sage Publications.

Bassett, B. R. (2010a). "Computer-based analysis of qualitative data: ATLAS.ti." In A. J. Mills, G. Durepos, & E. Wiebe (Eds.), *Encyclopedia of case study research* (Vol. 1, pp. 182–184). Thousand Oaks, CA: Sage Reference.

Bassett, B. R. (2010b). "Computer-based analysis of qualitative data: NVIVO." In A. J. Mills, G. Durepos, & E. Wiebe (Eds.), *Encyclopedia of case study research* (Vol. 1, pp. 192–194). Thousand Oaks, CA: Sage Reference.

Charmaz, K. (2006). *Constructing grounded theory: A practical guide through qualitative analysis*. London; Thousand Oaks, CA: Sage Publications.

Contreras, R. (2011). *Examining the context in qualitative analysis: The role of the co-occurrence tool in ATLAS.ti*. Newsletter No. 2011/2. Berlin: ATLAS.ti and EQR Training & Consulting, Inc.

Contreras, R. (2015). *The qualitative data analysis workbench: An overview*. Presentation by R. Contreras (August 2011).

Data Camp Team blog. (June 3, 2014). *What is the best statistical programming language?* Retrieved from https://www.datacamp.com/community/tutorials/statistical-language-wars-the-infograph

Fielding, N. (2012). The diverse worlds and research practices of qualitative software. *Forum Qualitative Sozialforschung/ Forum: Qualitative Social Research, 13*(2), Article 13, http://nbn-resolving.de/urn:nbn:de:0114-fqs1202124.

Friese, S. (2014). *Qualitative data analysis with ATLAS.ti*. London: Sage Publications.

Gibbs, G. R. (2014). "Using software in qualitative analysis." In U. Flick, K. Metzler & W. (Eds.), *The Sage handbook of qualitative data analysis* (pp. 277–296). London: Sage.

Graham, J. W. (2012). *Missing data: Analysis and design* (1st ed.). New York: Springer. doi:10.1007/978–1–4614–4018–5

Harvard Law School. (2016). *Analyzing data*. Retrieved from http://hls.harvard.edu/library/empirical-research-services/analyzing-data

Hatani, F. (2015). Analyzing high-profile panel discussion on global health: An exploration with MAXQDA. *Forum Qualitative Sozialforschung/Forum: Qualitative Social Research, 16*(1). Retrieved from http://nbn-resolving.de/urn:nbn:de:0114-fqs1501148

Humble, Á. M. (2010). "Computer-based analysis of qualitative data: MAXQDA 2007." In A. J. Mills, G. Durepos, & E. Wiebe (Eds.), *Encyclopedia of case study research* (Vol. 1, pp. 190–192). Thousand Oaks, CA: Sage Reference.

Hutchinson, S., Olmos, A., & Teman, E. (2013). *Adequacy of model fit in confirmatory factor analysis and structural equation models: It depends on what software you use.* American Evaluation Association, Washington, DC.

Killian, T. S., & Turner, M. J. (2014). Latent class typologies for emotional support among midlife and aging Americans: Evidence from the National Health and Human Nutrition Examination Survey. *Journal of Adult Development, 21*(2), 96–105.

Lewis, R. B. (2004). NVivo 2.0 and ATLAS.ti 5.0: A comparative review of two popular qualitative data-analysis programs. *Field Methods, 16*(4), 439–464. doi:10.1177/1525822X04269174

Longacre, M. L., Valdmanis, V. G., Handorf, E. A., & Fang, C. Y. (2016). Work impact and emotional stress among informal caregivers for older adults. *The Journals of Gerontology Series B: Psychological Sciences and Social Sciences, 2016*, 1–10. doi:10.1093/geronb/gbw027

Maietta, R. (2008). MAXQDA 2007: Resources for mixed methods research. *Journal of Mixed Methods Research, 2*(2), 193–198. doi:10.1177/1558689807314014

McKnight, P. E. (2007). *Missing data: A gentle introduction.* New York: Guilford Press.

Molenberghs, G., Fitzmaurice, G. M., Kenward, M. G., Tsiatis, A. A., & Verbeke, G. (2015). *Handbook of missing data methodology.* Boca Raton, FL: CRC Press.

Muenchen, R. A. (2011). *R for SAS and SPSS users.* New York: Springer. doi:10.1007/978–1–4614–0685–3

Muenchen, R. A. (October 2015). *The popularity of data analysis software.* Retrieved from http://r4stats.com/articles/popularity/

Newman, D. A. (2014). Missing data: Five practical guidelines. *Organizational Research Methods, 17*(4), 372–411. doi:10.1177/1094428114548590

Oliveira, M., Bitencourt, C., Teixeira, E., & Santos, A. C. (April 2013). *Thematic content analysis: Is there a difference between the support provided by the MAXQDA® and NVivo® Software Packages.* In Proceedings of the 12th European Conference on Research Methods for Business and Management Studies (pp. 304–314).

Osborne, J. W. (2013). *Best practices in data cleaning: A complete guide to everything you need to do before and after collecting your data.* Thousand Oaks, CA: Sage Publications.

Palmer, R. (2010). Missing data? Plan on it. *Journal of the American Geriatrics Society, 58*(Suppl 2), S343–S348. doi:10.1111/j.1532–5415.2010.03053.x

Rico-Uribe, L. A., Caballero, F. F., Olaya, B., Tobiasz-Adamczyk, B., Koskinen, S., Leonardi, M., & Miret, M. (2016). Loneliness, social networks, and health: A cross-sectional study in three countries. *PLoS One, 11*(1), 1–18. doi:10.1371/journal.pone.0145264

Sainani, K. (2015). Dealing with missing data. *Physical Medicine & Rehabilitation, 7*(9), 990–994. doi:10.1016/j.pmrj.2015.07.011

Salkind, N. J. (2014). *Statistics for people who (think they) hate statistics* (5th ed.). Thousand Oaks, CA: Sage Publications.

Schlomer, G. L., Bauman, S., & Card, N. A. (2010). Best practices for missing data management in counseling psychology. *Journal of Counseling Psychology, 57*(1), 1–10. doi:10.1037/a0018082

Smith, T. W., Marsden, P. V., & Hout, M. (2015). *General social surveys, 1972–2014: Cumulative codebook.* Principal investigator, Tom W. Smith; co-principal investigators, Peter V. Marsden and Michael Hout. National Data Program for the Social Sciences Series, no. 23, 3,505 pp., 28cm. (no. 23 ed.). Chicago: National Opinion Research Center.

Sweet, S. A., & Grace-Martin, K. (2012). *Data analysis with SPSS: A first course in applied statistics* (4th ed.). Boston: Pearson.

Wagner, W. E. (2015). *Using IBM SPSS statistics for research methods and social science statistics* (5th ed.). Los Angeles: Sage Publications.

Ward, B. W. (2013). What's better—R, SAS®, SPSS®, or STATA®? Thoughts for instructors of statistics and research methods courses. *Journal of Applied Social Science, 7*(1), 115–120.

Weil, J. (September 26, 2014). *Using ATLAS.ti for coding ethnographic and policy data.* ATLAS.ti Blog.

Wolf, D. A. (2014). Getting help from others: The effects of demand and supply. *The Journals of Gerontology Series B: Psychological Sciences and Social Sciences, 69*(Suppl 1), S59–S64.

Zhou, X., Zhou, C., Liu, D., Ding, X., & Ebooks Corporation. (2014). *Applied missing data analysis in health sciences.* Hoboken, NJ: John Wiley & Sons.

10

Ethical Issues and Concerns in Aging Research

Ethical issues are part of all research. This chapter outlines some ethical issues related to working with older populations. It balances realities of aging and federal rules for research with human subjects with commonly held misbeliefs about conducting research with older persons. The chapter reveals how some institutional boards continue to use age as an indicator of "vulnerability" status. Ethical codes of gerontological and social science organizations are included and compared. Recruitment issues of helicoptering, slash/crash and burn participant recruitment, and use of coercion are addressed as are possible protections for participants (e.g., the certificate of confidentiality, CoC, and Evaluation to Sign Consent, ESC, measure for consent). Ethical issues are also addressed by place/research site (e.g., issues for residents in the Continuum of Care) and those that are researcher based and design based (e.g., in qualitative, quantitative, mixed-methods designs). Questions to consider about ethics and gerontological research close the chapter.

Introduction: Role of Ethics in Aging Research

Ethics, in general, are codes of behavior that define what is right and what is wrong, or how we know what is right and what we consider wrong. More formally, "ethics may be conceptualized as a special case of norms governing individual or social action. In any individual act or interpersonal exchange, ethics connotes principles of obligation to serve values over and above benefits to the people who are directly involved" (Greenwald, 2001, p. 835; Nebelsick, 2016). When we think of ethics and aging research, ethics refer more to codes of conduct and the informed, fair treatment of the people we are studying.

Ethics discussed in this chapter will refer to those related to the practice of research with older persons or topics about aging. **Ethics in gerontological research** can be thought of as research principles that assess and weigh the rights of participants and those of researchers in pursuing studies that may advance the field. Ethics in gerontological studies "can raise questions about our conventional moral values and judgments and also reveal how relationships of power influences moral practices" (Holstein, Parks & Waymack, 2011, pp. 3–4). Others suggest that "ethics help define the nature, extent, and limits of the rights and obligations emerging from the relationships between gerontological professionals, patients/clients, families, facilities, third-party payers and reviewers, and society. Ethics also affect gerontological practice by drawing the professional into the social problems or disputes of the patient/client that require fair and just resolution" (Kapp, 2008, p. 66).

Institutional Review Boards and Research Ethics

Older persons were historically excluded from clinical and social research or **"orphaned" in research** (McHenry, Insel, Einstein, Vidrine, Koerner & Morrow, 2015; Ries, 2010, p. 578). Also, older persons were included in some studies with questionable ethics. Consider the following statements about alleged ethical abuses in research: "Live cancer cells were injected into 22 elderly human subjects as part of a study of immunity to cancer . . . the subjects were 'merely told they would be receiving some cells' . . . the word cancer was omitted," and "[i]dentification chips were implanted in 200 Alzheimer's patients and caregivers, quite possibly without permission." Which of these studies do you think is recent? Actually, the first statement refers a 1966 article by Henry Beecher, who reported about studies infecting convalescent elderly with cancer cells (Beecher, 1966, p. 1358; Israel, 2015; University of Miami, 2016). The microchipping example refers to allegations that a company implanted persons with Alzheimer's disease and their caregivers with microchips to track them as either a project or a study without consent (CBS News, 2010). Both examples illustrate participants utilized in a research study without disclosure and the informed consent of the participants.

Debates about consent and non-consensual involvement in studies are covered by Institutional Review Boards. **Institutional Review Boards (IRBs)** are bodies made up of at least five interdisciplinary, varied researchers and community members to make sure the rights of human subjects in research are protected. IRBs seek to ensure that participants agree to participate in a study through an informed consent based on knowledge of what is required as part of the study and potential related risks and benefits.

Box 10.1 Historical Documents in IRB Development/History

Belmont Report (April 18, 1979, the National Commission for the Protection of Human Subjects of Biomedical and Behavioral Research)

The National Commission for the Protection of Human Subjects of Research's summary of the ethical principles of research involving human subjects.
http://www.hhs.gov/ohrp/regulations-and-policy/belmont-report/

Declaration of Helsinki (1964, last amended 2013, World Medical Association)

Ethical principle statement for medical research involving human subjects, biological specimens, and data. http://www.wma.net/en/30publications/10policies/b3/

U.S. Department of Health and Human Services, Office for Human Research Protection, Code of Federal Regulations, Title 45, Part 46, the "Common Rule" (revised January 15, 2009)

Federal code governing research conducted on human subjects.
http://www.hhs.gov/ohrp/regulations-and-policy/regulations/45-cfr-46/index.html

National Institutes of Health (NIH) The HIPAA Privacy Rule: Information for researchers: Information about the research and the Health Insurance Portability and Accountability Act (HIPAA) Privacy Rule, protecting health information.
https://privacyruleandresearch.nih.gov/

The U.S. Department of Health and Human Services (DHHS), Office for Human Research Protection, Code of Federal Regulations, Title 45, Part 46, or **Common Rule** governs research conducted on human subjects. It defines key elements of the research process. A main key element is **informed consent**. According to DHHS: "The informed consent process involves three key features: (1) disclosing to potential research subjects information needed to make an informed decision; (2) facilitating the understanding of what has been disclosed; and (3) promoting the voluntariness of the decision about whether or not to participate in the research. Informed consent must be legally effective and prospectively obtained" (DHHS, 45 CFR 46.116 & 45 CFR 46.117).

Federally mandated at each university, medical center, or organization that conducts research involving human subjects, IRBs ask researchers to address several areas of their study: What will participants do, and how is a participant defined/identified? How and what types of data will be collected? How will participants be recruited? What are the risks on all levels—psychological, physical, social, emotional, etc.? How is the researcher planning to protect participants against these risks, and what are the benefits to participants as part of the study? Each IRB application must include a consent form outlining these items in clear, jargon-free language that is appropriate for the reading level of participants (Gitlin & Lyons, 2014, p. 235).

See Box 10.2 for an example of items that must be addressed in an IRB application.

Box 10.2 Example of Narrative of Institutional Review Board Application

A. **Purpose:** Includes research question. Hypotheses and supporting rationale (that includes brief review of literature) and justification of proposed category type: exempt, expedited, or full-board.
B. **Methods:** Includes a description of proposed sample/participants addressing age, vulnerable categories, and recruitment plan. Data Collection Procedures must detail how data will be collected, if deception is used, debriefing plans, and details about participant compensation (if used). Exact data analysis procedures should be noted, and data handling procedures outlined participants' identity protection. State plans for storage of files and original data (e.g., recordings, questionnaires) and the timeline for their destruction. The researcher should demonstrate that she or he understands confidential and anonymous data-collection differences. Any additional protection of participant measures are discussed here.
C. **Risks, Discomforts, and Benefits:** Level of risk must be stated and then justified with a full explanation. Risk must be justified in terms of research benefits with full disclosure of risk.
D. **Costs and Compensations:** Any compensation must be stated, and the role of compensation in influencing participation noted.
E. **Grant Information:** If the study is grant-funded, it must be noted.
F. **Consent Documents:** A sample study consent form must be included.
G. **Letters of Permission:** from research sites/partners must be included.
H. **Supporting Materials Can Include:** survey instruments questionnaires, interview questions/interview scripts, debriefing materials, and/or documentation of IRB training (for federally funded grants and full reviews).

Source: Adapted from the University of Northern Colorado's IRB Application Process, 2016.

An IRB review depends upon the **level of review** needed: exempt, expedited, or full board review. **Exempt reviews** are for projects that meet the Common Rule's definition of posing only minimal risk: "[T]he probability and magnitude of harm or discomfort anticipated in the research are not greater in and of themselves than those ordinarily encountered in daily life or during the performance of routine physical or psychological examinations or tests" (§46.102 Definitions, i). While the Common Rule does not name a specific IRB board member or role to review and exempt applications, each institution's IRB is encouraged to set up an exempt-status protocol. For exempt reviews, participants must be 18 years of age or older and not from a Common Rule's defined vulnerable group. Studies applying for an exempt review cannot include any activities that may put participants at criminal risk and cannot identify participants. They can include research in educational settings, some survey and interview procedures or observation of public behavior, secondary analysis of existing data, chart review, or taste/food quality evaluation.

Expedited reviews cover research that is judged to involve no more than minimal risk to subjects and includes appropriate informed-consent procedures with benefits to participants (Heflin, DeMeo, Nagler & Hockenberry, 2016). According to the Common Rule, several criteria must be present for an expedited review. The project must pose no more than minimal risk, not pose criminal risk, not include classified information, and be in one of the following seven categories: The medical category types include the study being a clinical or drug study, noninvasive biological data (such as blood draws), collection of non-invasive samples (nail clippings or teeth), and non-invasive procedures (such as x-rays). The social and behavioral categories include analysis of materials and data not collected for research purposes; data from video, audio, and digital recordings; and analysis of group behavior through focus groups, interviews, surveys, programs evaluation, and oral histories.

Full board review occurs for research that is judged to involve more than minimal risk. It must, therefore, be presented to the entire review board for discussion and consideration of approval. All members of the IRB meet and discuss these applications. Since deciding where a study fits can sometimes be complicated, a flowchart to help decide level of review is available at this *Human Subject Regulations Decision Charts* (2016) link: http://www.hhs.gov/ohrp/regulations-and-policy/decision-trees/index.html.

IRB and Age-Based Vulnerability

Much of the controversy about IRBs and older persons concerns defining whether or not older age means that a person will fall in the **"vulnerable subjects"** category. IRBs' protections follow the Federal Policy for the Protection of Human Subjects. This is called the Common Rule, Title 45—Department of Health and Human Services, Public Welfare, Part 46—Protection of Human Subjects. The latest revision of section 46.111, "Criteria for IRB approval of research," reads:

> When subjects are likely to be vulnerable to coercion or undue influence, such as children, prisoners, pregnant women, mentally disabled persons, or economically or educationally disadvantaged persons, additional safeguards have been included in the study to protect the rights and welfare of these subjects.
>
> (DHHS, 2009, §46.111, b)

While old age is no longer listed as a federally suggested vulnerable group, differences exist in IRBs' interpretation. Some university IRBs still consider "the elderly" and "the aged" as vulnerable or "protected populations" (Texas A&M, 2015) or "potentially vulnerable" (University of Chicago, 2016). University research statements written to include older persons (as general participants and not protected classes) reflect a more positive understanding of the inclusion of older persons in research:

> The elderly are, as a group, heterogeneous and not usually in need of special protections, except in two circumstances: cognitive impairment and institutionalization. It is now recognized conditions in institutional settings increase the chances for coercion and undue influence because of the lack of freedom inherent in such situations.
>
> (Virginia Tech, 2016, para. 1)

> Concerns of ageism arise if elderly populations are categorically excluded from a research protocol without justifiable scientific or moral reasons for doing so. Researchers cannot automatically assume that merely because a potential subject is elderly, that he/she is not competent to be involved in research.
>
> (University of Miami, 2016, para. 7)

Views on inclusion of older persons of all cognitive statuses in research are changing. A Canadian study examining risks and benefits of research participation for those with dementia found the majority of persons interviewed—from ethics boards, older persons, care providers, doctors, and researchers—felt older persons with dementia could be included in research when there was minimal risk. Only 2% felt that research should never be done with persons with substantial cognitive impairment (Dubois et al., 2011).

Proposed Changes to the Common Rule

The Common Rule is undergoing revision. The Department of Health and Human Services (HHS) formally issued a Notice of Proposed Rulemaking (NPRM) for **Revisions to the Common Rule in September 2015** (DHHS, 2016a). The proposed changes cover clinical and social research. Major changes for all researchers include a revision to the format of the informed-consent document with the most pertinent information about the study being stated clearly in ways the participant can understand. Broad informed consent will be required for bio-specimens used at a later date in secondary analysis. Use of waivers of signed consent will be expanded (if appropriate). The number of continuation reports will be reduced—making them needed for lesser types of studies and not needed if studies are completed. Some studies labeled as expedited studies will become exempt, and some current studies classified as exempt will be classified as excluded (not needing review—through the use of a tool to help in this process; DHHS, 2016a).

Social scientists see the three key changes to social research as follows: "1) changes to the format and layout of informed consent documents; 2) many social/behavioral studies now considered expedited will be exempt; and 3) many exempt studies will be excluded from review. A minor change that will affect sociologists minimally is that expedited studies will no longer require continuing review" (Kennedy & Van Valey, 2016, p. 3). A short summary and full text of proposed changes can be found at http://www.hhs.gov/ohrp/regulations-and-policy/regulations/nprm-home/#.

IRB Issues Related to Studying Differing Groups of Older Populations

Institutional Review Board issues can relate to the population being studied, the role of the researcher, or the type of study design. As alluded to earlier, the older population can receive the "vulnerable population" label, be susceptible to coercion (if they live in skilled nursing home care), or be seen as marginalized or as a group for unethical recruitment or treatment.

Can Persons with Cognitive Impairment (Dementia) Consent?

A review of **rates of cognitive impairment** by age group and gender is warranted before a discussion of ethical treatment of those with cognitive impairment in research. This review helps a researcher assess capacity to consent to participate in research. Figure 10.1, which uses 2002 Health and Retirement Study data, provides the proportion of people age 65 and older with moderate or severe memory impairment versus no or mild memory impairment. As expected, risk of impairment increases with chronological age. Also, women present lower levels of moderate and severe impairment when compared with their male counterparts.

Normal age-related memory changes include a slowing of working memory, which may impact an older person's ability to hold and process information while learning new instructions. Factual memory, word finding, and processing speed decreases. However, assessing mild cognitive impairment is not clear, though many reliable and valid screening tests exist to pick up severe cognitive impairment (Gomersall, Astell, Nygard, Sixsmith, Mihailidis & Hwang, 2015; Trzepacz, Hochstetler, Wang, Walker & Saykin, 2015). There is also little federal policy governing ways to consent someone with impaired cognitive status:

> HHS regulations are silent on consent procedures specific to subjects with impaired decision-making capacity, for example dementia, whether temporary, progressive, or permanent. The regulations require IRBs ensure safeguards are included in the study to protect all subjects that are "likely to be vulnerable to coercion or undue influence" [including aging populations].
>
> (DHHS, 2016b, Informed Consent FAQs, Question 21)

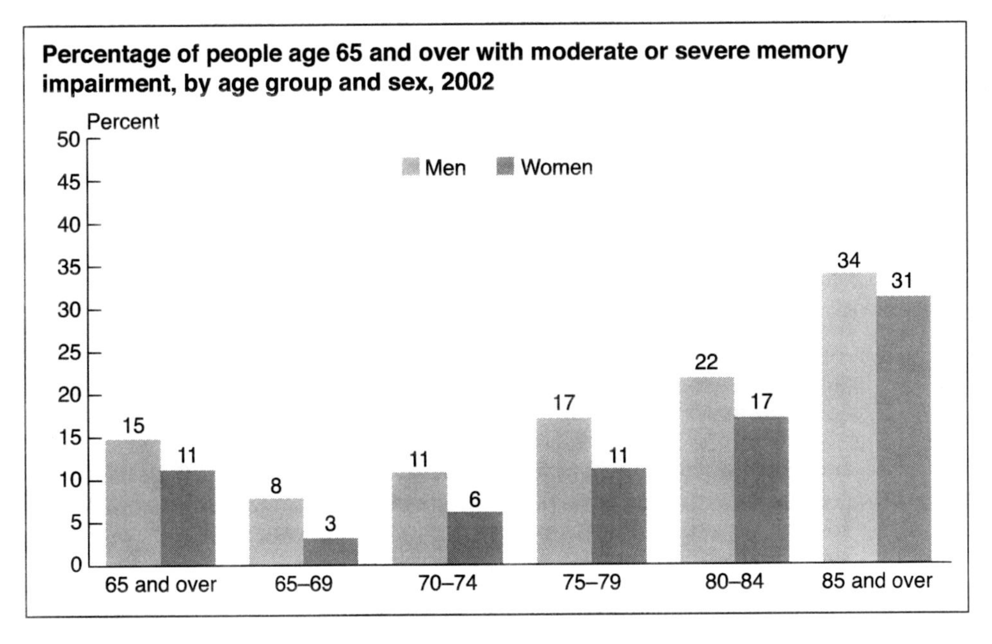

Figure 10.1 Percentage of People Age 65 and Older with Moderate or Severe Memory Impairment by Age Group and Gender

Source: Federal Interagency Forum on Aging-Related Statistics (2006, Indicator 17).

In the absence of a prescribed protocol, a review of studies conducted with those with dementia found a lot of differing approaches to the consent process. More stringent consent processes were being followed for clinical or drug studies (Black, Kass, Fogarty & Rabins, 2007). According to a review of the literature: "[T]here is no method for determining whether capacity to consent to research has been lost. Also, there are no national guidelines that Institutional Review Boards (IRBs) or investigators must follow when including cognitively impaired adults in research as there are for research with children, another vulnerable population" (Black, Kass, Fogarty & Rabins, 2007, p. 7). The Evaluation to Sign Consent Measure and the Partnership of Consent Protocol are two examples of screening procedures and processes created to address the lack of an established protocol for consenting persons with cognitive impairment.

The Evaluation to Sign Consent (ESC) Measure goes beyond a test of cognitive function and impairment such as the **Mini-Mental Status Examination (MMSE)** that attempts to assess the presence and level of delirium and dementia. The traditional MMSE developed by Folstein has 11 questions about orientation to time and place with some recall-based tasks. It has a maximum score of 30 with scores lower than 20 indicating problems in cognitive functioning. For the ESC, the potential participant must be asked several questions about study risks, expectation as a participant, what to do if she or he wants to stop, how to report discomfort, and who gets treatment or how selection for enrollment is decided. The researcher must also outline acceptable answers for each question (Resnick et al., 2007). If a person cannot pass the ESC, he or she gives verbal consent via assent, and a **proxy consent** form is signed by someone other than the older person.

The **Partnership of Consent Protocol**, based on a literature review of enrollment practices across many studies, created a flowchart to determine if informed consent or assent protocol can be used with individual participants. This protocol encourages researchers to really understand what are usual/typical states and behaviors of the persons with impairment, so he or she can fully assess discomfort or a change in willingness to participate (Batchelor-Aselage, Amella, Zapka, Mueller & Beck, 2014, p. 16). Surrogates/proxies were found to make participation decisions for those with cognitive impairment by choosing what was in the person's best interest. They did not simply rely on what the proxy felt was appropriate (Black, Wechsler & Fogarty, 2013). Proxies were found to refuse study participation for reasons other than ethics (Kim et al., 2010).

Box 10.3 Summary of the National Institutes of Health Research Involving Individuals with Questionable Capacity to Consent: Points to Consider

1. Assessing consent capacity using well-validated, practical methods. This included assessing consent capacity possibly with screening tools.
2. Add these assessments into recruitment plans.
3. Treat consent as an ongoing process.
4. Principal investigators are responsible for ensuring consent conditions are met.
5. IRBs are responsible for being knowledgeable of federal statutes. IRB members use their expertise and carefully review applications involving those with questionable capacity to consent.
6. IRBs in their review can determine if additional safeguards are needed.
7. Researchers must make clear the distinction between medical treatment and study procedures (addressing therapeutic misconception and conflicting roles).

8. Additional safeguards are available, so consider the use of consent or study monitors, as those not directly involved in the study to help assess consent and ongoing participation.
9. Information/educational techniques can be used before the study to discuss consent.
10. Waiting periods can be used to provide time to consider consent for study participation.
11. Carefully evaluate persons named as legally authorized representatives and in advance directives as sources of proxy consent/assent. This ability varies by state and document, and they may not know that person's research preferences.

Source: Created from *Research Involving Individuals with Questionable Capacity to Consent: Points to Consider* (November 2009), http://grants.nih.gov/grants/policy/questionablecapacity.htm.

Can Older Persons Who Might Be Coerced/in Skilled Care or Who Are Terminally Ill Consent?

Traditionally, older persons living in skilled nursing homes and those who were actively dying were thought to be at increased risk of coercion (Virginia Tech, 2016, para. 2). Institutional residence or dire illness has the potential to place older persons at increased risk for participation in research. Due to these concerns, many skilled-care facilities have internal boards and committees to assess research studies and allow researchers access. For example, a Canadian researcher wanted to conduct a study of the role of private-pay caregivers in skilled care. At the facility, both the Family Council and Personal Care Companion Council had issues with identification of subjects and risks of participation. They restricted the researcher's access. She modified her initial proposal completely and revised it into an interview-based study design to become a survey of 472 persons with only 30 interviews (Dergal-Serafini, 2010). To consider coercion, the Virginia Tech (2016) website "Research Involving Elderly or Terminally Ill Subjects" suggests researchers ask the following questions as safeguards: "Will the research take place in an institutional setting? And, has the possibility of coercion and undue influence been sufficiently minimized?" (Virginia Tech, 2016, para. 2).

Can Older Persons from Marginalized Groups Consent?

Due to historical mistreatment or forced participation in research groups, older persons might be excluded from research or misunderstood, which can reproduce stereotypes about groups. Researchers find indigenous older peoples at particular risk, emphasizing, "Research is probably one of the dirtiest words in the indigenous world's vocabulary" (Braun, Browne, Ka'opua, Kim & Mokuau, 2014, p. 1). Kathryn Braun, Colette Browne, Lana Sue Ka'opua, Bum Jung Kim, and Noreen Mokuau suggest that these groups may be **underrepresented in research** due to a fear that researchers may exploit them for the researchers' own needs. Or researchers may use **helicopter** and **"smash and grab"** tactics—only maintaining contact with the communities to gather data and rapidly leave. The research's results or benefits never reach or impact the communities from which the results are drawn, and power differentials remain. As a remedy, the researcher team suggests that indigenous IRBs are key, multiple voices must be recognized, and agency must reside with the elders being studied.

Literature suggests two other groups that can be **marginalized**: elders that are abused and older persons that are homebound. Conducting studies with older persons experiencing elder abuse raises questions as to whether the elder can give informed consent. Issues arise about being able to protect information learned in the study and the welfare of participants (Dresser, 2003). Others suggest that homebound older persons are at risk because they may see the researchers in a therapeutic role and should have a two-step consent process. Researchers first had a member of the existing home-care team, usually a nurse, bring up the study. Then researchers approached and consented only those interested (Locher, Bronstein, Robinson, Williams & Ritchie, 2006). A protocol for what constitutes abuse—utilizing debriefing (for the researchers) and community resources (for the participants)—are a good start in studies of elders experiencing abuse and of those homebound.

Protections and Ethics in Recruiting Older Participants

Researchers have several resources to ensure that they follow federal guidelines for studies with human subjects. Many institutions and federal funders require that researchers complete training modules and receive a certificate of training from organizations, such as the **Collaborative Institutional Training Initiative (CITI Program)**. CITI has more than 2,000 subscribing organizations and offers many online training modules, such as biomedical and clinical research, conflicts of interest, research/IRB administration, healthcare ethics committees, human subjects' research, information privacy and security, and responsible conduct of research. The human subjects' research and financial disclosure modules are common modules for social and behavioral sciences (Cushman, 2016).

Certificates of confidentiality (CoC) are another option if the researcher is working with a "sensitive health-related topic that collects names or other identifying characteristics of subjects, and that has been approved by an IRB"; they "allow researchers to refuse to disclose names or other identifying characteristics of research subjects in response to legal demands" (NIH, Certificates of Confidentiality, CoC Kiosk, para. 1). The National Institute of Health website offers some examples of study topics and types that could qualify for a CoC—research about:

- HIV/AIDS; sexually transmitted diseases; sexual attitudes, preferences, or practices
- Alcohol, drugs, or other addictive product use
- Illegal conduct
- Psychological well-being or mental health
- Information that is damaging to a participant's financial standing, employability, or reputation
- Information that could create social stigmatization or discrimination if released
- Behavioral interventions and epidemiologic studies

(NIH, 2016b, Eligibility for a Certificate)

In designing a study of Latino grandparents raising grandchildren and their service and program needs, a researcher delved deep into the literature and local setting. She anticipated that the legal status of some participants may put them at risk, as could potential issues of custody and alcohol and drug use. The researcher applied for, and received, a CoC as an additional layer of protection for her subjects (Mendoza, 2012). A CoC can also be useful in studying abused elders since the researcher may learn about behaviors (such as alcohol use or drug use) or other

Box 10.4 Ethical Recruiting: ROAR!

Recruiting Older Adults into Research (ROAR; https://www.nia.nih.gov/health/publication/roar-toolkit) is a project by several federal agencies (NIA/NIH, CDC, ACL) with the goals of increasing older adults' participation in research studies. ROAR has a downloadable toolkit for researchers and encourages adapting materials to meet an individual researcher's needs.

The toolkit includes the following:

- Multilingual participant-based materials about the benefits of being in a study, and general information about the research project; it includes a website (http://www.ResearchMatch.org/roar) and phone number (1–866–321–0259) for older persons who are interesting in registering to participate in trials
- Social media templates
- PowerPoint presentations (with presenter notes) to present studies to community members as possible participants
- Flyer templates
- A tip sheet for clinical trials and older people as participants

finances/sources of income that could jeopardize the participants' benefits or services received (Dresser, 2003).

In late 2014, a federal interagency effort produced a toolkit to aid researchers in ethically enrolling older participants in studies. The kit explains all aspects of research studies to potential participants and provides researchers with pre-made flyers and presentations to explain their research. See Box 10.4. The first research study emphasis is on enrollment in studies about Alzheimer's disease and dementia.

Researcher-Based Ethical Issues

Researchers may encounter situations that raise ethical dilemmas that must be addressed. For example, they may experience role conflict in the field. If the researcher is also a clinician and recognizes a pressing health issue, then how would she or she address the issue while in the researcher role? Is it ethical to not address the health concern?

Researchers may also witness or hear about potential abuses. If the subject is 75 years old and experiencing financial abuse, dire financial need, or isolation from social contact, a researcher must plan his or her action and response. If a researcher is doing research in an assisted-living or skilled-care facility and learns of suspected abuse or neglect, is there an obligation to report it? To whom—nursing home administrators? An ombudsman?

From being in a field setting, witnessing experiences, or finding outcomes in their data, researchers can experience secondary traumatic effects (Elder & Giele, 2009). How would the researcher navigate his or her own concerns while still conducting the study?

Fortunately, organizations have **codes of ethics** for members that can help delineate ethical practices. Some of these codes are presented in Box 10.5. Another strategy is for each researcher to create an ethical stance statement for each study he or she conducts. Some key questions that aid in the creation of an ethical stance are presented in Box 10.6.

Box 10.5 Researchers' Ethical Codes by Organizations Selections

Gerontological Society of America's (GSA) Code of Ethics (by the Research, Education, and Practice Committee) that relate to older persons as subjects: https://www.geron.org/code-of-ethics:

> To those we study we owe disclosure of our research goals, methods, and sponsorship. The participation of people in our research activities shall only be on a voluntary basis and only on research projects approved by an appropriate institutional review board . . .

The Association for Gerontology in Higher Education (AGHE) also follows GSA's Code.

The American Sociological Association's (ASA) Code of Ethics (http://www.asanet.org/about/ethics.cfm) lists a nondiscrimination clause that states:

> Sociologists do not engage in discrimination in their work based on age; gender; race; ethnicity; national origin; religion; sexual orientation; disability; health conditions; marital, domestic, or parental status; or any other applicable basis proscribed by law.
> (ASA, 1999/2008, Principle D)

The ASA has a Section on Aging and the Lifecourse (SALC; http://www.asanet.org/sections/aging.cfm) and its Mission Statement reads that its mission is:

> To examine the interdependence between (a) aging over the life course as a social process and (b) societies and groups as stratified by age, with succession of cohorts as the link connecting the two . . . both basic sociological research on age and its implications for public policy and professional practice . . .
> (2016, Mission Statement)

The American Psychological Association (APA) has *Ethical Principles of Psychologists and Code of Conduct* (June 1, 2003) with a 2010 Amendment. Principle E: Respect for People's Rights and Dignity covers non-differential treatment of older persons (http://www.apa.org/ethics/code/index.aspx). It states:

> Psychologists are aware of and respect cultural, individual, and role different needs, including those based on age, gender, gender identity, race, ethnicity, culture, national origin, religion, sexual orientation, disability, language, and socioeconomic status, and consider these factors when working with members of such groups . . .
> (ASA, 2016, Principle E)

The National Association of Social Workers has produced *Standards for Social Work Practice with Family Caregivers of Older Adults* (2010). One section of the document describes research practices with older adults: http://www.naswdc.org/practice/standards/index.asp.

> Differences in the wishes, perceptions, and capacity of older adults and family caregivers can present complex ethical and legal challenges to social workers. . . . Careful application of ethical principles is especially important when older adults or family caregivers have limited decision-making capacity or are experiencing or perpetuating mistreatment . . . (National Association of Social Workers, 2016, Standard 1).

The American Public Health Association's (APHA) Code of Ethics (2016) does not directly comment about age but includes several principles that are applicable to gerontological research (http://www.ncbi.nlm.nih.gov/pmc/articles/PMC1447186/). They are:

> Public health should advocate for/work for the empowerment of disenfranchised community members, ensuring that the basic resources and conditions necessary for health are accessible to all people in the community. Public health programs/policies should incorporate a variety of approaches that anticipate and respect diverse values, beliefs, and cultures . . .
>
> (APHA, 2016, Principles of Practice)

Box 10.6 Write Your Own Ethical Stance

Questions to ask to formulate your ethical stance:
Who am I as a researcher?
What goals do I set for my research?
How do I ensure that importance of the research process is valued over outcomes?

Adapted from: Lahman, Geist, Rodriguez, Graglia & DeRoche, 2011, p. 140.

Design-Based Ethical Issues

Ethical issues can also be unique to design type. Qualitative researchers often have been labeled as "**going in too deep**" (once called, problematically, "going native"), losing a researcher's perspective, and taking the cause of those studied. Quantitative researchers may face ethical concerns around issues of identifying subjects and consent when **linking individual datasets** (e.g., national datasets, Social Security, Medicare, etc.) into larger ones. Qualitative and quantitative researchers often must address ethical concerns of role mixing—of being a clinical or professional and also a researcher. Mixed-methods researchers can face qualitative and quantitative ethical issues and have additional ones. Mixed methods merge both data types and can be proven to reveal more data through data linking and use data for other purposes than the purpose for which the data were consented. See Hesse-Biber's (2010) work for more discussion of ethical issues arising from mixed-methods designs. Rules provided for ethical research practices with older adults can help researchers address ethical dilemmas while designing research and before beginning studies.

Box 10.7 Ten Rules for Ethical Research with Older Adults

1. Cognitive status is not a bar to study participation, and declining status should not be an assumption. Design a protocol to assess cognitive status/changes and follow it on an ongoing basis.
2. Altruistic motives should not be assumed, and incentives should be meaningful.
3. A researcher should explicitly state/write out his or her ethical stance in a particular study.

4. Consider your relationship and approach to the field setting/site of data collection. Are there any additional safeguards to put in place (e.g., skilled nursing care, etc.)?
5. Spend time at the data-collection site or make sure your findings are relayed back in some way to those studied. This avoids crash-and-burn tactics and lends reciprocity to the community.
6. Consider if your study matches the ethics of the cultural/SES group of older adults you intend to study.
7. Review your study design. Does it lean toward certain findings? Are you putting any groups at risk by your design?
8. Decide upon a plan for unexpected, reportable events that may happen in the study. Will you report them? Will you debrief? What resources are available for participants?
9. Co-create your study with older persons (e.g., as advisors or a focus group) and pilot it—to reduce or foresee places where ethical issues may emerge.
10. Consider the impact of publication and presentation of your research. Will it identify or put groups at risk? If so, consider available protections—such as NIH's Certificate of Confidentiality or the NIA's Recruiting Older Adults into Research (ROAR) toolkit's guidelines.

Ethical research practices must be the goal of all researchers who study aging. Codes of behavior are outlined by the Common Rule, federal guidelines, and ethical codes of organizations. Research studies conducted with older persons are reviewed by IRBs. Yet researchers may face unplanned ethical issues due to their role in the study, topic of the study, population of interest, or study design. The creation of ethical stances and protocols before beginning each study can provide additional layers of support in addressing ethical uncertainties.

Discussion Questions

- There are many views about people being considered vulnerable based on their age. Do you think that age 65+ makes a group be considered vulnerable? 85+? Living in a skilled-care institution? Explain the differing views in each of these cases.
- You are conducting an interview study of persons 80 and older at several points in time. At time 1, all participants are living in the community; at times 2 and 3, some are living in assisted and skilled-care settings, and others have cognitive impairment. One is in hospice. As a researcher, how would you address each of these conditions?
- You are asked to design a study of Navajo Native American elders' views about the Indian Health Service, federal health care system. What approach would you choose (quantitative or qualitative)? What data collection methods would you use (surveys, participant observation, etc.)? How would you address the group's history in research? How would you learn about, and respect, the cultural practices of the group?
- Look up the code of ethics for your own professional organization. Does it specifically address conducting research with older persons? How does it frame/discuss older participants? Does it mention cognitive status or dementia?
- Write your general ethical stance for your research using Box 10.6 as a guide. Modify this statement for each study you conduct.

Bibliography

American Psychological Association (APA). (2016). *Ethical principles of psychologists and code of conduct (June 1, 2003) with a 2010 amendment.* Principle E: Respect for people's rights and dignity. Retrieved from http://www.apa.org/ethics/code/index.aspx

American Public Health Association (APHA). (2016). *Principles of the ethical practice of public health.* Retrieved from http://www.ncbi.nlm.nih.gov/pmc/articles/PMC1447186/

American Society on Aging. (2016). *Legal and ethical issues.* Retrieved from http://www.asaging.org/blog/content-source/101

American Sociological Association. (2016). *Code of ethics.* Retrieved from http://www.asanet.org/about/ethics.cfm

American Sociological Association, Section on Aging and the Lifecourse. (2016). *Mission statement.* Retrieved from http://www.asanet.org/sections/aging.cfm

Batchelor-Aselage, M., Amella, E., Zapka, J., Mueller, M., & Beck, C. (2014). Research with dementia patients in the nursing home setting: A protocol for informed consent and assent. *IRB, 36*(2), 14–20.

Beecher, H. K. (1966). Ethics and clinical research. *New England Journal of Medicine, 274*(24), 1354–1360.

Black, B. S., Kass, N. E., Fogarty, L. A., & Rabins, P. V. (2007). Informed consent for dementia research: The study enrollment encounter. *IRB: Ethics & Human Research, 29*(4), 7–14.

Black, B. S., Wechsler, M., & Fogarty, L. (2013). Partner decision making for participation in dementia research. *American Journal of Geriatric Psychiatry, 21*(4), 355–363. doi:10.1016/j.jagp.2012.11.009

Blazer, D. G., Yaffe, K., & Liverman, C. T. (2015). *Cognitive aging: Progress in understanding and opportunities for action.* Washington, DC: National Academies Press.

Braun, K. L., Browne, C. V., Ka'opua, L. S., Kim, B. J., & Mokuau, N. (2014). Research on indigenous elders: From positivistic to decolonizing methodologies. *Gerontologist, 54*(1), 117–126.

CBS News. (March 18, 2010). *The controversy magnet: PositiveID "chips" Alzheimer's patients, quite possibly without permission.* Retrieved from http://www.cbsnews.com/news/the-controversy-magnet-positiveid-chips-alzheimers-patients-quite-possibly-without-permission/

Cushman, R. (2016). Personal correspondence, May 14.

Department of Health and Human Services (DHHS). (2009). *Common rule's code of federal regulations, Title 45- Public Welfare, Part 46, Protection of Human Subjects.* Retrieved from http://www.hhs.gov/ohrp/regulations-and-policy/regulations/45-cfr-46/

Department of Health and Human Services (DHHS). (2016a). *NPRM for Revisions to the Common Rule: HHS announces proposal to improve rules protecting human research subjects.* Retrieved from http://www.hhs.gov/ohrp/regulations-and-policy/regulations/nprm-home/#

Department of Health and Human Services (DHHS). (2016b). *Informed consent FAQs.* Retrieved from http://www.hhs.gov/ohrp/regulations-and-policy/guidance/faq/informed-consent/

Dergal-Serafini, J. (2010). "Power in numbers: research with families in long-term care." In D. L. Streiner, & S. Sidani (Eds.), *When research goes off the rails: Why it happens and what you can do about it* (pp. 65–73). New York: Guilford Press.

Dresser, R. (2003). "Ethical and policy issues in research on elder abuse and neglect." In National Research Council's Panel to Review Risk and Prevalence of Elder Abuse and Neglect (Ed.), *Elder mistreatment: Abuse, neglect, and exploitation in an aging America* (303–338). Washington, DC: National Academies Press. Retrieved from http://www.ncbi.nlm.nih.gov/books/NBK98782/

Dubois, M. F., Bravo, G., Graham, J., Wildeman, S., Cohen, C., Painter, K., & Bellemare, S. (2011). Comfort with proxy consent to research involving decisionally impaired older adults: Do type of proxy and risk-benefit profile matter? *International Psychogeriatrics, 23*(9), 1479–1488.

Elder, Jr., G. H., & Giele, J. Z. (2009). *The craft of life course research.* New York: Guilford Press.

Gerontological Society of America (GSA). (2002). *Code of ethics, research, education, and practice committee.* Retrieved from https://www.geron.org/code-of-ethics

Gitlin, L. N., & Lyons, K. J. (2014). *Successful grant writing: Strategies for health and human service professionals* (4th ed.). New York: Springer Publishing Company.

Gomersall, T., Astell, A., Nygard, L., Sixsmith, A., Mihailidis, A., & Hwang, A. (2015). Living with ambiguity: A meta-synthesis of qualitative research on mild cognitive impairment. *Gerontologist, 55*(5), 892–912. doi:10.1093/geront/gnv067

Greenwald, H. P. (2001). "Ethics in social research." In E.F. Borgatta & R.J.V. Montgomery (Eds.), *Encyclopedia of sociology* (2nd ed., Vol. 2, pp. 835–840). New York: Macmillan Reference.

Heflin, M. T., DeMeo, S., Nagler, A., & Hockenberry, M. J. (2016). Health professions education research and the institutional review board. *Nurse Educator, 41*(2), 55–59.

Hesse-Biber, S. N. (2010). *Mixed methods research: Merging theory with practice.* New York: Guilford Press.

Holstein, M., Parks, J. A., & Waymack, M. H. (2011). *Ethics, aging, and society: The critical turn.* New York: Springer Publication.

Israel, M. (2015). *Research ethics and integrity for social scientists: Beyond regulatory compliance* (2nd ed.). London: Sage Publications.

Kapp, M. B. (2008). Ethics education in gerontology and geriatrics. *Annual Review of Gerontology & Geriatrics, 28*, 61–71.

Kapp, M. B. (2014). "Research ethics." In B. Jennings (Ed.), *Bioethics* (4th ed., Vol. 1, pp. 129–131). Farmington Hills, MI: Macmillan Reference.

Kennedy, J., & Van Valey, T. (March-April 2016). Proposed changes to the common rule: The protection of human subjects. *American Sociological Association's Footnotes Newsletter. 44*(3). Retrieved from http://www.asanet.org/footnotes/marchapril16/common-rule_0316.html#sthash.mi8hAJUu.dpuf

Kim, S. Y., Uhlmann, R. A., Appelbaum, P. S., Knopman, D. S., Kim, H. M., Damschroder, L., & De Vries, R. (2010). Deliberative assessment of surrogate consent in dementia research. *Alzheimer's & Dementia, 6*(4), 342–350.

Kuo, K. (March 29, 2016). Personal email.

Lahman, M. K. E., Geist, M. R., Rodriguez, K. L., Graglia, P., & DeRoche, K. K. (2011). Culturally responsive relational reflexive ethics in research: The three Rs. *Quality & Quantity, 45*(6), 1397–1414. doi:10.1007/s11135-010-9347-3

Locher, J., Bronstein, J., Robinson, C., Williams, C., & Ritchie, C. (2006). Ethical issues involving research conducted with homebound older adults. *Gerontologist, 46*(2), 160–164. doi:10.1093/geront/46.2.160

McHenry, J. C., Insel, K. C., Einstein, G. O., Vidrine, A. N., Koerner, K. M., & Morrow, D. G. (2015). Recruitment of older adults: Success may be in the details. *The Gerontologist, 55*(5), 845–853.

Mendoza, A. N. (2012). *Grandparents raising grandchildren: A look at Latino cultural influences on needs and service usage*. Thesis, University of Northern Colorado.

National Association of Social Workers. (2016). *Standards for social work practice with family caregivers of older adults*. Retrieved from http://www.naswdc.org/practice/standards/index.asp

National Institute of Aging. (2016). *Recruiting older adults into research (ROAR) toolkit*. Retrieved from https://www.nia.nih.gov/health/publication/roar-toolkit

National Institutes of Health. (2016a). *Certificates of confidentiality (CoC) kiosk*. Retrieved from https://humansubjects.nih.gov/coc/index

National Institutes of Health. (2016b). *Eligibility for a certificate*. Retrieved from https://humansubjects.nih.gov/coc/faqs#definition-panel2

National Institutes of Health. (2016c). *Research involving individuals with questionable capacity to consent: Points to consider*. Retrieved from http://grants.nih.gov/grants/policy/questionablecapacity.htm

Nebelsick, A. (2016). Personal communication.

Resnick, B., Gruber-Baldini, A. L., Pretzer-Aboff, I., Galik, E., Buie, V. C., Russ, K., & Zimmerman, S. (2007). Reliability and validity of the evaluation to sign consent measure. *The Gerontologist, 47*(1), 69–77.

Ries, N. M. (2010). Ethics, health research, and Canada's aging population. *Canadian Journal on Aging, 29*(4), 577–580. doi:10.1017/S0714980810000565

Seppet, E., Pääsuke, M., Conte, M., Capri, M., & Franceschi, C. (2011). Ethical aspects of aging research. *Biogerontology, 12*(6), 491–502.

Staudinger, U., & Law, A. (2016). "Wisdom." In H. S. Friedman (Ed.), *Encyclopedia of mental health* (pp. 375–381). Waltham, MA: Academic Press.

Texas A&M. (2015). *Examples of vulnerable and protected populations*. Retrieved from https://vpr.tamu.edu/compliance/rcc/irb/sops/119

Trzepacz, P., Hochstetler, H., Wang, S., Walker, B., & Saykin, A. (2015). Relationship between the Montreal cognitive assessment and mini-mental state examination for assessment of mild cognitive impairment in older adults. *BMC Geriatrics, 15*, 107. doi:10.1186/s12877-015-0103-3

University of Chicago. (2016). *Social & behavioral sciences institutional review board: Vulnerable populations*. Retrieved from https://sbsirb.uchicago.edu/page/vulnerable-populations

University of Miami. (2016). *Geriatrics research issues: Elderly subjects in research*. Retrieved from http://www.miami.edu/index.php/ethics/projects/geriatrics_and_ethics/geriatrics_research_issues

Virginia Tech. (2016). *Research involving elderly or terminally ill subjects*. Retrieved from http://www.irb.vt.edu/pages/elderly.htm

11
Reporting Aging Research

Disseminating or sharing the research findings is one of the last steps in the research process. While there are many routes to dissemination, all share some common elements. This chapter outlines the basic elements of research-report writing across several types of written products. Good writing practice guidelines are provided. The grant-proposal process and scholarly, peer-reviewed academic journal submissions are outlined. Funding and ways to assess journal quality are provided. Federal and foundation-level funding information and the National Institute of Health scoring criteria close the chapter.

Good Writing Practices

The best writers write often. Granted, this is not an easy process, but it is a good habit to develop. Many **writing strategies** can be employed to stimulate writing, and each writer must find his or her individual preference and path. One strategy is to allocate the same time each day, 30–45 minutes or so, to sitting down and writing or doing research to forward an existing work. This works well for self-directed people, while joining writing groups (face-to-face or virtual) can provide forced deadlines and support for writers who need more external stimuli. Many "how-to" writing guides exist that break down the writing process into elements and provide contracts and timelines for authors—for example, Wendy Belcher's (2009) *Writing your journal article in 12 weeks*. Some universities require doctoral students to enroll in seminar courses that act as writing groups.

Electronic reminders, writing software programs, and distraction-blocking programs and apps can also aid in the writing process. Kathy Newman (2012) wrote an online piece in the *Chronicle of Higher Education* ("You are not alone") that explored the online Academic Ladder's Writing Club and the use of an app that blocks email and Internet access during devoted writing time. Non-academic and creative writing groups are other options and might be held at libraries or coffeehouses. See Box 11.1 for some fun online resources to diagnose your writing.

Box 11.1 Online Writing Screeners

Helen Sword's Writer's Diet: diagnoses cut-and-pasted text as "flabby or fit," "passives and prepositions, be-verbs and waste words"
http://writersdiet.com/?page_id=4

Hemingway Editor 2.0: evaluates cut-and-pasted text for readability and passive-voice use
http://www.hemingwayapp.com/

Grammarly: proofreads cut-and-pasted text for grammar and vocabulary use in context https://www.grammarly.com/

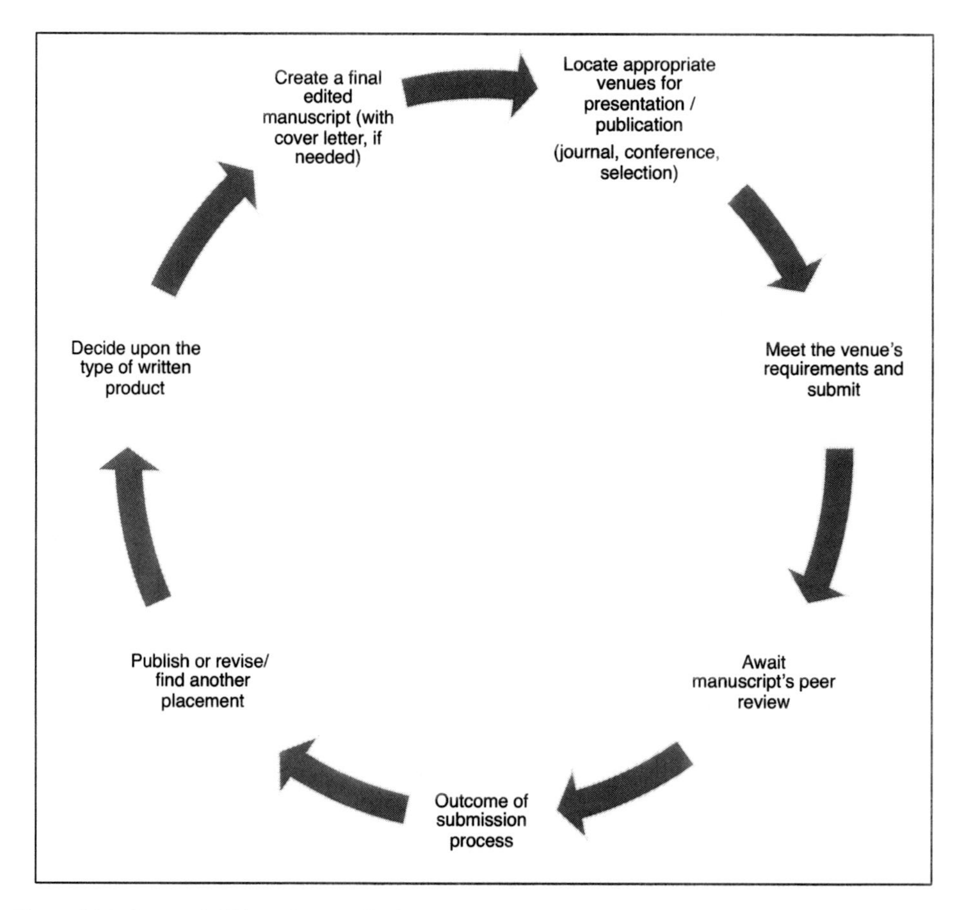

Figure 11.1 Research Writing Process/Cycle

Whatever the mode, the commitment to writing must be present. Then comes an understanding of the drafting/rewriting process and the merits of good peer review. **Drafting**—or writing, editing, rewriting—is essential to improve flow, logic, and readability of a document. **Peer review**, receiving peers' comments and addressing feedback, can be prickly but is necessary for the betterment of the work. It is helpful to provide readers with questions you have about your work or a rubric or guide for comments. See Figure 11.1 for the steps in the writing and publication process. Each is discussed in this chapter.

Interpretation and Write-Up for Publication or Presentation

The type of report determines how it is written in terms of language, style, jargon use, and level of statistical detail provided. Before writing, consider your writing goal and placement. Is your report an academic manuscript for a peer-reviewed journal, a conference presentation, a report to a funder, a report to an employer, or a presentation back to study participants? Each of these types of documents requires different considerations of audience, tone, style, and language or jargon use.

Academic manuscripts for a peer-reviewed journal require specific content organization and also writing and formatting styles. See published examples of articles within the field you are writing and style guides such as American Psychological Association (APA), American Sociological Association, or Chicago style. Some initial items to consider listing are author(s) with affiliations, abstracts, and keywords. Typical document **section headings** include an introduction, literature review/theoretical framework, research questions/hypotheses, methodology and design (sample/participants, data collection/procedure, and concepts/ indicators), data analysis (recoding/statistical tests), and findings/discussion/conclusion (limitations of current study, future directions, and policy implications). The end materials can be endnotes, references, authors' biographical information, sources of funding, and a statement of each author's contribution/conflict of interest.

Academic manuscripts do not have to be boring or lifeless. For example, Jill Schostak and John F. Schostak's (2013) book, *Writing research critically: Developing the power to make a difference*, takes the traditional academic elements (mentioned above) and actively includes peoples' voices and challenges existing ideas and power relationships. See Table 11.1 for a comparison of elements in many types of written reports.

Research proposals are an abridged version of a full manuscript or report. A proposal is an outline of the study or work that is planned—but not yet begun. It contains all the lead-in sections (the same as the manuscript) but stops at the proposed methods and design. It does not contain findings, discussion, or conclusion sections, since the project has not been completed. Research proposals can be part of theses, dissertations, or grant proposals.

Theses (at the master's level) and **dissertations** (at the doctoral level) can be parts of the requirements for master's and doctoral degrees. They are designed to be a unique contribution of the student author who also demonstrates his or her knowledge of current research and practices in his or her field. The traditional format and some non-traditional, or alternative, formats are noted in Table 11.1.

Books, edited volumes, and book chapters offer an author more space to write and more formatting options. Publishers can be university-based, academic, popular press, or based on self-publication. Each publisher requires a proposal that explains the originality of the proposed work in the field, its potential audience, and competition, and that provides outlines of the chapters. One or two full chapters are included with the proposal to give the editor and reviewers a sense of the author's writing style. It is best to give an early and latter chapter as examples. The proposal is then reviewed by experts in the field. Guided by the press's editor, the author is notified of the press's interest and needed revisions. Depending upon the press, chapters are exchanged, and the complete manuscript is reviewed and edited once more. Then the book receives cover art and is copyedited, proofed, and indexed.

A report to an employer or organization often takes the form of a **program evaluation**. The program evaluation is applied research used to make decisions about whether programmatic goals and objectives were met. For example, the Circle Talk program, a "relationship-centered program that transforms the person-to-person experience within senior residences to form warm, intimate communities of meaningful connections," takes residents in independent, assisted, and skilled care through 12 weeks of one-hour group-based activities. The

Table 11.1 Elements of Reports and Written Documents

Qualitative	Quantitative	Mixed Methods
Title	Papers or Journal Articles	Title
Abstract/Keywords	Title	Abstract
Introduction and Background	Abstract/Keywords	Literature Review Methods
Literature Review (but not if a Grounded Theory Design)	Introduction/Rationale	Data Analysis (includes a combination or comparison of both aspects of the design—often included in a tabular form)
Researcher's Stance	Literature Review/Conceptual Framework	Research Results / Findings
Research Question	Purpose Statement/Research Questions/Hypotheses	Discussion (of Findings)
Design and Data Collection	Methods / Research Design	Conclusion: data results only
Data Analysis	Data Analysis	References and End/Footnotes
Rigor	Reliability and Validity	
Appendix (can include Interview Script—if appropriate)	Research Results/Findings	
Research Results / Findings	Discussion (of Findings)	
Discussion (of Findings)	Conclusion	
Conclusion: data results only	References and End/Footnotes	
References and End/Footnotes	Tables, Figures, and Diagrams	
	Implications/ Acknowledgements	
	Conflict of Interest	

Research Proposals	Thesis/Dissertation	Federal, Larger Grant Proposal	Community Grant Proposal
Title	*Traditional Chapters*	Cover Letter	Letter of Intent or Inquiry
Abstract	Title	Title	Proposal Summary
Introduction and Background	Abstract	Project Summary	Goals/Objectives
Literature Review	Acknowledgement	Introduction	Methods
Purpose Statement/ Research Questions/ Hypotheses	TOC	Project Rationale	Evaluation
Proposed Methods/ Research	Body	Public Health Relevance	Sustainability
	Introduction	Research Strategy	Organizational Background
	Literature Review	Significance/Project Importance	Budget with Justification
	Methods	Innovation	Appendices—can include: letters of support, financial statements, data-collection tools, articles, etc.
	Findings	Specific Aims or Hypotheses	
	Conclusion	Approach	
	References and Appendices (can contain IRB approval and copies of instruments)	Preliminary Data	
	Nontraditional Chapters	Risk management	
	Introduction	Budget with justification	
	Literature Review	Human subjects protections	
	Methods and Procedures	Multiple Principle Investigator (PI) leadership plan	
	Article 1		
	Article 2		
	References		
	Appendices (can contain IRB approval and copies of instruments)		

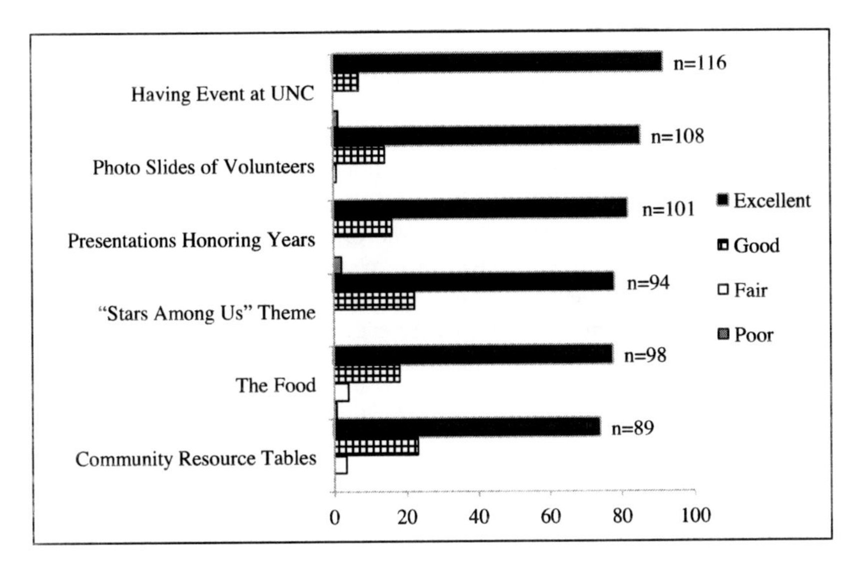

Figure 11.2 Volunteer/Guest Evaluation from a Summary Report Written for an Organization

Source: Collins, S. (2014). 2014 Weld County RSVP Volunteer Appreciation Breakfast Evaluation Report, University of Northern Colorado.

program's goals are to "create high engagement and a sense of community among participants; create a sense of routine and added structure to social interactions; and to tap into the 'whole person' and understanding residual abilities and previous roles and habits" (http://www.circletalk.org/programs/). These goals would be made into measurable objectives and each one assessed as being met or not met. The satisfaction of attendees and their ratings of the program would be included in the report. This information would help the organization understand what is working and not working in its program and also provide a way to relay this information to funders and clients.

Conference presentations often cover the same elements of a full academic paper but in an abridged format. Some conferences may require a full-paper submission; others do not. When working with older persons as co-researchers or as engaged participants and agencies within the aging network, it is common to present results back to these groups in **community presentations.** It is important to relay accurate information back without excessive use of jargon or identifying participants by either identity (name) or attributes (e.g., a 90-year-old, widowed farmer with a $300,000 annual income). While written more for those in age-related agencies, the following executive summary could be modified for use with older persons as participants. See Figure 11.2 for a bar chart from an executive summary for participants.

Getting Funded for Aging Research

Grant proposals and reports to funders also contain stylized elements. Grant proposals can be written for several levels of funders—from community-based and regional funding organizations to federal funders. Grants can be awarded to individuals, universities, or community organizations. **Requests for proposals (RFP)** or **funding announcement opportunities** (FOA) are the way organizations announce their funding opportunities and list the requirements for a proposal submission. The elements of each proposal follow a general pattern, but, as funding amounts and funders get larger, the amount of proposal requirements increase. A basic grant proposal for a community-based or smaller funder contains the following: a cover letter (describing significance), a summary or brief overview, a need statement that describes the issue, goals/objectives (sought to accomplish), methods or a description of programs and activities, evaluation or a plan for assessing the project (which can include a basic logic), sustainability, organizational background, budget (with direct and indirect costs), and appendices (including letters of support, financial statements, data-collection tools, articles). A federal or larger grant proposal, such as one for the National Institute of Health or National Institute of Aging, includes several commonly used elements. See Table 11.1 for elements of each grant-proposal type.

Foundation grants are geared toward nonprofit organizations that have received 501(c)(3) nonprofit status from the Internal Revenue Service. Examples include the Robert Wood Johnson foundation, the Daniels Fund, and Hartford Community funding. Professional organizations offer grants from organizations in their discipline—e.g., GSA or AGHE. Funding can also be based on regional/local grants—e.g., funding the Central Plains or Western Nebraska regions.

Box 11.2 Grant Resources and Starting Places

General Resources

General places to find background, mission, past funding by funders:
GuideStar: http://www.guidestar.org/AdvancedSearch.aspx
National Center for Charitable Statistics: http://nccs.urban.org/

Chronicle Guide to Grants: provides a selected list of fellowships, grants, institutes and workshops, and papers taken from an extensive list of forthcoming deadlines that appear each week in the *Chronicle of Philanthropy*; https://philanthropy.com/

*Aging Requests for Proposals (RFPs) Posted by the Foundation Center PND Digest**:
http://www.philanthropynewsdigest.org/rfps?search=1&tags_interest[]=aging

Grantmakers in Aging: provide links for gerontology discipline-specific funding about age-friendly communities; http://www.giaging.org/

Foundation Center: by the publisher of the *Foundation Directory*, provided a "Find Funders" menu; there are also two subscription-based databases for individuals for non-profit organizations; http://foundationcenter.org/

Idealist: contains links to over 15,000 organizations, publications, and directories in 90 countries and all 50 U.S. states; also provided is a comprehensive listing of Tools for Nonprofits, including sections on legal, fundraising, and management issues; see the "organizations" link; you may need to insert this URL into a browser: http://www.idealist.org/search/v2/?search_type=org

Non-for-Profit Best Practices Guide: great for ideas about good practices of non-profits; http://www.npgoodpractice.org/principles-and-practices

Foundations

John A. Hartford Foundation: provides grant awards around five areas: Interprofessional Leadership in Action, Linking Education and Practice, Developing and Disseminating Models of Care, Tools and Measures for Quality Care, and Policy and Communications by invitation
http://www.jhartfound.org/grants-strategy/current-strategies/

Robert Wood Johnson Foundations: can fund health-based studies
http://www.rwjf.org/en/how-we-work/grants-and-grant-programs.html

MetLife's Foundation: provides funding as part of their Health Aging initiative
https://www.metlife.com/metlife-foundation/apply/index.html?WT.ac=GN_metlife-foundation_apply

AARP Foundation's Opportunities for Funding:
http://www.aarp.org/aarp-foundation/grants/current-opportunities/
Alzheimer's Association: provides funding for Alzheimer's-based and caregiver research*
http://www.alz.org/research/alzheimers_grants/overview.asp
American Federation for Aging Research (AFAR): provides information about biomedical calls for proposals*
http://www.afar.org/research/funding/

Selected U.S. and Federal Government Resources

Grants.gov: pools requests for proposals and grant information from 32 federal agencies; http://www.grants.gov/
National Science Foundation: topics include advances in math and science research, Department of Health and Human Services' Grants Forecast—to read about forecasting of grant funding provided through the Department of Health and Human Services, see http://www.acf.hhs.gov/hhsgrantsforecast/; it also provides a Finding Funding option that allows searching by keyword for funding opportunities and for awards made the previous year: http://www.nsf.gov/funding/
National Institutes of Health provide an option to use keywords for searching for funding opportunities in the *NIH Guide for Grants & Contracts* as well as browsing active funding opportunities and recent policies and guidelines, and viewing weekly issues of the *Guide*: http://grants.nih.gov/funding/index.htm
National Institute on Aging: Inside NIA: A Blog for Researchers; http://www.nia.nih.gov/research/blog
Administration on Community Living (ACL) Funding Opportunity Announcements:*
http://www.acl.gov/Funding_Opportunities/Announcements/Index.aspx
National Association of Area Agencies on Aging: provided national and regional funding opportunities*; http://www.n4a.org/fundingopportunities

Subscription-Based Databases

SPIN: a database of over 40,000 grant programs from government, private, and non-profit sponsors; https://spin.infoedglobal.com/Home/GridResults
GrantSearch: produced by the Grants Resource Center, a division of the American Association of State Colleges and Universities that helps its member institutions become more competitive in pursuing grant funding: http://www.aascu.org/grc/gs/Default.aspx

Faculty and Student Grant Resources

Emerging Scholar and Professional Organization (ESPO) of the Gerontological Society of America (GSA) and AGHE, ASA, etc.: http://gsa.dev.confluencecorp.com/membership/emerging-scholar-and-professional-organization/awards
NIH, NIA, and federal agencies' websites for post-doctoral and summer training: https://www.nia.nih.gov/research/publication/finding-your-way-resources-early-career-researchers

* *Source:* Michigan State University's Grants for Nonprofits: The Aged (2016).

Government/federal grants for aging research have larger funding amounts and are awarded to researchers at larger institutions. If awarded, the leading individuals, or Principal Investigators, add on fees to the budget that are given to the university, called **Facility and Administration (F &A) or Indirect Costs Rates (IDCs)**. These fees cover the services that the university provides the researcher, such as electricity and place, informational and technology help, and library resources. Federal funders include the National Institutes of Health (NIH),

National Institutes on Aging (NIA), Department of Health & Human Services (DHHS), the Agency for Healthcare Research and Quality (AHRQ), and the Centers for Disease Control. Grant-funding mechanisms are coded to help the researcher select the best route. NIH types include Research Grants (R series), Career Development Awards (K series), Research Training and Fellowships (T & F series), and Program Project/Center Grants (P series). Federal grant proposals offer all technical and content details and are submitted electronically using two platforms: Grants.gov and eRA Commons. A cover letter that indicates which **Scientific Review Group (SRG)** is best to review that specific proposal must be included. Federal agencies provide a Program Officer who can help clarify the process or points in the FOA.

Once the SRG gets proposals, two levels of review might occur. At the first, the proposal can be either moved toward discussion by the full panel at the group's meeting or stopped. Proposals stopped at the first review may be scored by each member of the review panel prior to the section's in-person meeting but **not discussed** ("ND") by the full panel when they meet. Or, if there are major concerns with ethical issues, or with the human subjects' protections sections, a proposal may receive an "NR" or **not recommended.** These proposals do not move forward in the process because the problems make the project considered "not fundable."

If a proposal is reviewed, ranked, and scored at the second review by the SRG, those funded will receive a **Notice of Award** (NoA) and begin executing the grant's activities. For proposals that are not funded, the next steps in the potential resubmission process include providing a list of changes to the Program Officer and discussing resubmission via the same Funding Opportunity Announcement (FOA) or others. From submission to outcomes, it takes about 9 to 13 months (NIH, Peer Review Process). For an overview of the NIH Grants Process, see the video "The Big Picture" (at https://www.youtube.com/watch?v=rNwsg_PR90w); or for an overview of the NIH SRG peer-review process, see https://www.youtube.com/watch?v=fBDxI6l4dOA&feature=relmfu). Box 11.3 provides NIH review criteria, and Figure 11.3 illustrates NIH's scoring criteria and interpretation.

Box 11.3 NIH Peer Review Criteria

Overall Impact. What is the overall impact of this study or project in the field if funded and completed?

Scored Review Criteria. Reviewers in a study section/group will score each of the five criteria from 1 (exceptional) to 9 (poor).

- **Significance.** Will the study or project improve a critical issue or need in the field? Will the work generate meaningful applications to use for future interventions?
- **Investigator(s).** Depending on the principal investigators' career stage, do they have the skills, training, expertise, or track record to lead and complete the project?
- **Innovation.** What aspects of design, implementation, or population are novel? Move the research or thinking in the field forward?
- **Approach.** How sound and well planned is the design and analysis? Did the proposal plan for problems and also protect subjects included in the study? Was the approach inclusive?
- **Environment.** What are the resources and capabilities/capacity of the university or setting to support the proposed research—from infrastructure to personnel?

Additional Review Criteria. These are often required and included in the proposal's merit evaluation but do not contribute to the proposal's score:

Protections for Human Subjects
Inclusion of Women, Minorities, and Children
Vertebrate Animals
Biohazards

Additional Review Considerations. These items are only reviewed but do not contribute to the proposal's score.
Applications from Foreign Organizations
Select Agent
Resource Sharing Plan

Adapted from: National Institutes of Health, NIH (2015). "Peer Review Process." Retrieved December 26, 2015, http://grants.nih.gov/grants/peer_review_process.htm.

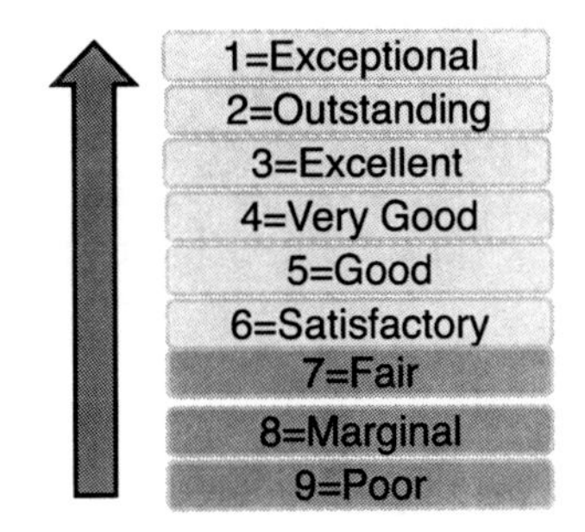

Figure 11.3 NIH Scoring Criteria Interpretation

Adapted from: National Institutes of Health, NIH (2015). "Scoring System and Procedure." https://grants.nih.gov/grants/peer/guidelines_general/scoring_system_and_procedure.pdf.

Publish, Not Perish: Finding a Journal

Journals are a common venue to publish research results. They are scholarly, peer-reviewed publications that select manuscripts from authors to print at scheduled intervals (2 to 12 times) throughout the year both in print and online. Online journals will also publish ahead of print versions of accepted articles and publish additional materials—such as supplementary data sets. The mechanics of publication begin with the selection of a journal as an appropriate place to publish an individual manuscript.

Several approaches can be taken. First, authors tend to see the journals that publish similar work and review the journals in their bibliography. Carefully reviewing the aims and scope of the journal is a key to success—do they fit the manuscript? Many journals have sign-up emails lists to have tables of contents emailed to you when a new issue is published. Journals' calls for papers about a specific theme or topics that are of interest can be a way to match a manuscript with a journal. Peers who publish in the same areas or type of article you have written can act as resources. For example, does the journal of interest publish literature review articles? Quantitative articles? Qualitative articles? Mixed-methods ones? Commentaries? Do they embrace student authors? Online tools exist to aid in journal selection, such as Taylor and Francis's "How to choose the right journal" (http://authorservices.taylorandfrancis.com/how-to-choose-a-journal/). This book's companion website contains a list of some gerontological journals.

Overall **audience** is another deciding factor in journal selection. Is the ideal reader an academic researcher? A practitioner working in the field? A policymaker? Journals vary by intended audience. Gerontology journals are inter- and multidisciplinary, covering a wide range of aspects of gerontology, so the field must be considered when selecting a journal to make sure the article is received by the right readership.

Authors must make some important decisions in the publication process in terms of readership. Journals are ranked by how often published articles are cited by others. These ratings are called **impact factors**. Journals with higher scores have more of their articles cited. Note that since gerontology encompasses many fields (psychology, sociology, social work, public health, etc.), journals may have different rankings based on the field of journals to which they are compared. Authors must also decide if they want their manuscript published online vs. in print or through both formats—and if the manuscript is available to all (as open access) or available only by a fee or subscription. Authors must decide if they will pay a fee-to-publish.

Once a journal is selected and the manuscript (along with a cover letter) is submitted according to guidelines, the submission materials will be uploaded or emailed to an editor. The editor, then, conducts an initial review and decides if the manuscript should move forward to his or her reviewers. Reviewers, as academic peers, review the manuscript according to the journal's guidelines, and each provides a decision of acceptance with no revision, acceptance with minor revision, acceptance with major revision, or rejection. The editor culls the reviewers' comments and recommendation and sends his or her decision back to the author(s) with narrative comments.

Publication Process Perils: Establishing Co-authorship, Conflict of Interest, Predatory Publishers

Articles written by multiple authors may require some planning to assure authorship ordering and credit. Journals are increasingly calling for each author listed to also have an associated **contributed-to-work statement** at the end of the manuscript. If this is not the case, establishing (and keeping to) an assigned and written authorship order can eliminate any issues that may arise. Having a process for authors who leave the project and for student authors is helpful. Intellectual property rights for students and ownership of student data have been of concern. Ways to address students' rights and power differentials in authors' titles along with access to data when students graduate are being debated (Foster & Ray, 2012; Oberlander & Spencer, 2006; Russell, Hogan & Junker-Kenny, 2013). Additionally, an author must **disclose conflicts of interest**. For example, if one or more authors receive funding for the research, it must be stated so that the information and possible influence can be taken into consideration when reading the findings. Many people have difficulty distinguishing real journals from more "fake" ones with similar-sounding names. Jeffrey Beall has created a searchable blog-like list of what he calls **"predatory journals"** and book-publishing companies to address these concerns (https://scholarlyoa.com/publishers/). Best practices of report writing exist to counteract the negative aspects of the publication process. Box 11.4 offers these guidelines.

Box 11.4 Best Practices for Report Writing

- Make sure to address/follow all the guidelines.
- Make sure to include all components.
- Know the writing style: APA, ASA, Chicago, MLA.
- Use a multiple draft system; writing and rewriting is the key.

- Have a person or persons proofread.
- Cite sources.
- Provide ample time for revision.
- If there are multiple authors, assign and follow that order.
- Make sure there is a clear voice and flow to the writing.
- Eliminate noise and text that distracts from the main argument.
- Make sure the level of language or writing style matches the call (i.e., writing an academic article differs from a community grant proposal vs. a federal grant proposal).

Although the last step in a study, the dissemination of results is key. Locating the right venue and matching the type of report to that venue increases publication potential. Knowing the elements of your written report ahead of time, using a multiple draft and peer-review process, and establishing authorship order sets the process up for success. Choosing a well-matched journal or funder for your work can provide a new platform and extend the positive reach of your research.

Discussion Questions

- Choose a manuscript you are working on (by abstract or title), and use resources in this chapter to find a couple of potential journals that might be a good fit.
- Describe the process of converting a presentation into a manuscript for publication. How does each differ?
- What are some guidelines you would use when establishing authorship order? Define the circumstances when and if you would change authorship. How would you handle some power differentials in authorship and establishing roles?
- How does a grant proposal differ from a journal article? Use your research interest, and create a topic for a proposal you would like to have funded. Use the links in this chapter to locate some potential funding sources.
- Since real and predatory journal names can sound similar, review Beall's list of predatory journals in this chapter. Then review some real, scholarly, peer-reviewed journals on the list in this book's companion website. What are some differences between these two groups?

Bibliography

Beall, J. (March 28, 2016). *Predatory journals and other scholarly publishing-related perils.* Presentation, University of Northern Colorado, slide 10.

Belcher, W. L. (2009). *Writing your journal article in 12 weeks: A guide to academic publishing success.* Thousand Oaks, CA: Sage Publications.

Collins, S. (2014). 2014 Weld County RSVP Volunteer Appreciation Breakfast Evaluation Report, Greeley, CO: University of Northern Colorado.

Foster, R. D., & Ray, D. C. (2012). An ethical decision-making model to determine authorship credit in published faculty-student collaborations. *Counseling and Values, 57*(2), 214.

Gump, S. (2004). Writing successful covering letters for unsolicited submissions to academic journals. *Journal of Scholarly Publishing, 35*(2), 92–102. doi:10.3138/jsp.35.2.92

Hessler, K., & Weil. J. (March 31, 2016). *So you want to write a book. . . .* Center for Education Teaching and Learning (CETL), University of Northern Colorado, Greeley, CO.

Michigan State University's Grants for Nonprofits: The Aged. (2016). http://staff.lib.msu.edu/harris23/grants/2aged.htm

Nettina, S. (2011). "Writing a book or book chapter." In C. Saver (Ed.), *Anatomy of writing for publication for nurses* (pp. 229–244). Indianapolis, IN: Sigma Theta Tau International.

Newman, K. M. (April 2012). You are not alone. *The Chronicle of Higher Education*, *58*(31). http://www.chronicle.com/article/You-Are-Not-Alone/131323/

Oberlander, S. E., & Spencer, R. J. (2006). Graduate students and the culture of authorship. *Ethics & Behavior*, *16*(3), 217–232. doi:10.1207/s15327019eb1603_3

Russell, C., Hogan, L., & Junker-Kenny, M. (2013). *Ethics for graduate researchers: A cross-disciplinary approach* (1st ed.). Amsterdam and Boston: Elsevier.

Schostak, J., & Schostak, J. F. (2013). *Writing research critically: Developing the power to make a difference.* New York: Routledge.

Appendix A

Overview of Past Methodological Research Design Work in Gerontology

Seminal Initial Texts in the 1980s

Sinnott, J., Harris, C., Block, M., Collesano, S., & Jacobson, S. (1983). *Applied research in aging: A guide to methods and resources.* Boston, MA: Little, Brown.

McAuley, W. J., & Blieszner, R. (1987). *Applied research in gerontology.* New York: Van Nostrand Reinhold.

Research Design Guide, One Specific Design, Qualitative

Reinharz, S., & Rowles, G. (1988). *Qualitative gerontology.* New York: Springer.

Gubrium, J. F., & Sankar, A. (1994). *Qualitative methods in aging research.* Thousand Oaks, CA: Sage.

Rowles, G. D., & Schoenberg, N. E. (2002). *Qualitative gerontology: A contemporary perspective.* New York: Springer.

Leontowitsch, M. (2012). *Researching later life and ageing: Expanding qualitative research horizons.* London, UK: Palgrave Macmillan.

Research Design Guide, One Specific Design, Quantitative

Schaie, K. W., Campbell, R. T., Meredith, W. M., & Rawlings, S. C. (Eds.). (1988). *Methodological issues in aging research.* New York: Springer.

Lawton, M. P., & Herzog, A. R. (1989). *Special research methods for gerontology.* Amityville, NY: Baywood.

Skinner, J., Teresi, J., Holmes, D., Stahl, S., & Stewart, A. (2002). *Multicultural measurement in older populations.* New York: Springer Publishing Company.

Bergeman, C. S., & Boker, S. M. (2006). *Methodological issues in aging research.* Mahwah, NJ: Lawrence Erlbaum.

Overview of Qualitative and Quantitative Designs

Peace, S. M., & British Society of Gerontology. (1990). *Researching social gerontology: Concepts, methods and issues.* London, UK: Sage.

Jamieson, A., & Victor, C. R. (2002). *Researching ageing and later life: The practice of social gerontology.* Buckingham and Philadelphia: Open University Press.

Guidebooks for a Specific Technique

Birren, J. E., & Cochran, K. (2001). *Telling the stories of life through guided autobiography groups.* Baltimore, MD: Johns Hopkins Press.

de Medeiros, K. (2014). *Narrative gerontology in research and practice.* New York: Springer.

Elder, Jr., G., & Giele, J. (2009). *The craft of life course research.* New York: Guilford Press.

Research Methods Related to Aging and Health

Curry, L., Shield, R., & Welte, T. (2006). *Improving aging and public health research: Qualitative and mixed methods.* Washington, DC: American Public Health Association.

Bosworth, H. B., & Hertzog, C. K. (2009). *Aging and cognition: Research methodologies and empirical advances.* Washington, DC: American Psychological Association.

Riby, L. (October 2016). *Handbook of gerontology research methods: Understanding successful aging.* New York: Routledge.

Book Chapters

Cavanaugh, J. C., & Whitbourne, S. K. (1999). *Research methods in gerontology: An interdisciplinary perspective.* New York: Oxford University Press.

Rubinstein, R. (2002). The qualitative interview with the older informant. Some key questions. In G. Rowles, & N. Schoenberg (Eds.), *Qualitative aging research* (pp. 137–153). New York: Springer.

Wenger, G. C. (2002). Interviewing older people. In J. F. Gubrium, & J. A. Holstein (Eds.), *The handbook of interview research: Context and method* (pp. 259–278). Thousand Oaks, CA: Sage.

Victor, C., Westerhof, G., & Bond, J. (2007). Researching ageing. In J. Bond, P. Coleman, & S. Peace (Eds.), *Ageing in society* (pp. 83–112). London: Sage.

Appendix B

Sample Research Report

This manuscript is a proposal for a research study and contains sample IRB forms. It is a sample report. It uses APA style and first-person voice. Color-coded notes provided throughout indicate differences that would be incorporated if this were another type of qualitative study, a quantitative one, or a mixed-methods one.

Each style guide — APA, MLA, ASA, and Chicago — provides its own specific guidelines about sections and headings a researcher must include in a report. Dissertations, theses, grant proposals, and other report types all have their own required elements.

These notes are qualitative.

These notes are quantitative.

These notes are mixed methods.

Meaningful Interactions: Reminiscence with Mild Cognitively Impaired and Non-Cognitively Impaired Older Adults

The **title page** offers a title that reflects the main theme of the report in a jargon-free way. Authorship and affiliations are also noted.

Rebecca L. Artzer
McNair Scholars Program
University of Northern Colorado
Mentor: Dr. Joyce Weil, School of Human Sciences

An **Acknowledgement** would go here, if the study was sponsored by a funder or presented at a conference.

If this were a full report, an **Abstract** would go here. Abstracts range from 100–250 words and tell the reader the purpose (goal/objectives/hypotheses), design and methods, and findings (or results) and larger application/implications of the study.

Keywords can also be present. They are the terms that express the overall ideas of the study.

Meaningful Interactions: Reminiscence with Mild Cognitively Impaired and Non-cognitively Impaired Older Adults

Definitions

Qualitative studies often begin with a page of definitions for terms.

The current research will explore the types of reminiscence and themes of meaningful events that develop in interactions with older adults. Reminiscence is defined as "personal memories in which the person recalling them was either a participant or an observer" (Wong & Watt, 1991, p. 272). Wong and Watt (1991) identified the different types of reminiscence: integrative, instrumental, transmissive, narrative, escapist, and obsessive. In integrative reminiscence, an individual incorporates life experiences as valuable despite trials or challenges. Instrumental reminiscence is goal directed and involves learning from life events to solve concerns. With transmissive reminiscence, the person passes down his or her personal history or advice to the listener. Narrative reminiscence does not have a clear purpose but involves cultural references to older values and wisdom. Escapist (aka defensive) reminiscence involves exalting the past and putting down the present; exaggerations are common. In obsessive reminiscence, the person feels regret from certain life experiences and often has not resolved these feelings. Wong and Watt's (1991) definitions became useful to later researchers who were also exploring reminiscence, and they will be used in the current study.

Meaningfulness is distinctive from meaning. Life can have meaning without having value. In contrast, meaningfulness is when an event, goal, decision, or, in this case, life in general has "significant value" (Kirkland, 2015). Meaningfulness is present in a life event or experience that is significant enough to an individual that it impacts how he or she perceives values and the world; the memory of this event often stays with the person for the rest of his or her life (Allen, 2009). An example of an event that is meaningful could be as simple as traditions with family members or as complicated as a major event in history.

One group of adults in this study will have mild cognitive impairment (MCI), and the other group will not have cognitive impairment. Cognitive impairment is defined in the literature as a level of diminishing mental abilities that has not reached the point of Alzheimer's disease but that is significant enough to be noticed in daily life and occasionally by other people (Barnabe, Whitehead, Pilon, Arsenault-Lapierre & Chertkow, 2012). Differences or similarities between these two groups in the ways they use reminiscence will be studied.

With medical capabilities increasing, more people are living longer and thus will have more opportunities to reminisce than people in the past who did not live as long. Decreased depressive symptoms, loneliness, and time to recall memories as well as an increase in life satisfaction and positive interactions are just some benefits of reminiscence (Allen, 2009; Allen et al., 2014; Allen, Hilgeman, Ege, Shuster, John & Burgio, 2008; Chiang et al., 2010). With older populations, there is also a higher number of people who have cognitive impairments. Researchers suggest that these impairments can likely be alleviated to some extent through the use of reminiscence (Barnabe, Whitehead, Pilon, Arsenault-Lapierre & Chertkow, 2012; Bohlmeijer & Westerhof, 2014; Cohen-Mansfield, Papura-Gill & Golander, 2006). It is noteworthy to point out that, in Allen (2009), reminiscence did not seem to decrease depressive and lonely moods. This is in contrast to the other research that found an association between the integration of focused reminiscence and decreased negative emotions (Allen, 2009; Allen et al., 2014; Bohlmeijer & Westerhof, 2014; Chiang et al., 2010). The dissimilar association that Allen found should serve as a motivator for researchers to carefully examine results and not exclude findings that are contrary to societal expectations. Exploring the types of reminiscence older adults engage in as well as observing differences or similarities in reminiscence for those with contrasting cognitive abilities can increase the current understanding of reminiscence.

Review of the Literature

Purposes and Benefits of Reminiscence for Non-cognitively Impaired Older Adults

Researchers have supported the usefulness of reminiscence in older adults. Bohlmeijer and Westerhof (2014) conducted an extensive review of studies between 1963 and 2013 and noticed patterns in the purpose of reminiscence such as social, instrumental, and integrative functions. Social purposes would include opportunities to converse with family or friends about life events. An example of an instrumental function would be using reminiscence to cope with or work through emotions from past events. Integrative functions are a combination of the previous two factors or an unforeseen element of reminiscence that was useful to the person. Each is a clear rationalization for the use of reminiscence to age successfully. Bohlmeijer and Westerhof also found that reminiscence focuses more on positive life events rather than a spectrum like in life review or a narrative. This is not to say that negative experiences are barred from reminiscence. Rather, if the negative event is part of a healing process for the individual and he or she is dealing with unsettled emotions, exploration is encouraged.

> For grounded-theory studies, some suggest no literature review is needed. If one is required, attention must be paid so that the review does not unduly influence the grounding or creation of new theory. Other qualitative studies (narrative analysis, ethnography, grounded theory, case studies, and phenomenological accounts) include literature reviews—but the weight of a qualitative report is in its findings that use rich, thick text.
>
> This study is narrative analysis using reminiscence to look at themes in the stories and how stories are told.

The value of reminiscence was furthered by the studies with the Legacy Project. In the Legacy Project, a participant, family member, and gerontology professional focus on reminiscence with the participant. The family member serves as a quality check to ensure the accuracy of the memories and to enjoy the time with his or her loved one. The professional compiles a memory book or recording of the memories discussed. Allen, Hilgeman, Ege, Shuster, John, and Burgio (2008) created a study where professionals were randomly assigned to participants for life review. Allen's study is some of the initial research using the Legacy Project. Participants reported higher levels of well-being and improved connections with family, but a decrease in depressive mood was not reported (Allen, Hilgeman, Ege, Shuster, John & Burgio, 2008). Allen found more positive reports in later studies with the Legacy Project. In the second study, participants and professionals were paired based on interests. The case studies found that the value of experience and connections with family were reported as well as decreases in depressive symptoms (Allen, 2009). This improvement could be due to the case-study focus instead of randomization. It also could be due to Allen's improved design or the specific group that she used. Increasing positive results are seen in subsequent studies. Allen et al. (2014) studied whether volunteers conducting the Legacy Project would have levels of success that are similar to professionals conducting the project. With appropriate training, volunteers were shown to have the same competency and equally positive results as gerontology professionals (Allen et al., 2014). Because the studies on reminiscence with the Legacy Project had increasing success with varying methods, the current study will likely provide similar emotional benefits to participants.

Benefits of Reminiscence for Cognitively Impaired Older Adults

Reminiscence has had specific uses for older adults with dementia and thus may offer similar benefits to the mild cognitively impaired group in this study. Past research has shown that reminiscence can increase positive mental health, improve self-esteem, and better communication abilities (Dempsey et al., 2014). Dempsey et al. examined reminiscence as a therapeutic method for those with dementia. A main goal was to ensure a stable quality of life for participants by using reminiscence. Participants and their families engaging in reminiscence together was particularly adaptive and helpful to the older adults. Families reported that their loved ones—from the beginning to the end of the study—seemed to have improved their self-efficacy and well-being (Dempsey et al.). The current study will not specifically be using reminiscence as a therapy, but engagement with reminiscence in any form is likely to hold these benefits for mild cognitively impaired older adults. However, examining reminiscence with cognitively impaired people will fill a gap in the literature because much of the present research is on dementia and Alzheimer's disease rather than MCI.

Other studies have also shown reminiscence to progress the quality of life for older adults with dementia. Whether as a therapy or used more casually between older adults, reminiscence is commonly used in long-term-care settings for most older adults and especially those with dementia (O'Shea et al., 2014). Researchers do suggest that caution be taken. O'Shea et al. explain that reminiscence is frequently used and appears to show benefits, but its effectiveness is ambiguous. This may be due to the fact that there is not one universal definition of reminiscence that all researchers use for reminiscence. In addition, a tool has not been developed to specifically measure how reminiscence is impacting participants and whether a tangible, traceable change is occurring. A more precise method for measurement would be useful, but it may not be feasible given the nature of reminiscence research. Given the co-dependent conversational atmosphere that reminiscence requires, it would be difficult and nearly impossible to measure effectiveness in a calculated way. This is not to say that a method cannot be developed to better measure reminiscence. It is just that this method should not be expected to meet the precision of a mathematician or a chemist; reminiscence—personal interactions—cannot be quantified in that way.

Another benefit that is supported by Cooney et al. (2014) and Dempsey et al. (2014) is the engagement the person has with his or her staff and family members in long-term-care settings. The family and staff who had reminisced with participants on at least one point in time explained that they felt they understood the person better (Cooney et al.). By learning of the participant's past, family and staff were better able to accommodate for confusion behaviors (Cooney et al.). Research conducted with individuals who have dementia may be transferable to older adults with MCI. If this is not seen in the current study, my research will fill a gap in the literature that distinguishes benefits of reminiscence for people with dementia and benefits for people with MCI. In addition, differences between the MCI group and non-cognitively impaired group will deepen knowledge about how reminiscence types are used by each. This comparison will be important to professionals in the field as well as individuals that are personally affected by MCI to identify potential differences when engaging with these types of older adults.

Purpose and Research Questions

My study will fill several of the gaps explained above. In the proposed project, I will explore the impact that different types of reminiscence have on a sample of older adults. I particularly want to see how the meaningfulness of life events is connected to the type of reminiscence used for reflection. A new direction that my research will take is demonstrating the differences seen between reminiscence themes for mild cognitively impaired and non-cognitively impaired groups. Other specific gaps in the literature are seen because most studies have involved nurses or other older adults conducting reminiscence with participants (Allen et al., 2014). Although the literature has examined the authenticity of reminiscence types, it has not explored the most salient reminiscence types for a group of people. This will be discovered by analyzing themes for which types of reminiscence are used most often. The design and goals of the current study will add new insight to the body of literature as a whole.

I will study the types of reminiscence and themes of meaningful events that develop in interactions with older adults. The research questions I would like to study are (1) which types of reminiscence are associated with the most meaningful life experiences and (2) what differences are seen in regard to meaningfulness for mild cognitively impaired and non-cognitively impaired older adults? These questions are central to expanding upon which life events are most important or meaningful to older adults. This understanding will be relevant to most people because knowing which life events will be meaningful in later life may allow individuals to enjoy the moment more. Knowing what will be relevant 20 to 40 years down the road may increase determinedness to enjoy the present moment. Exploring reminiscence in non-cognitively impaired and mild cognitively impaired older adults can shed light on whether similar enjoyment of reminiscence is experienced by these two groups. Additionally, I will conduct the current research as a volunteer at the facility rather than as staff or a fellow senior. Literature is limited on the combination of factors that I will explore; this study will build on the need for research on significantly meaningful events, reminiscence, and cognitive impairment in conjunction with each other.

> Research questions can be broad.

> Descriptive studies are not testing a relationship; they seek to describe events with summary statistics. If the study's focus is on description, the research question states the goal of the study. If the design is inferential, the research question leads to the statement of hypothesis(es). Hypotheses must have direction (with the exception of those including nominal-level data) and degree of change. For example, how much will the independent variable cause a change in the dependent variable? Researchers should set P-values for significance levels—p≤0.05 (*), p≤0.01 (**) or, p≤0.001. Hypothesis(es) must later be matched to appropriate statistical tests later in the report.

> Mixed-methods designs can use a combination of research questions and hypotheses—depending upon their design.

Methods

Design

A qualitative approach will be used to address my research questions. I will conduct an open-ended, guided interview study with some observational aspects. The interview process will be semi-structured with five to seven questions to prompt and focus the reminiscence (see Appendix A). I am taking a social constructivism approach because this

> Each quantitative methodological choice (surveys, single-case study, pre-testing/post-testing or experimental design, causal comparative, correlation, and structured observation) is suited to a particular application. Factors to consider when choosing a design include the purpose of your research design, population and sample options (design, size), availability of data, time needed for the project, time-constraint issues, planning, resources, existing materials, access to data, researcher's level of comfort with quantitative work, and comfort with older persons as co-researchers. Narrowing down these choices can help select the most suitable design type.
>
> **As a quantitative study**, this project could be a pre-test/post-test quasi-experiment running the full Legacy intervention of nine weeks of structured reminiscence (as the intervention) or usual dementia groupwork (as the control group). The Alzheimer's Disease Related Quality of Life (ADRQL)instrument will assess quality of life as an outcome measure.

research will be guided by the experiences of each participant and my interactions with them. We will engage in a co-constructed experience. This approach allows for openness in the research process and is based on the idea that people construct understanding through shared experiences. I realize that I will have an influence on the stories participants tell and how they tell them. I feel that the meaningful interactions I have in the interviews with participants are still relevant to the field as a whole and necessary to achieve a shared experience. Learning more about the experiences of others will increase overall understanding of reminiscence. This approach fits best with the research questions and the aim of the study.

Mixed-method research designs are classified according time order (do quantitative and qualitative parts occur at the same time or does one follow the other?) and paradigm emphasis (do quantitative and qualitative parts have equal status or does one part having a dominant status?). Mixed-methods design types are sequential explanatory, sequential exploratory, convergent parallel, embedded, transformative, and multi-level.

As a mixed-methods study, this project could be a convergent parallel design that simultaneously combines qualitative reminiscence with older persons and a quantitative structured survey with care providers about the benefits of reminiscence across cognitive statuses.

Researcher Stance

I must acknowledge my role and researcher's stance and realize that they will affect data interpretation. I am developing this study as I prepare myself for a career in gerontology and serving older adults. Over my lifetime, I have had a strong interest in cognitive impairment and dementia. Having had relatives with dementia, I am particularly intrigued by it, but I am choosing to begin my study in this area with MCI because it often does not have the higher levels of impairment that come with more advanced dementia. I have chosen to use reminiscence because of its conversational nature. I am a verbal processor, meaning I work through problems and make decisions by talking through the circumstances with someone. This is part of why I value reminiscence. Another component is that, while interning at a care facility, I encountered many older adults that wanted to discuss their lives with me. In fact, most of the residents wanted to do this. So, I truly feel that reminiscence is a well-fitted technique to use in research with older adults. From personal interest and experience, I am a strong supporter of taking a reminiscence approach with MCI older adults. My experiences should be recognized when considering my research.

Note the researcher's perspective and the researcher's reflection of her stance and role in the study. Adding this stance can help assess the interactive effect of the interviewer upon the interview.

Stating a philosophy or worldview applies to quantitative work as well. While a formal researcher's stance is not included, a researcher can briefly state his or her reasoning for a study design and selection of instruments/measures.

Sample

The convenience sample will be gathered from a local care facility. Older adults that live independently in the community will not be used because research has identified important differences in demographics between community dwellers and those in institutions (Locher, Bronstein, Robinson, Williams & Ritchie, 2006; Wong & Watt, 1991). Participants will be recruited with the help of institution

A quantitative study needs to describe how a sample was defined and collected. What were the eligibility criteria for inclusion in the sample? Was the sample probability or non-probability based? How was sample size calculated/determined? Are there weights attached to the sample? What was the response rate among respondents? If applicable—as in the case of a longitudinal or repeated measure—what were the attrition rates or amounts of missing data? Did those who left the sample have similar characteristics—such as being frail or living in a particular setting? For pre- and post-tests or quasi-experimental designs, was any cross-contamination between groups present? The text should also note the reason a particular sampling method was selected and the advantages and disadvantages of this particular method. Sample size and power would be discussed based on all types of statistical tests to be performed. Rationale/justification for sample size would be included with a table of participants' descriptive characteristics (of central tendency and variation along demographic and other key variables).

staff (see Appendix B). I will be in contact with the staff members and will ask them for a list of non-cognitively impaired and cognitively impaired older adults who would likely be interested in and capable of participating in the study. From these lists, I will begin the process of advertising the study and talking with the potential participants. Mental abilities to consent will be assessed using the Evaluation to Sign Consent measure (ESC) (see Appendix C). The Mini-Cognitive Assessment, which has a word recall and clock drawing element, will be used to determine whether potential participants are MCI or non-cognitively impaired (see Appendices D and E). Any interviews or meetings with older adults will be private and not in groups. Meeting will occur in the older adult's room or another appropriate and quiet location. The sample-size goal is 6 to 14 people aged 75 to 100. The older adults will likely have moderate to high economic status because they are able to afford long-term institutional care. This data will not be collected, but it is important to acknowledge the differences between this sample and the community population.

Since we are assigning pre- and post-test groups, the sample would include information about eligibility, inclusion/exclusion criteria, and how random sampling was achieved.

Here, staff are key informants and offer help in recruiting a sample. Some ethical issues about cognitive status and residence in skilled care are addressed later in the report.

Mixed-methods sampling designs are based upon the relationships of participants in each of the quantitative or qualitative parts of the design. Identical sampling has the same participants in all parts of the design; parallel sampling, nested sampling, or multilevel sampling can take multiple samples from different populations. Traditional mixed-methods designs use a nomenclature involving capitalization and arrows or plus signs. The prioritized method is in all capital letters; the lesser prioritized methods are in lowercase letters. A plus sign is used for methods occurring at the same time. Arrows are used to indicate the order of designs in that follow each other in time order. In this convergent parallel design—each design is equally weighted and done together in time:

QUAL

QUANT

Tools

Evaluation to Sign Consent Measure

A concern is whether participants with MCI are able to offer their consent. The ESC consists of five evaluative questions to determine if the older adults have the mental understanding to offer their consent in the study (Resnick et al. 2007). Resnick et al. tested the validity and reliability of the Evaluation to Sign Consent (ESC) measure. The researchers found that more studies should be conducted with the ESC, but it has demonstrated consistent screening ability with multiple MCI groups. Researchers have been able to successfully dismiss potential participants who are too memory impaired to consent. This measure will be used in the current study.

Explicit operationalization of variables, scoring, and psychometric properties are stated. Initially, the researcher should define all concepts in the study with unambiguous, operationalized definitions. Measures of reliability for scales should be included that show the measure is appropriate/applicable for the intended population of interest. Suitability of measures is not universal but specific to group, language, and place.

Mini-Cognitive Assessment

It is essential to be aware that participants who are mild cognitively impaired are a vulnerable and challenging population to study. The Alzheimer's Association and Barnabe, Whitehead, Pilon, Arsenault-Lapierre, and Chertkow (2012) are just two examples of successful involvement with this group. The cognitive assessment toolkit provided by the Alzheimer's Association is a resource full of evaluative measures that professionals in the organization use frequently to screen for levels of impairment. In fact, the current study will use one of the assessments from this freely available resource. The Mini-Cognitive Assessment will be used to determine the level of cognitive impairment (specifically memory) that the potential participant has incurred (Alzheimer's Association, 2015). This measure was selected to aid in the division of eligible participants into two groups: mild cognitively impaired (those with mild memory or other cognitive impairments) and non-cognitively impaired (those who are functioning at a high level). A score of one or two recalled words and an abnormal clock drawing task or a score with no recalled words will be sufficient to eliminate a participant from the study due to more severe cognitive impairment.

Interview Protocol

After final participant selection, I will conduct semi-structured interviews with participants over a minimum time frame of six weeks and possibly longer depending on scheduling. A digital recording device will be used in the interview to ensure authenticity of participant voice; the recordings will be stored on a password-protected computer on the UNC campus. I will also take minimal notes during the interview to record direct observations (describing the setting) and inferential notes (the participant appears tired during the interview). These notes will be kept in one notebook that I will use for the research.

See the Interview Script at the end of this paper. The researcher would want to take field notes or memos to record what he or she witnesses in observational work. As far as reflexivity, some suggest keeping research diaries, frequent/daily personal notes, creating visual representations, and talking with others (peers and participants) on and off your project as being helpful in a researcher's understanding and relaying his or her role.

Procedure

I am collecting important life events in the lives of older adults as well as the type of reminiscence they use to reflect on these events during the interview. Institutional Review Board approval will be obtained. Before the interviews, I will be in contact with the administrator of a local care facility to determine which residents would be interested in serving as participants. I will give my information to the administrator to pass on to family members or caretakers in case they would like to know more about or be involved in the process. Older adults who are interested in participating will be asked to contact me. When this has occurred, I will schedule a meeting with each older adult based on how our schedules match up. Meetings and interviews will be private, and the resident's information will not be shared outside of the research group. During this meeting, I will explain and administer the ESC measure to screen the potential participant on his or her ability to consent. Older adults who fail the screening measure will not be interviewed, and the process will end with me thanking them for their time. If participants pass the ESC, I will go through the consent document with them, allow them to ask questions, let them sign it if they choose to do so, and provide them with their own copy. The form will contain information for debriefing: contact information for counseling services and whom to contact

The types of statistical tests chosen, with rationale and relationships between variables are stated. Mediation, moderation, and control variables and way of addressing causality are noted.

For this example, test options include a Paired t-test: is there a difference in means in the pre- and post-test scores in all participants in the study—regardless of group? And, a repeated-measures ANOVA: do means differ between the intervention/Legacy group and control/regular activity group at time 1 (pre-test) and time 2 (post-test)?

For the qualitative interviews with older persons: codes and themes are developed. From the quantitative structured surveys with care providers: (based on level measurement) descriptive analysis of perceived views of reminiscence groups, crosstab/other bivariate analysis correlations, and possible multivariate analysis may be run.

with questions or concerns. The consent forms will be kept on campus for three years due to researcher policy requirements. If we do have remaining time left in the interview after completing the ESC and consent document, the participant and I will schedule another time to meet. In the next meeting (or continuation of the first meeting if there is time), the participant will choose a pseudonym for the interview and the assessments. They will be labeled with the pseudonym. The next assessment (hopefully to also be completed in this first interview) is the Mini-Cognitive Assessment. Each participant will complete this measure, and I will use their results to divide them into a MCI group and a non-cognitively impaired group. I will explain to those who do not meet non-cognitive impairment standards that they will likely still reap the benefits of reminiscence, and I just want to see how they engage in the process differently or similarly to another group.

This initial contact and screening will occur in the first two to three months depending on resident and researcher availability. When the groups are composed, I will begin the process of scheduling interviews where the older adults individually engage in reminiscence as I record their words on a digital recorder and take basic observational notes. Interviews will occur at a separate time from the initial assessment and will be based on how my schedule and each participant's schedule align. The interview will be held in a private location of the participant's choosing, such as the participant's room if appropriate or a quiet room in the facility. Initial ice-breaker questions will initiate the process. The important events in each participant's life and the natural flow of the conversation will dictate the direction of the interview. The interview will be allowed to occur for as short as the participant prefers (about 20 minutes) or as long as is reasonable (no longer than one hour). I have designed the interview so the conversation will flow naturally and with the length that the participant prefers. Immediately after each interview, I will ask each participant if I can contact him or her for a follow-up meeting after completing my analysis.

Data collection includes a description of the entire data-collection process: time interval of data collection, data collector (individual/team), instruments or tools used to collect the data, and problems that arose and how they were addressed (or not addressed) during the study. Secondary data require a description of the original use and intention behind the first data collection, along with the source of data collection and funder, if applicable.

Data cleaning examines raw data to check for values or answers that are out of range. Most often, data-analysis software, such as the Statistical Package for the Social Science (SPSS), Statistical Analysis System (SAS), or R Data Analysis Software, are used to assist with both data management and data analysis.

After cleaning, the data may be transformed/recoded. Good recoding practice mandates that a copy of the original dataset be kept, along with all variables (both recoded and original) and their operationalized definitions, in a codebook.

Mixed-methods data cleaning, reduction, and consolidation or transformation follows the practices of both qualitative and quantitative designs. For the quantitative data, frequency distributions and descriptive statistics help review data and identify outlying values. Variables can be recoded or collapsed. Qualitative data can be pooled with established coding criteria. Codes are created and made into larger code groups, or families, and discrepant cases/codes/counternarratives are noted.

Data Analysis

Before the second interview with willing participants, I will listen to the interview recordings and reread my observational notes. Then I will transcribe the initial interviews and reread what I typed in the transcription to ensure accuracy for each participant. I will code each transcription for the types of reminiscence used to tell life events. Next, I will run qualitative software, such as Atlas.ti or NVivo, to detect the number of times

Coded data lead to creation of themes (as ways to represent the data) with counter-narratives (of different views) included. Looking for types of reminiscence categories is a deductive approach that uses categories of analysis (called codes) planned before the analysis begins. But, looking for concepts and ideas that arose while analyzing data and creating themes is part of an inductive approach. Here, a content-analysis approach is used to generate themes from the text.

different reminiscence types are encountered as well as the significant life events that interviewees discuss. From this analysis, I will develop themes for the connection between reminiscence types and significant life events. I will also evaluate the results for differences or similarities in themes between mild cognitively impaired and non-cognitively impaired older adults. Then, I will compile and write a general discussion (to be used in the follow-up interview) of the most salient themes from the first interviews.

While software may assist in the data-analysis process, it should never drive analysis. The advantages include managing large amounts of textual, audio, and visual data, assistance with organizing codes and categories, and ways to graphically/visually represent the data. Limitations include being more removed from the data, the software learning curve, and the risk of overreliance on technical (and not methodological) design. The goal of software in analysis should never be to quantify qualitative work.

Data Handling

In the second interview, each participant and I will individually ensure trustworthiness (member checking) of my interpretations by determining if the overall themes and impressions I coded accurately depict what they were communicating. If not, we will make note of this together and adjust my interpretation.

The screening assessments will have actual participant names on them but will be kept in my mentor's secure filing cabinet that only my mentor and I will have access to. Confidentiality will be maintained. After analysis for reminiscence types and themes, the assessments and the included names will be permanently destroyed. The interviews will be private, and participants will have a pseudonym of the participant's choice and will be separated from the measures with names on them after analysis is complete. The notes taken will have the pseudonym on them. Digital recordings will be permanently destroyed after analysis is complete. Screenings, assessments, and recordings will not be kept longer than one month after the final analysis has been conducted and secured for the purpose of the project. Transcripts will not include identifiable information and thus will be kept indefinitely.

Data analysis consists of taking cleaned/recoded data and applying them to the statistical tests chosen as part of the design of the project. It is important to recheck that the data meet the requirements and assumptions of the test. Any variation should be stated. Steps in the process must be clearly stated. Significance levels of results must be reported as they detail the level by which results are real and not by chance. Yet, it must be noted that significant results do not necessarily mean meaningful or important results; that is where the researcher's interpretation comes into play.

Mixed-method designs include constant comparative design and triangulation. Post-cleaning and condensing of data, qualitative data's themes can be compared and combined or synthesized. Descriptive (frequency distribution, summary statistics) and inferential analysis can occur (cluster analysis, correlation, ANOVA, multivariate, SEM, path) for quantitative data. Qualitative themes and quantitative variables for the same constructs can be compared. Integration of quantitative and qualitative elements data and findings is the goal of mixed-methods designs. True data integration can happen in three ways: Data are integrated by building through sequential integration. Also, data are integrated by merging or bringing the quantitative and qualitative elements together. Integration can also be embedded and happening repeatedly throughout the ongoing data analysis.

In this convergent parallel example, data are integrated by comparison and merging. Mixed methods often use visual displays and/or matrices to help the reader see how the data from each design have been integrated and work together.

Trustworthiness

Assurance of quality will be obtained through two means: member checking and definition of reminiscence types (Wong & Watt, 1991). The follow-up or second interview will ensure that I analyze and report what the participants actually meant to say. When coding data, I will use the definitions for reminiscence types that Wong and Watt developed when identifying the types. This is so I can clearly know that Participant A was talking about reminiscence Type B when discussing Event C. My research will examine the phenomenon of reminiscence from a different point of view. This will increase overall understanding of reminiscence.

In qualitative studies, rigor is called trustworthiness (which includes credibility transferability, dependability, and confirmability). If a team analyzes data, consider inter-coder reliability or inter-coder agreement.

Timeline and Intended Outcome

This study will occur over a five-month to six-month time period. The first month will involve recruiting and screening potential participants. Then, I will begin the cognitive assessments and interviews with quality checks for up to two months. The final step will be data analysis for themes as well as a full manuscript of the study (abstract, methods, literature review, results, discussion, etc.). The last three to six months will be this process. I also plan to submit my research for publication in a peer-reviewed journal and will present at several conferences.

IRB and Ethical Concerns

Some mild frustration may occur when screening with ESC and the cognitive assessment occurs. If needed, I will provide documents in larger text for older adults who are undergoing vision changes. Only older adults who can consent will participate. I will clearly tell the older adults that they may stop at any time. Their wishes will be respected. Participants may experience mild to moderate emotional discomfort if they choose to discuss events from the past that are upsetting. I, as the researcher, will not probe for these types of events but will let the participants determine how much they feel comfortable sharing. If there is excessive distress, I will ask the participants if they would like to change the subject or if they would like to continue at all. I will respect their decision to cease participation if that is what they choose.

Potential costs include digital recorder, paper and ink for the two screening measures, and access to qualitative analysis software. The primary cost to participants is their time. This should be considered when they are deciding whether to consent or not, but, if they decide to leave the study at any point, this decision will not reflect negatively on them in any way.

There may also be benefits for the older adults from their engagement in this research. Conversing with the researcher may serve as a friendly social visit for participants. This could be particularly beneficial to older adults who do not get many visitors at the care facility. Engaging in reminiscence for their own enjoyment, working through unresolved emotions, and offering advice to the researcher through reminiscence are possible benefits during this process. There are also indirect benefits. In the bigger picture, participants will be contributing to literature in the gerontology field about reminiscence and mild cognitive impairment in older adults.

> Validity questions whether the right concept is being measured. In other words, is the researcher really measuring the concept that he or she intends to measure (e.g., face validity, construct validity, content validity, concurrent validity, etc.)? Reliability refers to stability or consistency of a measure over a brief time interval (e.g., test-retest reliability, intra-observer, or intra-rater reliability, inter-item reliability, alternate-form reliability, etc.). If a team analyzes data, consider interrater reliability in data collection and analysis. Researchers generally cover the basics of reliability and validity in reporting, such as Cronbach's alpha, to show Likert-scale reliability or interrater reliability if there is a research-data collection team. Face validity is often assumed through the explicit operationalization or definition of variables. But, content or criterion validity, as well as other forms of both validity and reliability, should be discussed because they directly impact the researchers' choice of measures.

> A mixed-methods study maintains the individual integrity of each part of the design. Quantitative and qualitative standards and vocabulary need to be used and matched to that element. For quantitative parts, discuss reliability and validity, and for qualitative parts, address rigor. Issues of representativeness (in the quantitative part) and saturation (in the qualitative designs) should be addressed. In mixed-methods designs, legitimization addresses validity, while inference transferability allows researchers to apply findings of one study to other settings. Inference transferability refers to how well and in what settings a mixed-methods study's results can be applied more broadly.

> For those with impaired cognitive status (such as dementia), qualitative researchers have found ethical concerns about persons with impairment being silent, answering in shorter phrases or the affirmative, echoing the answers of caregivers, or not understanding study requirements. Researchers suggest the consent process be an ongoing process rather than a one-time event. Researchers also warn that gatekeepers can exclude participation when the person with dementia may wish to consent. Residents living in care settings may also be subject to gatekeepers making their own decisions about consent and possible inclusion in a study for their residents without including the resident in the process. These gerontology-related ethical issues encountered, and how they were addressed, should be reported.

Quantitative research requires statistical skill or access to software to conduct analysis. Analyses can be run with differing significance levels, parameters, and tests to achieve significance results. Research can conflict (or be confused) with clinical treatment in some designs. There is the potential for data linking, or merging older persons' records with other data sources and across studies. The quantitative researcher is present throughout the work—from initial design to operationalization of variables, data collection, and choice of test for the analysis, and writing of the report. Researchers should state their choice of design/method, crossover with medical or other roles, protection of participants' information, and sensory and cognitive changes that could impact quantitative work.

A mixed-methods study's ethical issues are a combination of the designs used in the study.

If this was a complete report (not a proposal), several sections would appear here with findings from the data. These sections are as follows:

Research Results/Discussion of Findings:
Be explicit about your coding or other data-analysis processes. The reader wants to know how you developed codes (deductive, inductive coding, etc.) and who did the coding. The write-up of analysis needs to be more than one sentence, such as "thematic content analysis was used to code data"—especially for readers less familiar with qualitative designs. Do not feel you have to make the report of your findings narrow or fit cookie-cutter molds. Use the deep, thick, rich text descriptions that are an essential feature of the work. Blocks of direct participants' quotes are the hallmark of good qualitative writing.

Conclusion:
Tell the readers what your study adds to the body of literature and (in the case of grounded theory) what new theories or frameworks were created because of your study.

Research Results/Discussion of Findings:
Findings from statistical tests are presented in narrative and tabular form with levels of significance.

Conclusion:
Findings need to be linked back to the research questions and hypotheses. Were they "proven" or supported via statistical testing? Were these findings interpreted beyond statistical significance and applied back to the original goals of the study? Were the findings tied back to either theoretical premises or a conceptual model? Were plausible explanations given as to why the proposed relationship was not found? Limitations and appropriate groups to generalize results to are noted. Did the authors provide both implications of their findings to practice and the field and give future directions for additional research?

Research Results/Discussion of Findings:
The key to mixed-methods results discussion is to talk about how the results of the individual designs work together to inform each other.

Conclusion:
Mixed-methods theorists suggest that meta-inferences are stated. Meta-inferences are analogous to a conclusion or a summary section in other designs. Mixed-methods conclusions need to detail the ways findings are applicable to other groups.

Authorship Contribution: Many journals require each author listed to disclose his/her contribution to the article. Typical roles include conceiving the study's idea anddesigning the study, collecting and analyzing data, performing specialized analysis, etc. Establishing authorship order and assigned roles at the onset of a study is a good practice.

Conflict of Interest Statements: may also appear here if the author financial support for the study or other relationships that may influence the study.

Bibliography

Allen, R. S. (2009). The legacy project intervention to enhance meaningful family interactions: Case examples. *Clinical Gerontologist, 32*, 164–176. doi:10.1080/07317110802677005

Allen, R. S., Harris, G. M., Burgio, L. D., Azuero, C. B., Miller, L. A., Shin, H. J., & Parmelee, P. (2014). Can senior volunteers deliver reminiscence and creative activity interventions? Results of the legacy intervention family enactment randomized controlled trial. *Journal of Pain and Symptom Management, 48*, 590–605. Retrieved from http://www.journals.elsevier.com/journal-of-pain-and-symptom-management/

Allen, R. S., Hilgeman, M. M., Ege, M. A., Shuster, J., John, L., & Burgio, L. D. (2008). Legacy activities as interventions approaching the end of life. *Journal of Palliative Medicine, 11*, 1029–1038. doi:10.1089/jpm.2007.0294

Alzheimer's Association. (2015). *Health care professionals and Alzheimer's: Cognitive assessment toolkit*. Retrieved from http://www.alz.org/healthcareprofessionals/cognitive-tests-patient-assessment.asp

Barnabe, A., Whitehead, V., Pilon, R., Arsenault-Lapierre, G., & Chertkow, H. (2012). Autobiographical memory in mild cognitive impairment and Alzheimer's disease: A comparison between the Levine and Kopelman interview methodologies. *Hippocampus, 22*, 1809–1825. doi:10.1002/hipo.22015

Bohlmeijer, E. T., & Westerhof, G. J. (2014). Celebrating fifty years of research and applications in reminiscence and life review: State of the art and new directions. *Journal of Aging Studies, 29*, 107–114. doi:10.1016/j.jaging.2014.02.003

Chiang, K., Chu, H., Chang, H., Chung, M., Chen, C., Chiou, H., & Chou, K. (2010). The effects of reminiscence therapy on psychological well-being, depression, and loneliness among the institutionalized aged. *International Journal of Geriatric Psychiatry, 25*, 380–388. doi:10.1002/gps.2350

Cohen-Mansfield, J., Papura-Gill, A., & Golander, H. (2006). Utilization of self-identity roles for designing interventions for persons with dementia. *Journals of Gerontology, Series B, Psychological Sciences and Social Sciences [H.W. Wilson—SSA]*, *61B*(4), P202.

Cooney, A., Hunter, A., Murphy, K., Casey, D., Devane, D., Smyth, S., O'Shea, E. (2014). "Seeing me through my memories": A grounded theory study on using reminiscence with people with dementia living in long-term care. *Journal of Clinical Nursing, 23*, 3564–3574. doi:10.1111/jocn.12645

Dempsey, L., Murphy, K., Cooney, A., Casey, D., O'Shea, E., Devane, D., Hunter, A. (2014). Reminiscence in dementia: A concept analysis. *Dementia, 13*, 176–192. doi:10.1177/1471301212456277

Kirkland, R. (Fall 2015). *Chapter 4: Person-environment interactions and work*. PowerPoint slides. Retrieved from the University of Northern Colorado Blackboard website, https://unco.blackboard.com/

Locher, J. L., Bronstein, J., Robinson, C. O., Williams, C., & Ritchie, C. S. (2006). Ethical issues involving research conducted with homebound older adults. *The Gerontologist, 46*, 160–164. doi:10.1093/geront/46.2.160

O'Shea, E. Devane, D., Cooney, A., Casey, D., Jordan, F., Hunter, A., Murphy, K. (2014). The impact of reminiscence on the quality of life of residents with dementia in long-stay care. *International Journal of Geriatric Psychiatry, 29*, 1062–1070. doi:10.1002/gps.4099

Resnick, B., Gruber-Baldim, A., Pretzer-Aboff, I., Galik, E., Buie, V., Russ, K., & Zimmerman, S. (2007). Reliability and validity of the evaluation to sign consent measure. *Gerontologist, 47*(1), 69–77. doi:10.1093/geront/47.1.69

Wong, P. T. P., & Watt, L. M. (1991). What types of reminiscence are associated with successful aging? *Psychology and Aging, 6*, 272–279. doi:10.1037/0882-7974.6.2.272

Sample Research Report Appendix A

Potential Interview Questions: Semi-Structured

Begin: Hi, I'm Rebecca, a student at the University of Northern Colorado and am here to interview you about your significant life experiences. We can treat this like a casual discussion, and the only requirement is that you discuss at least two events that have had a major impact on your worldviews, relationships, faith, or life in general. Does that sound good to you? (*Recall: I will have already conducted two assessments with the participant at this point.)

Ice breakers if needed:

(1) How have you been today?
(2) What are some of your hobbies? What did you do for work before?

Conversation encouragers/probes if needed:

(3) How did your parents make a living?
(4) How many brothers and sisters did you have?
(5) Who has had the greatest influence on your life?
(6) What were some of your family traditions?
(7) What are some of your hobbies? How did you pick them up?
(8) How old were you when you got married?
(9) Where have you visited? What places did you like the most?
(10) Where have you lived?
(11) What was your greatest challenge? How did you meet it?
(12) What do you feel is your greatest achievement?
(13) What are the societal changes you have seen taking place in your lifetime?

This interview script is a starting point with suggested questions to guide the interview.

Sample Research Report Appendix B

Letter of Permission for Research

I, ______________________________, allow permission for ______________________________
to enter this care facility on [scheduled dates] for the purpose of collecting data in research that has received Institutional Review Board approval. Rebecca Artzer may engage in the approved cognitive assessments and interviews with residents who are able to give and have given their consent.

____

Facility Administrator Signature (Date)

____

Researcher Signature (Date)

> Since this study is at a skilled-care facility, a letter from the Nursing Home Administrator is needed for the Institutional Review Board (IRB) and shows the facility's support of the study.

Sample Research Report Appendix C

ESC Questionnaire and Acceptable Answers

The ESC protocol is used to assess understanding of the study's specific requirements. Questions and acceptable answers to questions are listed here.

1. What are two potential risks? Frustration; emotional upset; physical discomfort while sitting during interview; no risk.
2. What is expected from you, the resident? Complete assessments; answer questions; converse with Rebecca; discuss life events.
3. What if you don't want to continue? Ask to stop.
4. What if you experience discomfort? Say something; ask to stop.
5. How is it decided who gets to participate in this study? Voluntary participants; ability to give consent; recommended from staff or fellow residents.

Sample Research Report Appendix D

Mini-Cog™ Questions

Appendices D and E would include some mental assessments and screening tests. These are not needed for all studies with older persons (of course); they are included for this study because it includes people across the cognitive spectrum.

The Mini-Cog™ that includes word recall and clock-drawing tasks is not reproduced here. This test is not in the public domain. To reproduce the tests, researchers should contact the test creators who hold the copyright. See Borson, S., Scanlan, J., Brush, M., Vitaliano, P., and Dokmak, A. (2000). The Mini-Cog: A cognitive 'vital signs' measure for dementia screening in multi-lingual elderly. *International Journal of Geriatric Psychiatry*, 15, 1021–1027.

Sample Research Report Appendix E

Mini-Cog™ Clock Drawing

Appendices D and E would include some mental assessments and screening tests.These are not needed for all studies with older persons (of course). They are included for this study because it includes people across the cognitive spectrum.

The Mini-Cog™ that includes word recall and clock-drawing tasks is not reproduced here. This test is not in the public domain. To reproduce the tests, researchers should contact the test creators who hold the copyright. See: Borson, S., Scanlan, J., Brush, M., Vitaliano, P., and Dokmak, A. (2000). The Mini-Cog: A cognitive 'vital signs' measure for dementia screening in multi-lingual elderly. *International Journal of Geriatric Psychiatry*, 15, 1021–1027.

Sample Research Report Appendix F

Large-Print Consent Document for the Visually Impaired (Can Be Made Larger or Formatted as Needed)

University of Northern Colorado

Consent Form for Human Participants in Research University of Northern Colorado

Project Title: Reminiscence with Mild Cognitively Impaired and Non-cognitively Impaired Older Adults

Researcher: Rebecca Artzer, Undergraduate Researcher
(970) 351–2403
Advisor: Joyce Weil, Ph.D., School of Human Sciences
(970) 351–1583

An example of an Informed-Consent document. The document should be formatted to meet the needs of the group studied.

Purpose of the study: I am a student at the University of Northern Colorado. I am studying the life stories of older adults. I want to compare the stories of people who have no memory problems with the stories of people who have just a little trouble with their memory or thinking. I would like to interview you, asking questions like: Who has had the greatest influence on your life? Where have you lived?

Tests and interview schedule: If you agree to participate in this study, here is what would be expected of you: The interview schedule would be:

- A 20-minute introductory test to measure your understanding of the consent process. I want to be fair in asking you to make a decision about participating in this study
- Consent form process: 20 minutes or more if needed
- A 15-minute test of your memory and thinking skills

Then, depending on results of tests:

- One or two interviews (30–60 minutes)
- Follow-up interview (20 minutes, optional)

Confidentiality: You may choose a fake name in place of your real name so what you say cannot be tied to you personally. I will use this fake name if I talk about your stories to other people in my field. I cannot promise complete privacy at [nursing facility name here] because nurses or your neighbors may walk in during my conversations with you, but I will do my best to allow for privacy. I will use an electronic recorder in our interviews so that later I can type up what we talk about.

After I have typed up our meetings, I will permanently get rid of the recordings. I will also take a few hand-written notes as reminders for me about our interview. Your test results and my hand-written notes will be locked in my research advisor's office, Gunter Hall 1250, at the University of Northern Colorado.

Participation: Risks involved in this study are minimal, likely to not be greater than those encountered on a daily basis by older adults in care facilities. If you desire, you may seek counseling from [care facility service's name] and can contact them at [(000) 000–000].

Participation is voluntary. You may decide not to participate in this study, and if you begin participation you may still decide to stop and withdraw at any time. Your decision will be respected and will not result in loss of benefits to which you are otherwise entitled. Having read the above and having had an opportunity to ask any questions, please sign below if you would like to participate in this research. A copy of this form will be given to you to retain for future reference.

If you have any concerns about your selection or treatment as a research participant, please contact Sherry May, IRB Administrator, Office of Sponsored Programs, 25 Kepner Hall, University of Northern Colorado Greeley, CO 80639; 970–351–1910.

Please feel free to phone the researcher if you have any questions. Having read the above and having had an opportunity to ask any questions, please sign below if you would like to participate in this research. You will receive one copy of this form for future reference. If you have any concerns about your selection or treatment as a research participant please contact the Office of Sponsored Programs, Kepner Hall, University of Northern Colorado Greeley, CO 80639; 970–351–2161.

____

Participant's Signature (Date)

____

Researcher's Signature (Date)

Sample Research Report Appendix G

Read-Aloud Common Language Consent Section

Participation

Having a verbal script to read to participants can help assure study requirements are known when consent is given.

Being in this study is completely your choice. You can choose not to participate at any time, and I will not question your choice. Your choice about being in the study or not being in it will not impact the care you are getting. You will not have any specific benefits from being in this study. But you will help me and those in my field to know more about life stories from older adults like you. By participating, you will face risks that are likely to not be more than what you see on a day-to-day basis. If you desire, you may seek counseling from [care facility service's name] and can contact them at [(000) 000–000]. Please let me know at any time about any questions or problems you have with doing this study. If you do not feel comfortable talking to me, you can contact Sherry May, IRB Administrator, Office of Sponsored Programs, 25 Kepner Hall, University of Northern Colorado Greeley, CO 80639; 970–351–1910.

Glossary

Abduction/abductive approach: using the researcher's own questions or curiosity about problems he or she encounters in daily life as the starting point for solving problems with research. Using intuition, rather than theory or data, to begin formal study. (See Deductive and Inductive approach.)

Academic manuscripts: papers/reports, written to submit to peer-reviewed journals, that generally have a specific format, content organization, and writing and formatting styles.

Activities of Daily Living (ADLs): tasks performed as part of routine daily activities. These include bathing, dressing, grooming, eating, transferring from bed to chair, walking around one's home, and toileting. See IADLs.

Activity theory: this theory suggests it is participation in, or maintenance of, a group of activities that influences an older person's well-being throughout life. An older person's own view of himself or herself that is supported by this engagement with the external environment or society. Developed to challenge the idea that disengagement is a natural or expected part of the aging process. See Disengagement Theory; Successful Aging; Socioemotional Selectivity Theory.

Age effects: These are the changes that happen over a person's life and include normal age-related and developmental changes that happen with the passage of chronological time. (See Age-period-cohort [APC] effects.)

Age-period-cohort (APC) effects: Term used to describe the combination of these three time elements in studies of aging. There are changes that occur with age (age effects), changes that occur owing to a period of time experienced by all (period effects), or changes due to the group into which one is born (cohort effects).

Age Stratification Theories: focus attention on the process of dividing members of a society into strata, or social groups by age, and the conflicts that arise between age groups of "young" versus "old." Examples include spending on Social Security programs for the Baby Boomers versus federal aid to families with young children; or older persons placing an excessive burden both upon their families and upon the healthcare system.

Aging in place: traditionally described as the ability to remain in one's own home or community over one's life, until old age, and is often associated with the availability of resources of all kinds to do so. The definition of aging in place has been expanded to include those aging in place in the same formal, continuum-of-care institution—including those in assisted living moving to skilled-nursing and/or memory-care settings in the same place.

Alternate-form reliability: compares individuals' answers to slightly different versions of survey questions (i.e., slightly reworded questions) to make sure answers are consistent across questions about the same concept.

Alternate hypothesis: is where the real relationship between groups is stated.

Ambulatory difficulty: difficulty with walking or stair climbing. Can include the use of personal devices or equipment (such as a cane or walker).

Amnestic: mild cognitive impairment can be experienced as periods of forgetfulness without changes in executive function.

Analysis of covariance (ANCOVA): builds upon ANOVA by removing the influence of an independent variable, or "controlling for it," as covariate upon a dependent variable.

Analysis of variance (ANOVA): tests for significant difference in the means of *two or more groups* upon a dependent variable. It is like t-testing in its use of group comparisons for hypothesis testing, but ANOVA expands the number of groups used in t-testing.

Analysis topologies: have been created to review stories from the point of view of the storyteller and the listener. Also called story analysis.

Analytical memos: go beyond description and include examination and evaluation of materials and observations.

Anatomical changes: physical changes in the brain, including a reduction in brain mass/size, decrease in white matter, and pre-frontal grey matter loss affecting executive functioning (controlling organization and emotional regulation).

Anti-aging medicine: a discipline looking to halt or reverse the effects of aging (or aging, itself) and seek prolongevity, or life extension. Such groups make up an anti-aging consumer market with appearance-based products and services. Theories focus on stem-cell research, gene therapy, calorie restriction, nanotechnology, and technology-enhanced aging.

Applied research: research that seeks a solution to an everyday issue or to solve practical problem.

Asynchronous: refers to data-collection timing in digital ethnography. For example, a researcher would be reading transcripts of texts posted in a chat room or blog *after* they were posted and not chatting "live"/in real time with a participant.

Attributes: are the quantified or numeric values assigned to response choices or categories of data. Often used in mixed-methods computerized software. Also called variables.

Audience: the intended readership of an article or report.

Autoethnography: a first-person account of an individual that also reflects upon societal structure and larger societal/social influences upon his or her life. Types of autoethnography include emotional, evocative, or heartful, where researchers include their own emotions/reactions in the writing.

Axial codes: take the open and *in vivo* codes and suggest relationships (e.g., hierarchies or categories and subcategories) between these codes to create larger elements or ideas.

Baltes's lifespan perspective: adds the consideration of biological, social, historical, and cultural differences to the development processes throughout a person's life.

Bar charts: are the most commonly used visual display; depict counts or percentages of responses in a bar graph.

Biography: older person-based narrative; other-written.

Bivariate correlation: also called zero-order correlation; tests a relationship between two variables.

Bivariate measures of association: provide a researcher with a number quantifying the relationship between the two variables. In some cases, depending upon a variable's level of measurement, the number provides the strength of the relationship.

Books, edited volumes, and book chapters: offer an author more space to write and more formatting options. Publishers can be university based, academic, popular press, or based on self-publication.

Bounded cases: cases that have naturally occurring limits (such as the case of older persons living in a particular rural county in 2015), or cases can be made into a bounded group—that is, grouped by the researcher for his or her own purposes (e.g., the first several persons to move into elder co-housing or men experiencing widowhood).

Boxplots: show the distribution of a variable or variables including a depiction of central tendency and variation.

Case studies (qualitative): can have one individual as a focus or include multiple persons or levels as part of the case—individuals, social institutions, societies, or even larger geographic units, such as countries. Also called extended case studies. See Bounded cases, Intrinsic cases, etc.

Case study analysis (qualitative): pattern-matching compares what is found in data to the researcher's expectations and explanation-building, or looks for alternative explanations and lists any problems encountered. A researcher can perform time-series analysis for cases, look for changes over time, or employ logic models to examine the relationship of different types of outcomes that are defined and tested. Researchers may explore cross-case synthesis, comparing the case of interest to other cases, including those in literature.

Causal comparative approach (quantitative): tests causal relationships after they have occurred or after the fact (*ex post facto*). This design can test how changes in an independent variable effect changes in a dependent variable or how two preexisting, naturally occurring groups differ on a dependent variable. This design is a good choice when data already exists to address a research question at hand and the researcher seeks to assign cause and effect.

Causality (quantitative): quantitative designs can establish causality among independent variables as cause and among dependent variables as effect. Several elements are needed to establish basic causality: (1) the independent variable occurring before the dependent variable; (2) an association must exist between the independent and dependent variables; (3) the relationship between the independent and dependent variables must not be caused by another variable (spuriousness); (4) the change in the independent must precede and cause the change in the dependent; and (5) the change in the independent variable effects change across the dependent variable.

Certificates of Confidentiality (CoC): a safeguard issued by the National Institutes of Health (NIH) for IRB-approved (Institutional Review Board) studies that deal with NIH-defined "sensitive" topics (for example, behavioral practices, health issues, or illegal activities). A researcher can request a CoC for his or her study, which will help him or her avoid disclosing participants' data if requested by a court or legal system.

Chi-square (x^2): tests for significant differences in observed vs. expected values for two groups. It is a common test because it can be used by variables of all levels of measurement.

Closed-ended questions: survey questions with fixed or pre-formatted responses categories.

Cluster sampling: is similar to stratified sampling, except the units are naturally occurring clusters or groups. The sampling occurs in a series of each cluster. Each cluster becomes a sampling frame from which cases are drawn. Selecting different types of clusters may help the sample from becoming too homogenous.

Codebook: records all aspects of variables in a dataset—including variable names, position in the dataset, the narrative or text variable labels (providing a longer description of what the variable is), the variable's level of measurement, and its technical aspects (type: string/numeric, number of characters, number of decimal places, etc.). The codebook also addresses how missing values for a variable are coded or noted. Software producers' codebooks are a starting place, but adding more details to the generated codebook is of benefit to the researcher.

Code families or trees: groups of individual codes.

Codes: ways of organizing qualitative data gathered from a variety of sources including interview transcripts, field notes, participant observation, documents, etc. Codes are used to generate themes. See Axial, *In vivo*, Open, and/or Selective code families.

Coding: is the process of assigning labels to similar segments of text, video, or audio elements in the analysis. Codes can be predetermined before analysis or generated from the data, themselves. Qualitative software lets a researcher apply several types of codes (or nodes) to each case.

Coding Analysis Toolkit (CAT): software that calculates inter-rater reliability and coding consistency for teams conducting qualitative research.

Cognitive impairment rates: vary by age group and gender. Risk of impairment increases with chronological age. Women present lower levels of moderate and severe impairment when compared with their male counterparts.

Cognitive plasticity: the ability to learn or acquire new skills. Theories debate whether cognitive training with high-order, executive-function-based mental strategies and tasks, along with increased blood supply, help with cognitive plasticity.

Cognitive reserve: ways the brain is resilient to loss; can potentially mitigate memory losses and keep functioning at a high level.

Cognitive speed: the ability to process information and respond verbally; slows with age.

Cohort (birth cohort) effect: a cohort is the group into which one is born and with whom one ages across one's lifespan. Cohorts are heterogeneous, cover a wide time span, and have subgroups within them. The cohort into which a person is born affects his or her attitudes, views and experiences, health and functional abilities, and place in society. See Age-period-cohort (APC) effects.

Collaborative Institutional Training Initiative (CITI Program): online training modules for ethics, Institutional Review Board training, and conflicts of interest in human subjects' research in biomedical, social, and behavioral sciences.

Color vision: may be distorted. Eyes become dry with a reduced peripheral visual field and more sensitivity to glare.

Common Rule: informal name for the U.S. Department of Health and Human Services' (DHHS), Office for Human Research Protection, Code of Federal Regulations, Title 45, Part 46. It governs research conducted on human subjects. It defines key elements of the research process. DHHS formally issued a Notice of Proposed Rulemaking (NPRM) for Revisions to the Common Rule in September 2015.

Community-based participatory research (CBPR): keeps researchers and older community members as true equals with no power differentials.

Community presentations: a vehicle for presenting study results back to older persons as co-researchers or as engaged participants and agencies within the aging network. It is important to relay accurate information back without excessive use of jargon or directly identifying participants by name or attributes.

Computer-Assisted/Aided Qualitative Data Analysis Software (CAQDAS): programs to aid in the analysis of data. Commonly used, general quantitative software options include the Statistical Package for the Social Sciences (SPSS), Statistical Analysis Software (SAS), Stata software by Stata Corp, and R software that offers options for statistical analysis. Also available are more specialized quantitative program options such as MPlus (a program for latent variable modeling) and Lisrel (which is commonly used for Structural Equation Modeling [SEM]). Commonly used qualitative options include ATLAS.ti and Nvivo. Some other qualitative software options include HyperRESEARCH, QDA Miner, AnSWR, Qualrus, RQDA, and Ethnograph. MAXQDA is suggested as a program for mixed-methods data analysis.

Conception of Adult Development: a theory using life-cycle eras to create an adult-transition phase (ages 60 to 85) as a "season of life" where one experiences major health events and some loss of societal status.

Conceptual consistency: inferences made from the data in mixed-methods designs match both the data and theory.

Conceptualization: simply specifying what a term means. See operationalization.

Concurrent validity: occurs when a score on a measure predicts another.

Conference presentations: use the same elements of a full academic paper but in an abridged format. Some conferences may require a full-paper submission; others do not.

Conflicts of interest: author's disclosure statement of any information and possible influence that must be taken into consideration when reading the findings, for example, receiving funding for the research.

Confirmability: researchers include their own self-reflections about their role as data collectors and interpreters including any potential biases. Adding discrepant cases or counternarratives that challenge the existing findings aid in confirmability. Confirmability can be generally related to the concept of objectivity in quantitative analysis. See trustworthiness.

Constant comparative method: a process of continued comparison and contrasting of the data, as an ongoing, recurrent part of the qualitative data-collection and analysis process. The more types of narrative data (from interviews, written stories, printed materials), the stronger the comparative process in producing differing ideas and avenues of study.

Constructionism: philosophical perspective or worldview that seeks to capture the way individuals construct or create reality. Research is centered upon participants' views and ways of constructing meaning in their daily worlds.

Construct-level missing data: data that, when missing, eliminate an entire construct or set of variables from analysis.

Construct validity: "proves" soundness of a measure by grounding the measure in a theory or model and defining the concept the researcher is measuring.

Contamination: occurs when the lines between the two groups, the experimental and control, are crossed and the knowledge or treatment (designed to affect only the experimental group) begins to affect both groups.

Content validity: assures that the measure captures all dimensions of the concept the researcher is measuring.

Continuity Theory: suggests with older age comes a way to balance and adapt to changes both on internal levels (such as values, ideas) and on external levels (such as experiences within society or in social networks) to maintain a sense of the self over time. The continuity-achieving process is dynamic, flexible, and ongoing.

Continuous: a unit of analysis that can be infinitely divided (such as age). See also Discrete.

Continuum of care: the network of care setting including assisted living, skilled-nursing, and memory-care settings in the same place.

Contributed-to-work statement: work on the manuscript is outlined by author. Optional but can eliminate any authorship issues that may arise.

Control group: group not receiving the intervention.

Convenience (or availability) sampling: participants are selected based on ease of accessibility or availability by the researcher and are often used for pilot testing.

Convergent parallel designs: a mixed-method design that does not have one dominant method; instead, this design uses each method (quantitative or qualitative) equally and takes the findings from each to explain the research question at hand.

Convoy Model of Social Relations: visually depicts types of social relationships older persons have-using a series of concentric circles.

Co-occurrence table: an option in qualitative analysis that compares the amount of times codes appear together. Some qualitative software produces a C-Coefficient with values 0–1 indicating the strength of the co-occurring relationship between the codes.

Correlation designs (quantitative): examine the association between variables. This approach cannot impose causal order—stating which instance or variable affected the other—but can describe co-occurring changes and strength and magnitude of the association.

Counternarratives: differing or discrepant voices or themes.

Creative research methods: humanities and arts have merged with gerontological approaches in study design, such as video, drawing, and art.

Credibility: confirmation of findings through the use of multiple data sources, multiple methods, and/or several researchers. As a comparison for those more familiar with only a quantitative approach, credibility can be thought of as similar to internal validity in quantitative models. See Trustworthiness.

Criterion validity: is achieved when the item the researcher is measuring is similar to another separate, established indicator that measures the same concept.

Critical discourse analysis: examines power dynamics and the role of age, race, class, and gender of the speaker and the relationship of the speaker to hegemonic (dominant) societal norms. Types include dispositive analysis and linguistic analysis of speech and text.

Critical ethnography: represents a multitude of participants' voices (with a focus on those of groups often voiceless) or centers around exposing existing inequalities.

Critical gerontology: critical gerontologists adapted Marxist philosophy to include the impact of the power of social structures (the State, societal institutions) upon the individual experience of aging.

Critical perspective or worldview: in a study, a philosophical approach that includes the role of power and political dynamics of oppressed/marginalized groups and societal influences upon these groups.

Cronbach's alpha (α): calculated to see if the items measured in the index relate to the same concept reliably. It can be used to report the strength of relationships (with a range of 0–1).

In the social sciences, 0.70 to 0.79 is acceptable/adequate; 0.80–0.89 is very good; and 0.90 or above is very good.

Crosstabulation (crosstabs): is used to examine the relationships between two (or more) variables.

Crystallized intelligence: accumulated knowledge; increases with age or at least shows little decline with aging.

Cultural gerontology: when conducting research, seeks to place the study of gerontology in cultural context and, therefore, recognizes the role of a way of life and attitudes, language, customs, race, and ethnicity of a specific group of older persons.

Culture: refers to the way of life, practices, beliefs, and attitudes of a particular group of persons.

Cumulative Advantage/Disadvantage (CAD) theories: see inequalities as lifelong, not simply a result of a later period or stage in life. Theorists suggest that avoiding the impact of society on lifelong development would paint an incomplete the picture of aging. Also called Cumulative Inequality Theory.

Data cleaning: in quantitative studies, raw data are examined to check for values or answers that are out of range or are outliers. After cleaning, the data may be transformed or recoded.

Data files: in quantitative software are the actual numerical values for the information the researcher has collected. Each program assigns a different extension to these files, but they are the primary building blocks for your data analysis. Data in the data editor window look like an Excel spreadsheet, and they contain the actual coded responses from study participants.

Data harmonization: process of standardizing variables and responses so that a concept can be tracked, linked, and followed in more than one dataset.

Data linking: merging older persons' records with other data sources (e.g., large national datasets), which can lead to identification of older individuals.

Decolonizing strategies: methods of conducting research with indigenous older persons that addresses power differentials and marginalization of indigenous people in research. These methods avoid a Eurocentric/ethnocentric view of participants and acknowledge the role of culture and cultural practices.

Deduction/deductive approach: using theory to generate and test hypotheses (see Abductive and Inductive approach).

Deductive coding: also called top-coding. In qualitative analysis, deductive codes (or categories) are planned before the analysis begins. The researchers then highlight text that matches the deductive code.

Deep mapping: the use of ethnography and multimedia to create a sense of what place, setting, or geography is like for a person.

Dementia theater: theatrical work (such as a play) created by or about persons with cognitive impairment with performances relaying the subjects' lived experiences.

Dependability: assurance that findings are based only on the data—even if the field setting or study direction change. Dependability is similar to reliability in quantitative models. See Trustworthiness.

Descriptive approach (or descriptive research): seeks to describe, or summarize, the sample's characteristics using variables in quantitative studies.

Descriptive statistics: depict one variable in a frequency distribution (or table that summarized counts or percents in each category of a variable) or visually in charts or graphs.

Descriptive studies: quantitative studies that do not seek to test a hypothesis. They describe or paint a picture of the phenomena you are studying with numerical data.

Diaries and journaling: older person-based, self-written narratives.

Diaries for people with dementia: first-person reflection in any form (photos, audio, written, or in combination), to include elders' own voices and as advocacy measures in research.

Dichotomous variables: variables with yes/no (Y/N) response choices.

Digital ethnography: also called cyber ethnography, virtual ethnography, or netnography; expands the medium of traditional ethnographic practice. In digital ethnography, the field is an online setting or virtual reality made up of social networks. Data can be collected via phone/tablet apps, mapping or geographic information systems (GIS), and video-calling interfaces, such as FaceTime or Skype.

Discourse analysis: a process of interpreting conversation and content of language with critical reflection upon the analysis. Discourse analysis examines a person's expression of ideas through words, voice, intention, activeness, or passiveness of language. This analysis can focus on the form, structure, and meaning of the conversation or take a more linguistic approach, focusing on syntax, argument cohesion, or changes in the tone of the voice.

Discrete: the smallest unit of analysis that cannot be divided further (such as residents of cohousing). See also Continuous.

Disengagement theory: suggests that as one ages, one withdraws from society until the final disengagement (of death). This reverse-socialization process is unidirectional and not reversible. The removal from societal participation makes the way for younger generations to fill and take over roles once held by older persons. Now debunked.

Divided attention: splitting one's attentions to accomplish several tasks at once.

Drafting: process of writing, editing, rewriting—essential to improve flow, logic, and readability of a document.

Ecological fallacy: unit of analysis-based error, studying individuals and making statements about groups. See also reductionist fallacy (i.e., if you are studying groups but then apply your findings to individuals, that is a reductionist fallacy).

Ecological Model: (Urie Bronfenbrenner) describes lifespan development as the process of an individual's personal characteristics interacting with many levels of his or her social and physical environments—called microsystems, mesosystems, exosystems, macrosystems, and chronosystems.

Ecological Model of Person-Environment Fit: (M. Powell Lawton and Lucille Nahemow) includes a sense of place with the experience of aging. One's ability to remain in place is examined in terms of how well one fits in within one's own home environment or geographic setting. The fit of person and place is assessed by the match of an older person's personal capabilities and level of autonomy to that person's environmental demands.

Elderly mystique: a societal view of aging and expectations of older people that is based on ageism and, therefore, limited and not portraying real accounts of aging.

Embedded mixed methods design: include both quantitative and qualitative elements together with one element enhancing ("supplementing") another. Embedded designs can be both sequential and concurrent.

Embodiment: using the body and its interaction with the social world in research.

Emergent methods: methods moving beyond and integrating aspects of quantitative, qualitative, and mixed-methods designs. For example, researchers becoming more enmeshed in the data and research process, using participants' words as performance, advocating for a group as part of the group, or being openly aware of power differentials and conflicting roles.

Emergent theories: new theories in gerontology. Some focus more deeply at the cellular levels to expose the biological agents of the aging process. Others add additional political and economic determinants, as well as the impact of societal stereotypes about age, or culture-based theories along with spiritual, intra-individual ones.

Emic: term for studying a group when one is inside, or part of, a group.

Episodic memory: remembering personal daily details.

Error Theories of Biological Aging: see aging as a mistake or abnormal change in biological processes.

Ethics: codes of behavior or practice. Ethics in aging research refer mainly to codes of conduct and the informed, fair treatment of the people being studied. Research principles that assess and weigh the rights of participants and those of researchers in perusing studies that may advance the field.

Ethnodrama: the process of taking interview or written/recorded text from an individual being studied and creating a dramatic interpretation or performance of that work. The performance can be filmed or audio recorded.

Ethnodramatic practices: include the researchers in the narrative process and let them act out or perform stories of those they study. Can be in the form of visual stories and poetry.

Ethnogerontology: (Jacqueline Johnson) includes the role of race, ethnicity, and culture in research on biological, psychological, and social processes related to aging.

Ethno-Goggles: eyeglasses that take video and photos of what the researcher is viewing. The goggles also include a microphone to capture the researcher's spoken reflections.

Ethnographer as instrument: the researcher records data and his or her own observations, field notes, printed materials, and audio and visual materials; can act as the data.

Ethnography: a qualitative method of studying a group of people in a society or social setting. This method has been integral to the understanding of older persons and their lived experiences and social worlds from the individual's perspective. The researcher becomes embedded with the persons he or she is studying and remaining with the group for a long period of time. The goal of ethnographic work is to understand an experience or events from a participant's point of view without having the researcher impose his or her own point of view on the events as they happen. See Autoethnography, Critical ethnography, Digital ethnography, Participatory ethnography, and Performance ethnography.

Ethnopoetics: the use of poetry or the creation of poetry through participants' own words.

Etic: term for studying a group when one is outside, or not part of, a group.

Evaluation to Sign Consent (ESC) measure: asks persons with potential cognitive impairment about the risks, benefits, and ways to withdraw from a study before they participate. The researcher outlines acceptable answers for each question, and the participant must discuss them to be included in the study.

Executive function: higher-cognitive skills needed to perform complex tasks, organize information, think abstractly, and adapt to new situations and act.

Exempt Reviews: cover research that meets the Common Rule's definition of posing only minimal risk: the same level of discomfort of harm in everyday life/usual activities. For exempt reviews, participants must be 18 years of age or older and not from a Common Rule's defined vulnerable group. Studies applying for an exempt review cannot include any activities that may put participants at criminal risk and cannot identify participants. The studies can include research in educational settings, some survey and interview procedures or observation of public behavior, secondary analysis of existing data, chart review, or taste/food quality evaluation.

Exogenous change: occurs when other events not part of the study itself happen during the study. These outside events, then, can impact your findings.

Expansion of hierarchical Age-Period-Cohort (APC) designs: include the application of latent class analysis at the individual and group levels and increased use of hierarchical APC models.

Expedited Reviews: cover research that is judged to involve no more than minimal risk to subject and includes appropriate informed-consent procedures with benefits to participants. According to the Common Rule, the project must pose no more than minimal risk, not pose criminal risk, not include classified information, and be in one of the following seven categories. The medical category types include the study being a clinical or drug study, noninvasive biological data (such as blood draws), collection of non-invasive samples (nail clippings or teeth), and non-invasive procedures (such as x-rays). The social and behavioral categories include analysis of materials and data not collected for research purposes; data from video, audio, and digital recordings; and analysis of group behavior through focus groups, interviews, surveys, program evaluations, and oral histories.

Experimental group: group receiving the intervention.

Explanatory studies: (also called "confirmatory") quantitative studies that seek to find a relationship for a phenomenon or events being studied to generate more research.

Exploratory studies: quantitative studies that seek to begin to research an issue of interest via a pilot or smaller-scale study.

Face validity: asks the question: on its face, or by general reading, does the question or instrument relate to the concept the researcher is claiming to study?

Facility and Administration (F &A) or Indirect Costs Rates (IDCs): fees added to the budget of grant proposals submitted by universities. These fees cover the services that the university provides the researcher, such as electricity and place, informational and technology help, and library resources.

Federal Grant Outcomes: after review by a Scientific Review Group, a proposal can be either moved toward discussion by the full panel at the group's meeting or stopped. Proposals stopped at the first review may be scored by each member of the review panel prior to the section's in-person meeting but not discussed ("ND") by the full panel when it meets. If major concerns with ethical issues, or with the human subjects' protections sections exist, a proposal receives an "NR" or not recommended. These proposals do not move forward in the process. If a proposal is reviewed, ranked, and scored at the second review by the SRG, those funded will receive a Notice of Award (NoA) and begin executing the grant's activities.

Feminist gerontological theory: focuses on the difference gender creates in the process of aging to understanding the lived experience of both aging and being a woman.

Fence-sitters: those who cling to the middle or neutral value of a scale with an odd number of responses. Eliminating the neutral/middle value by using a second prompt is a good option. This prompt lets the respondent provide a non-neutral opinion. See Prompt.

Field notes: a researcher's personal reflections and observations of people, actions, and events, as participant or participant observer in the field, are key data and may include direct narrative and quotes of participants. These should be written (by hand or electronically) or audio recorded throughout the course of the study while the experiences are fresh in the researcher's mind.

Filter questions: assess eligibility or appropriateness of other questions that follow.

Fluid intelligence: problem solving in new settings decreases with age.

Foundation grants: grant awards geared toward nonprofit organizations that have received 501(c)(3) nonprofit status from the Internal Revenue Service. They can be offered by foundations, professional organizations, and regions.

Free Radical or Oxidative Stress Theory: states that cells need oxygen to live, but, if unattached (as an unpaired electron, free energy, bonded with other molecules), oxygen can damage cells. This process has been linked to late-onset diabetes, arthritis, cataracts, hypertension, and atherosclerosis.

Freewriting: a writing exercise using a fixed interval of time to brainstorm and write the first thoughts one has about a topic. Freewriting is free from grammar and punctuation rules. The goal is to further an idea or develop a new one by writing or drawing a conceptual map.

Frequency distribution: table summarizing counts or percent for each category of a variable.

Full Board Review: occurs for research that is judged to involve more than minimal risk. It must, therefore, be presented to the entire review board for discussion and consideration of approval. All members of the IRB meet and discuss these applications.

Gaming: a research-design option, such as trivia, map/treasure hunting, or online personalities/images, avatars.

Gatekeeper: a person who is key in getting access to the site and may help in the researcher's first contact with participants.

Geographic information systems (GIS): computerized systems mapping positions of people and places on earth. GIS have been used to track and analyze older peoples' movement in their neighborhoods.

Geriatrics: the study of the medical, biological, and health-related aspects of the aging process and older persons.

Gerontological imagination: building upon C. Wright Mills's sociological imagination, the gerontological imagination looks at both the individual-level and the societal-level factors that impact aging.

Gerontology (social gerontology): the study of the biological, psychological, and social processes and changes that occur as part of aging and in older populations. Gerontology, though often used interchangeably, must be differentiated from the term "geriatrics," which has a more biomedical focus.

Gerotranscendence: (Tornstam) describes changes in an older person's developmental processes and relationship to the outside world. Gerotranscendent persons develop a more fluid sense of time—the cosmic view of the past felt as present or the past and present merge. The individual feels more connected to the universe and sees deeper meaning and insights into everyday events. There is a broadmindedness, acceptance of all positive and negative aspects of one's life, new openness to seeing the world, and comfort with the unknown.

"Going native" ("going in too deep"): a negative label or accusation that a researcher is losing his or her perspective and taking the cause of those studied.

Government/federal grants: grant opportunities for aging research. They offer larger funding amounts and are awarded to researchers at academic and research institutions. See Grant-funding mechanisms.

Grant-funding mechanisms: the National Institutes of Health (NIH) use codes to help researchers select the best funding route. NIH types include Research Grants (R series), Career Development Awards (K series), Research Training and Fellowships (T & F series), and Program Project/Center Grants (P series). Federal grant proposals offer all technical and content details and are submitted electronically using two platforms: Grants.gov and eRA Commons.

Grant proposals: reports to funders that contain stylized elements. Grant proposals can be written for several levels of funders—from community-based and regional funding organizations to federal funders. Grants can be awarded to individuals, universities, or community organizations.

"Grey digital divide": term indicating that older persons were left out of technology use.

Groundedness: counts of individual codes and code groups as frequencies in qualitative software programs.

Grounded theory: (Barney Glaser and Anselm Strauss) a qualitative method that develops theory from an ongoing, open-ended questioning process with participants. The interrelatedness of concepts leads to the development of theory of how the events of processes studied relate to each other. The grounded-theory process involves several elements in creating theory from data. These key elements are an inductive process, rich data, theoretical sampling, constant comparative method, memo use, saturation, researcher's self-reflexiveness, theory production, and a different approach to the literature review.

Grounded theory coding practices: in a grounded-theory approach, several types of coding practices are used, ultimately, to generate a theory. Coding to ground theory is iterative—meaning the transcripts and data are read and reviewed. The sequence is often thought of as open/*in vivo* coding → axial coding → selective coding. See Open coding, *In vivo* coding, Axial coding, and Selective coding.

Guided autobiography: older person-based; self-written narrative; led through group processes.

Hawthorne Effect: refers to the impact of a researcher, or the effect of the experience of being studied, upon the behaviors of those studied. People in a study may modify their behaviors because they are being studied and want to be seen a certain way or live up to the researcher's expectations.

Healthy Aging: a popular theme in the discourse on aging. Healthy aging theories were featured in the U.S. 2015 White House Conference on Aging and the National Institutes of Health–created web-based "senior" healthy-aging topic directory.

Hearing changes: begin at age 40 or 50 with noticeable changes noted after 60, when about 30% of people report some hearing loss. Rates of hearing difficulty increase with age. Normal age-related changes include hearing loss, presbycusis (loss of high-pitched and other frequencies), and tinnitus (or ringing in the ears).

Histograms: a visual display, with the categories or responses of a variable using bars to represent counts or percentages.

"Hit and run," helicopter, and "smash and grab" tactics: a negative label or accusation that a researcher is maintaining contact with the communities only to gather data and rapidly leave.

Human-Computer Interaction (HCI): examines the relationship between aging and technologies as a remedy for health concerns and physical and cognitive decline.

Hypothesis statement: contains two variables (one independent and one dependent). A typical hypothesis statement would be: "If the independent variable increases (or decreases or changes), then the dependent variable will increase (or decrease or change)."

Hypothesis testing: involves two hypotheses. The null hypothesis states that there is "no difference" between the groups being tested. The alternate hypothesis is where the real relationship between groups is stated. In a two-tailed hypothesis test, the researcher seeks only to find difference between groups tested. In a one-tailed hypothesis test, the alternate hypothesis is making a directional statement about the relationship between the groups tested (e.g., with greater-than or less-than statements).

Identical sampling: uses the same sample of participants in all the parts of a mixed-methods design.

Identity politics: the idea of basing decisions and actions on shared common characteristics with a person or group.

Idiosyncratic variation: a question reading differently to someone because of the way the question is constructed.

Impact factors: scores used to rank journals. Journals with higher scores have more of their articles cited. Since gerontology encompasses many fields (psychology, sociology, social work, public health, etc.), a journal may have a different impact factor depending upon the field in which it is grouped.

Independent t-tests (or two sample-t tests): test hypotheses and look at significant differences in means of two groups or interventions on a dependent variable.

Index (index score): a summary measure compiled from answers to several questions about a topic.

Induction/inductive approach: using data to generate theory (see Abductive and Deductive approach).

Inductive coding: (also called bottom-up coding) in qualitative analysis, inductive codes arise from concepts and ideas noted when analyzing data. They are not pre-determined categories.

Inference transferability: allows researchers to apply findings of one mixed-methods study to other settings. It refers to how well and in what settings a mixed-methods study's results can be applied more broadly. Inference transferability depends upon design quality and interpretive rigor.

Inferential statistics: use findings from a sample or samples to generalize back to the larger population. The most commonly selected type of inferential-statistics process is hypothesis testing.

Informed consent: standard set by the Department of Health and Human Services' (DHHS) Common Rule for research with human subjects. Includes three key elements: information about the study, risk, and benefits are provided so participants can make an informed decision; the information is relayed in a way the participant can understand; and the participant must understand that participation is voluntary.

Institutional Review Boards (IRBs): are bodies made up of at least five interdisciplinary, varied researchers and community members to make sure the rights of human subjects in research are protected. IRBs seek to ensure that participants agree to participate in a study through an informed consent based on knowledge of what is required as part of the study and potential related risks and benefits. See Exempt Review, Expedited Review, or Full Board Review.

Instrumental Activities of Daily Living (IADLs): complex tasks performed as part of routine daily activities. These include using the telephone, shopping, completing housework, driving/using transportation, taking medication, doing laundry, and/or managing finances. Also see ADLs.

Integrated Model of Social Gerontology: (Gretchen Alkema and Dawn Alley) builds upon the inclusion of societal forces on aging and includes cultural, economic, political, environmental, and historical influences.

Interactive effect: recognition that the presence of the interviewer and his or her personal characteristics and reactions to a story impacts the way a story is told.

Inter-coder reliability or inter-coder agreement: a way to measure consistency in coding when a team approach is used in qualitative research. To establish inter-coder reliability, two or more coders code independently and then compare the matching or sameness of coding. The percentage of code matching by the team is reported. Coding differences are reconciled through discussion and agreement. If a different code or value was assigned by a researcher, both researchers discuss the case and resolve the issue through consensus and refined coding strategies moving forward in analysis. See Inter-Coding Reliability (ICR) statistic.

Inter-Coding Reliability (ICR) statistic: can calculate inter-coder reliability while removing the possibility that the matching codes were made by chance. One method is providing pre-highlighted text blocks selected by one researcher to other researchers, and then having the second researcher or group assign codes. Another option is to have coding matched on deductive (pre-determined) codes only, which may work better than assessing matching on inductive or emergent coding. An example of an IRC statistic is Klaus Krippendorff's alpha.

Intergenerational exchange: sharing of time and resources among groups of different generations.

Inter-item reliability: (also called internal consistency) means that the researcher has included enough items or questions to measure all aspects of the concept being measured.

"International spotlights": feature created in a gerontology journal to highlight the need to understand aging globally.

Inter-observer reliability or inter-rater reliability: implies agreement between many observers.

Interpretative agreement: the inferences made in a mixed-methods design make sense for all groups being studied.

Interrater coefficients: indicate the percent of agreement between scores or raters.

Intersectionality: builds upon earlier concepts of multiple jeopardy (or the combination of marginalized statuses in society) and attempts to bring in all social positions and the role of society in viewing, constructing, and regulating aging into one model to research. It includes the interaction of many identities but does not use the concept of a master status or dominant identity as more important than other identities.

Interval-ratio: refers to items with an equal or fixed distance between items (e.g., age in number of years) or a true zero.

Intra-individual variability: lifespan theories focus on allowing for more heterogeneity in developmental processes and paths for each individual.

Intra-observer or intra-rater reliability: observations made by the same observer should be in agreement.

Intrinsic case: a case chosen because of interest in that specific, distinct case.

"Investigator's imprint": term describing the researcher's presence and effect upon the narrative process.

***In vivo* codes:** codes based on or created from the direct quotes or text of documents to reflect the individual's language. These codes arise from exact words or phrases uttered by a participant.

Item-level missing data: data missing for a person from individual items (or questions) on a survey.

Journal Decisions: after peer review, a journal editor provides the author with a decision of acceptance with no revision, acceptance with minor revision, acceptance with major revision, or rejection. The editor culls the reviewers' comments and recommendations and sends his or her decision back to the author(s) with narrative comments.

Journal headings: standard section headings for journal articles: an introduction, literature review/theoretical framework, research questions/hypotheses, methodology and design (sample/participants, data collection/procedure, and concepts/indicators), data analysis (recoding/statistical tests), and findings/discussion/conclusion (limitations of current study, future directions, and policy implications). The end materials can be endnotes, references, authors' biographical information, sources of funding, and a statement of each author's contribution/conflict of interest.

Journals: a common venue to publish research results. They are scholarly, peer-reviewed publications that select manuscripts from authors to print at scheduled intervals (two to 12 times) throughout the year both in print and online. Online journals will also publish ahead of print versions of accepted articles and publish additional materials—such as supplementary data sets. The mechanics of publication begin with the selection of a journal as an appropriate place to publish an individual manuscript.

Jung, Carl: saw development as not fixed but lifelong. He suggested that midlife, the "afternoon" of one's life, involves a transition where goals and expectations are evaluated. During this time of change, concerns about one's physical self move toward achieving balance or being in harmony with nature.

Key informants: (also called stakeholders or gatekeepers) are from the group being studied or knowledgeable about the topic of the study. They help the researcher gain access to participants by building trust and rapport with those in the field.

Language abilities: vocabulary and comprehension of words remains stable with age, and some say are better than a younger person's aptitude. Aspects of language negatively affected by age include language production, having lesser idea density in speech, less ability to understand distorted speech, and word loss ("words on the tip of one's tongue").

Latent class analysis predictors: are underlying factors (indicating group membership) that may cause the relationship between variables.

"Leave-behind" questionnaire: self-administered and printed survey use include a questionnaire or survey left with the respondent and can be completed and returned at his or her convenience.

Legitimization: addresses validity in mixed-methods designs.

Level of measurement: ways of classifying variables. Nominal variables are those that are names or labels (e.g., gender, race, ethnicity, geographic location). Ordinal variables are those that can be ranked or ordered (e.g., ratings of skilled-care facilities' treatment of residents—low, medium, high—or health as excellent, good, fair, poor), and interval-ratio refers to items with a true zero and equal or fixed distance between items (e.g., age in number of years).

Lifecourse Perspective (or Approach): (Glen Elder) examines how transitions during the early years in one's life, the time in which one lives, and social connections shape lived experiences. In this theory, individuals have agency, or the ability, to exert their influence and make changes within the worlds in which they live.

Life histories: older person's self-story; told to another.

Life history graph approach: plots multiple dimensions of life events and levels of population at once, like the true lifecourse approach, which places individual lives in a societal and temporal context.

Life review: older person's self-story; told to another with explicit evaluative or resolution-based purpose; can be guided.

Life stories: older person's self-story; told to another or written by self; a more generic term.

Likert scale: a five-point (or seven-point) scale with non-dichotomous answers (i.e., 1 = strongly disagree to 5 = strongly agree) to be synonymous with the survey method. When using scales, it is important to address *fence-sitters*, those who cling to the middle or neutral value of a scale with an odd-number of responses—for example, those choosing a "3" on a scale of 1 to 5. This middle-value choice does not reflect an opinion of either agreement or disagreement.

Listwise deletion: removes a case with *any* missing data from analysis. Some warn, though, that this is often a software default; the missing cases may differ from those remaining in the data and create issues of representativeness and bias and can remove data that are important to the study.

Logic models: a model or framework used in program evaluation. It assesses relationships among resources, activities, outputs, outcomes, and goals.

Logistic regression: a multivariate test to examine which independent variables significantly predict variation in a *dichotomous* dependent variable.

Longitudinal designs: collecting data over several time points. They are used to fix the ordering of variables in time, and are one way to address causal ordering in research design. A *(fixed) panel design* follows the same group of people throughout time periods (or waves) and best establishes causal changes within those studied.

Macro-level forces: influences at the level of society, culture, and country.

Map: (or mapping) a visual representation of the relationship between codes in qualitative data. Mapping helps a researcher understand that codes are related to each other as codes and subcodes or related codes at the same level.

Marginalized: a term used for persons or groups assigned/given lesser power or status in a society.

Master narratives: cultural scripts for behaviors or actions that exist in a particular society that may work their way into an individual's own story or narrative.

Matching: participants in a quasi-experiment can be matched on several characteristics. They may have great differences in other non-matched characteristics. These non-matched characteristics may introduce difference and bias.

Measures of central tendency: describe the most common or central values for data by level of measurement. The arithmetic mean is the average of all values of the variable. The median is the value that divides the distribution in half. The mode is the value, or values, that occur most frequently.

Measures of variation: describe the range, dispersion, or spread of values for data by level of measurement. The standard deviation is used to tell how far values are from the mean, and the range shows the spread of scores from lowest to highest. The range calculates the distance between the highest and lowest scores.

Meditating variables: are a causal link or those through which the independent variables operate to impact the dependent variable. Mediator variables connect (or intervene with) the independent and dependent variables' relationship. Four criteria must be established for a mediation: (1) the independent variable predicts the dependent variable; (2) the independent variable predicts the mediator variable; (3) the mediator variable predicts the dependent variable; and (4) mediation is complete when, after the mediator is introduced, the relationship between the independent and dependent variables no longer exists.

Memoirs: older, person-based, self-written narratives with memories of times and events as a focus.

Memos: serve as ways to record decision making during the data-analysis process, to collect the researcher's reactions and thoughts, and as an analytical tool. Memos also track coding definitions and coding decisions. Memos in software can aid in coding or rethinking and examining the relationship between codes/concepts throughout the analysis. They can be analytical (an examination of the materials/observations), methodological (record thoughts/ongoing issues with methodology), or theoretical in nature (exploring relationships between concepts and how they relate to each other, to form a theory or conceptual framework).

Meta-inferences: tell the reader which groups mixed-methods finding can be applied to—similar to generalizability in quantitative studies or transferability in qualitative ones.

Meta-reviews: summarize and provide an overview of literature published about a topic to date. Meta-reviews also outline current debates, critical issues, and key authors writing about a topic in the field.

Method: the process a researcher uses to collect data as part of the study. A research method is the way a researcher actually carries out and conducts his or her research. Methods are often confused with methodology but are a part of an overall methodology. See Methodology.

Methodological memos: provide an opportunity to record thoughts and any ongoing issues with your methodology—e.g., difficulties with questions or the interview script, locating participants, etc.

Methodology: an underlying philosophy a researcher uses as a basis to conceptualize and design all elements of a study—from selection of theory to presentation of findings. It includes the researcher's use of an underlying philosophy (worldview or epistemological perspective) that is the basis of the study's design and his or her approach and relationship to participants. Methodology includes rules of how a study is conducted and is broader than the method alone, and it can be a quantitative approach (using numerical data), a qualitative approach (using textual data), or a mixed-methods approach (using both data types).

Mini-Mental State Exam (MMSE): test developed by Folstein to assess memory and for the presence of cognitive impairment.

Missing at random (MAR): occurs when data missed on one variable is related to answers on another question, variable, or event. The data are missed due to a relationship with another data point.

Missing cases or data: occur as part of the data-collection process in aging/gerontological research and cause problems in analysis if not handled correctly. Data can be intentionally missed—meaning respondents can refuse to answer a question or say they "don't know," or a question can be "non-applicable" to that particular respondent. Each of these responses can be coded with a researcher-defined value. Questions or items unintentionally left blank or data omissions, made when entering data, are truly missed data. A researcher must describe missing data by its being expected/unexpected, the scope of the missing data, and possible patterns that exist in the data. Variables with missing data can be deleted (or removed) or have values imputed (filled in).

Missing data completely at random (MCAR): implies there is no pattern to the way data are missing. It is difficult to determine MCAR, but data are in this category are thought to not greatly influence outcomes.

Missing-data patterns: can be completely at random (MCAR), missing at random (MAR), or missing not random (MNAR).

Missing not random (MNAR): missing data are related to the nature of a particular question.

Mixed-methods approach: uses numerical and textual data types.

Mixed-Methods Designs: the combination of quantitative and qualitative designs is classified according to two major dimensions: time order (do quantitative and qualitative parts occur at the same time, or does one follow the other?) and paradigm emphasis (do quantitative and qualitative parts have equal status, or does one part having a dominant status?). Types of mixed-methods designs are sequential explanatory, sequential exploratory, convergent parallel, embedded, transformative, and multi-level.

Mixing of biological, performance-based measures: studies now combine self-rated and performance-based measures with biomarkers circulating in an older person's blood to define physical performance and disease risk across the lifespan.

(Model of) Successful Aging: (John Rowe and Robert Kahn) social components to theories of aging and health. Successful aging is defined by (1) the ability to maintain low risk of disease and disease-related disability; (2) high mental and physical functioning; and (3) an active engagement with life. A revised version of this theory, Successful Aging 2.0, is underway.

Mode of administration: surveys can be delivered in a variety of ways: self-administered, telephone, and as a face-to-face interview. Surveys can be sent by mail or via the Internet.

Moderating variables: are those that interact with the independent variables to produce different outcomes in the dependent variables. In moderation, the relationship between the independent and dependent variables changes across levels of the moderator.

Modernization, Theory of: the idea is that as a society becomes more industrialized and undergoes an economic modernization, older persons lose their former, traditional, and respected roles. At the time of its introduction, this theory introduced structural elements, such as economic changes in society, into a largely individualistic and psychologically based view of the aging process.

Motivational Theory of Life-Span: (Richard Schulz and Jutta Heckhausen) sees the motivation to meet goals as an ongoing process throughout life. The theory includes primary control (where older persons change the external world to meet their needs) and secondary control (where older persons adapt themselves to meet changes in the external world).

Multilevel sampling: takes multiple samples in a mixed-methods design.

Multiphase designs: mixed-methods studies done in more than two phases.

Multiple imputation: technique that uses existing information from other variables for that case to create data to fill in for the missing data.

Multiple Jeopardy, Theory of: examines the impact of a multitude of social statuses that one may occupy simultaneously upon the experience of aging or being old. Old age can add to any existing group status, such as an older person's race, ethnicity, gender, sexual orientation, social class, and health. An older person with non-hegemonic (i.e., non-dominant) societal statuses in more than one of these categories faces multiple jeopardy.

Multiple regression: a multivariate test for the significant effects of multiple independent variables in predicting variation on a dependent variable. The procedure tests how much each independent variable—and how much all independent variables combined—contribute to variance in the dependent variable.

Multivariate analysis of covariance (MANCOVA): tests for significant difference in two or more groups upon *two or more/multiple-outcome or dependent variables* (like MANOVA) but adds in control or other covariates that might impact the dependent variable. See MANOVA.

Multivariate analysis of variance (MANOVA): tests for significant difference in two or more groups upon *two or more/multiple-outcome or dependent variables.* See ANOVA.

Narrative analysis: a qualitative design that is an analysis of the content of the story and how it conveys meaning on the part of the teller. Or the analysis can be about the way a story is told, of the text and dialogue itself. Narrative accounts can be spoken or written. The narrative process is not about assessing a universal "truth" but analyzing the story, itself, from many vantage points. Narratives can be self-written or collected on the part of the older person with the older person as author and also recorder of the story.

Narrative analysis options: include content analysis, thematic analysis, use of elements of case studies, discourse, or conversations as data for analysis. The *holistic approach* examines the whole text, while the *categorical* reviews parts of it. A *content-analysis approach* generates themes from the text, while a *form-based analysis* examines the story's structure and the way it is told. One can also look at the story, in its entirety, for the self-assigned role of the storyteller in the story, the story in relation to the larger culture, ways the story may be retold, the storyteller's interpretation of the story and its structure, and unique features of a story.

Nested sampling: means that the entire mixed-methods study uses the same sample of participants. One part of the nested design uses the whole sample, and another part of the design uses only a smaller part of that same sample of participants.

Neural plasticity: the ability of the brain to change and compensate for loss. Can refer to neuronal changes (the growth, change, or loss of neurons and dendrites in the brain).

Nomenclature: in mixed-methods designs, the prioritized method in all capital letters and the lesser prioritized methods in lowercase letters. A plus sign is used for convergent methods, and arrows are used for sequential methods. For example, a mostly qualitative study—with some quantitative aspects—in which the qualitative work leads to the quantitative would be noted: QUAL —> quant. Methodologists are calling for extension of this notation system.

Nominal variables: are those that are names or labels (e.g., gender, race, ethnicity, geographic location).

Non-amnestic: mild cognitive impairment can be experienced as periods of forgetfulness with changes in executive function.

Non-probability-based sampling technique: non-random sampling options. They include *convenience (or availability) sampling* (selecting readily available cases and are often used for pilot testing), *quota sampling* (selecting a sample based on a characteristic of note, but these selection items are not matched to their representation in the population), *purposive sampling* (each element of the sample selected for a specific reason or purpose, such as knowledge about an issue or expertise), and *snowball sampling* (begins with one participant who then recommends another who recommends another; it is used with populations or groups that do not have a sampling frame or are tough to reach/locate).

Non-response reasons: notation as to why a person refused to respond to a question of a survey.

Normative age-related sensory changes: physical health changes in sight, touch, taste, smell, and sensory-perception that accompany normal chronological aging impact research with older persons.

Notice of Award (NoA): notification by a funder that a proposal will be funded.

Not discussed ("ND"): a term assigned to federal grant proposals that are stopped at the first review. They may be scored but are not discussed by the review group when they meet.

Not recommended ("NR"): a term assigned to federal grant proposals when major concerns with ethical issues, or with the human subjects' protections sections, exist. These proposals do not move forward in the process.

Null hypothesis: states that there is "no difference" between the groups being tested.

Objectivism: a philosophical stance or belief in the existence of an objective, external reality that can be measured and tested.

Omit (omitted) narratives: researchers may seek to leave out segments of text or phrases from coding that marginalize groups further or oppress groups—because reproducing the text may perpetuate the oppression. Instead, researchers place blanks or stricken-through text in their place. Or researchers can actively include resistance narratives in the data analysis, exploring the reasons behind the participants' refusal to participate.

One-tailed test: in a one-tailed hypothesis test, the alternate hypothesis is making a directional statement about the relationship between the groups tested (e.g., with greater-than or less-than statements).

Online methodologies: research design in gerontology using online environments and technology—can refer to online surveys, email questionnaires, online groups, a smartphone, a tablet, social media, online communities, and gaming or extend to sensors and robots. See online or virtual environment.

Online or virtual environment: site of conducting research using an online setting or tools. Can be online chatting, email, smartphone-based visual conversations (via Skype, FaceTime, or Hangouts), blogs (for comment posting) and interactive webpages where users can co-create content (wikis), or posts on social media (tweets).

Open codes: codes that arise from the data and are not predetermined by the researcher. While reviewing the data many times, the researcher begins to see patterns and categories arise in the data. These categories are recorded or noted as open codes.

Open-ended questions: survey questions with space for narrative comments. Open-ended questions generally begin with a prompt, and the respondent can then answer in his or her own words.

Operationalization: defining concepts in the study in detail, making them into variables that can be measured. See Conceptualization.

Oral histories: stories about an older person collected by another.

Ordinal variables: are those that can be ranked or ordered (e.g., ratings of skilled-care facilities' treatment of residents—low, medium, high—or health as excellent, good, fair, poor).

"Orphaned in research": term referring to older persons being historically excluded from clinical and social research or older persons included in some studies with questionable ethics.

Output or results windows: in quantitative software programs, these windows display the result of tests and transformations dictated by syntax or point-and-click commands. In SPSS, the Output window contains the results of all the calculations done by the quantitative software program and displays results in tabular form. Log columns are included as a window within the output or results windows and provide an alert for errors that occur when running analysis.

Paired t-test: uses repeated measures to look for significant differences in a mean for the same group at two different times. A paired t-test is often used for pre- and post-test comparisons.

Pairwise deletion: a way to address missing data by removing cases only if they have missing data on variables that are of key interest in the study's research questions, hypotheses, or analysis.

Paradata: data about the process of data collection. Can be tracing of typed keys, how a person navigates in an online survey, or timing in answering a question.

Parallel sampling: involves different samples or participants in each part of a mixed-methods design, but all participants are selected from the same underlying population.

Partial correlational designs (partial or control tables): introduce a third variable and look at the association between the two original variables in the presence of the third variable. This third variable is also called a control variable.

Participatory action research (PAR): designs in which persons impacted by an issue or problem define the problem and seek to find solutions.

Participatory ethnographic videos: researchers and the community in the study create a video that addresses a community-based issue in a shared, ongoing process.

Partnership of Consent Protocol: flowchart to determine if informed consent or assent protocol that can be used with individual participants. This protocol encourages researchers to really understand what are usual/typical states and behaviors of the persons with impairment so the researcher can then fully assess discomfort or a change in willingness to participate.

Path analysis: examines significant indirect and direct relationships between variables and upon the dependent variable. Independent variables are called exogenous, and dependent variables are call endogenous.

Pearson's correlation coefficient (r): a measure of bivariate association, ranges from -1 to $+1$, indicating the strength of the relationship between the variables. Values closer to zero indicate a weak relationship, and ±1 is a strong relationship.

Peer review: comments and feedback from reviewers as part of the publication process. Reviewers' identities are not known to the author(s).

Peer-reviewed journals: these journals publish academic articles after they have been reviewed for rigor and edited by other researchers active in the field. Journal articles have a general format or structure: title, author(s) with affiliation, abstract, keywords, introduction, literature review/theoretical framework, research questions/hypotheses, methodology and design (sample/participants, data collection/procedure, and concepts/indicators), data analysis (theme coding/statistical tests), findings/discussion/conclusion (limitations of current study, future directions, and policy implications), notes, references, authors' biographical information, sources of funding, a statement of each author's contribution/conflict of interest, and received and accepted publication dates.

Performance ethnography: blends research and artistic expression (such as spoken word or dance) to address social issues.

Period effects: these are changes that occur across calendar years or time intervals. A period effect is the result of all of society experiencing an event or phenomenon that occurs during the study period. The event or experience is not unique or restricted solely to older adults (see Age-period-cohort [APC] effects).

Person-level missing data: occurs when a particular individual did not respond to *any* questions; his or her responses are missing entirely.

Phenomenological accounts: used by researchers when they want to understand how an individual makes his or her own personal meaning of a situation or experience. These accounts see the participant as the one who deciphers meaning and assigns cause and effect to events, using his or her own worldview. Participants give the researcher access to their lifeworld and how they give conscious meaning to or interpret their lived experiences, how they organize thoughts and feelings, and how they interpret all the encounters in their daily social world. It is important that researchers are aware of their own assumptions and do not apply their view to the individual(s) studied; participants must interpret and assign their own meaning to events.

Philosophical standpoint: the overall philosophy underlying how a researcher sets up a study. See Positivist, Constructionist, Subjectivist, Transformative, and Pragmatist.

Photovoice (or self-photography): a research method providing participants with cameras or other devices to record, capture, and reflect upon their self-created pictures of their daily lives. The photos themselves can be analyzed for the intention of the picture taker or the theme and content of the photo. Photos can also be analyzed for artistic content and merit (e.g., lighting, angle, color, positioning of items within the frame).

Pie charts: depict responses as portions or sections of a circle.

Placebo effect: when positive effects are seen without administering a treatment or intervention.

Poetry: older person-based, self-written narrative.

Political economy of aging: (Carroll Estes) these theories state there is a dominant (hegemonic), negative view of older people in society. Social institutions, such as social services and laws, are designed to support and keep this view alive in debates. Social institutions, then, have the power to regulate older peoples' lives and control aging and older people by the policies they create.

Population: a sampling frame that includes all possible elements—for example, conducting a census, like the U.S. Decennial Census. If drawn systematically from the entire population, sampling is a good way to conduct studies with smaller groups and infer/refer back to the entire population.

Positivism: a philosophy or worldview associated with the traditional quantitative "scientific approach" to study people. A positivist approach argues studies are objectively generalizable; post-positivists use the scientific method with variables, hypotheses, and theory to quantify and explain reality.

Pragmatism: a philosophy or worldview that avoids construction-of-reality debates and lets the researcher apply methods in the real world. The researcher is not interested in getting at a universal truth or being linked to only one philosophy—the real goal is problem solving, or how the data and outcomes can help solve real-world problems.

"Predatory journals": "fake" or questionable publishers with similar-sounding names to real ones. Jeffrey Beall created this term and created a list of predatory journals to help distinguish real publishers from more "fake" ones.

Predictive studies: quantitative studies that seek to establish cause and effect among variables in a study.

Pre-post testing and experimental design: a quantitative design with roots in experimental methods. The two groups are either the group receiving the intervention (experimental) or the group not (control). Often, the researcher will choose naturally existing groups. He or she may also match persons in each group based on similar characteristics (such as age, race, ethnicity, gender, age, socioeconomic status, etc.) so that these other aspects of one's social position do not impact the study. See Control groups, Experimental groups, Intervention, and Matching.

Probability-based sampling technique: random-based sampling options. When the sample is selected, it closely represents the underlying population from which it is drawn, so findings can be generalized back to the population from which the sample was selected. See Simple random sampling (with/without replacement), Systematic sampling, Cluster sampling, and Stratified sampling.

Procedural memory: learning new skills.

Program evaluation: a report to an employer or organization used to make decisions about whether programmatic goals and objectives were met.

Programmed Theories: suggest cells have an inherent "lifespan" and die/lose effectiveness over time.

Prompt: a guided question after a neutral response on a scale. A prompt lets the respondent provide a non-neutral opinion—for example, "If you had to choose a non-neutral value, would you say you: strongly agree, agree, disagree, or strongly disagree?" See Fence-sitters.

Prospective memory: remembering future tasks and events.

Proxy: another person (other than the person of interest in a study) who provides information.

Proxy consent: consent for research that is given by someone other than the older person or person of interest.

Pseudonyms: fictitious names of participants/those studied.

Purposive sampling: each element of the sample is selected for a specific reason or purpose, such as knowledge about an issue or expertise.

P-values: relate to the chance of making a Type I error. Errors can occur when a researcher makes decisions during hypothesis testing. An alpha (α) or Type I error occurs if a researcher rejects the null hypothesis (of "no difference") when it is true. In other words, the researcher finds differences between the sample and populations he or she is testing or two samples he or she is testing—when there is no difference. Researchers set P-values (from lowest to highest significance level) at $p \leq 0.10$ (marginal significance), $p \leq 0.05$ (*), $p \leq 0.01$ (**), or $p \leq 0.01$ (***). The lower the p-value, the less likely a relationship is found by chance—or, conversely, the more confident a researcher can be that the relationship he or she finds is not due to chance. P-values are affected by both large and small samples sizes. See Type I and Type II errors.

Qualitative analysis: consists of taking narrative data and applying them to the coding options chosen as part of the design of the project. It can take on several forms: thematic analysis (as in qualitative content analysis or grounded-theory construction) or narrative analyses (as in conversation, discourse, and critical-discourse analysis).

Qualitative approach: uses textual data.

Qualitative design: best used when the researcher seeks to explore a topic in aging about which little is known or where more in-depth, first-person accounts are needed. A qualitative approach can be seen as a shift from a more positivistic view of reality that sees it as objective or something external that can be independently measured to a stance that believes reality and social life are socially constructed or created by individuals. There are multiple realities and viewpoints of reality. Qualitative methods employ a general philosophy of constructivism or subjectivism—how meaning is attached to experiences or events.

Quantitative approach: uses numerical data.

Quantitative studies: best used when the researcher seeks to numerically represent or test relationships about topics in aging. Follows the view of reality that sees it as objective or something external that can be independently measured. Quantitative studies have four main functions: description, explanation, exploration, and prediction. See Description, Explanation, Exploration, and Prediction.

Quota sampling: selecting a sample based on a characteristic of note, but these selection items are not matched to their representation in the population.

Recent biological theories: focus on loss of cellular protein in cells as a cause of aging, while some scientists are focusing on the relationship between inflammation and chronic diseases—e.g., heart diseases, cancer, frailty, and loss of cognitive functioning.

Recoded: the process of changing, combining, or collapsing the response categories of a variable to match research questions. Data-transformation options include combining or collapsing variable responses into new ones or counting response types in a variable or across a couple/several variables and combining them into a summed measure or index.

Recruitment site vs. study site: describes the way a researcher sees the study site—either as a place to recruit participants only or as a place the researcher will spend a significant amount of time doing research.

Redefining of age: redefining the boundaries or demarcation of what is "old" and "very old/ oldest old" in terms of chronological age. For example, "being old" at age 65 or "oldest old" at 85 or 90 years of age are no longer the case. These age markers were tied to eligibility for social program, benefits (Social Security, Medicare), or retirement age, but they no longer reflect these age markers in contemporary society.

Reductionist fallacy: a unit of analysis-based error. It occurs when a researcher studies groups but then applies his or her findings to individuals. See also Ecological fallacy.

Reliability: refers to stability or consistency of a measure over a brief time interval. See Test-retest reliability, Intra-observer, Intra-rater reliability, Inter-observer reliability, Inter-rater reliability, Inter-item reliability, Cronbach's alpha (α), and Alternate-form reliability.

Reminiscence: older person's directed storytelling to another.

Repeated cross-sectional designs: studies about the same topic repeated with different groups of people at each study interval. They mimic longitudinal approaches, and they do not track the same people over time, which impacts causality. However, repeated cross-sectional designs may have higher response rates that longitudinal studies and reflect trends over time.

Requests for proposals (RFPs) or Funding Announcement Opportunities (FOAs): ways organizations formally announce their funding opportunities and list the requirements for a proposal submission.

Research: a way or systematic process of seeking an answer to a question that arises in a gerontologist's mind, experience, or practice, or time in the field. It can be "blue skies" research, or research for the sake of research, without immediate application. It can be applied research or research that seeks a solution to an everyday issue or to solve a practical problem.

Research proposals: are an abridged version of a full manuscript or report. A proposal is an outline of the study or work that is planned—but not yet begun. It contains all the lead-in sections (the same as the manuscript) but stops at the proposed methods and design. It does not contain findings, discussion, or conclusions sections, since the project has not been completed. Research proposals can be part of the thesis, dissertation, or grant-proposal-writing process.

Research questions: questions about the issue that is of the researcher's interest, or the phenomena he or she seeks to investigate, relayed to others in a statement.

Rich, thick, description: (Clifford Geertz) the recording of all events in the field in great detail. Included are taking extended, detailed quotations from interviewees; recording field notes about the setting and events from the researcher's perspective; and including items from the field (newsletters, photos, etc.) in the data-collection process. The goal is to gather enough information to aid the researcher in understanding the many factors of the issue he or she is studying from the participants' point of view.

Sample size (qualitative): the needed number of cases is driven by the research question and approach and not an "n" or predetermined sample size. While researchers have tried to generate sample-size guidelines, these golden numbers do not exist. General, wide-ranging estimates say the "right" sample size for your study can be one person (in the case of a phenomenological or case study), four or five people for case studies, six to nine persons for focus groups, and range up to 30 or more (for grounded theory creation) or 30 to 50 or more (for an ethnographic study).

Sample size (quantitative): referred to as "N" for the total number of persons in a sample if a study has only one sample. If a study has multiple samples or one is referring to a smaller part of the total sample, use "n." Adequate sample size is important because it gives the researcher confidence that he or she can conduct certain statistical tests or that he or she is reaching parameter estimates. General sample-size ideas are a larger size can decrease error, the more complex the design the larger the sample, sample size should be adequate for all statistical tests in the study, and weaker relationships need larger samples. Online programs, such as G*Power, can calculate sample size.

Sampling, case selection: quantitative software programs (SPSS, SAS, and R) can draw simple random samples, cluster samples, and stratified samples. In addition to helping select a sample from a larger population of cases, quantitative software can also help apply sampling weights.

Sampling, mixed methods: mixed-methods sampling techniques draw from both quantitative and qualitative options. There is additional sampling terminology unique to mixed methods' designs. See Identical sampling, Parallel sampling, Nested sampling, and Multilevel sampling.

Sampling error (quantitative): since sampling units are being selected from the population, if the sample statistics differ from the population's parameters, some error can exist. Probability sampling includes some error from the general design, but other error can be introduced if other sampling frames are incomplete, the sample does not represent the entire population, or systematic patterns in the cases are ignored in the sampling process.

Sampling frame: a list of all possible participants or elements in the population from which the sample is drawn.

Sampling weights: help adjust the sample and its characteristics to match those of the original population from which they are drawn. This reduces error when running statistical analyses from the sample.

Saturation: (also called theoretical saturation) is a saturation of knowledge and ideas about the issue you are studying. No new data, ideas, themes are generated.

Scale: measures various aspects of a concept. A summed scale provides an overall score for all the items. The score is interpretable with higher scores indicating more support for the concept of interest.

Scatterplots: show the relationship between scale-level or higher variables and can be plotted against a regression line.

Scientific Review Group (SRG): the groups of peers that review federal grant proposals. Submitters can indicate their SRG preferences or conflicts of interest in a cover letter submitted with the proposal.

Secondary data analysis: a form of research in which the data collected and processed by one researcher are reanalyzed—often for a different purpose—by another. This method of analysis extracts knowledge that was not the original focus of the survey and uses new research questions and novel interpretation of existing data. Advantages include low cost, less time spent on data collection, expertise of original data collectors, reinterpretation of the data, and exploration of missed opportunities in the existing data. Disadvantages include availability or accessibility of the data, a need to be able to read and recode the data from its original form, differences in coding of the data from what is stated in the documentation, and amounts/ways the original investigators handled missing data.

Selection bias: refers to the composition of participants or the way they have been chosen to participate in the study. If participants are not randomly chosen, they may not represent the population about which you wish to make statements.

Selective attention: focusing on and filtering events and tasks in one's social environment.

Selective codes: (also called substantive codes) build axial codes into elements of theory.

Selective Optimization with Compensation (SOC): (Paul Baltes and Margaret Baltes) defines aging well as an outcome of how one adapts to environmental changes. When aging, individuals select important activities or developmental goals they see as key in defining themselves. Then they optimize the activities they do well as part of a task to address any loss of functioning and compensate, or change, the way they may carry out a task due to physical changes.

Semantic memory: factual, fact-based memory.

Sensor technology: electronic devices used to track older persons' health measurements. Examples include digital homes that integrate the use of technology and the homeowner's preferences and transmitter use in settings both inside and outside the home.

Sequential explanatory design: a mixed-methods design that begins with a quantitative method and then is followed by a qualitative method to further explain the findings of the first, quantitative approach.

Sequential exploratory design: a mixed-methods design that first uses a qualitative approach to explore a phenomenon and then uses knowledge gained in testing by quantitative designs. This sequential exploratory design is often used in survey/instrument development.

Severe vision difficulty: having serious difficulty seeing or chance of blindness.

"Shadow" or hidden stories: stories within a story. Often, themes or other messages relayed to the listener when the main story is told.

"Silences in the data": absences and gaps in the narratives or text being analyzed. There is a need to focus on omissions and missing data or items absent from discussion and to create codes about these themes.

Simple random sample: chooses elements from a *sampling frame* (or list of all possible participants), using random selection sometimes in the form of a random numbers table, to create this type of sample. This process ensures that each element has the same chance/probability of being selected.

Single-case studies (quantitative): research design that can have one participant or subject or a naturally occurring group as a subject model. This is similar to experimental designs, but, since there are no comparison groups, this design focuses on the impact of interventions (independent variables) upon outcomes (dependent variable) for an individual or individual group over time.

Single imputation: technique that replaces one missing value in a dataset with a valid one. This can be done by using existing data to extrapolate a plausible data value.

Skip pattern: based on answers provided to earlier questions, some questions are appropriately and intentionally "missed" (or skipped) because they do not apply to that respondent.

Snowball sampling: begins with one participant who then recommends another who recommends another; it is used with populations or groups that do not have a sampling frame or are tough to reach/locate.

Social Breakdown and Competence models: (J.A. Kuypers, Vern Bengston & Jane Meyers) theorizes the relationship between an older person's social world and the view an older person has about himself or herself. The two opposite processes are circular processes or wheels. In the social-breakdown cycle, a negative change/role loss makes older persons feel society is labeling them as "other" (i.e., weak, frail, dependent) and that role is internalized. The older person matches his or her behavior to meet these lowered expectations, which causes skills to be lost over time and promotes more negative labeling. In the social-competence cycle, the older person's value is restored; the person is seen as valuable for what he can do instead of what he cannot. This reinforces one's sense of ability, which fosters new skill building and resistance to negative labeling.

Social Construction: the idea that reality is created by people and societal views.

Socioemotional Selectivity Theory: (Laura Carstensen) older persons seek more meaningful interactions based on greater satisfaction from close friendships and less from peripheral friendships.

Sociogenic hypothesis: (Dale Dannefer) adds the role of society and social structures as heavily influencing later lifespan developmental processes.

Software Use for Statistical Analyses and Tests: the strength of quantitative software is its ability to run a wide range of uni- and multivariate statistical analyses on large amounts of data in a relatively short period of time. Each test can be identified by the user to account for missing data and run the user's preferences.

Somatographic analysis: the use of body-based or arts-based work to record and critically analyze data.

Source memory: keeping memories in context or remembering links between people and events.

Spectrum Model of Aging: (Diane Martin and Laura Gillen) lets each person create a self-defined, customized plan to age well with less focus on only activity or ability as the most important elements.

Stage Theory of Development: (Erik and Joan Erickson) divides lifespan development into a series of eight sequential stages. Each stage has two sides of a psychosocial crisis requiring conflict resolution to move to the next stage. The last and eighth stage of late adulthood (called "Old Age") has the conflict of ego integrity versus despair—with the result of this conflict being "wisdom" through reflection upon all prior lifelong stages. A ninth stage called "Extreme Old Age" was added in which all prior stages are evaluated.

Stratified random sample: random sampling using several classes or strata. After strata are determined, cases are randomly selected from within each stratum. Either each stratum can have the same characteristics as the population from which it is drawn, or a stratum can differ in how its characteristics are represented in the population.

Structural equation modeling (SEM): uses several statistical techniques to take many observed variables to create latent (inferred) variables and test their relationships while reducing measurement error.

Structured observation (quantitative): like experimental design without random assignment to experiential and control groups.

Subjectivism: posits that our views of reality are filtered or seen through individual viewpoints or vantage points.

Sub-scales/measures: surveys will often break down complex concepts into several questions about a larger concept.

Survey construction (question wording): if questions are not clearly worded, there is more room for different and incorrect interpretations among respondents. Begin with questions that ask most directly about the survey's topic to gather data about the topic of interest and cue the respondent in to the survey's main focus. Keep these questions straightforward and interesting. Keep any sensitive questions to the end of the instrument. Questions should also have a time frame of reference for the item being measured.

Surveys (quantitative): measure attitudes, behaviors, and beliefs and also collect demographic information. Survey questions can be closed (with fixed responses) or open ended (with space for narrative comments). See closed-ended questions, open-ended questions, Likert scale, fence-sitters, prompt, survey construction, filter questions, idiosyncratic variation, sub-scales/measures, non-response reasons, mode of administration, and leave-behind questionnaire.

Sustained attention: when the ability to concentrate or focus on a particular task does not decline with age.

Symbolic Interactionism: explores how people attach meaning to their experiences in the world based on their interaction with society.

Synchronous: means data collection, researcher, and participants are all interacting at the same period of time.

Syntax: this is the direct programmatic language specifying the exact conditions of the tests or data transformation being conducted. Syntax can be written in program-specific codified language; however, in many cases, writing syntax or programmatic language has been augmented with drop-down or query menus and a point-and-click option making the analysis more widely applicable.

Syntax window: in quantitative software, programs looks like a Word document. This area is the place where syntax/commands are typed that tell the quantitative software program which tests to do and which numbers to calculate.

Systematic random sampling: builds upon a simple random sample, selecting cases using a sampling interval. The first case is randomly selected, as is every nth case thereafter. This process requires a complete sampling frame and, unfortunately, is subject to periodicity, or patterns in the sample frame or list.

Test-retest reliability: if a researcher administers/applies the measure a second time, those results will be the same as the first assessment.

Themes: ways to summarize or represent data.

Theoretical memos: (often associated with grounded theory development) are a place to explore relationships between concepts and how they may relate to each other to form a theory or conceptual framework.

Theoretical sampling: (Lincoln and Egon Guba) cases or participants are selected to aid in the development of theory because they represent a category or element of the theory. Cases can be selected throughout the course of the study and need not be completed prior to the study or pre-arranged ahead of time. See Grounded theory.

Theory: informs the research questions and methods in an investigation. Theory helps explain the reasons why events happen, lets the researcher integrate knowledge, guides interventions, and influences practitioners' work and public policy.

Theory of Adult Development: (George Valliant) sees the developmental task of old age as being a "keeper of meaning."

Theory of Human Potential: (Gene Cohen) finds that human potential and creativity (in many forms) increase with age. The developmental phases are midlife reevaluation (ages 40s–50s midlife, people on a path of quest, not crisis), liberation (ages 60s–70s, brings a renewed sense of personal freedom), summing up (ages 70+, placing life's context in larger meaning), and encore (ages 80+, assessing one's final impact and completion of life's loose ends).

Theses: theses (at the master's level) and dissertations (at the doctoral level) can be parts of the requirements for master's and doctoral degrees. They are designed to be a unique contribution of the student author, who also demonstrates his or her knowledge of current research and practices in his or her field.

Thriving: suggests an alternative to the "failure to thrive" concept. In thriving theory, a person and his or her human and built environments interact to create positive ties to society, meaning in his or her life, and resiliency.

Traditional images of an ethnographer: present someone jotting field notes in a physical notebook while a cassette tape runs as data-collection methods. This image now also includes digital ethnography, or audio and video recording, and performance-based methods.

Transcription: the process of typing all spoken or recorded speech, audiotapes, or digitally recorded files into a written document for qualitative analysis. Software programs can aid in transcription.

Transferability: description of instances where the findings of the current study are applicable or relatable to other studies. The closest quantitative comparison is external validity. See Trustworthiness.

Transformative mixed-methods designs: address issues of injustice or marginalization and include acceptance of multiple realties of those in the study (e.g., researchers, participants) instead of assuming one view or a universal reality. Power differentials for those in the study due to each person's social position are recognized. Transformative mixed-methods designs can be sequential or concurrent.

Trustworthiness: (Yvonne Lincoln and Egon Guba) rigor in qualitative work consisting of four elements. See Credibility, Transferability, Dependability, and Confirmability.

Two-tailed test: tests only to find difference between groups tested.

Type I error: (also called an alpha, α, error) occurs if a researcher rejects the null hypothesis (of "no difference") when it is true. In other words, the researcher finds differences between the sample and populations he or she is testing or two samples he or she is testing—when there is no difference.

Type II error: (also called a beta, β, error) occurs if a researcher accepts the null hypothesis (of "no difference") when it is false, he or she is making a Type II error. Here, researchers find no difference in the sample and populations of two samples they are testing—when there is difference.

Types of files (qualitative software): qualitative data-analysis programs use a wide array of files as cases or individual pieces of data. These files include text documents (as in Word files), audio files, videos, and survey data (as from Excel). Some also incorporate data from Google Earth's geospatial data and social media.

Types of files (quantitative software): quantitative software programs have three types of files: data, syntax, and output. See Data, Syntax, and Output.

Typology tables: a function in mixed-methods software that quantifies codes and provides additional statistics for the relationship between the quantified codes and variable categories.

The statistics are in either the form of numbers and percent or means and standard deviations based on variables' level of measurement.

Underrepresented in research: groups of older people not included in research or groups that fear researchers may exploit the group for the researchers' own needs.

Units of analysis (UOA): elements of the sample. UOAs can range from individuals to entire settings such as an organization or country.

Univariate: data or data analysis referring to one variable.

Validity: a measure must capture the concept a researcher intends to measure/evaluate in his or her study. Types of validity include face validity, construct validity, content validity, criterion validity, and concurrent validity.

Value labels: attach text or narrative to each numerical response category.

Variable names: since variable names may have character limits, variable names allow the researcher to add a longer description to define what that variable is about.

Variables: are the way concepts are operationalized or discussed in a study. Variables must have values that vary. They are the quantified or numeric values assigned response choices or categories of your data.

Vicarious trauma: researchers working on projects that include traumatic events can also experience trauma when working on the study.

Video diaries: offering participants a camera or other device to record video about their personal experiences.

Vision changes: start in the 30s or 40s and increase when a person reaches his or her 60s. Changes can include a need for reading glasses, decrease in acuity or sharpness, and loss of near vision. Contrast between light and dark is more difficult, and more light is needed to read.

Visual displays (qualitative): representation of the codes in the data. Can include visual word clouds of codes or maps of codes.

Visual displays (quantitative): depictions of data. Can include pie charts, histograms, or boxplots and scatterplots.

Voluntary consent: participating in a study by choice without coercion. See Common Rule, Institutional Review Board.

Vulnerable subjects: term in the Common Rule to identify research participants who may need additional safeguards when enrolling in a study. Common Rule examples include children, prisoners, pregnant women, mentally disabled persons, or economically or educationally disadvantaged persons. While old age is no longer listed as a federally suggested vulnerable group, differences exist in IRBs' interpretation with some IRBs still considering older age groups as vulnerable populations. Those with cognitive impairment, residing in skilled care, or actively dying in hospice are more generally accepted examples of vulnerable populations.

Wear-and-Tear Theory: suggested that, with time, an organism wears out and was the precursor of many "failure to repair" theories that see aging as an accumulation of injury and damage from the environment. However, advances in molecular and cell biology made wear-and-tear theory outdated.

Word cloud: visual representation of codes in qualitative data. More frequently occurring codes appear in a larger font in the cloud.

Working memory: allows one to retain the partial results while solving an arithmetic problem without paper to combine the premises in a lengthy rhetorical argument.

Writing strategies: techniques to stimulate writing. Each writer must find his or her individual preference and path. Strategies include allocating the same time each day, 30–45 minutes or so, to sitting down and writing or doing research to forward an existing work or joining writing groups (face-to-face or virtual) to provide forced deadlines.

Yellow filter effect: the eye lens yellows with age and viewing color may be distorted.

Zing: software that lets several people use their keyboards simultaneously online to participate in online focus groups.

Author Index

Subject Index